Shojo Beat

Story & Art by

Kazune Kawahara

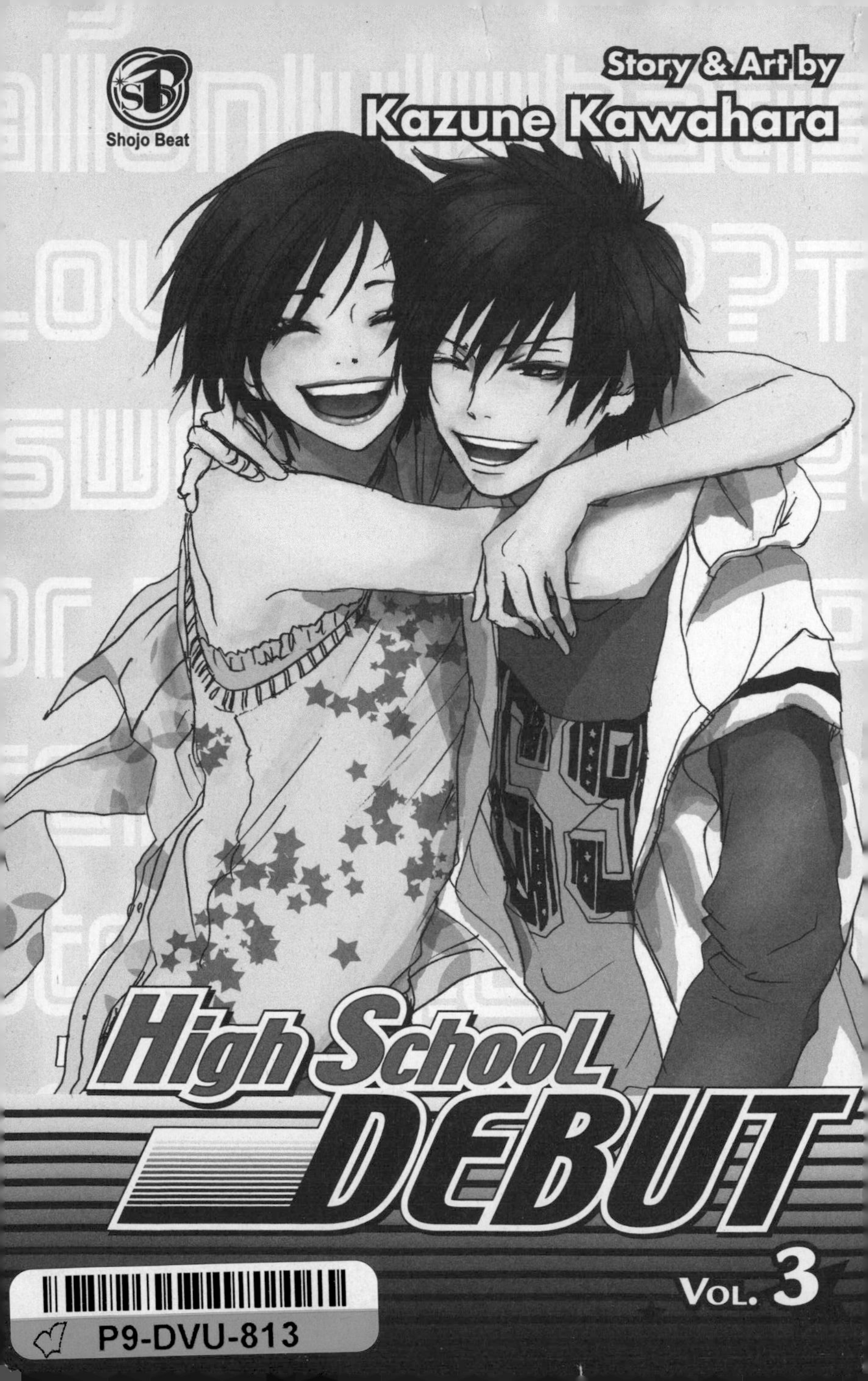

High School DEBUT

Vol. 3

High School DEBUT

Story Thus Far...

High school freshman Haruna was a sporty girl and an ace player for her softball team back in junior high. Now that she's in high school, she wants to give her all to finding true love instead! She gets Yoh, a guy who knows how to be popular, to be her "love coach" and falls in love for the first time with his friend Fumi. When her heart is broken, she's able to pick herself back up with Yoh's support and an optimistic attitude. However, she doesn't find herself drawn to other guys as she starts to notice Yoh more and more.

At a school sports competition, Haruna is chosen to be the pitcher for the softball team. However, worried that Yoh's ex-girlfriend is the complete opposite of her, she refrains from using her true althletic abilities. Yoh, who came to cheer her on, becomes upset at her reasoning and tells her, "I really can't stand you right now." Awakened by these harsh words, Haruna decides to give her all to the game and helps her team win the championship. At the same time, she now fully realizes that she likes Yoh...

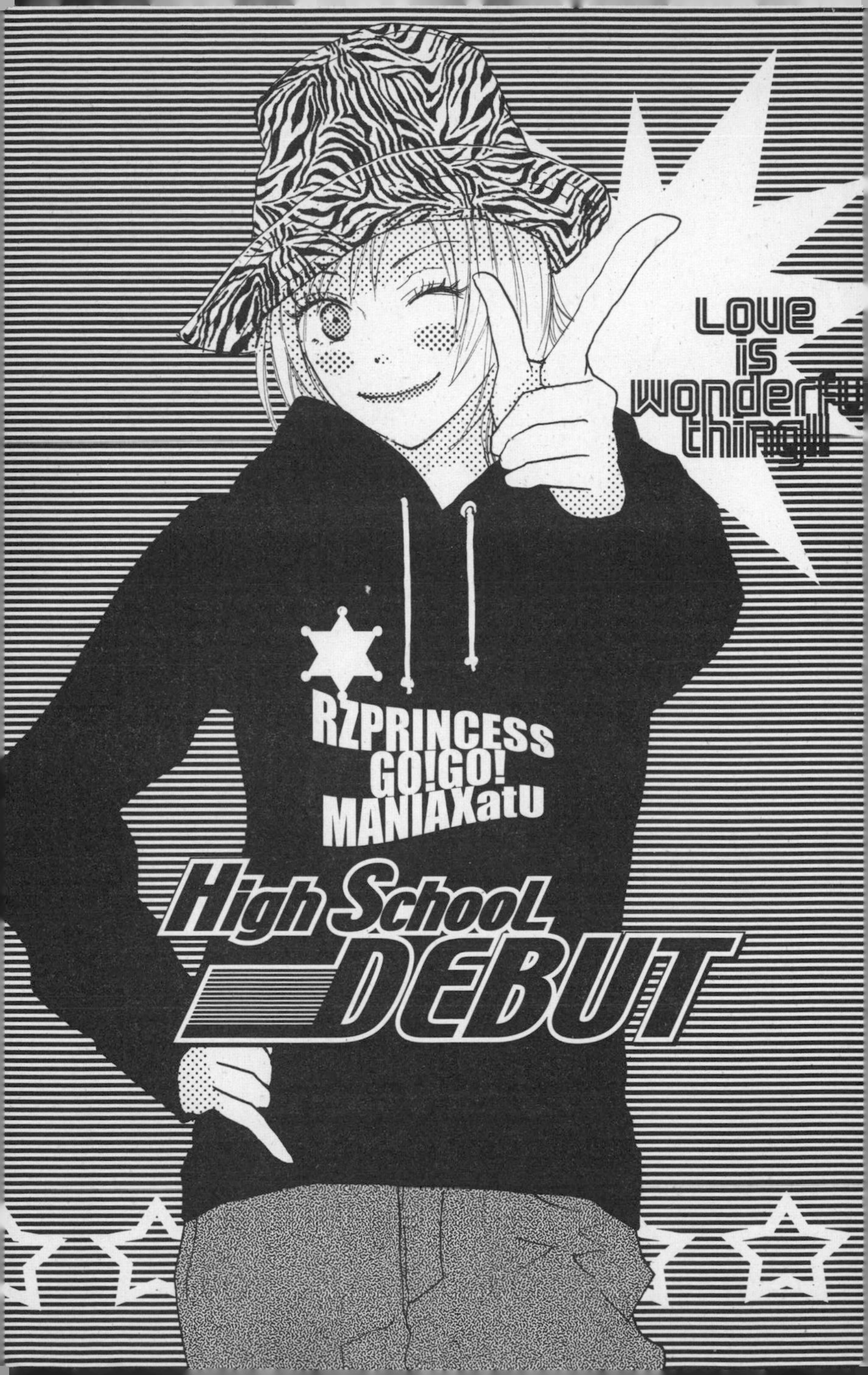
Love is wonderfu thing!!
RZPRINCESS
GO!GO!
MANIAXatu
High School
DEBUT

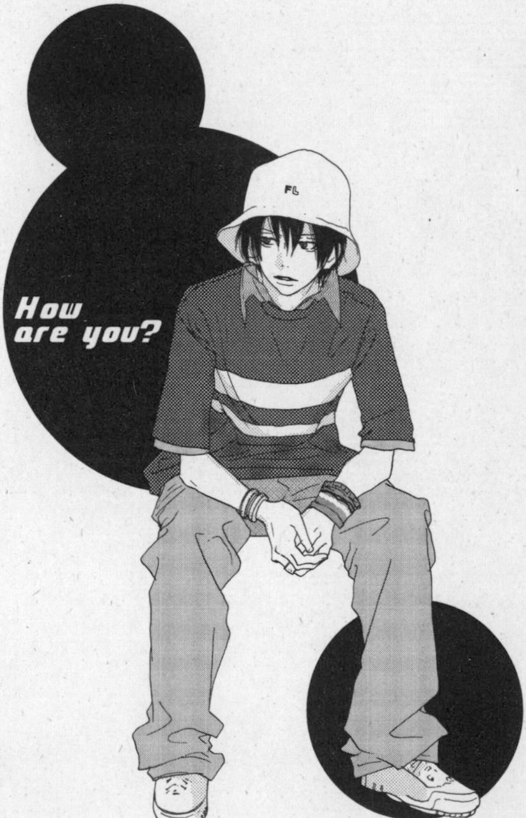
How
are you?

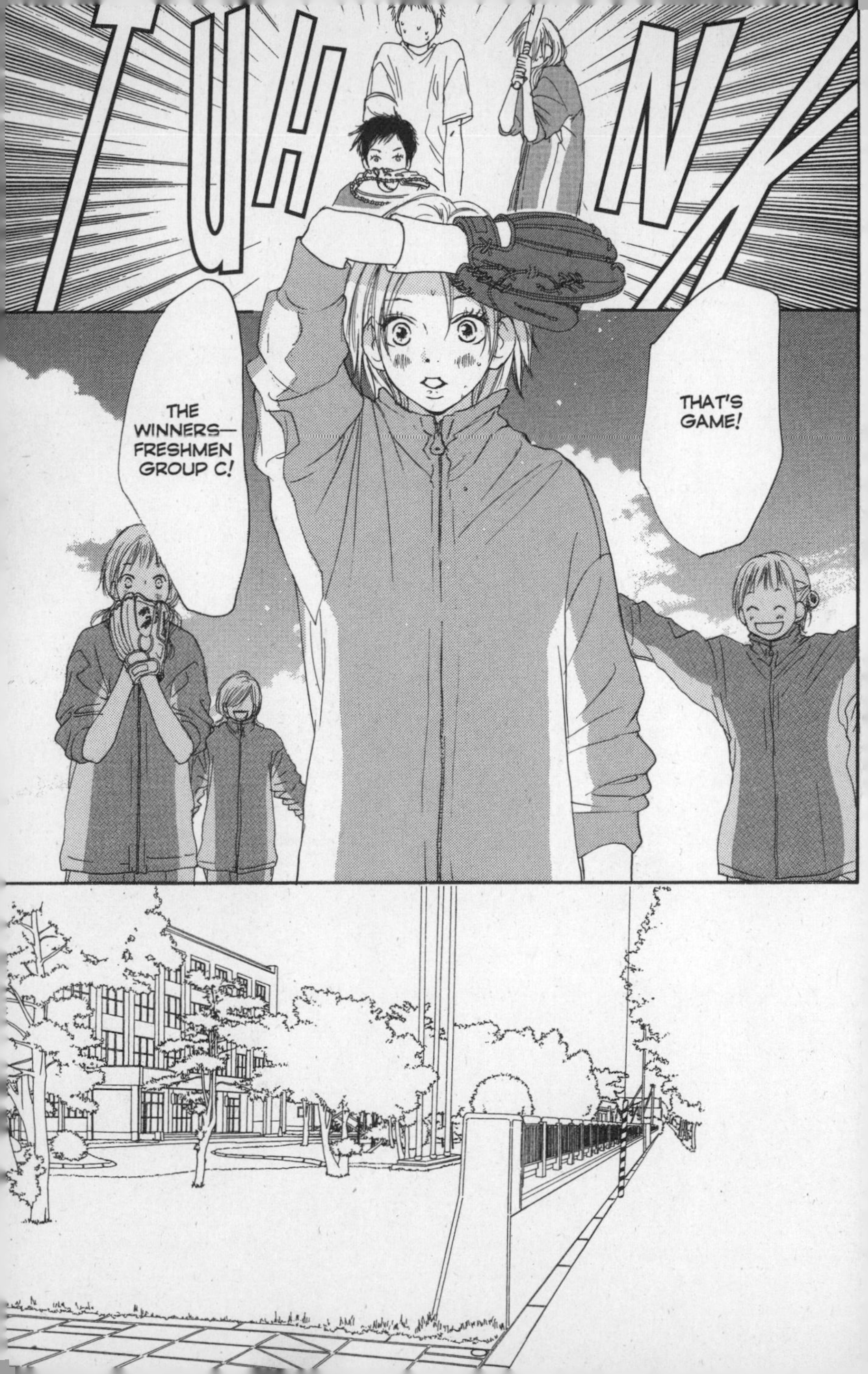
THUNK
THAT'S GAME!
THE WINNERS—FRESHMEN GROUP C!

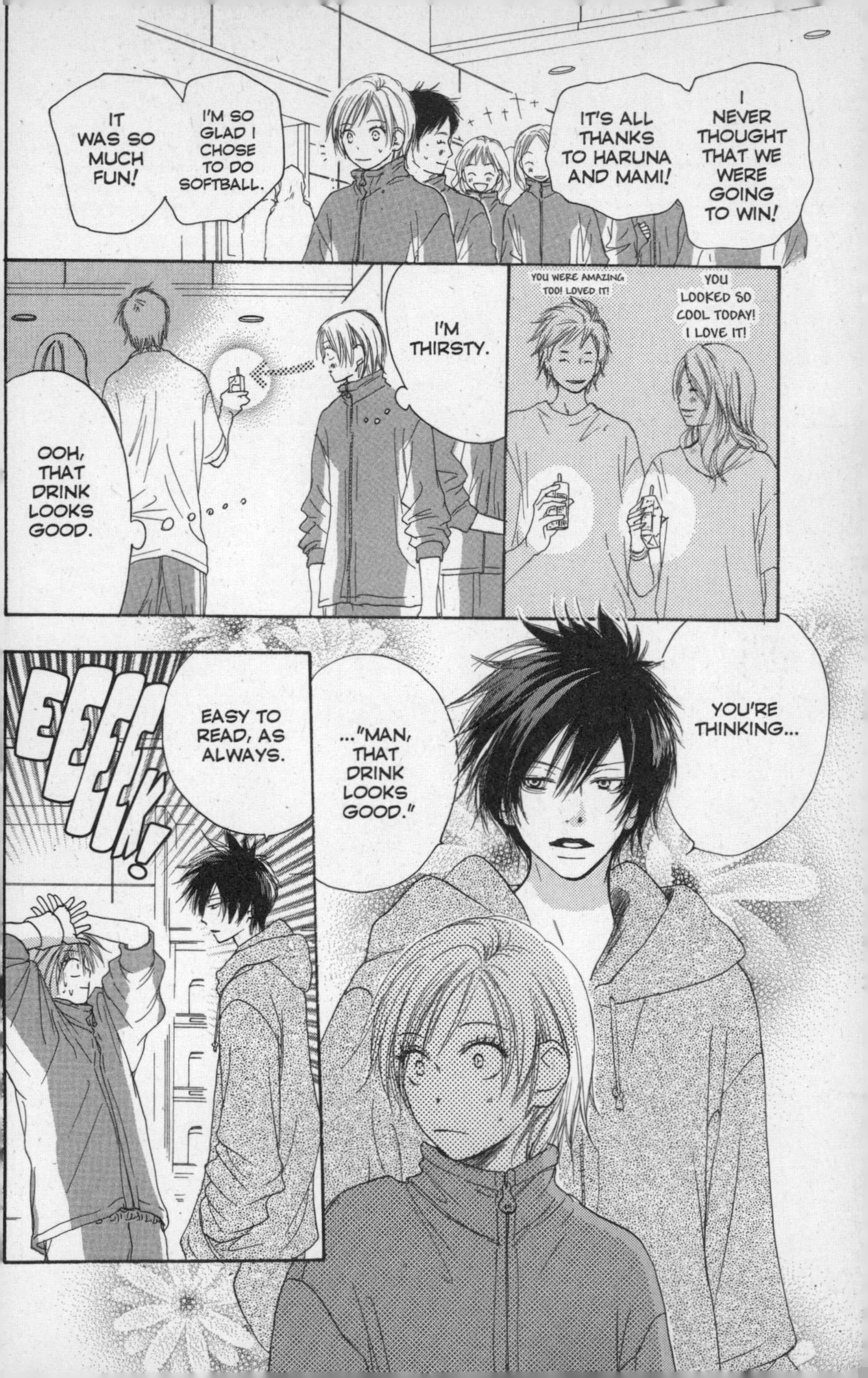
I NEVER THOUGHT THAT WE WERE GOING TO WIN!
IT'S ALL THANKS TO HARUNA AND MAMI!
I'M SO GLAD I CHOSE TO DO SOFTBALL.
IT WAS SO MUCH FUN!
YOU LOOKED SO COOL TODAY! I LOVE IT!
YOU WERE AMAZING TOO! LOVED IT!
I'M THIRSTY.
OOH, THAT DRINK LOOKS GOOD.
YOU'RE THINKING...
..."MAN, THAT DRINK LOOKS GOOD."
EASY TO READ, AS ALWAYS.
EEEEK!

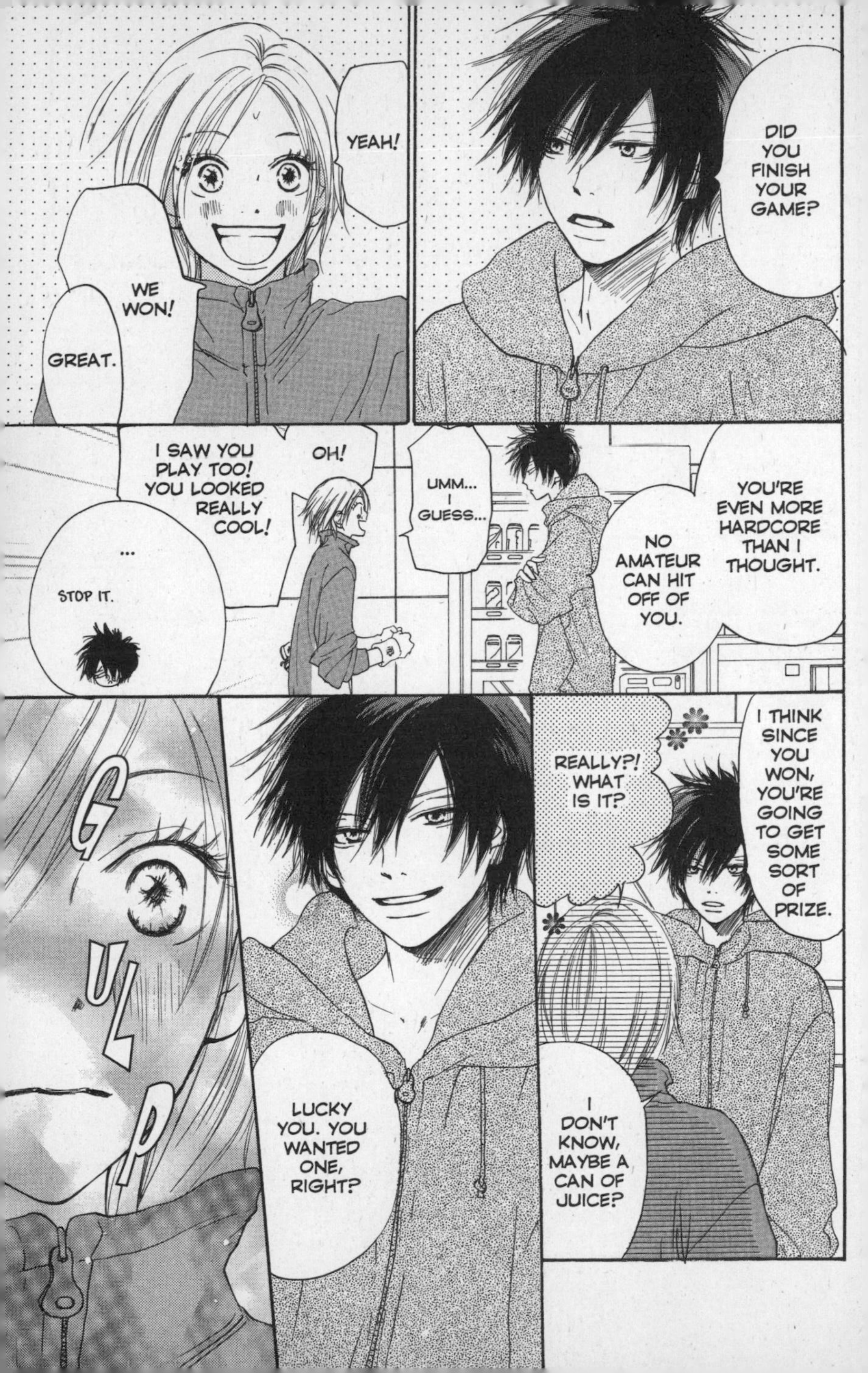
DID YOU FINISH YOUR GAME?
YEAH!
WE WON!
GREAT.
YOU'RE EVEN MORE HARDCORE THAN I THOUGHT.
NO AMATEUR CAN HIT OFF OF YOU.
UMM... I GUESS...
OH!
I SAW YOU PLAY TOO! YOU LOOKED REALLY COOL!
...
STOP IT.
I THINK SINCE YOU WON, YOU'RE GOING TO GET SOME SORT OF PRIZE.
REALLY?! WHAT IS IT?
I DON'T KNOW, MAYBE A CAN OF JUICE?
LUCKY YOU. YOU WANTED ONE, RIGHT?
GULP

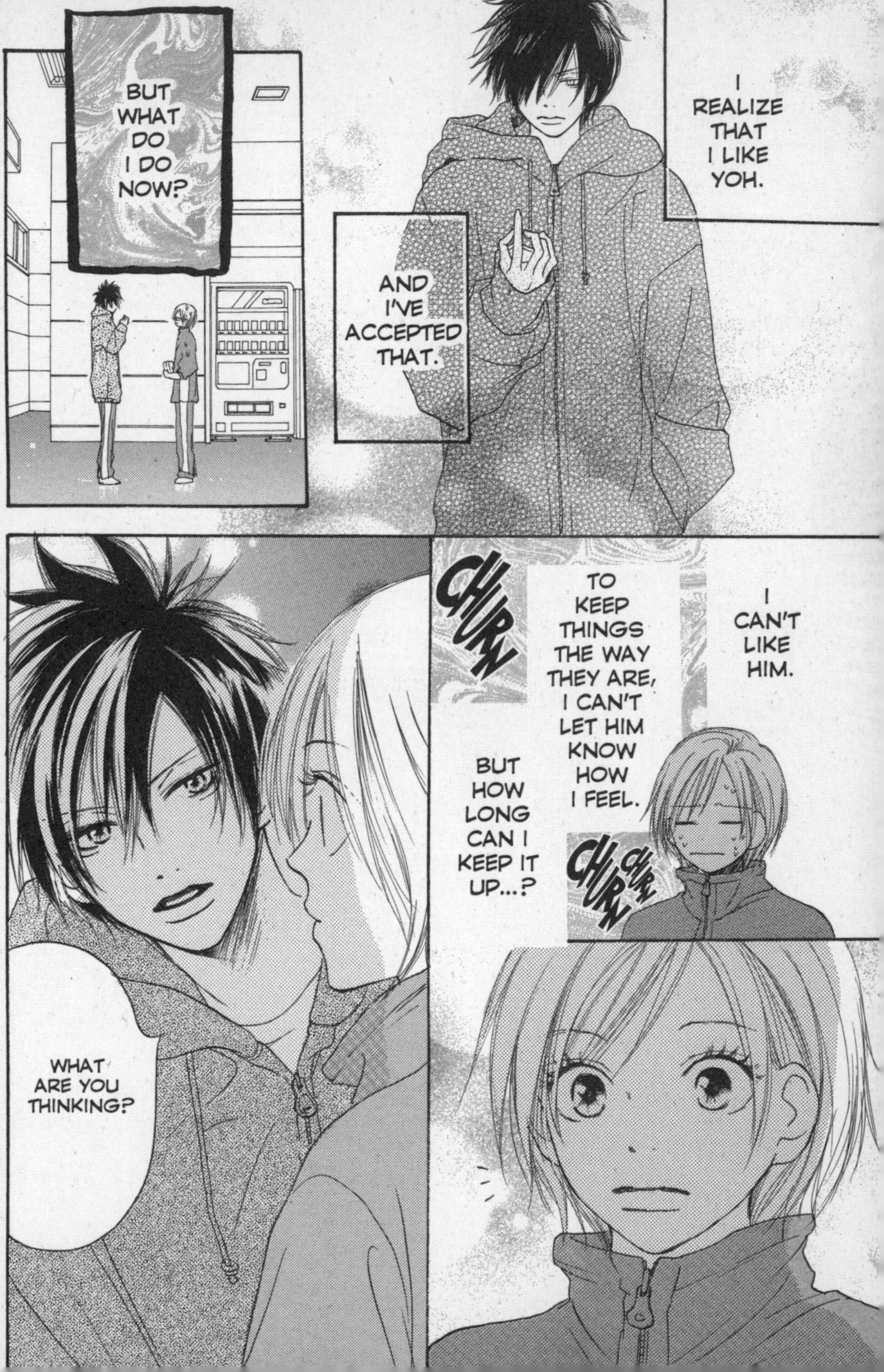
I REALIZE THAT I LIKE YOH.
AND I'VE ACCEPTED THAT.
BUT WHAT DO I DO NOW?
I CAN'T LIKE HIM.
CHURN
TO KEEP THINGS THE WAY THEY ARE, I CAN'T LET HIM KNOW HOW I FEEL.
BUT HOW LONG CAN I KEEP IT UP...?
CHURN CHURN
WHAT ARE YOU THINKING?

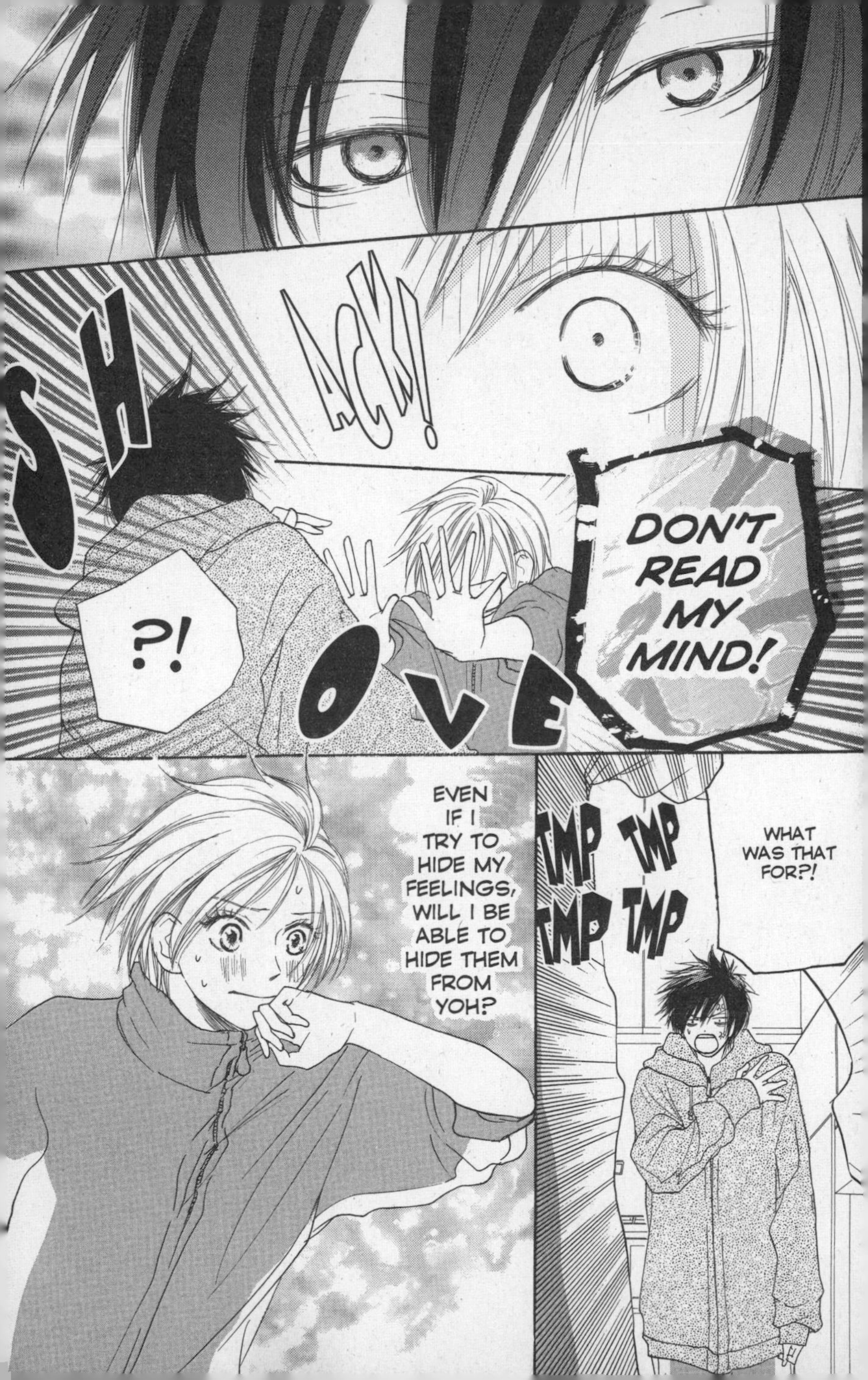
ACK!
DON'T READ MY MIND!
SHOVE
?!
WHAT WAS THAT FOR?!
TMP TMP TMP TMP
EVEN IF I TRY TO HIDE MY FEELINGS, WILL I BE ABLE TO HIDE THEM FROM YOH?

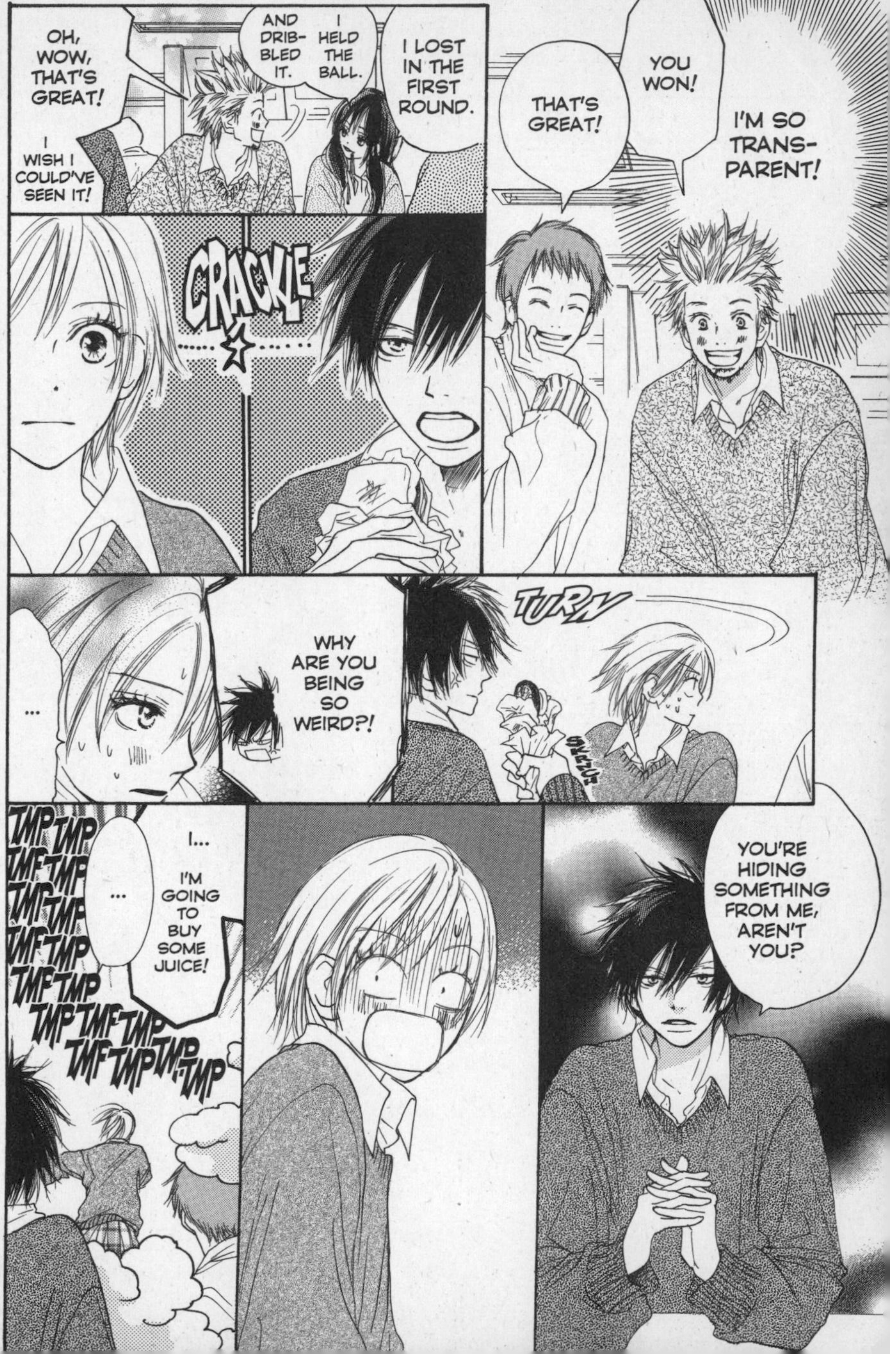
YOU WON!
THAT'S GREAT!
I'M SO TRANS-PARENT!
I LOST IN THE FIRST ROUND.
I HELD THE BALL.
AND DRIB-BLED IT.
OH, WOW, THAT'S GREAT!
I WISH I COULD'VE SEEN IT!
CRACKLE
TURN
SKRNCH
WHY ARE YOU BEING SO WEIRD?!
...
YOU'RE HIDING SOMETHING FROM ME, AREN'T YOU?
I...
I'M GOING TO BUY SOME JUICE!
...
TMP TMP TMP TMP TMP TMP TMP TMP TMP TMP TMP TMP TMP TMP TMP TMP TMP TMP

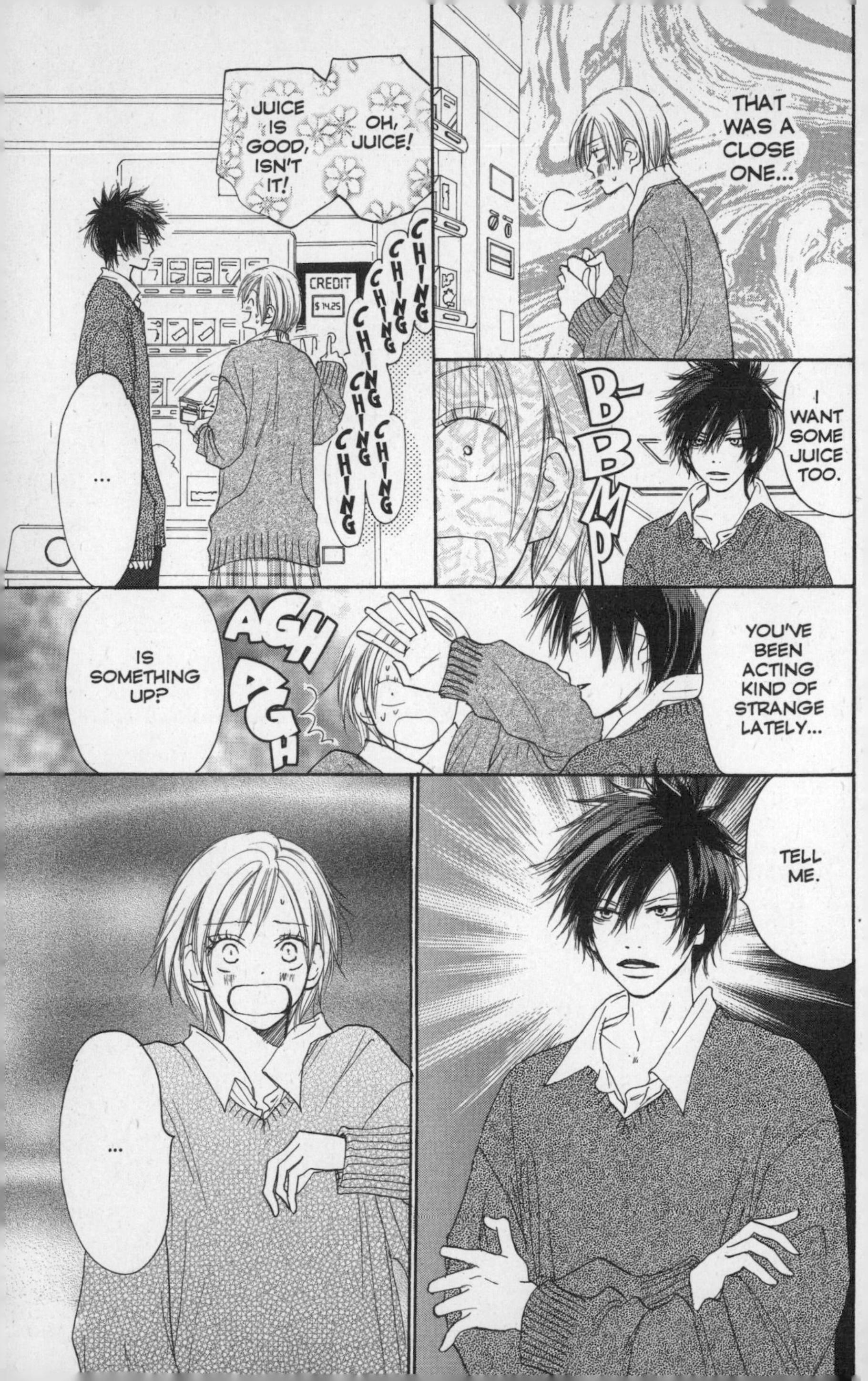
THAT WAS A CLOSE ONE...
I WANT SOME JUICE TOO.
B-BBMP
OH, JUICE!
JUICE IS GOOD, ISN'T IT!
CREDIT
$14.25
CHING CHING CHING CHING CHING CHING
...
YOU'VE BEEN ACTING KIND OF STRANGE LATELY...
AGH AGH
IS SOMETHING UP?
TELL ME.
...

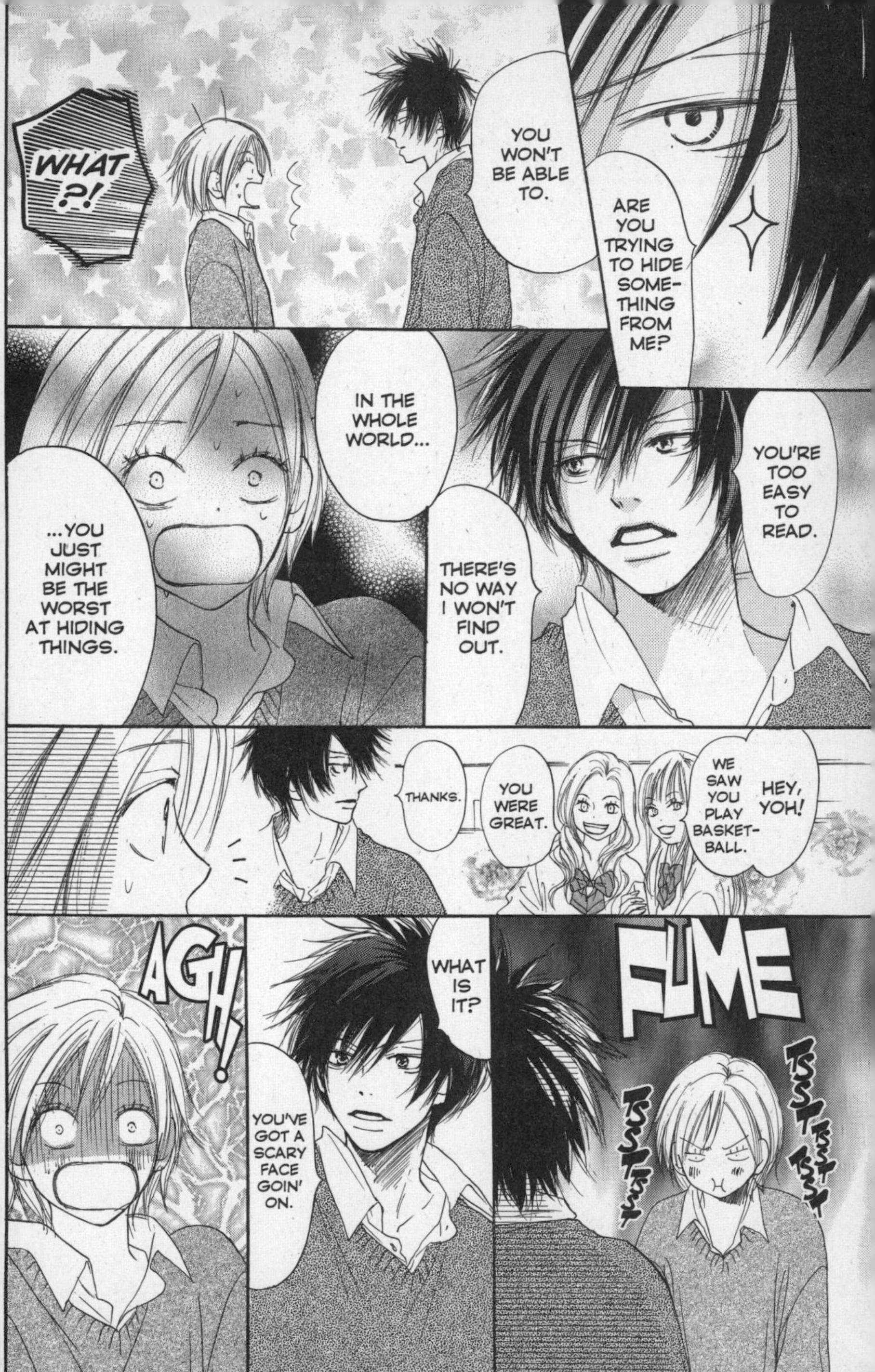
ARE YOU TRYING TO HIDE SOME-THING FROM ME?
YOU WON'T BE ABLE TO.
WHAT?!
YOU'RE TOO EASY TO READ.
THERE'S NO WAY I WON'T FIND OUT.
IN THE WHOLE WORLD...
...YOU JUST MIGHT BE THE WORST AT HIDING THINGS.
HEY, YOH!
WE SAW YOU PLAY BASKET-BALL.
YOU WERE GREAT.
THANKS.
FUME
TSST TSST
TSST TSST
WHAT IS IT?
YOU'VE GOT A SCARY FACE GOIN' ON.
AGH!

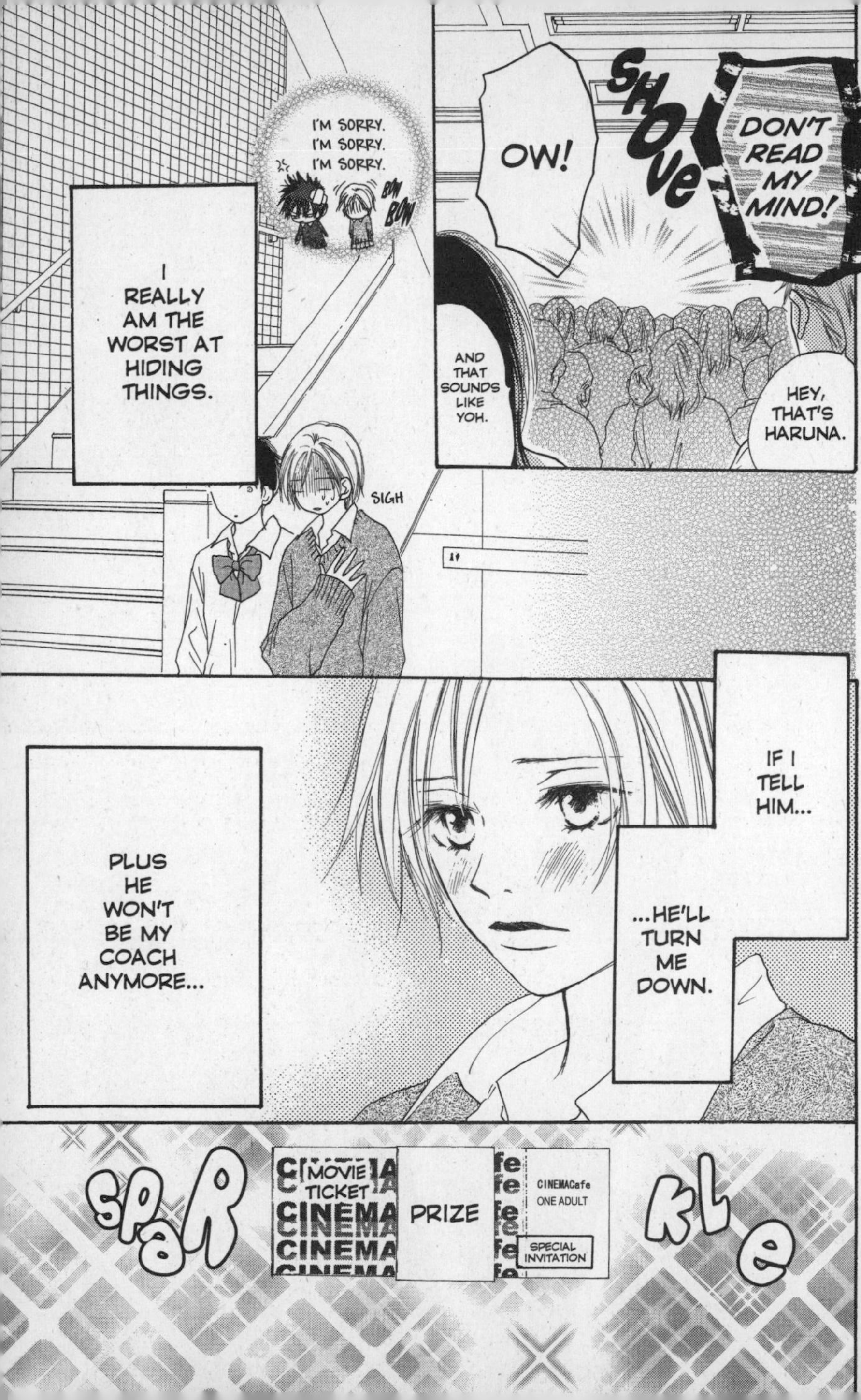
DON'T READ MY MIND!
SHOVE
OW!
HEY, THAT'S HARUNA.
AND THAT SOUNDS LIKE YOH.
I'M SORRY. I'M SORRY. I'M SORRY.
BOW BOW
I REALLY AM THE WORST AT HIDING THINGS.
SIGH
IF I TELL HIM...
...HE'LL TURN ME DOWN.
PLUS HE WON'T BE MY COACH ANYMORE...
SPARKLE
MOVIE TICKET
PRIZE
CINEMACafe
ONE ADULT
SPECIAL INVITATION

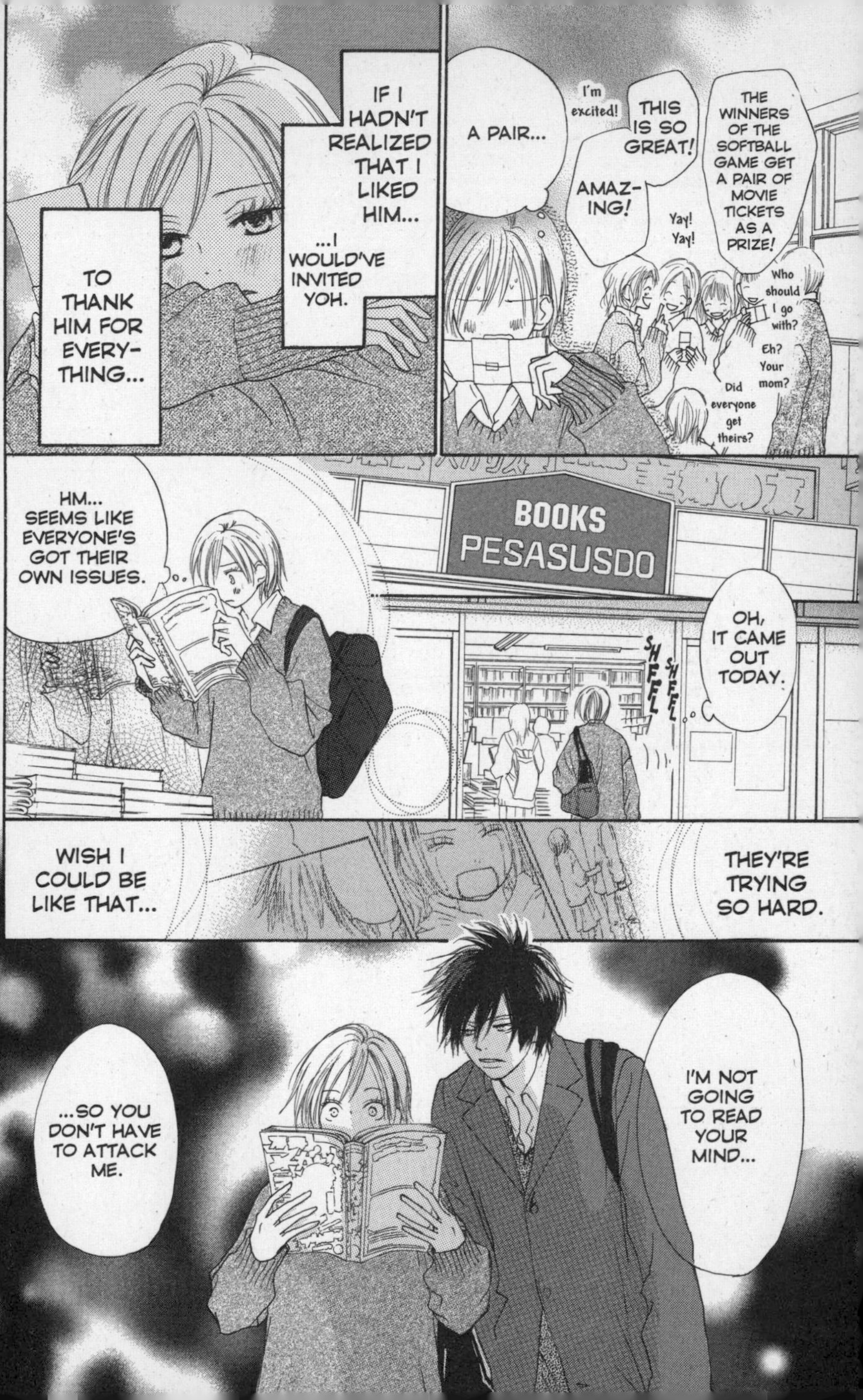
THE WINNERS OF THE SOFTBALL GAME GET A PAIR OF MOVIE TICKETS AS A PRIZE!
THIS IS SO GREAT!
I'm excited!
AMAZ-ING!
Yay! Yay!
Who should I go with?
Eh? Your mom?
Did everyone get theirs?
A PAIR...
IF I HADN'T REALIZED THAT I LIKED HIM...
...I WOULD'VE INVITED YOH.
TO THANK HIM FOR EVERY-THING...
BOOKS PESASUSDO
OH, IT CAME OUT TODAY.
SHFFL SHFFL
HM... SEEMS LIKE EVERYONE'S GOT THEIR OWN ISSUES.
THEY'RE TRYING SO HARD.
WISH I COULD BE LIKE THAT...
I'M NOT GOING TO READ YOUR MIND...
...SO YOU DON'T HAVE TO ATTACK ME.

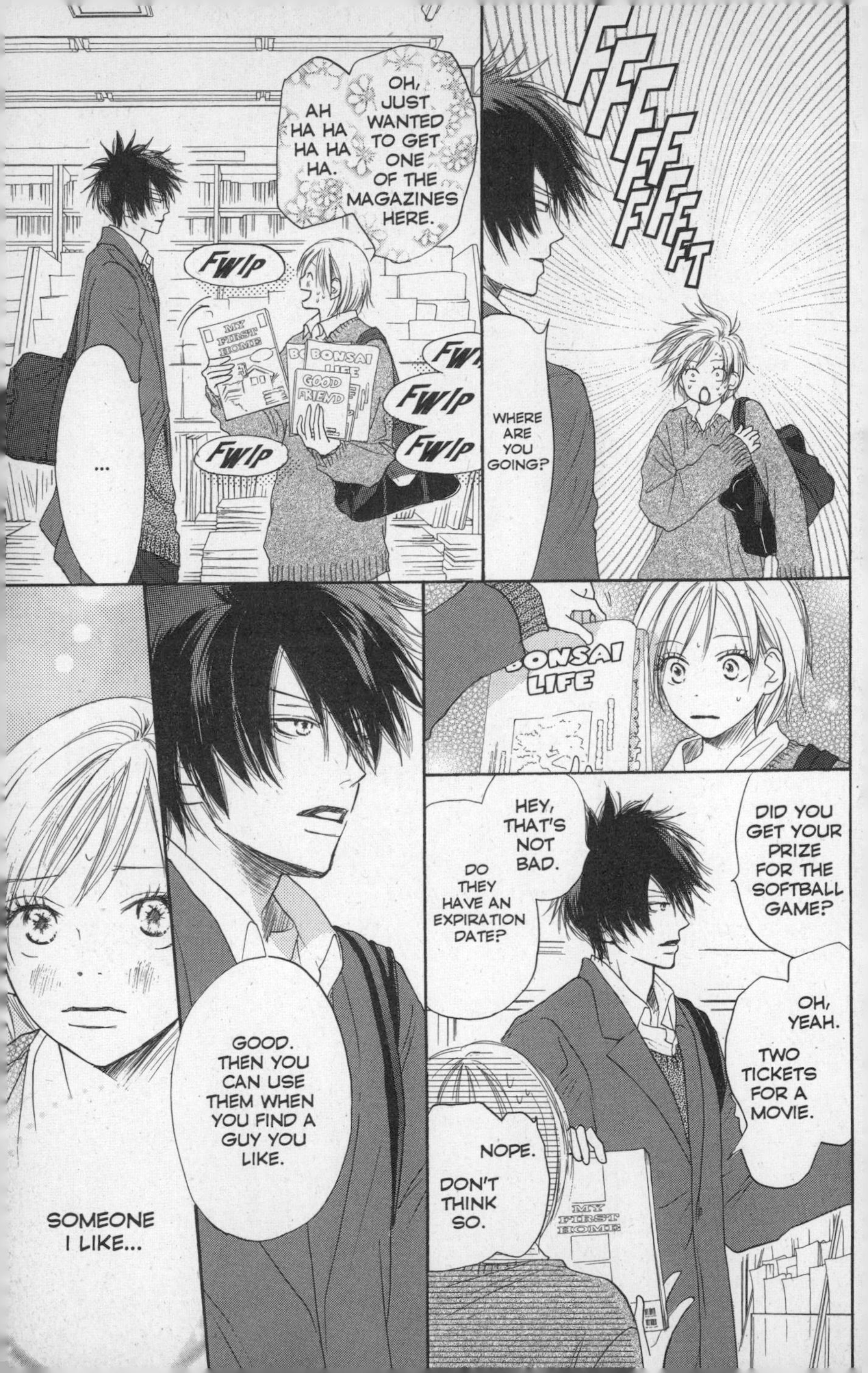
FFFFFFFFT
WHERE ARE YOU GOING?
OH, JUST WANTED TO GET ONE OF THE MAGAZINES HERE.
AH HA HA HA HA HA.
FWIP
FWIP
FWIP
FWIP
FWIP
MY FIRST HOME
BONSAI LIFE
GOOD FRIEND
...
BONSAI LIFE
DID YOU GET YOUR PRIZE FOR THE SOFTBALL GAME?
OH, YEAH.
TWO TICKETS FOR A MOVIE.
HEY, THAT'S NOT BAD.
DO THEY HAVE AN EXPIRATION DATE?
NOPE.
DON'T THINK SO.
MY FIRST HOME
GOOD. THEN YOU CAN USE THEM WHEN YOU FIND A GUY YOU LIKE.
SOMEONE I LIKE...

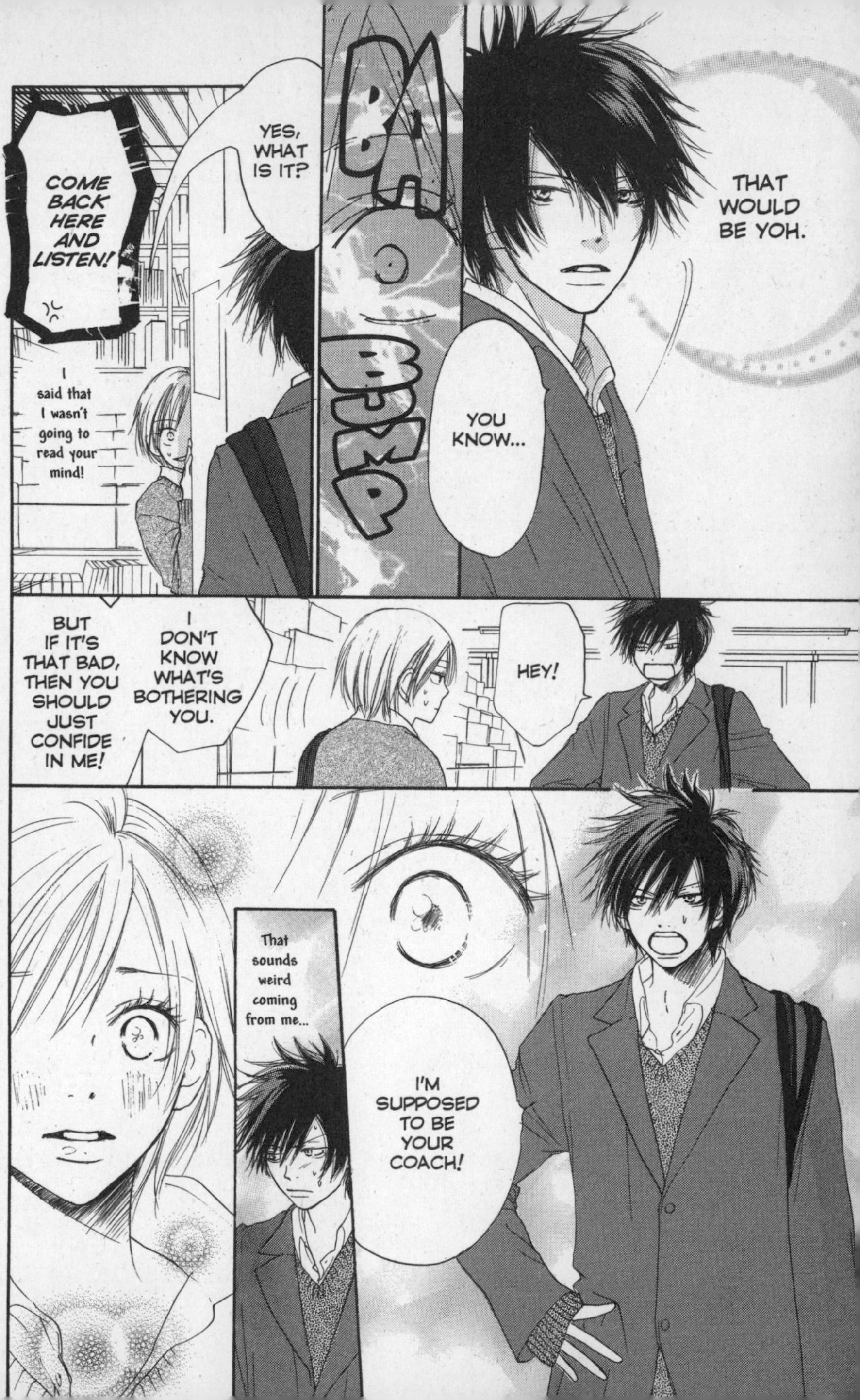
THAT WOULD BE YOH.
YOU KNOW...
BA
BUMP
YES, WHAT IS IT?
COME BACK HERE AND LISTEN!
I said that I wasn't going to read your mind!
HEY!
I DON'T KNOW WHAT'S BOTHERING YOU.
BUT IF IT'S THAT BAD, THEN YOU SHOULD JUST CONFIDE IN ME!
I'M SUPPOSED TO BE YOUR COACH!
That sounds weird coming from me...

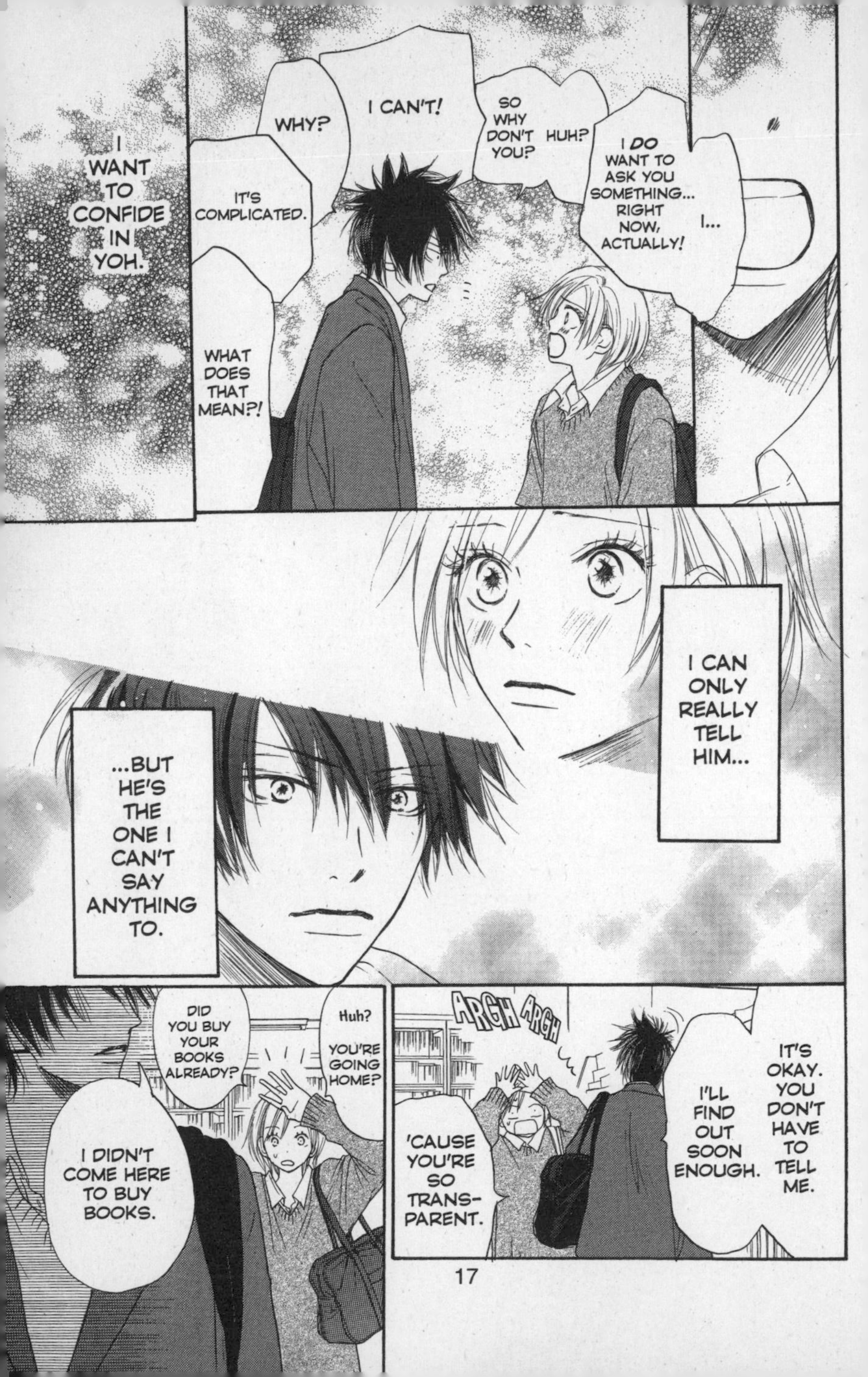
I...
I DO WANT TO ASK YOU SOMETHING... RIGHT NOW, ACTUALLY!
HUH?
SO WHY DON'T YOU?
I CAN'T!
WHY?
IT'S COMPLICATED.
WHAT DOES THAT MEAN?!
I WANT TO CONFIDE IN YOH.
I CAN ONLY REALLY TELL HIM...
...BUT HE'S THE ONE I CAN'T SAY ANYTHING TO.
IT'S OKAY. YOU DON'T HAVE TO TELL ME.
I'LL FIND OUT SOON ENOUGH.
'CAUSE YOU'RE SO TRANS-PARENT.
ARGH ARGH
Huh? YOU'RE GOING HOME?
DID YOU BUY YOUR BOOKS ALREADY?
I DIDN'T COME HERE TO BUY BOOKS.

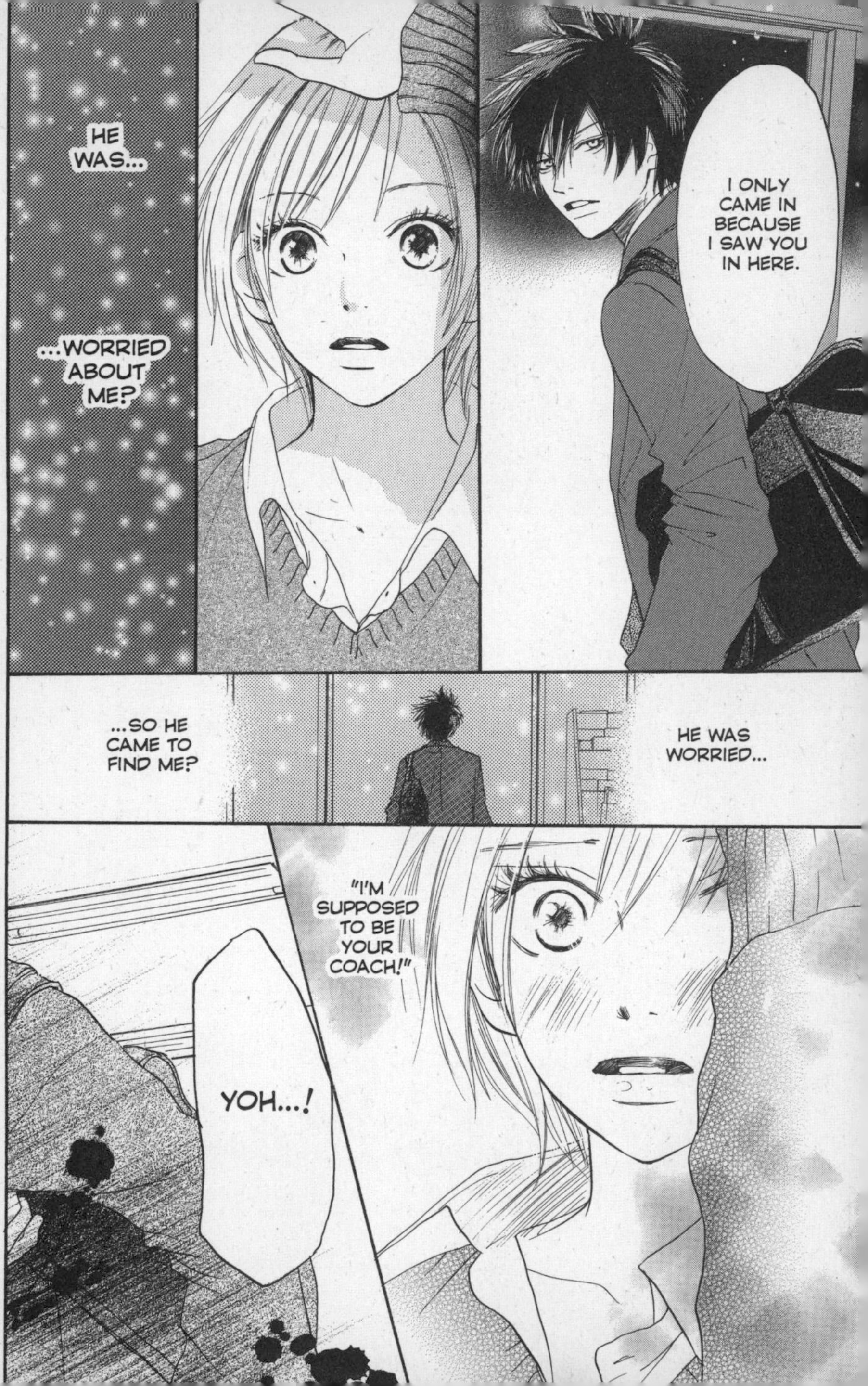
I ONLY CAME IN BECAUSE I SAW YOU IN HERE.
HE WAS...
...WORRIED ABOUT ME?
HE WAS WORRIED...
...SO HE CAME TO FIND ME?
"I'M SUPPOSED TO BE YOUR COACH!"
YOH...!

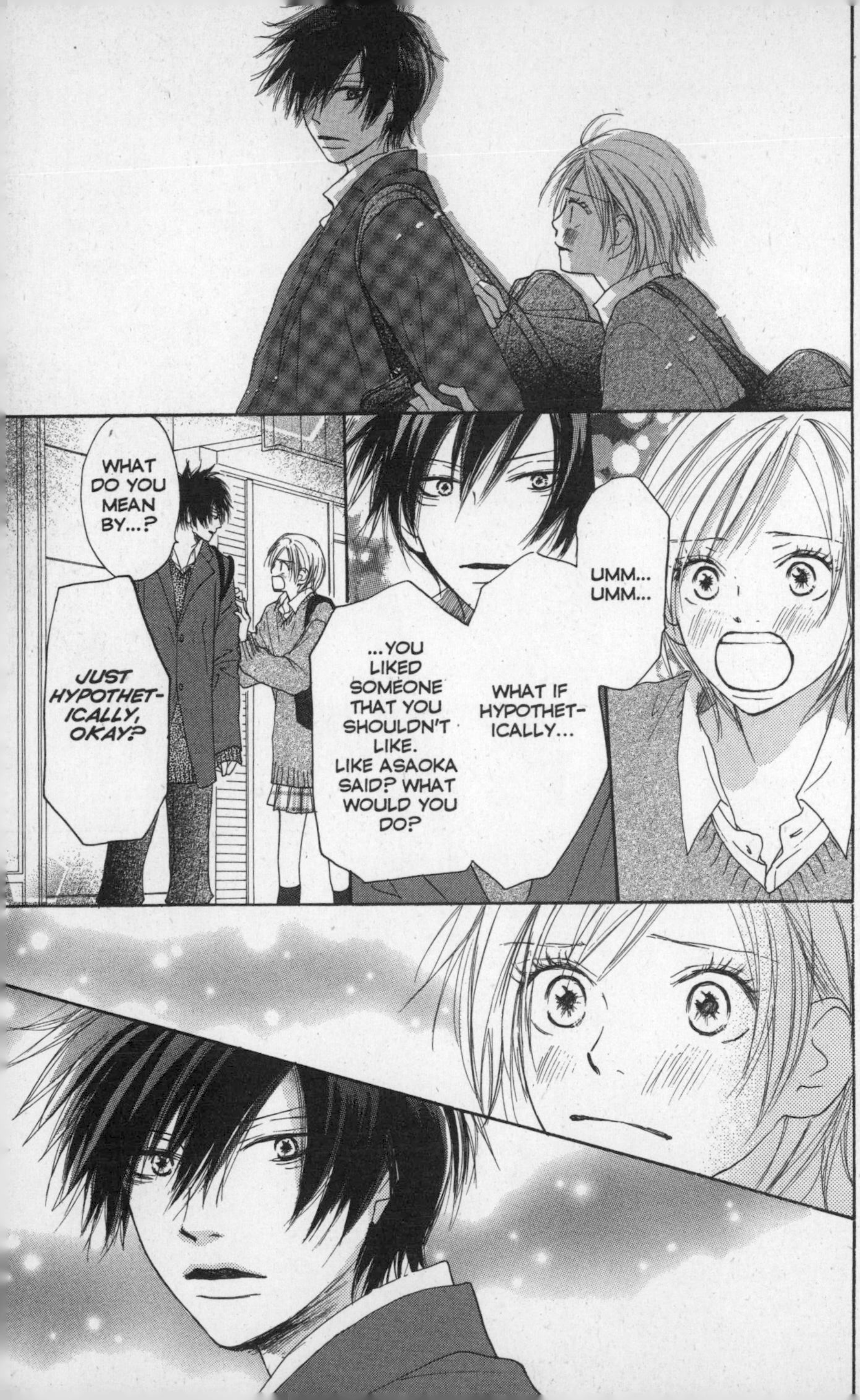
UMM... UMM...
WHAT IF HYPOTHETICALLY...
...YOU LIKED SOMEONE THAT YOU SHOULDN'T LIKE. LIKE ASAOKA SAID? WHAT WOULD YOU DO?
WHAT DO YOU MEAN BY...?
JUST HYPOTHETICALLY, OKAY?

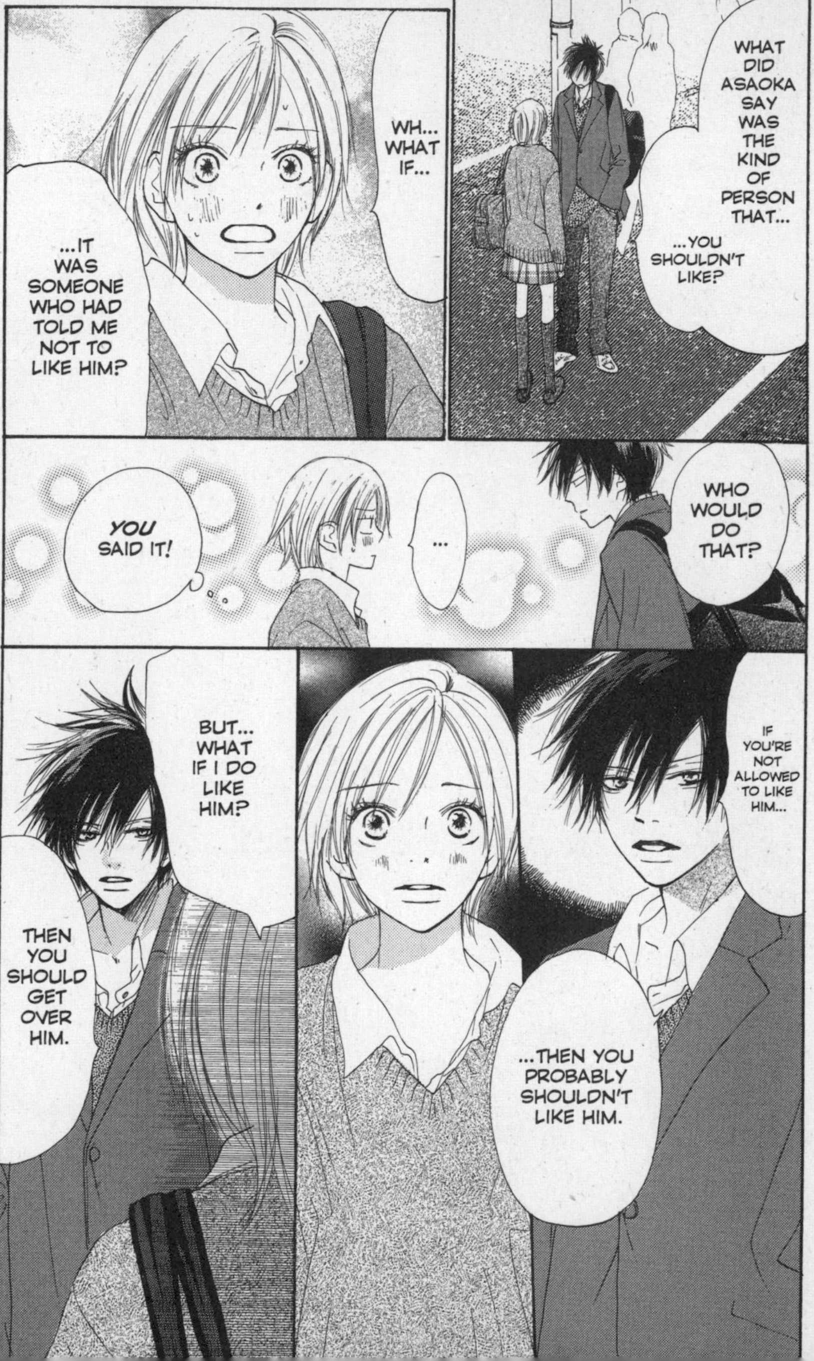
WHAT DID ASAOKA SAY WAS THE KIND OF PERSON THAT...
...YOU SHOULDN'T LIKE?
WH... WHAT IF...
...IT WAS SOMEONE WHO HAD TOLD ME NOT TO LIKE HIM?
WHO WOULD DO THAT?
...
YOU SAID IT!
IF YOU'RE NOT ALLOWED TO LIKE HIM...
...THEN YOU PROBABLY SHOULDN'T LIKE HIM.
BUT... WHAT IF I DO LIKE HIM?
THEN YOU SHOULD GET OVER HIM.

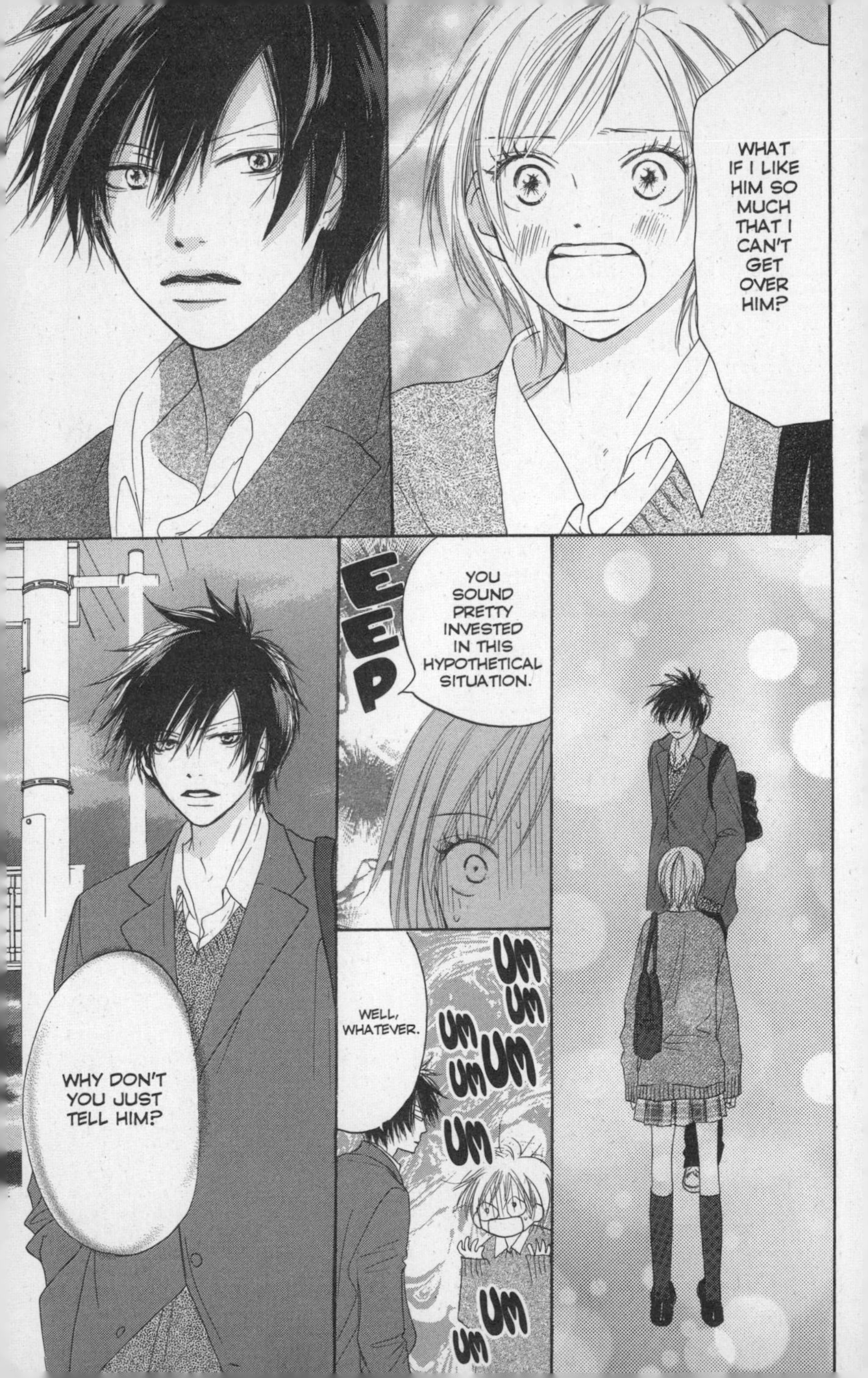
WHAT IF I LIKE HIM SO MUCH THAT I CAN'T GET OVER HIM?
YOU SOUND PRETTY INVESTED IN THIS HYPOTHETICAL SITUATION.
EEP
WELL, WHATEVER.
UM UM UM UM UM UM UM UM UM
WHY DON'T YOU JUST TELL HIM?

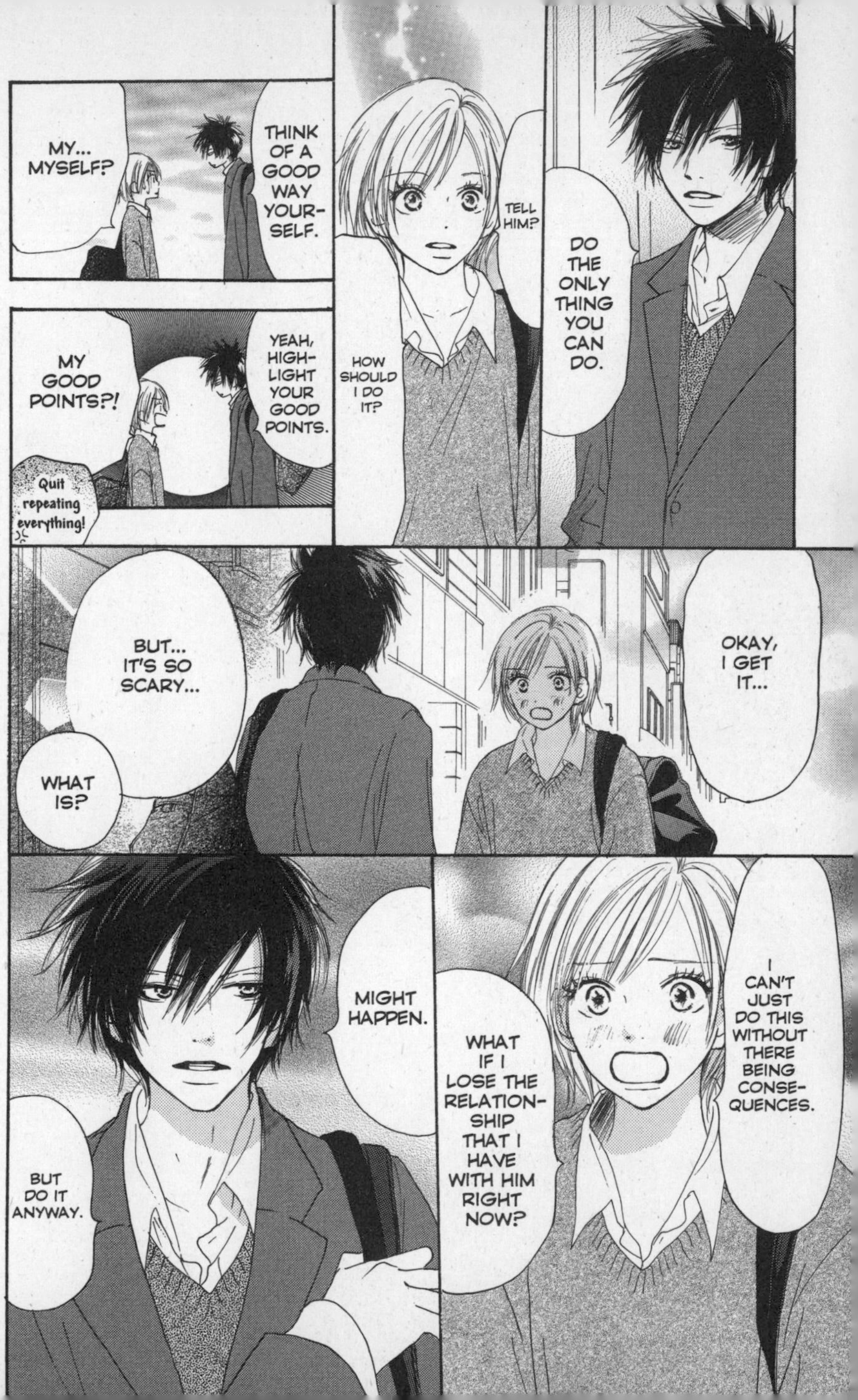
DO THE ONLY THING YOU CAN DO.
TELL HIM?
HOW SHOULD I DO IT?
THINK OF A GOOD WAY YOURSELF.
MY... MYSELF?
YEAH, HIGHLIGHT YOUR GOOD POINTS.
MY GOOD POINTS?!
Quit repeating everything!
OKAY, I GET IT...
BUT... IT'S SO SCARY...
WHAT IS?
I CAN'T JUST DO THIS WITHOUT THERE BEING CONSEQUENCES.
WHAT IF I LOSE THE RELATIONSHIP THAT I HAVE WITH HIM RIGHT NOW?
MIGHT HAPPEN.
BUT DO IT ANYWAY.

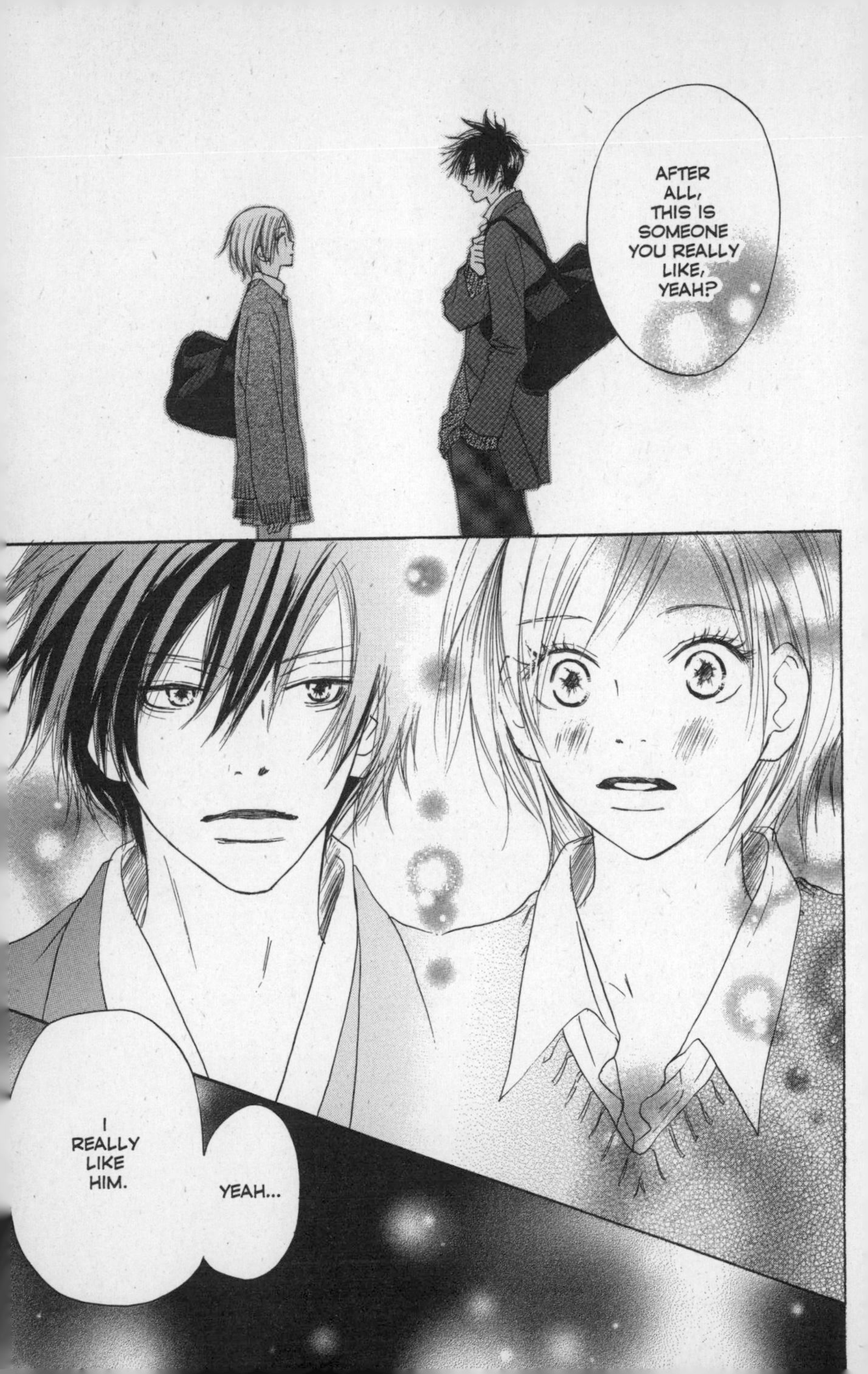
AFTER ALL, THIS IS SOMEONE YOU REALLY LIKE, YEAH?
YEAH...
I REALLY LIKE HIM.

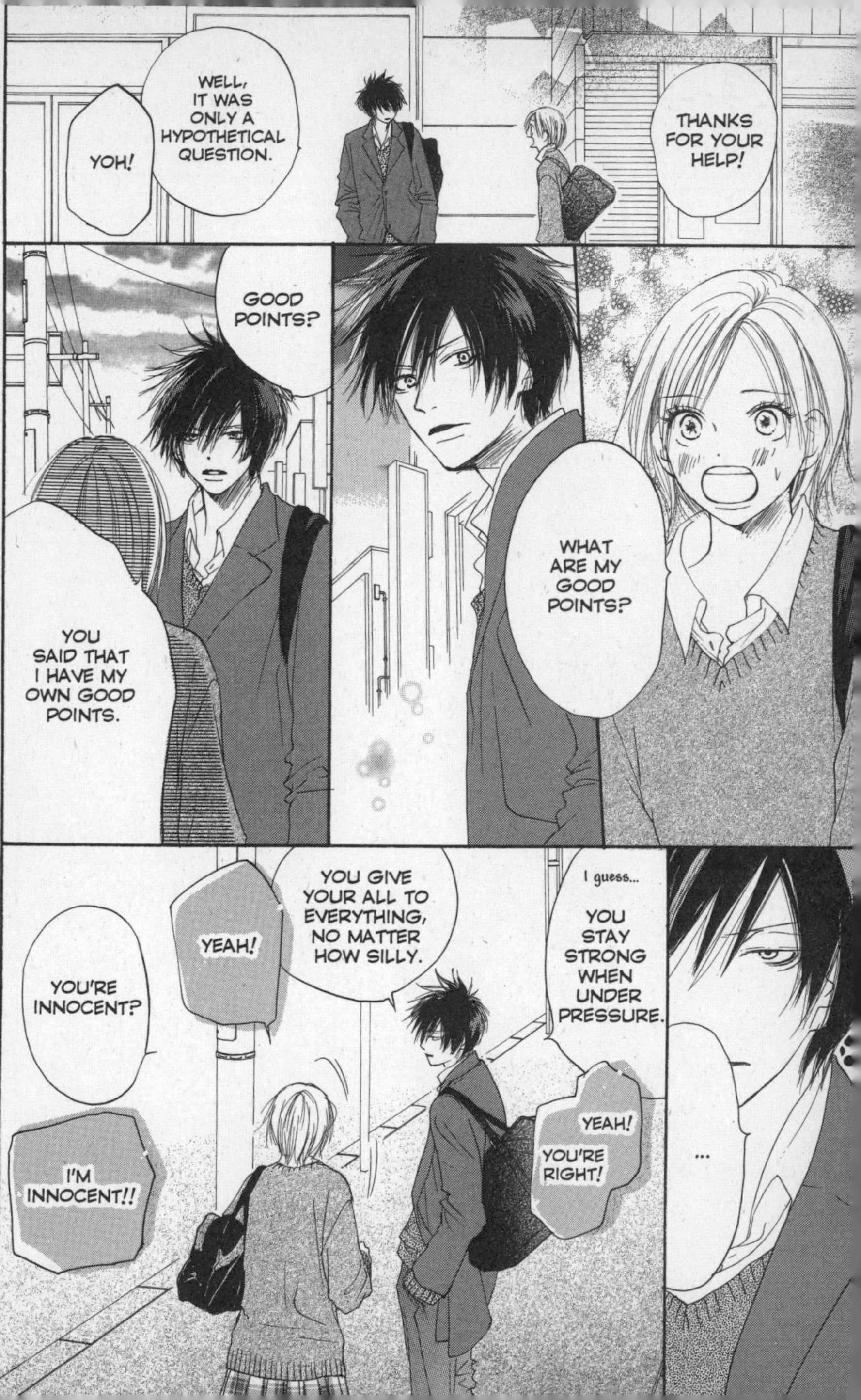
THANKS FOR YOUR HELP!
WELL, IT WAS ONLY A HYPOTHETICAL QUESTION.
YOH!
WHAT ARE MY GOOD POINTS?
GOOD POINTS?
YOU SAID THAT I HAVE MY OWN GOOD POINTS.
...
I guess...
YOU STAY STRONG WHEN UNDER PRESSURE.
YEAH!
YOU'RE RIGHT!
YOU GIVE YOUR ALL TO EVERYTHING, NO MATTER HOW SILLY.
YEAH!
YOU'RE INNOCENT?
I'M INNOCENT!!

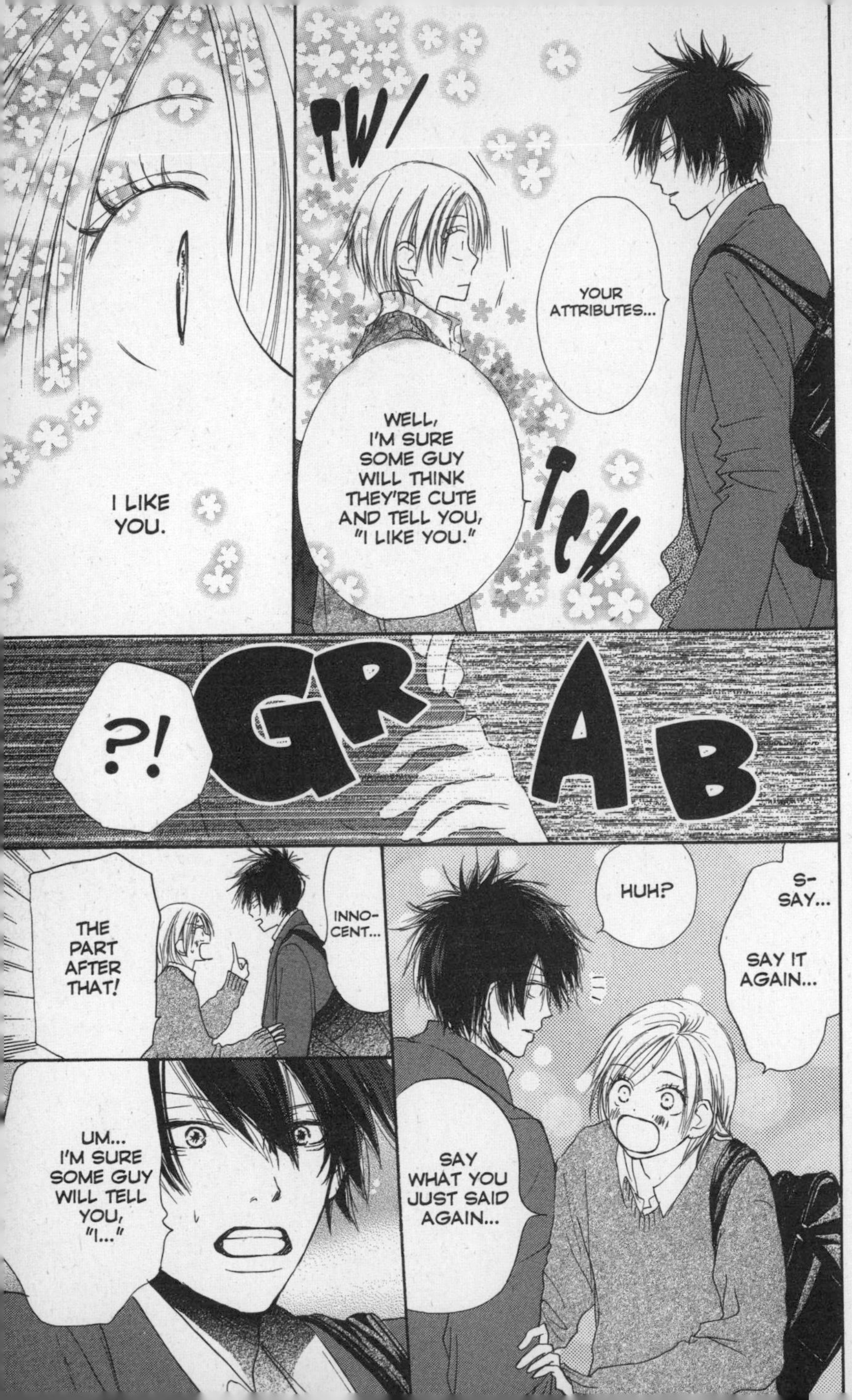
YOUR ATTRIBUTES...
TWI
WELL, I'M SURE SOME GUY WILL THINK THEY'RE CUTE AND TELL YOU, "I LIKE YOU."
TCH
I LIKE YOU.
GRAB
?!
S- SAY...
SAY IT AGAIN...
HUH?
SAY WHAT YOU JUST SAID AGAIN...
INNO-CENT...
THE PART AFTER THAT!
UM... I'M SURE SOME GUY WILL TELL YOU, "I..."

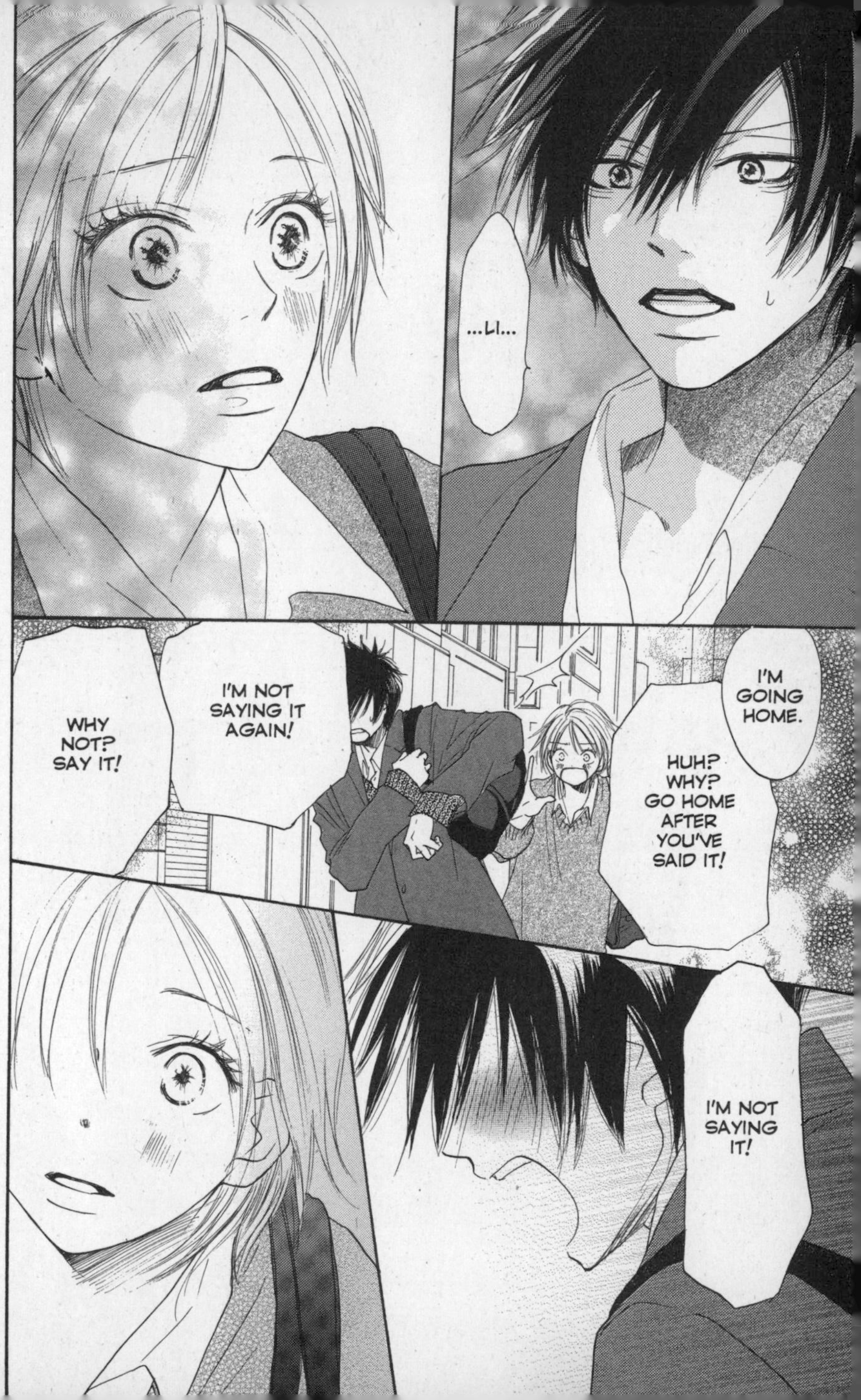
...LI...
I'M GOING HOME.
HUH? WHY? GO HOME AFTER YOU'VE SAID IT!
I'M NOT SAYING IT AGAIN!
WHY NOT? SAY IT!
I'M NOT SAYING IT!

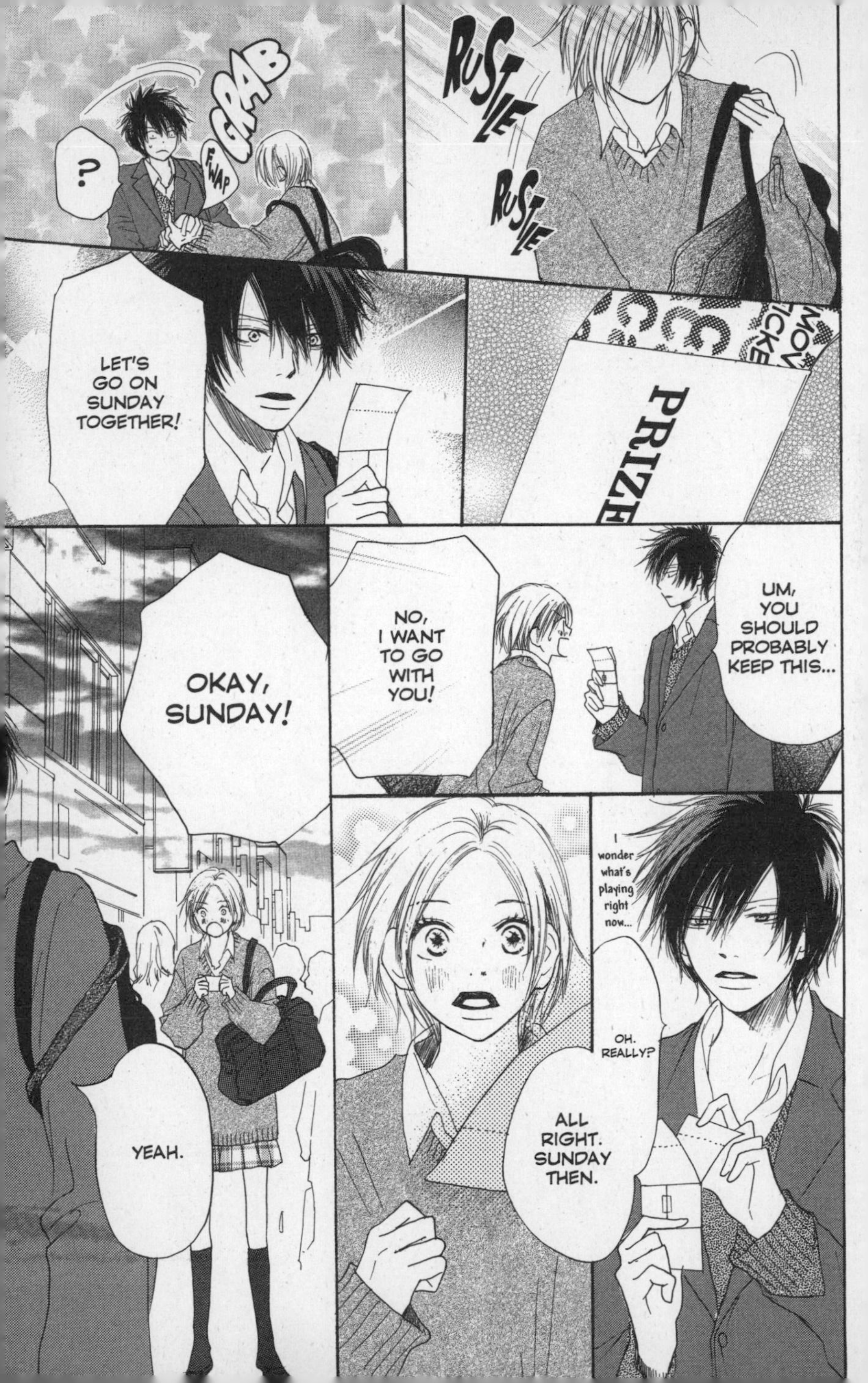
RUSTLE
RUSTLE
GRAB
FWAP
?
MOV TICKE
PRIZE
LET'S GO ON SUNDAY TOGETHER!
UM, YOU SHOULD PROBABLY KEEP THIS...
NO, I WANT TO GO WITH YOU!
I wonder what's playing right now...
OH. REALLY?
ALL RIGHT. SUNDAY THEN.
OKAY, SUNDAY!
YEAH.

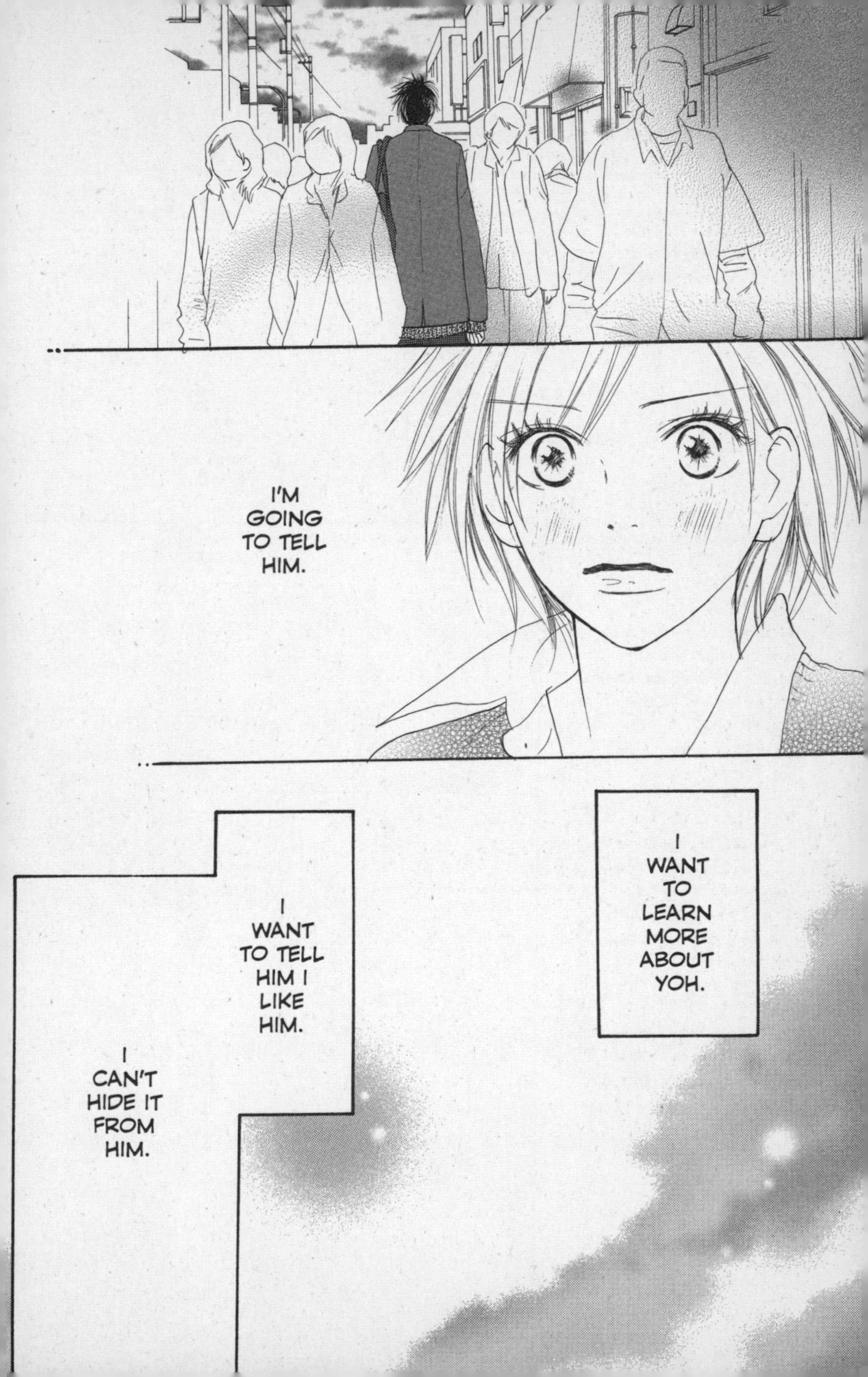

I'M GOING TO TELL HIM.
I WANT TO LEARN MORE ABOUT YOH.
I WANT TO TELL HIM I LIKE HIM.
I CAN'T HIDE IT FROM HIM.

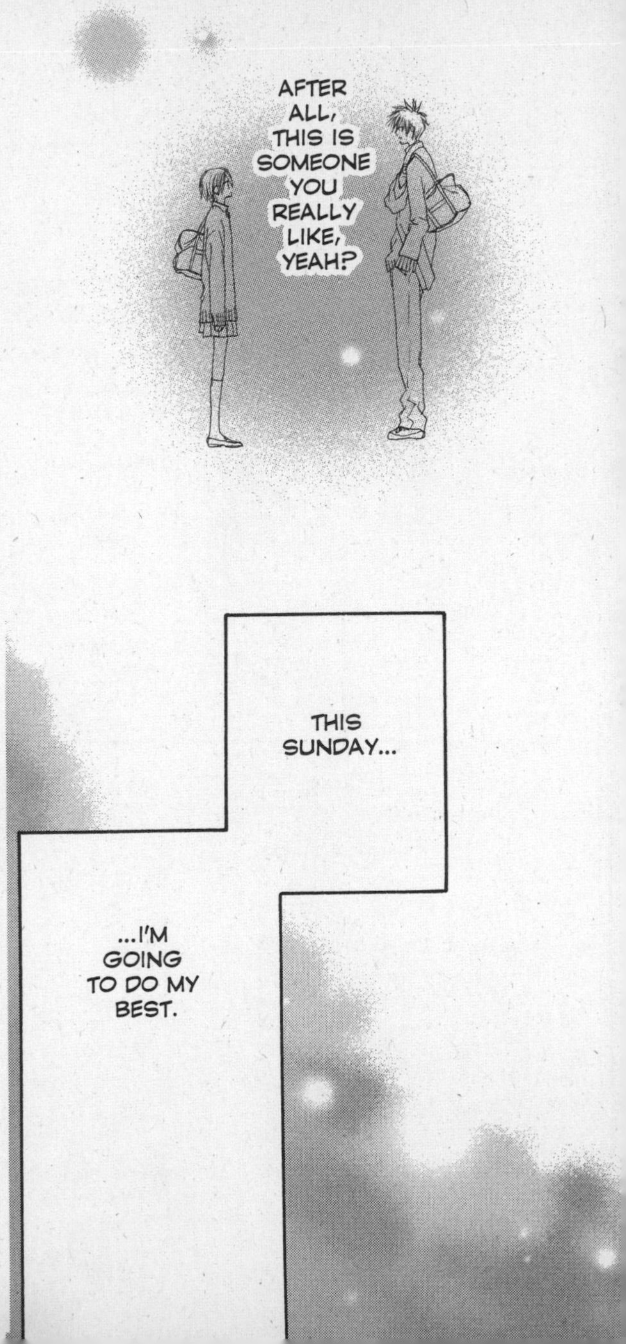
AFTER ALL, THIS IS SOMEONE YOU REALLY LIKE, YEAH?
THIS SUNDAY...
...I'M GOING TO DO MY BEST.

1

Hello. Are you all doing well? I'm doing just fine. Recently, the windshield wipers on my car broke. It was a big hassle.

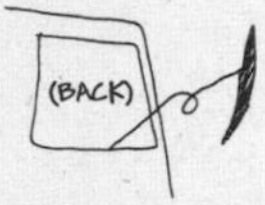
(BACK)

"What a piece of junk!" I got mad for a second, but then when I calmed down, I thought it looked kind of funny and was kind of glad it happened.
So I regained my senses and proceeded to back up, but I hit a Harley that was parked behind me. (I guess I hadn't fully regained my senses after all). The Harley was without a scratch, but there was a round dent on my car. I guess if you put something that's 660cc against something that's 1000cc, the 1000cc is just that much stronger. Since the dent didn't affect my car's performance, I left it alone. However, I'm starting to think I should get it fixed because other people keep asking me, "What happened?"

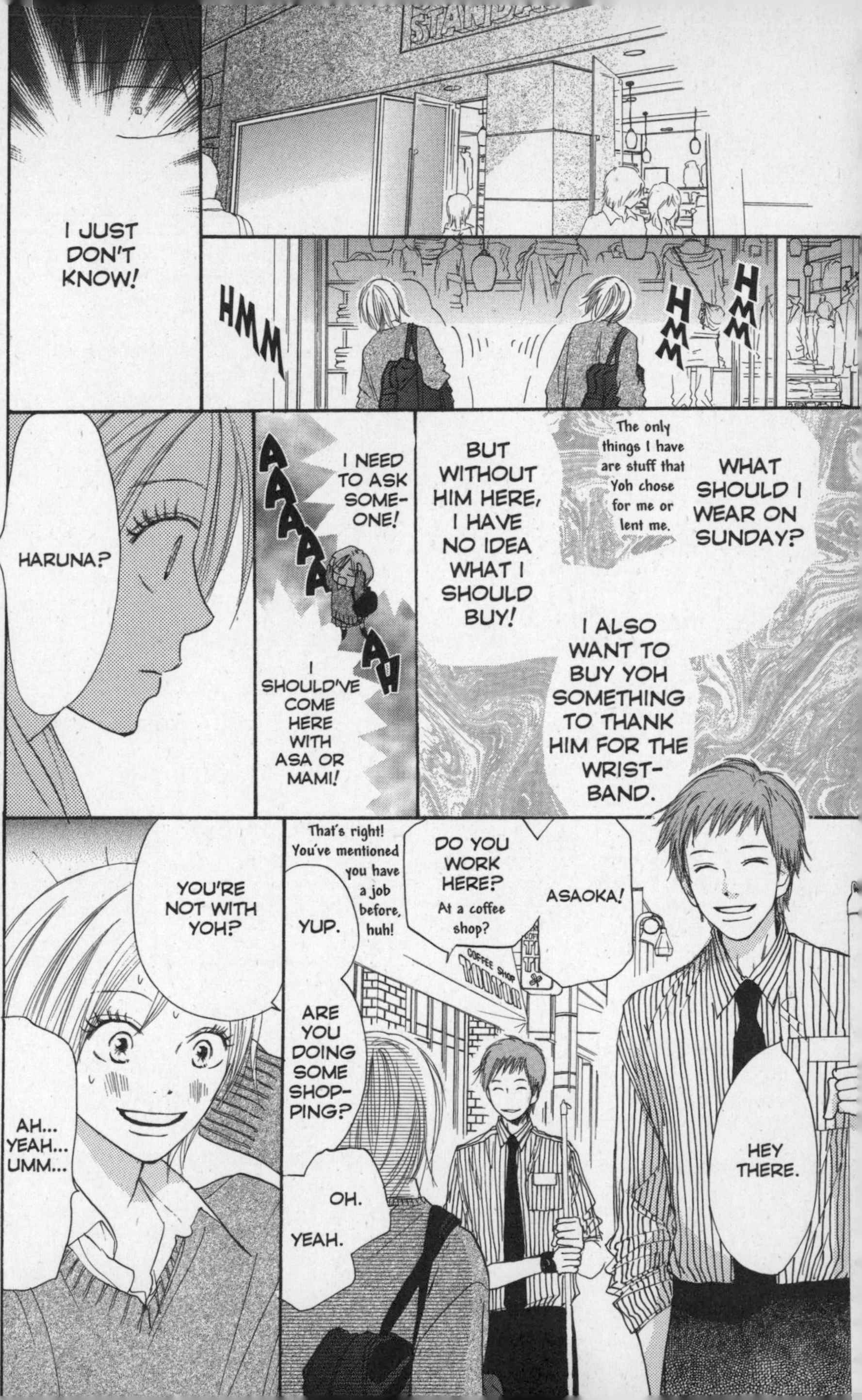
HMM
HMM
HMM
I JUST DON'T KNOW!
WHAT SHOULD I WEAR ON SUNDAY?
The only things I have are stuff that Yoh chose for me or lent me.
BUT WITHOUT HIM HERE, I HAVE NO IDEA WHAT I SHOULD BUY!
I ALSO WANT TO BUY YOH SOMETHING TO THANK HIM FOR THE WRIST-BAND.
I NEED TO ASK SOME-ONE!
AAAAAAAH
I SHOULD'VE COME HERE WITH ASA OR MAMI!
HARUNA?
HEY THERE.
ASAOKA!
DO YOU WORK HERE?
At a coffee shop?
COFFEE SHOP
That's right! You've mentioned you have a job before, huh!
YUP.
ARE YOU DOING SOME SHOP-PING?
OH.
YEAH.
YOU'RE NOT WITH YOH?
AH... YEAH... UMM...

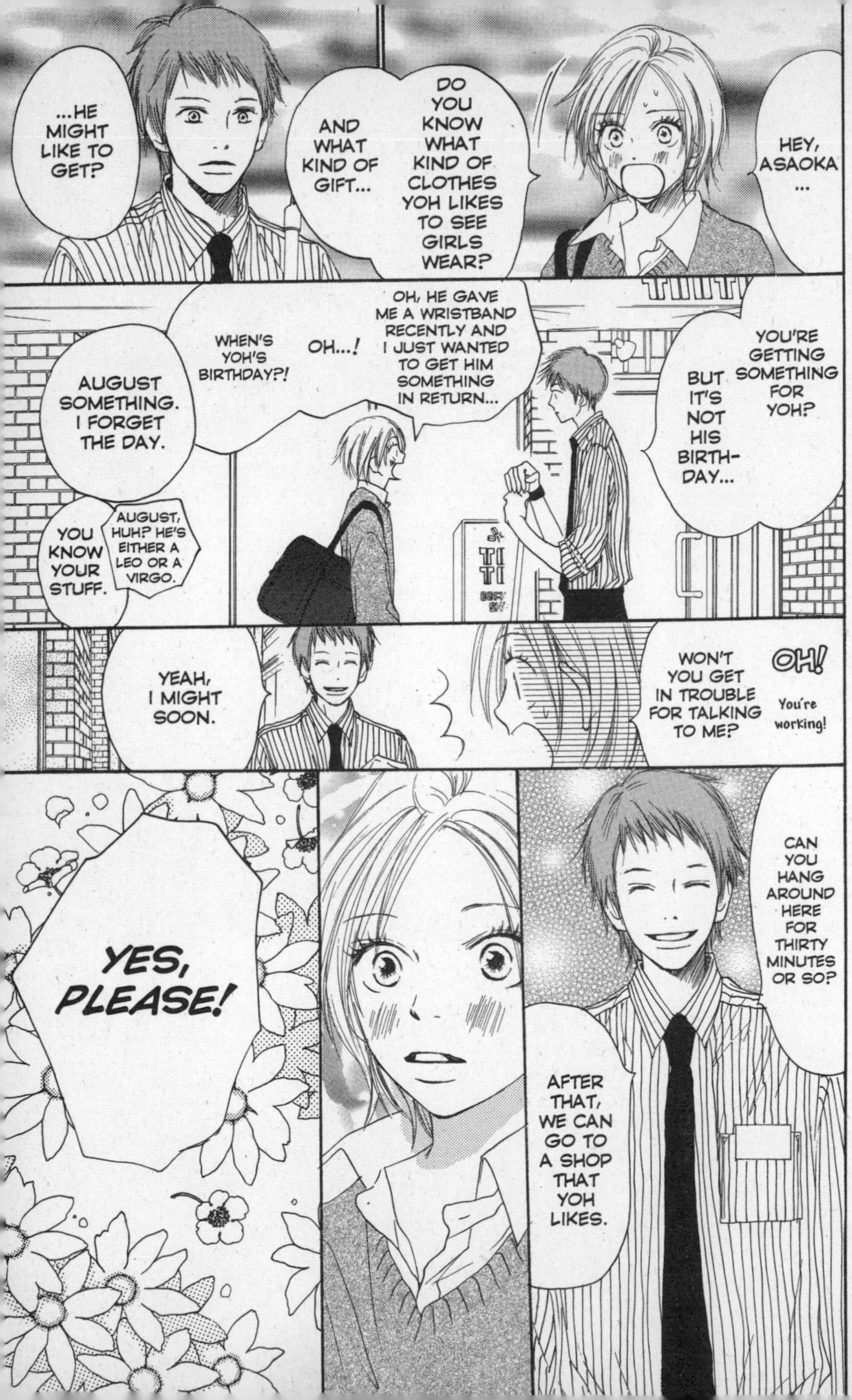
HEY, ASAOKA ...
DO YOU KNOW WHAT KIND OF CLOTHES YOH LIKES TO SEE GIRLS WEAR?
AND WHAT KIND OF GIFT...
...HE MIGHT LIKE TO GET?
YOU'RE GETTING SOMETHING FOR YOH?
BUT IT'S NOT HIS BIRTHDAY...
OH, HE GAVE ME A WRISTBAND RECENTLY AND I JUST WANTED TO GET HIM SOMETHING IN RETURN...
OH...!
WHEN'S YOH'S BIRTHDAY?!
AUGUST SOMETHING. I FORGET THE DAY.
AUGUST, HUH? HE'S EITHER A LEO OR A VIRGO.
YOU KNOW YOUR STUFF.
OH!
You're working!
WON'T YOU GET IN TROUBLE FOR TALKING TO ME?
YEAH, I MIGHT SOON.
CAN YOU HANG AROUND HERE FOR THIRTY MINUTES OR SO?
AFTER THAT, WE CAN GO TO A SHOP THAT YOH LIKES.
YES, PLEASE!

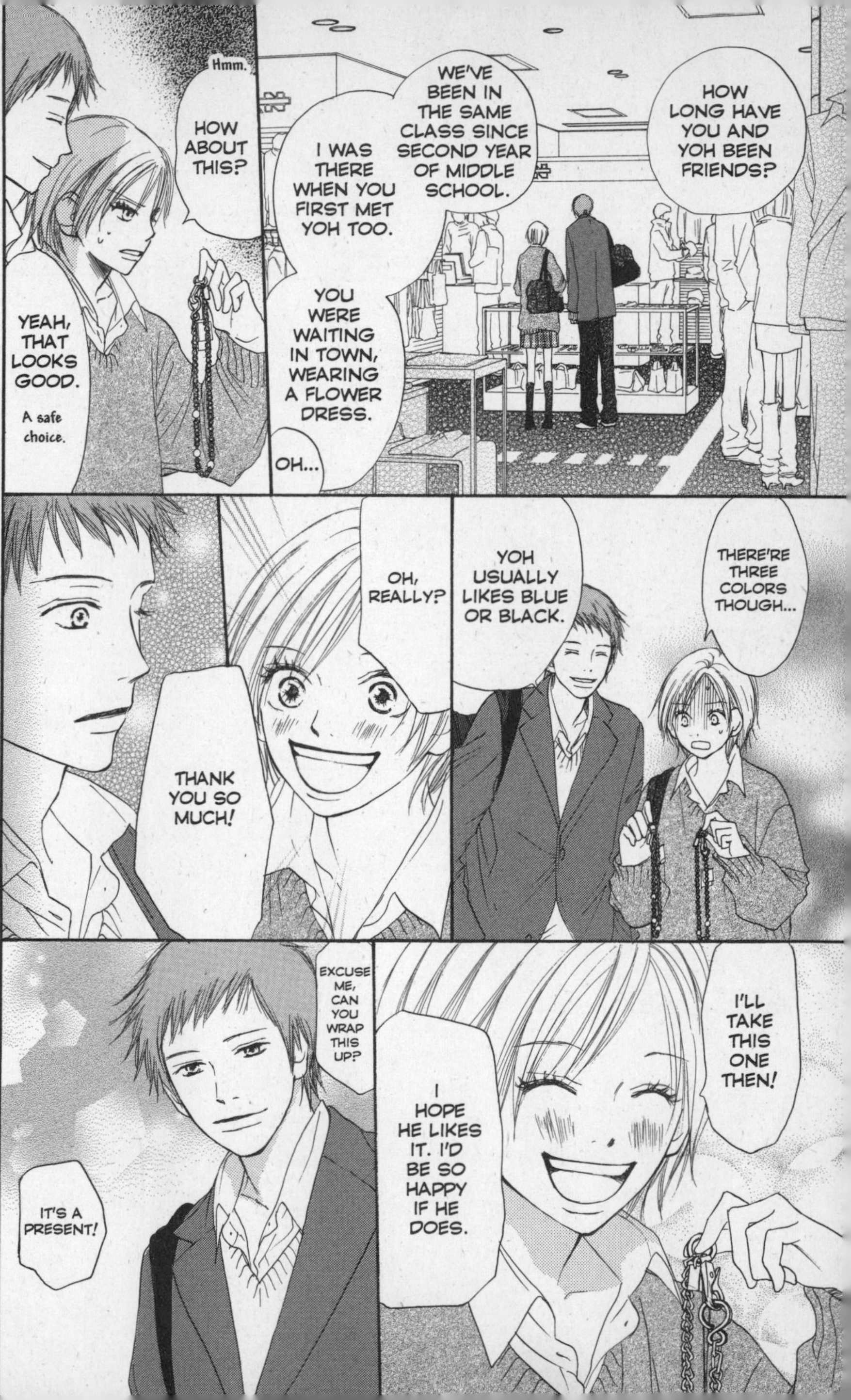
HOW LONG HAVE YOU AND YOH BEEN FRIENDS?
WE'VE BEEN IN THE SAME CLASS SINCE SECOND YEAR OF MIDDLE SCHOOL.
I WAS THERE WHEN YOU FIRST MET YOH TOO.
YOU WERE WAITING IN TOWN, WEARING A FLOWER DRESS.
OH...
Hmm.
HOW ABOUT THIS?
YEAH, THAT LOOKS GOOD.
A safe choice.
THERE'RE THREE COLORS THOUGH...
YOH USUALLY LIKES BLUE OR BLACK.
OH, REALLY?
THANK YOU SO MUCH!
I'LL TAKE THIS ONE THEN!
I HOPE HE LIKES IT. I'D BE SO HAPPY IF HE DOES.
EXCUSE ME, CAN YOU WRAP THIS UP?
IT'S A PRESENT!

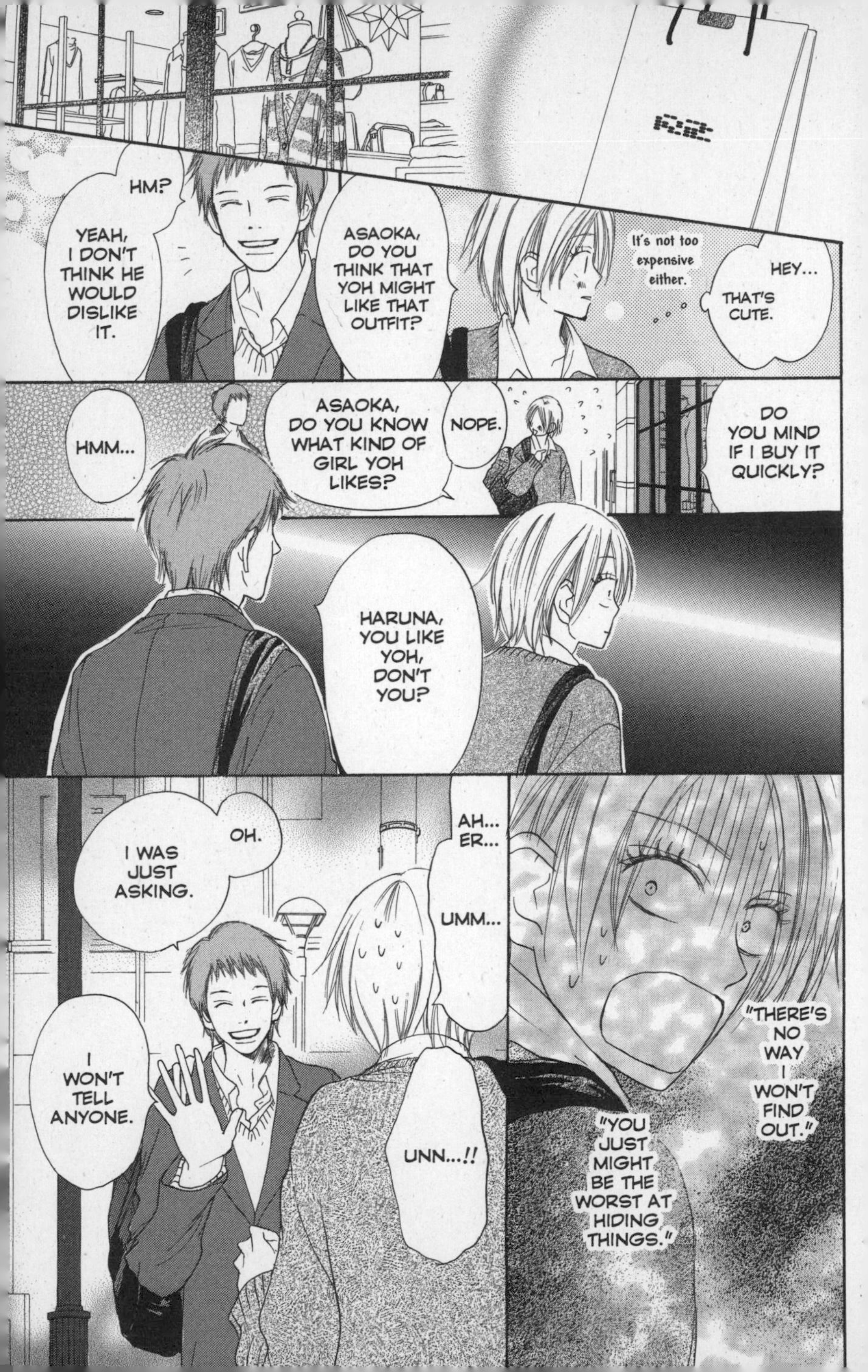

HEY... THAT'S CUTE.
It's not too expensive either.
ASAOKA, DO YOU THINK THAT YOH MIGHT LIKE THAT OUTFIT?
HM?
YEAH, I DON'T THINK HE WOULD DISLIKE IT.
DO YOU MIND IF I BUY IT QUICKLY?
NOPE.
ASAOKA, DO YOU KNOW WHAT KIND OF GIRL YOH LIKES?
HMM...
HARUNA, YOU LIKE YOH, DON'T YOU?
"THERE'S NO WAY I WON'T FIND OUT."
"YOU JUST MIGHT BE THE WORST AT HIDING THINGS."
AH... ER...
UMM...
OH.
I WAS JUST ASKING.
UNN...!!
I WON'T TELL ANYONE.

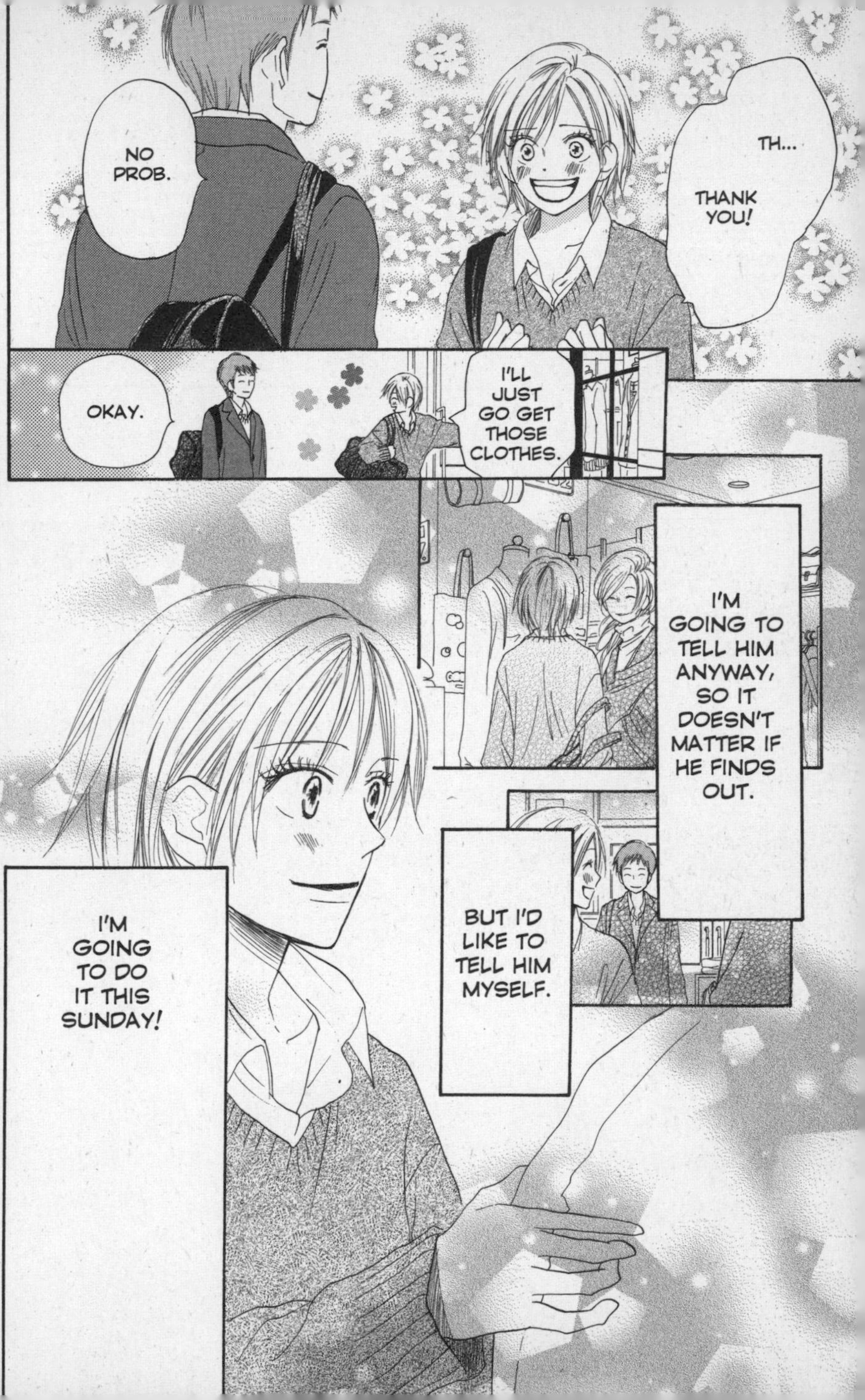
TH...
THANK YOU!
NO PROB.
I'LL JUST GO GET THOSE CLOTHES.
OKAY.
I'M GOING TO TELL HIM ANYWAY, SO IT DOESN'T MATTER IF HE FINDS OUT.
BUT I'D LIKE TO TELL HIM MYSELF.
I'M GOING TO DO IT THIS SUNDAY!

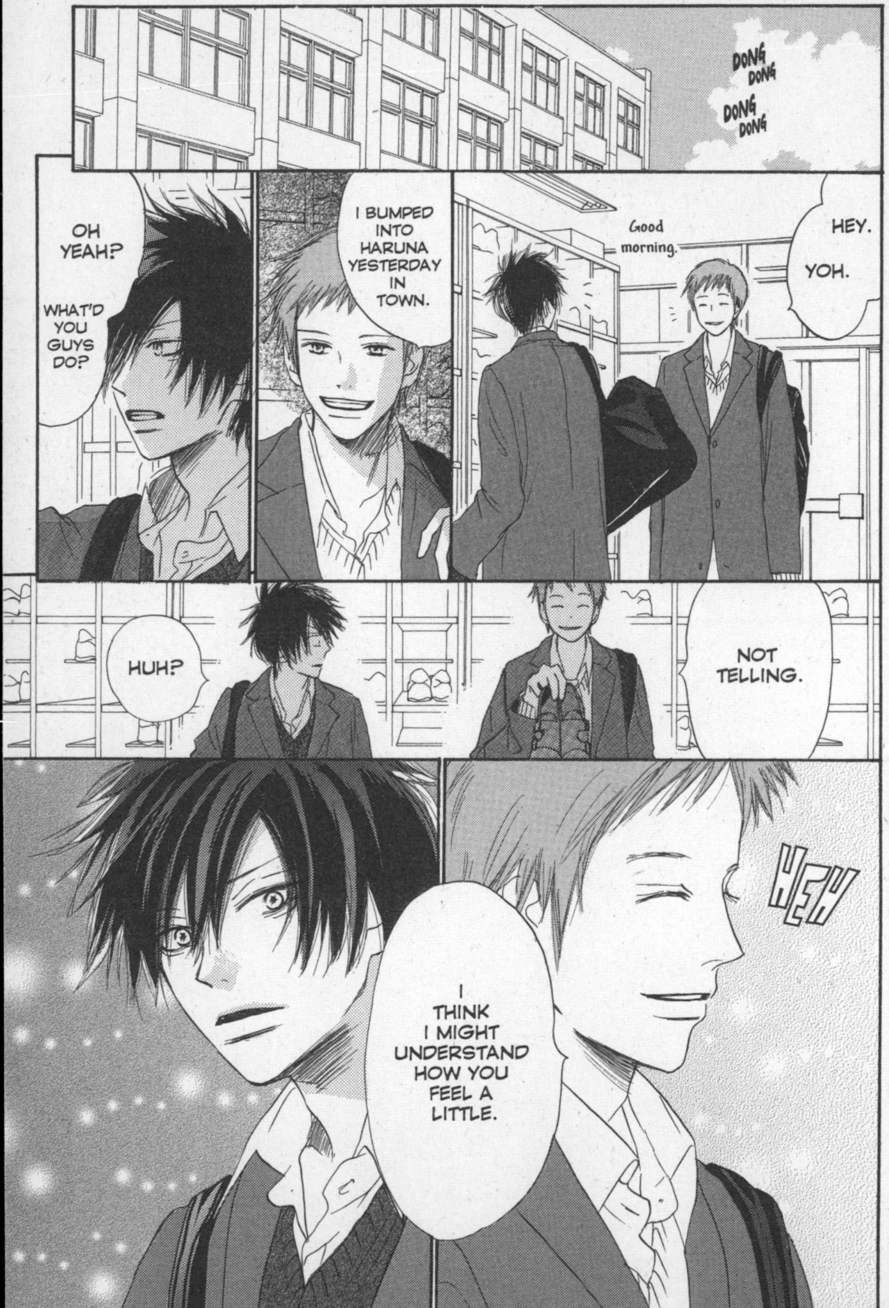
DONG DONG
DONG DONG
HEY.
YOH.
Good morning.
I BUMPED INTO HARUNA YESTERDAY IN TOWN.
OH YEAH?
WHAT'D YOU GUYS DO?
NOT TELLING.
HUH?
HEH
I THINK I MIGHT UNDERSTAND HOW YOU FEEL A LITTLE.

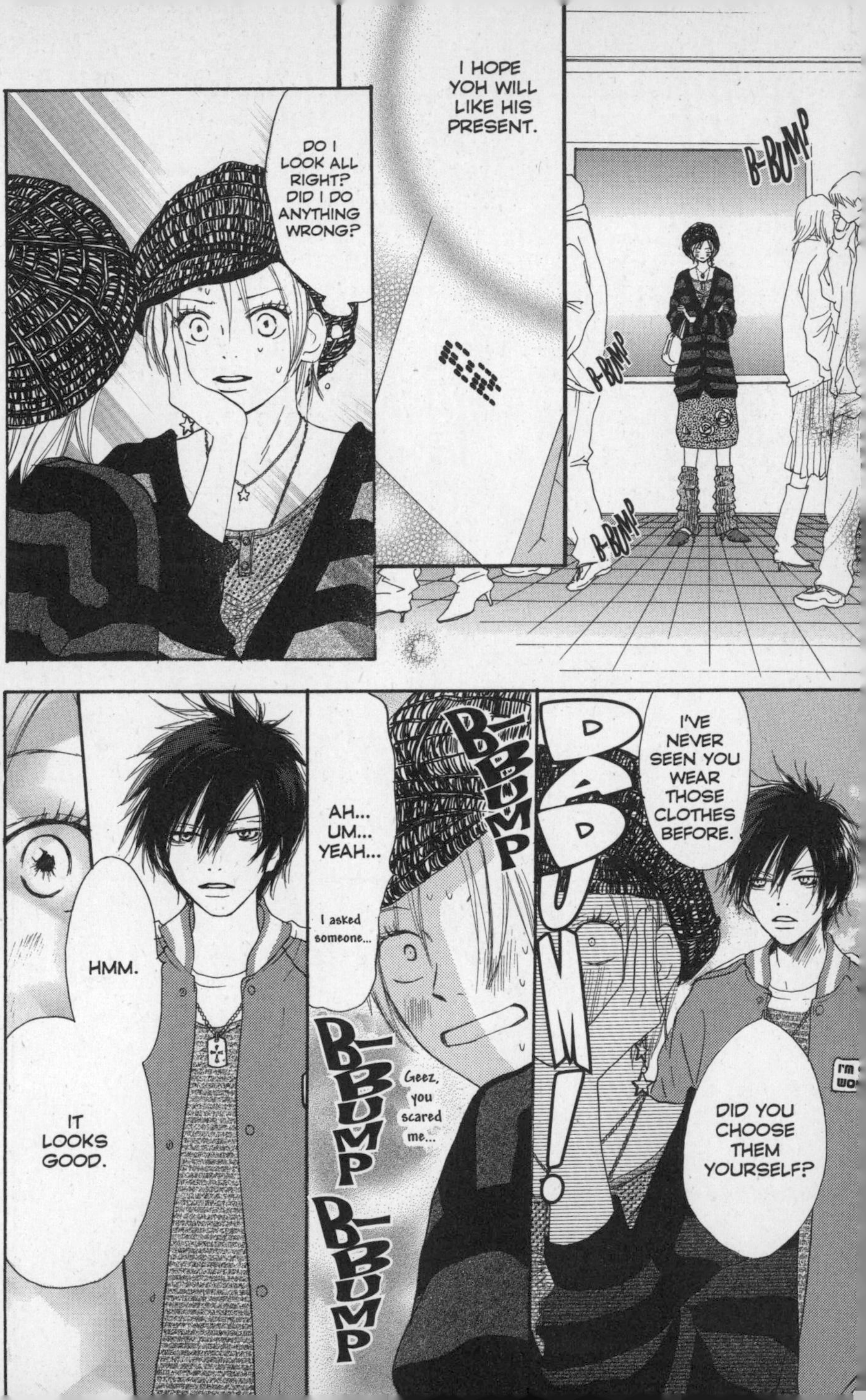
I HOPE YOH WILL LIKE HIS PRESENT.
B-BUMP
B-BUMP
B-BUMP
DO I LOOK ALL RIGHT? DID I DO ANYTHING WRONG?
I'VE NEVER SEEN YOU WEAR THOSE CLOTHES BEFORE.
DADUM!
DID YOU CHOOSE THEM YOURSELF?
B-BUMP
AH... UM... YEAH...
I asked someone...
B-BUMP
Geez, you scared me...
B-BUMP
HMM.
IT LOOKS GOOD.

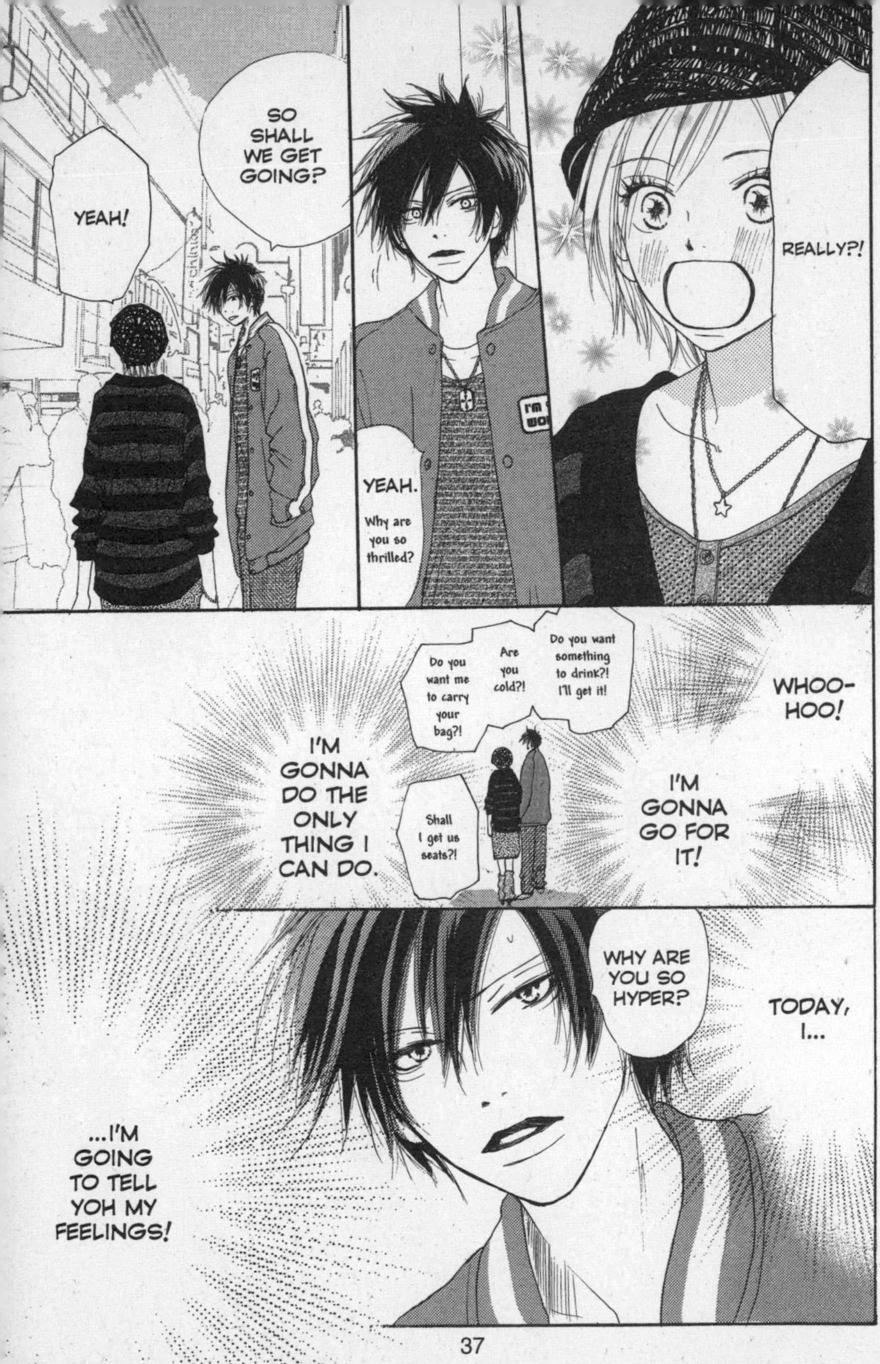
REALLY?!
YEAH.
Why are you so thrilled?
SO SHALL WE GET GOING?
YEAH!
WHOO-HOO!
I'M GONNA GO FOR IT!
Do you want something to drink?! I'll get it!
Are you cold?!
Do you want me to carry your bag?!
Shall I get us seats?!
I'M GONNA DO THE ONLY THING I CAN DO.
WHY ARE YOU SO HYPER?
TODAY, I...
...I'M GOING TO TELL YOH MY FEELINGS!

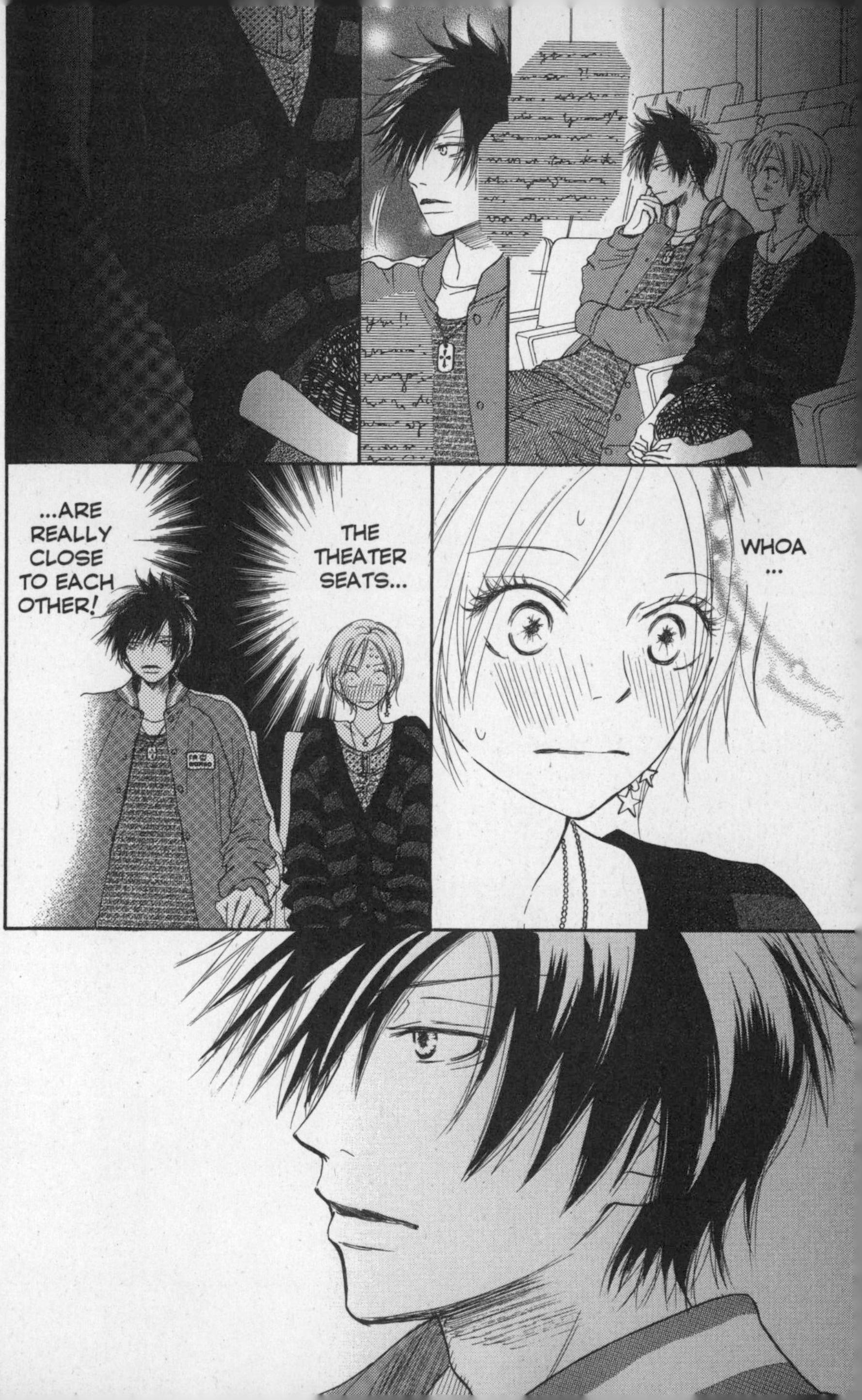
WHOA ...
THE THEATER SEATS...
...ARE REALLY CLOSE TO EACH OTHER!

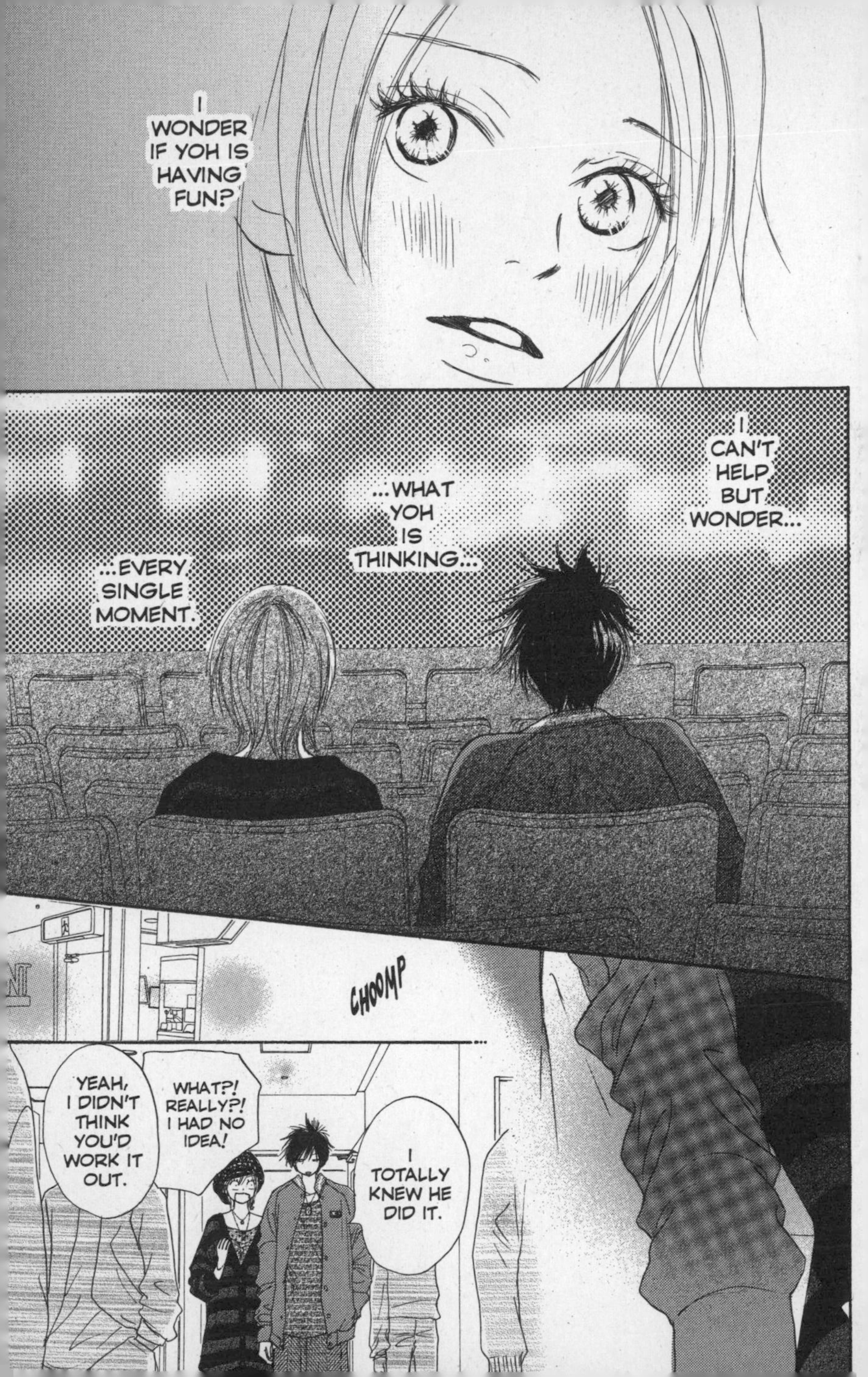
I WONDER IF YOH IS HAVING FUN?
I CAN'T HELP BUT WONDER...
...WHAT YOH IS THINKING...
...EVERY SINGLE MOMENT.
CHOOMP
I TOTALLY KNEW HE DID IT.
WHAT?! REALLY?! I HAD NO IDEA!
YEAH, I DIDN'T THINK YOU'D WORK IT OUT.

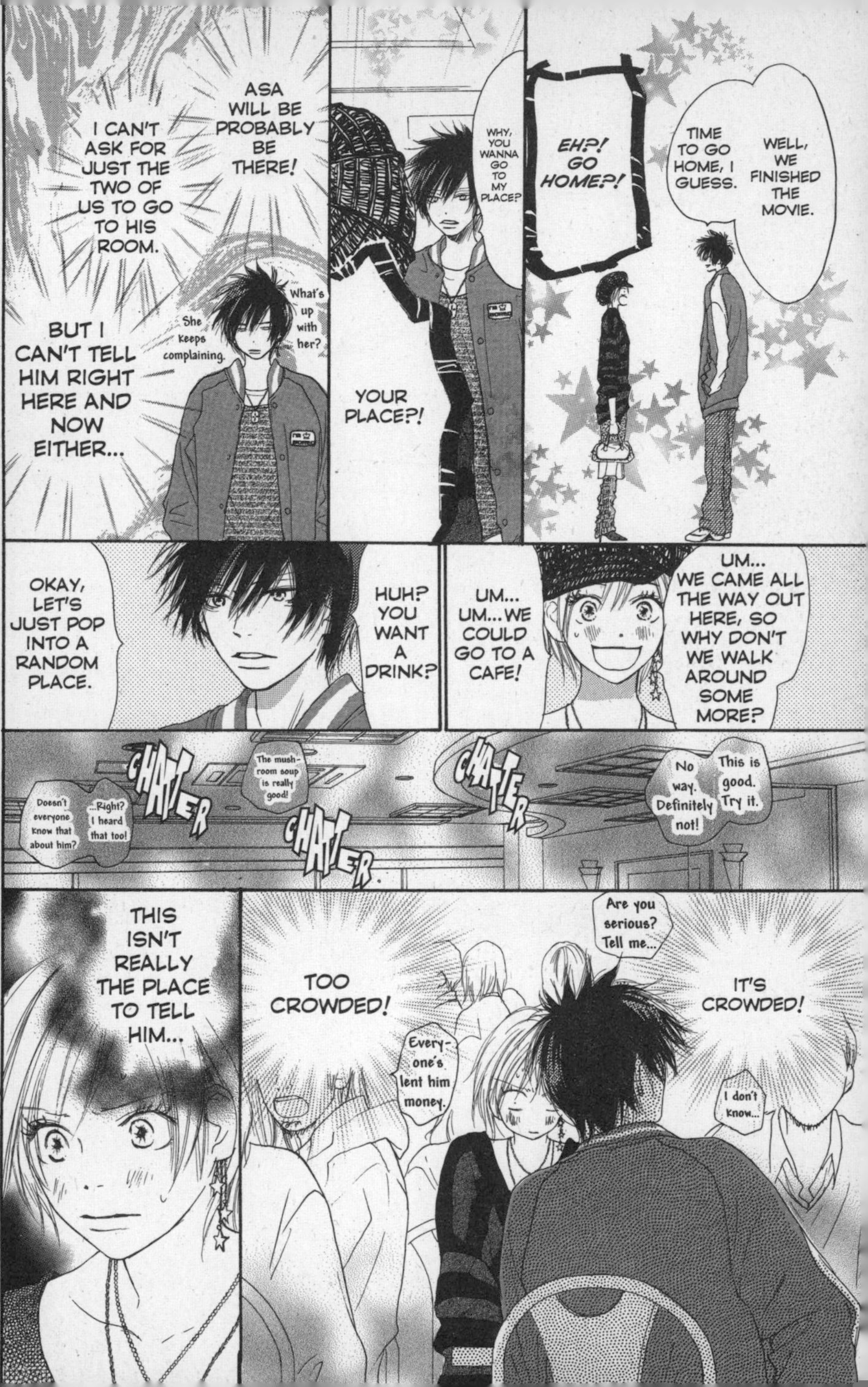
WELL, WE FINISHED THE MOVIE.
TIME TO GO HOME, I GUESS.
EH?! GO HOME?!
WHY, YOU WANNA GO TO MY PLACE?
YOUR PLACE?!
ASA WILL BE PROBABLY BE THERE!
I CAN'T ASK FOR JUST THE TWO OF US TO GO TO HIS ROOM.
What's up with her?
She keeps complaining.
BUT I CAN'T TELL HIM RIGHT HERE AND NOW EITHER...
UM... WE CAME ALL THE WAY OUT HERE, SO WHY DON'T WE WALK AROUND SOME MORE?
UM... UM...WE COULD GO TO A CAFE!
HUH? YOU WANT A DRINK?
OKAY, LET'S JUST POP INTO A RANDOM PLACE.
This is good. Try it.
No way. Definitely not!
CHATTER
The mush-room soup is really good!
CHATTER
CHATTER
...Right? I heard that too!
Doesn't everyone know that about him?
IT'S CROWDED!
Are you serious? Tell me...
I don't know...
TOO CROWDED!
Every-one's lent him money.
THIS ISN'T REALLY THE PLACE TO TELL HIM...

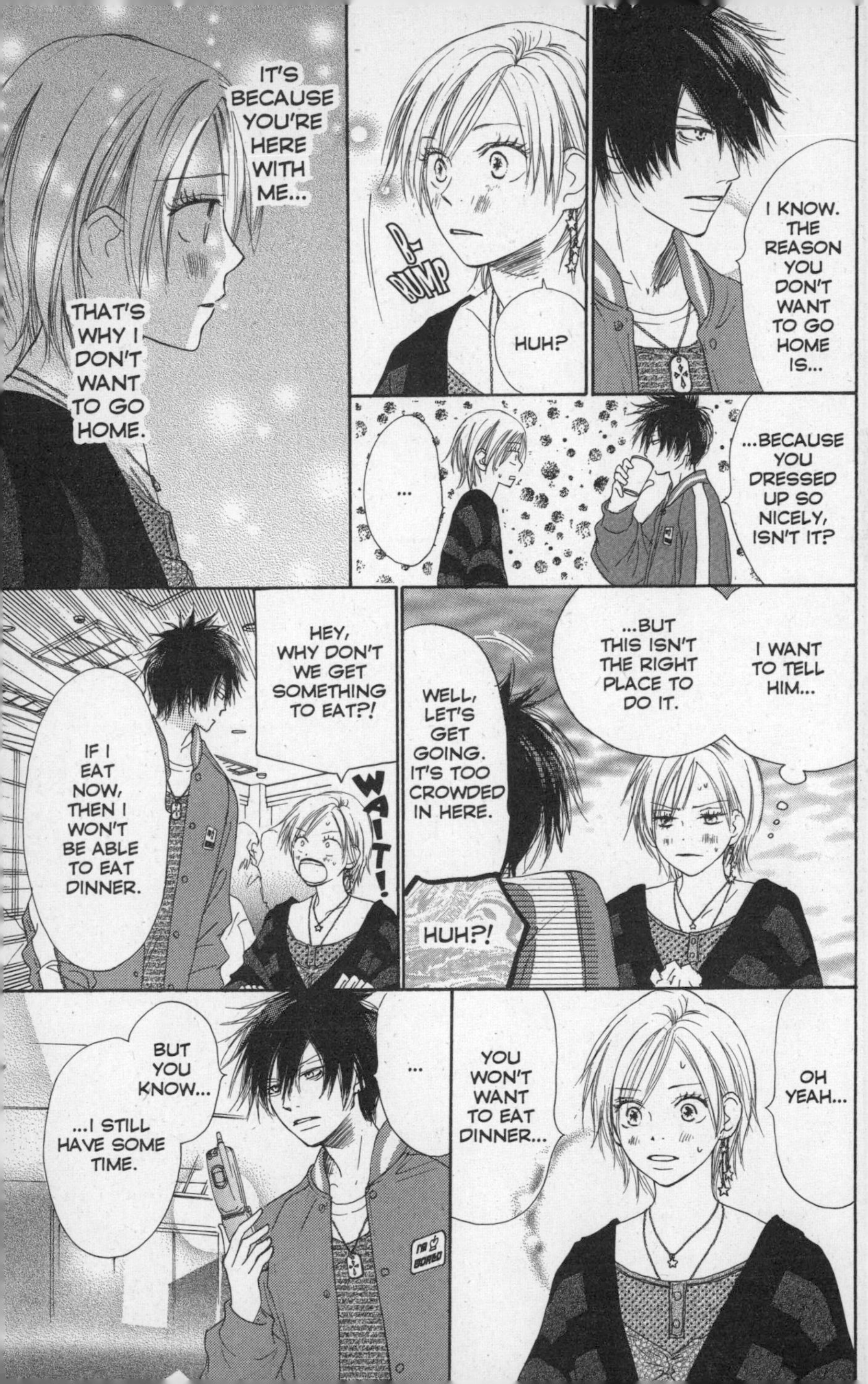
I KNOW. THE REASON YOU DON'T WANT TO GO HOME IS...
B-BUMP
HUH?
...BECAUSE YOU DRESSED UP SO NICELY, ISN'T IT?
...
IT'S BECAUSE YOU'RE HERE WITH ME...
THAT'S WHY I DON'T WANT TO GO HOME.
I WANT TO TELL HIM...
...BUT THIS ISN'T THE RIGHT PLACE TO DO IT.
WELL, LET'S GET GOING. IT'S TOO CROWDED IN HERE.
HUH?!
HEY, WHY DON'T WE GET SOMETHING TO EAT?!
WAIT!
IF I EAT NOW, THEN I WON'T BE ABLE TO EAT DINNER.
OH YEAH...
YOU WON'T WANT TO EAT DINNER...
...
BUT YOU KNOW...
...I STILL HAVE SOME TIME.

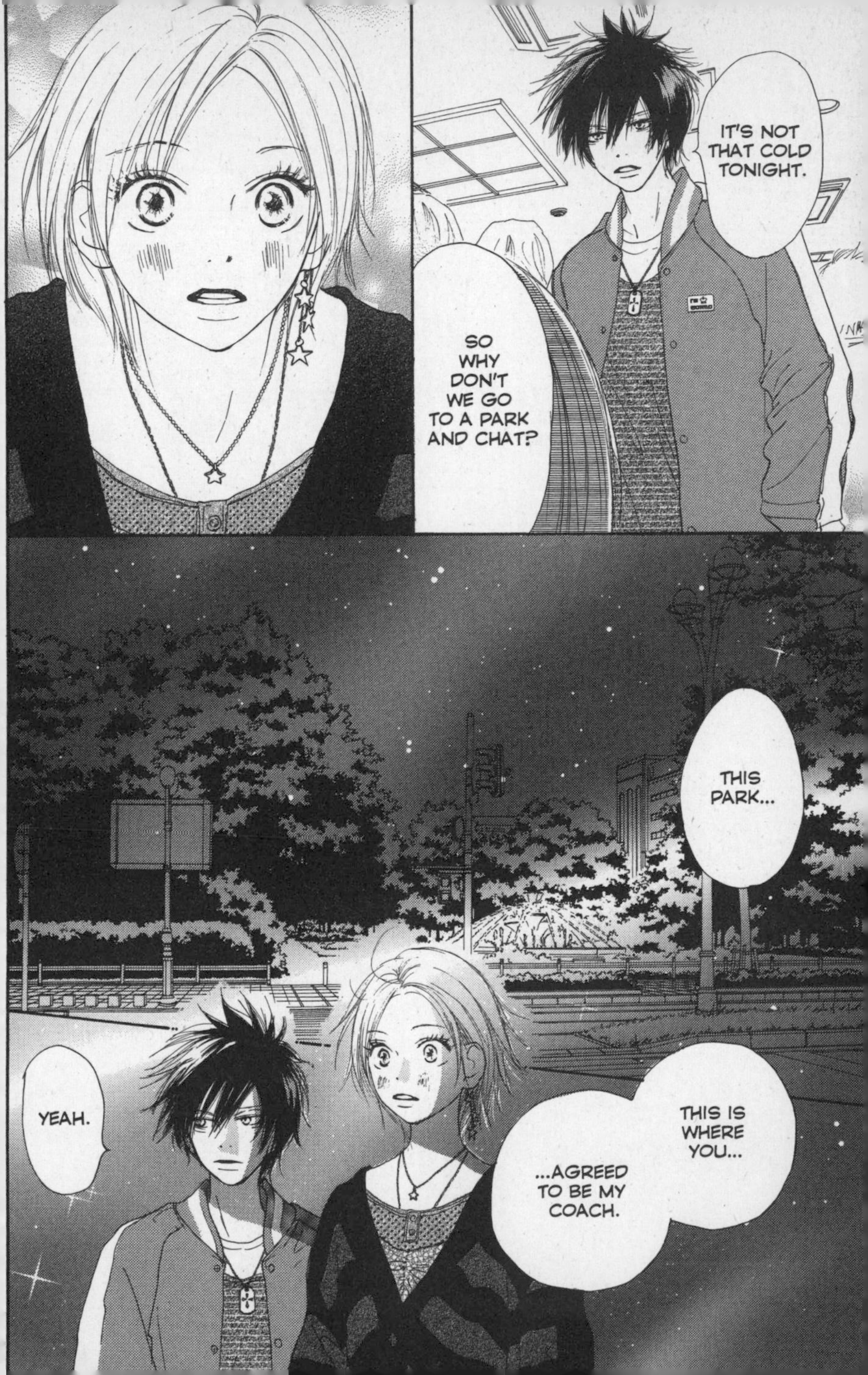
IT'S NOT THAT COLD TONIGHT.
SO WHY DON'T WE GO TO A PARK AND CHAT?
THIS PARK...
THIS IS WHERE YOU...
...AGREED TO BE MY COACH.
YEAH.

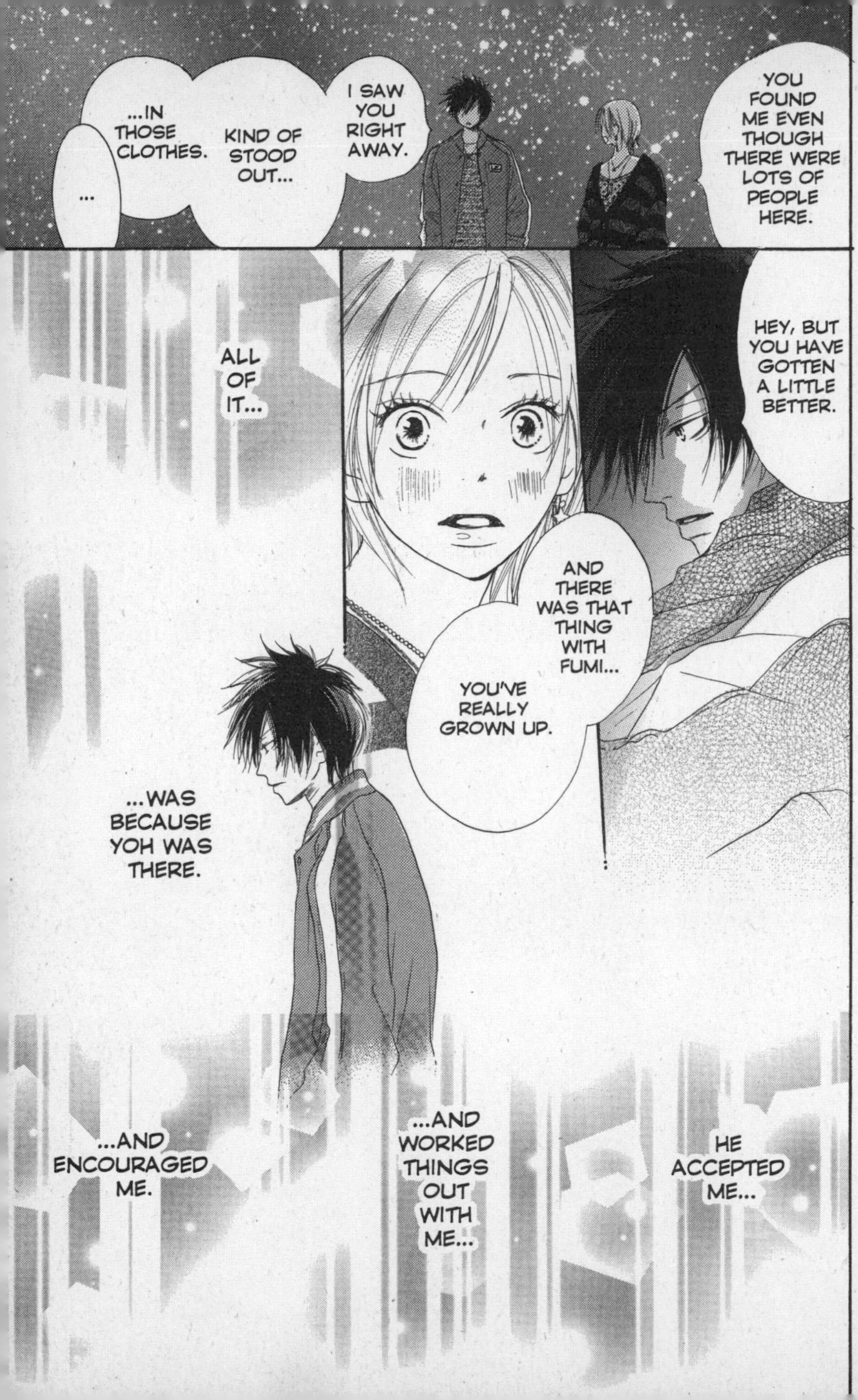
YOU FOUND ME EVEN THOUGH THERE WERE LOTS OF PEOPLE HERE.
I SAW YOU RIGHT AWAY.
KIND OF STOOD OUT...
...IN THOSE CLOTHES.
...
HEY, BUT YOU HAVE GOTTEN A LITTLE BETTER.
AND THERE WAS THAT THING WITH FUMI...
YOU'VE REALLY GROWN UP.
ALL OF IT...
...WAS BECAUSE YOH WAS THERE.
HE ACCEPTED ME...
...AND WORKED THINGS OUT WITH ME...
...AND ENCOURAGED ME.

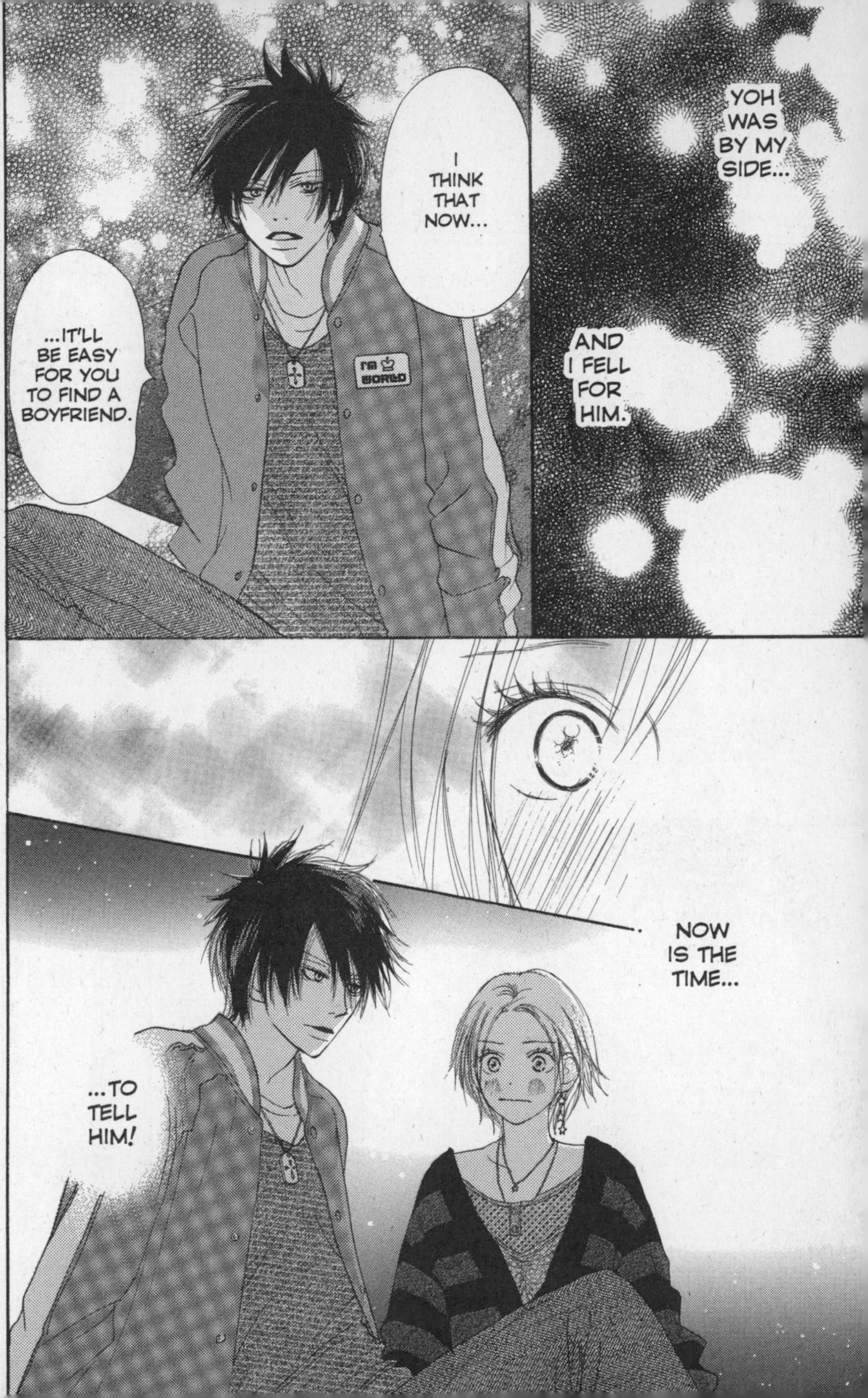
YOH WAS BY MY SIDE...
AND I FELL FOR HIM.
I THINK THAT NOW...
...IT'LL BE EASY FOR YOU TO FIND A BOYFRIEND.
NOW IS THE TIME...
...TO TELL HIM!

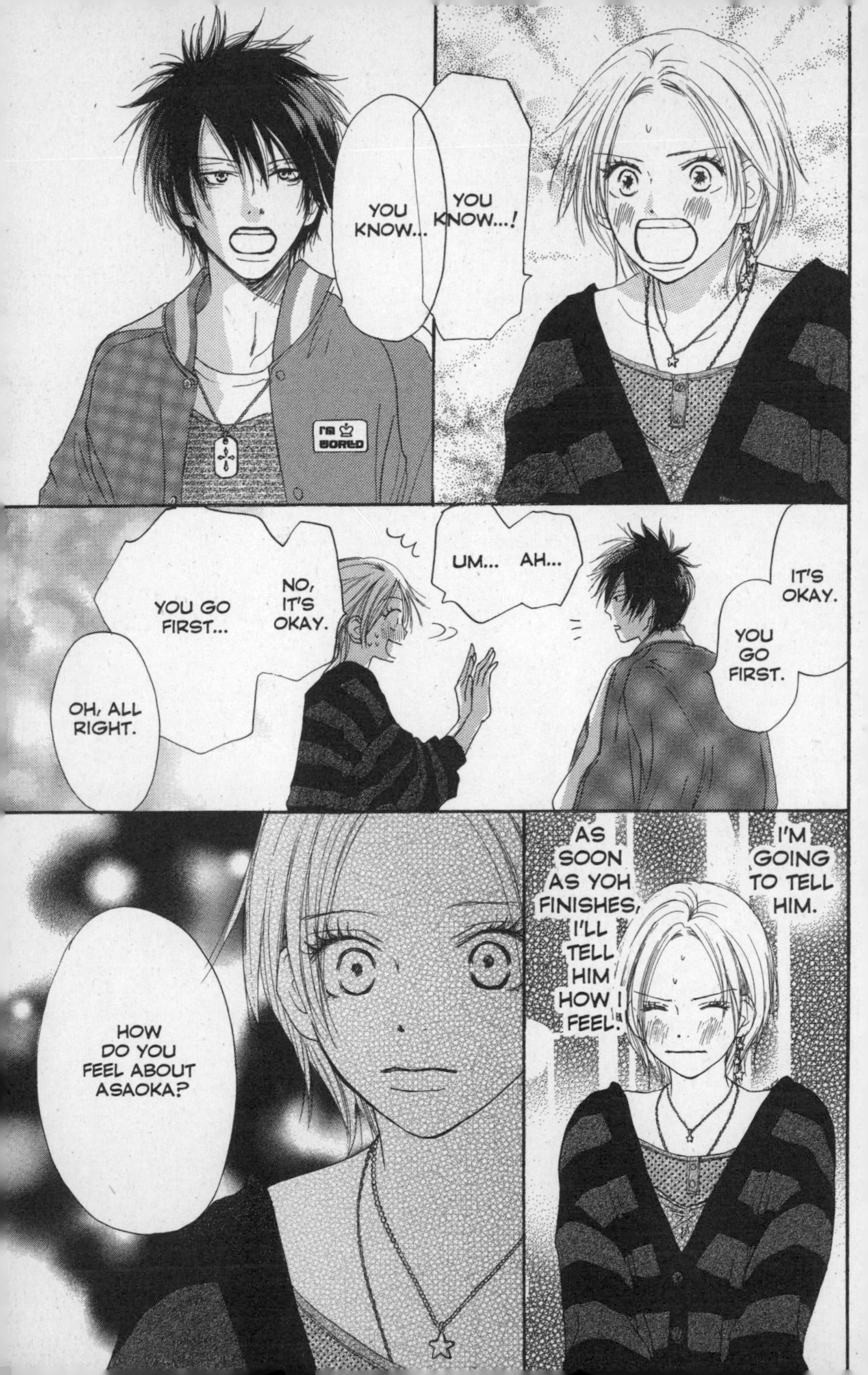
YOU KNOW...!
YOU KNOW...
I'M WORLD
IT'S OKAY.
YOU GO FIRST.
UM... AH...
NO, IT'S OKAY.
YOU GO FIRST...
OH, ALL RIGHT.
I'M GOING TO TELL HIM.
AS SOON AS YOH FINISHES, I'LL TELL HIM HOW I FEEL.
HOW DO YOU FEEL ABOUT ASAOKA?

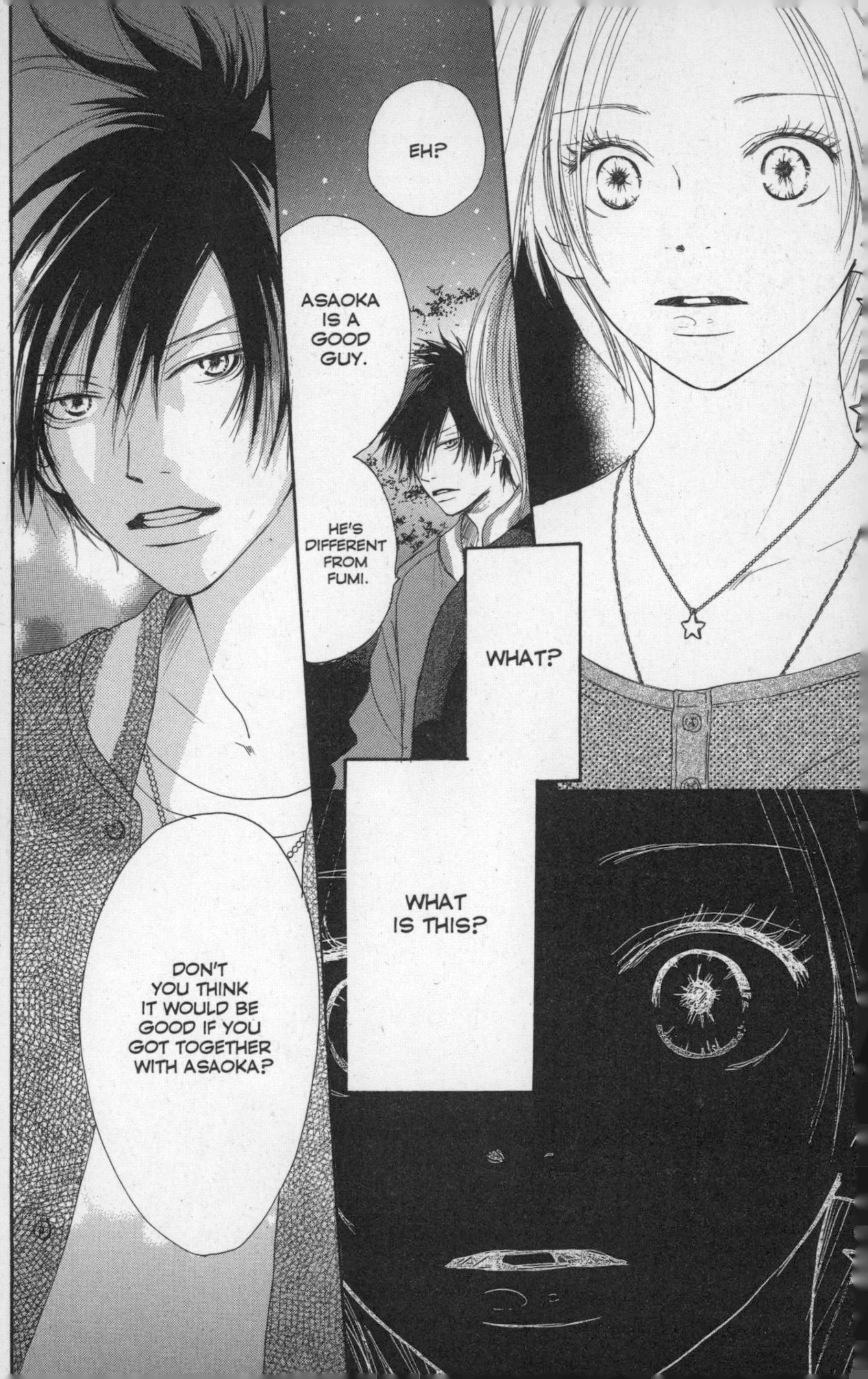
EH?
ASAOKA IS A GOOD GUY.
HE'S DIFFERENT FROM FUMI.
DON'T YOU THINK IT WOULD BE GOOD IF YOU GOT TOGETHER WITH ASAOKA?
WHAT?
WHAT IS THIS?

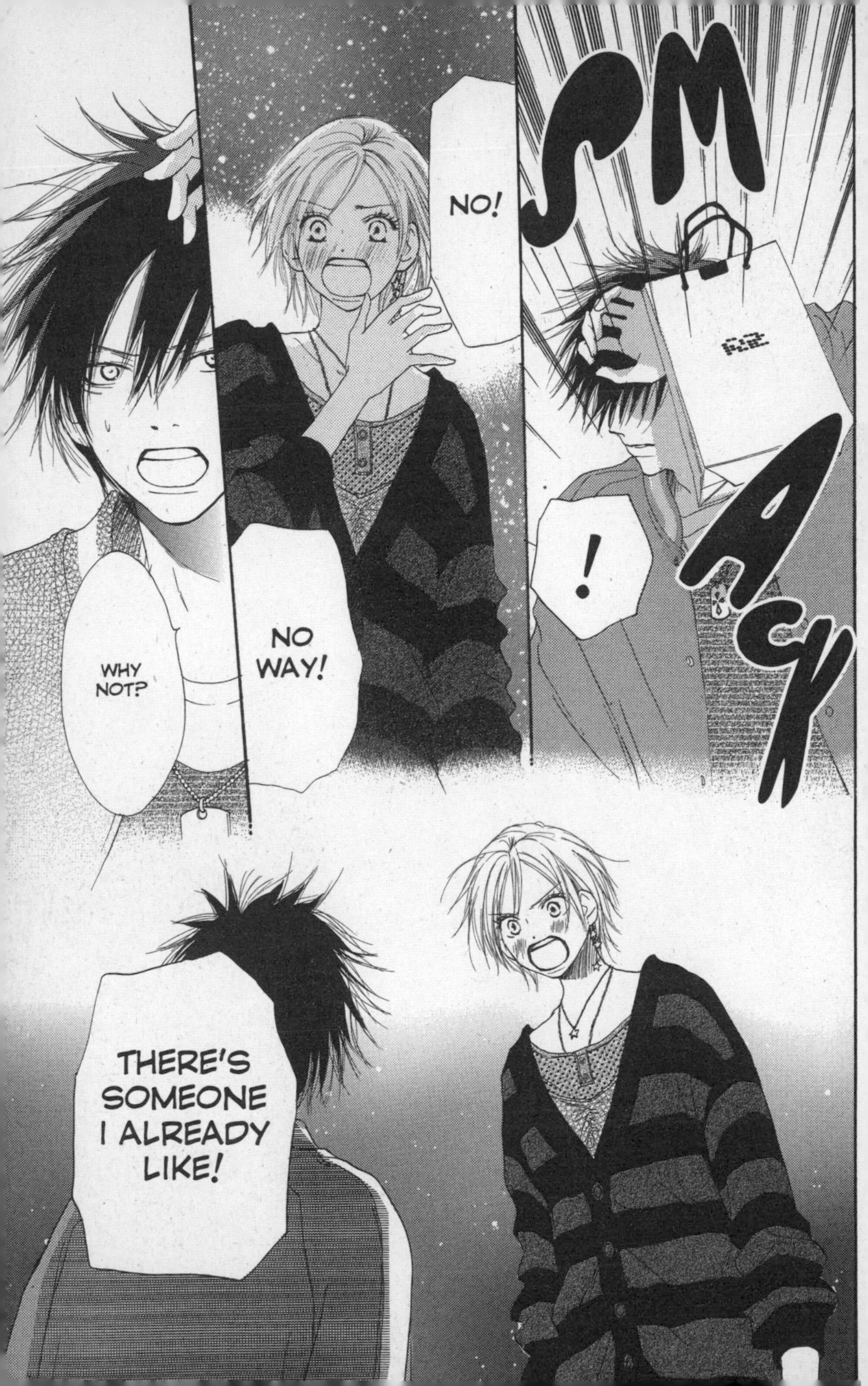
SMACK
!
NO!
NO WAY!
WHY NOT?
THERE'S SOMEONE I ALREADY LIKE!

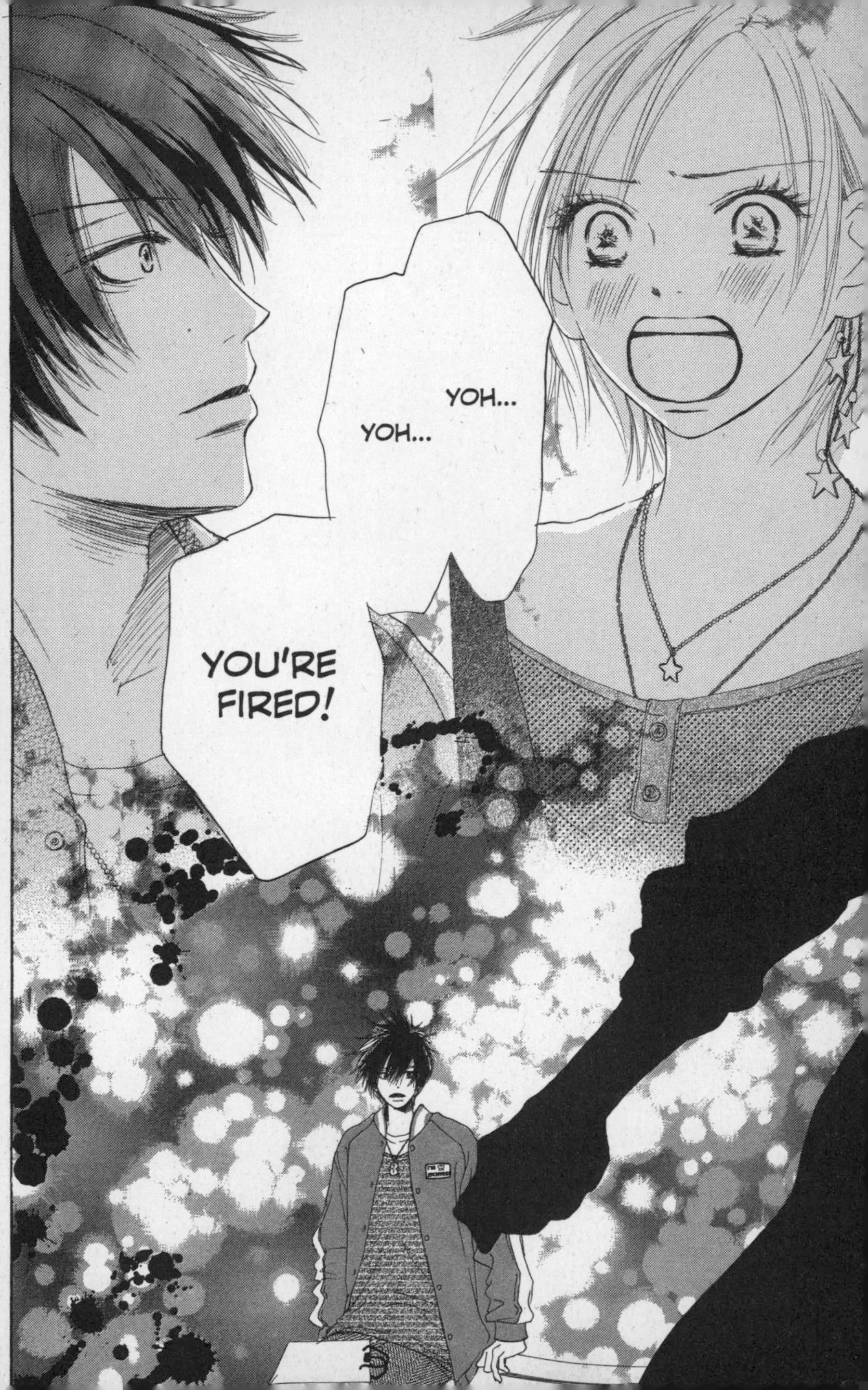
YOH...
YOH...
YOU'RE FIRED!

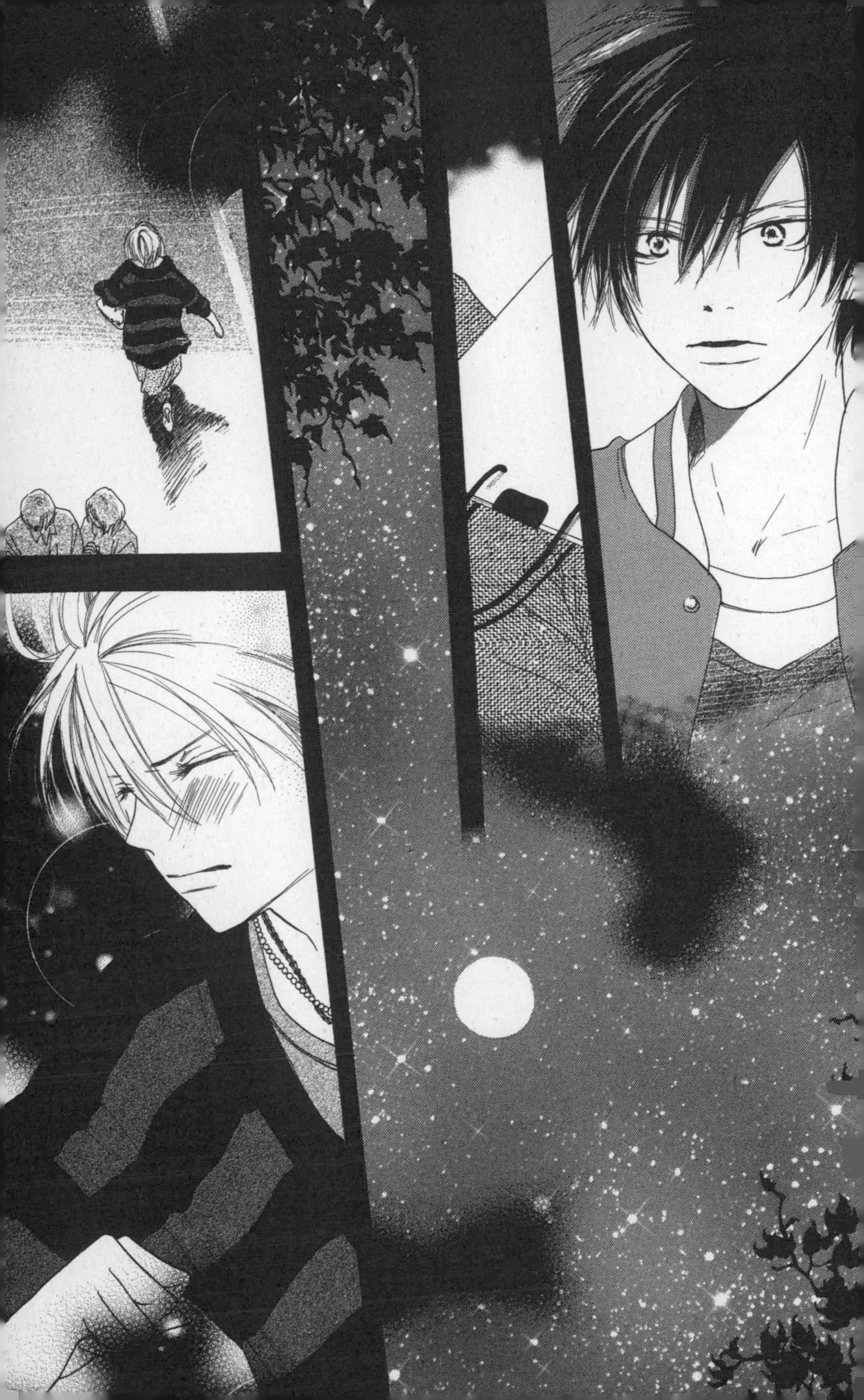

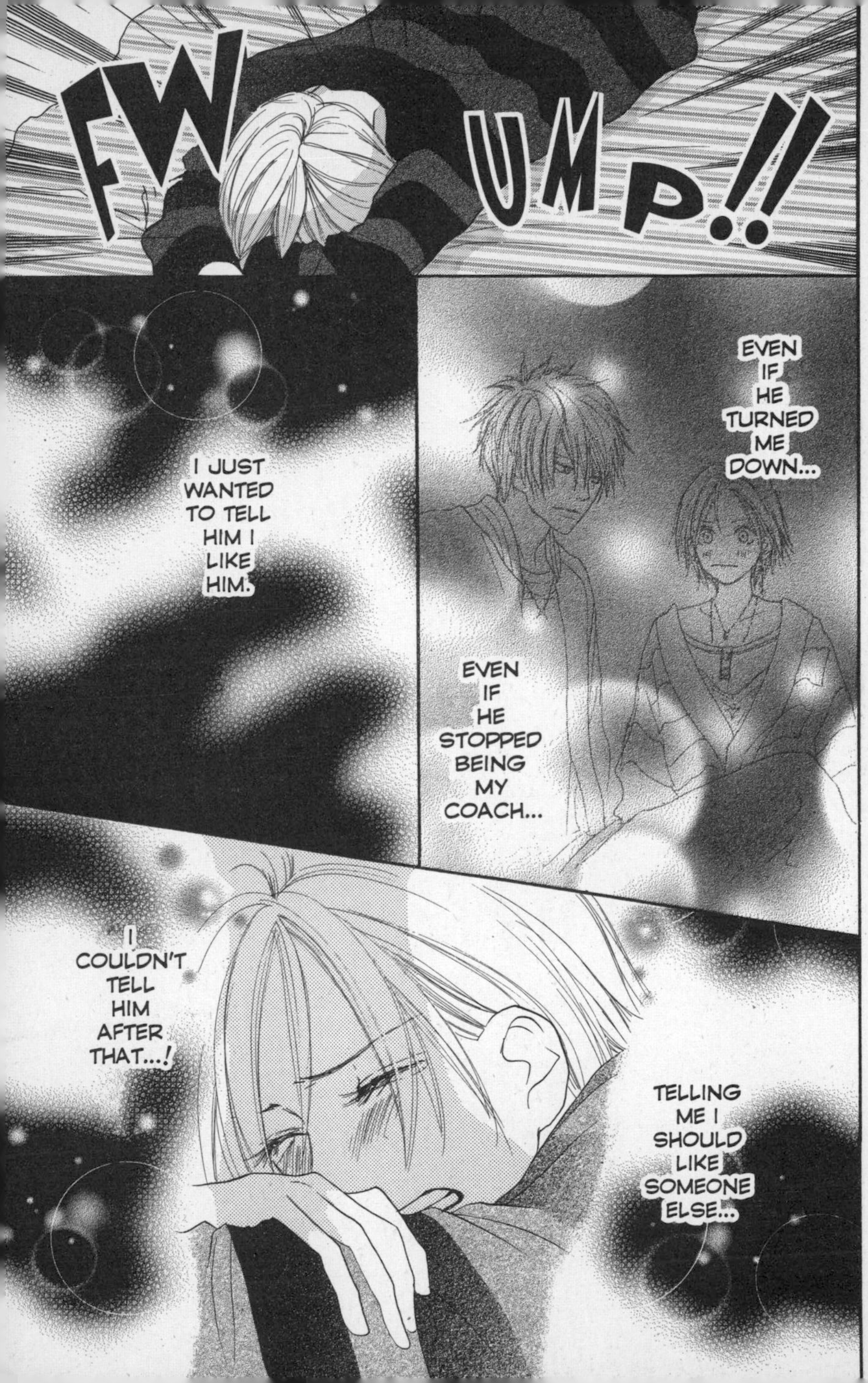
FWUMP!!
EVEN IF HE TURNED ME DOWN...
EVEN IF HE STOPPED BEING MY COACH...
I JUST WANTED TO TELL HIM I LIKE HIM.
TELLING ME I SHOULD LIKE SOMEONE ELSE...
I COULDN'T TELL HIM AFTER THAT...!

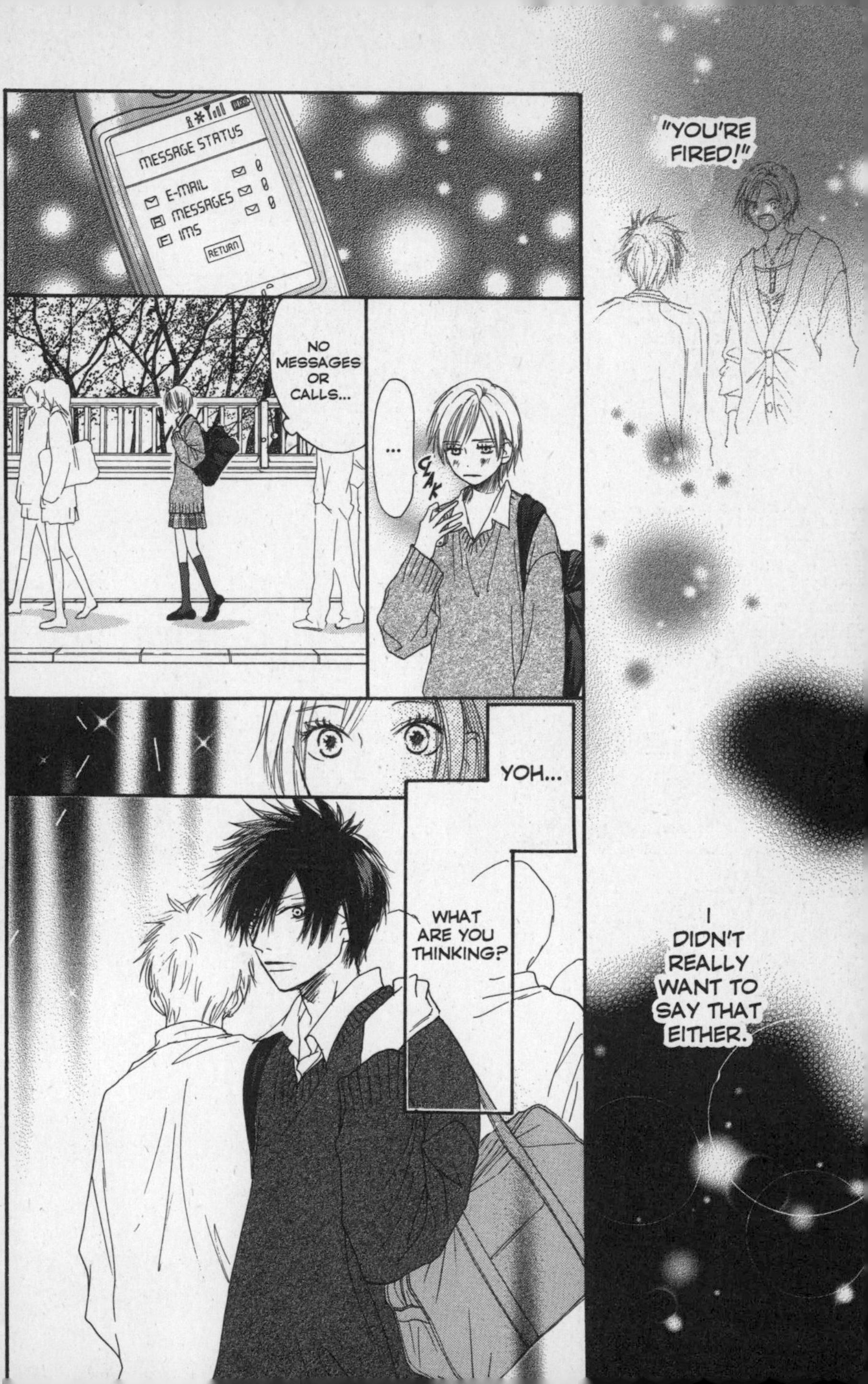
"YOU'RE FIRED!"
I DIDN'T REALLY WANT TO SAY THAT EITHER.
MESSAGE STATUS
E-MAIL 0
MESSAGES 0
IMS 0
RETURN
...
CLAK
NO MESSAGES OR CALLS...
YOH...
WHAT ARE YOU THINKING?

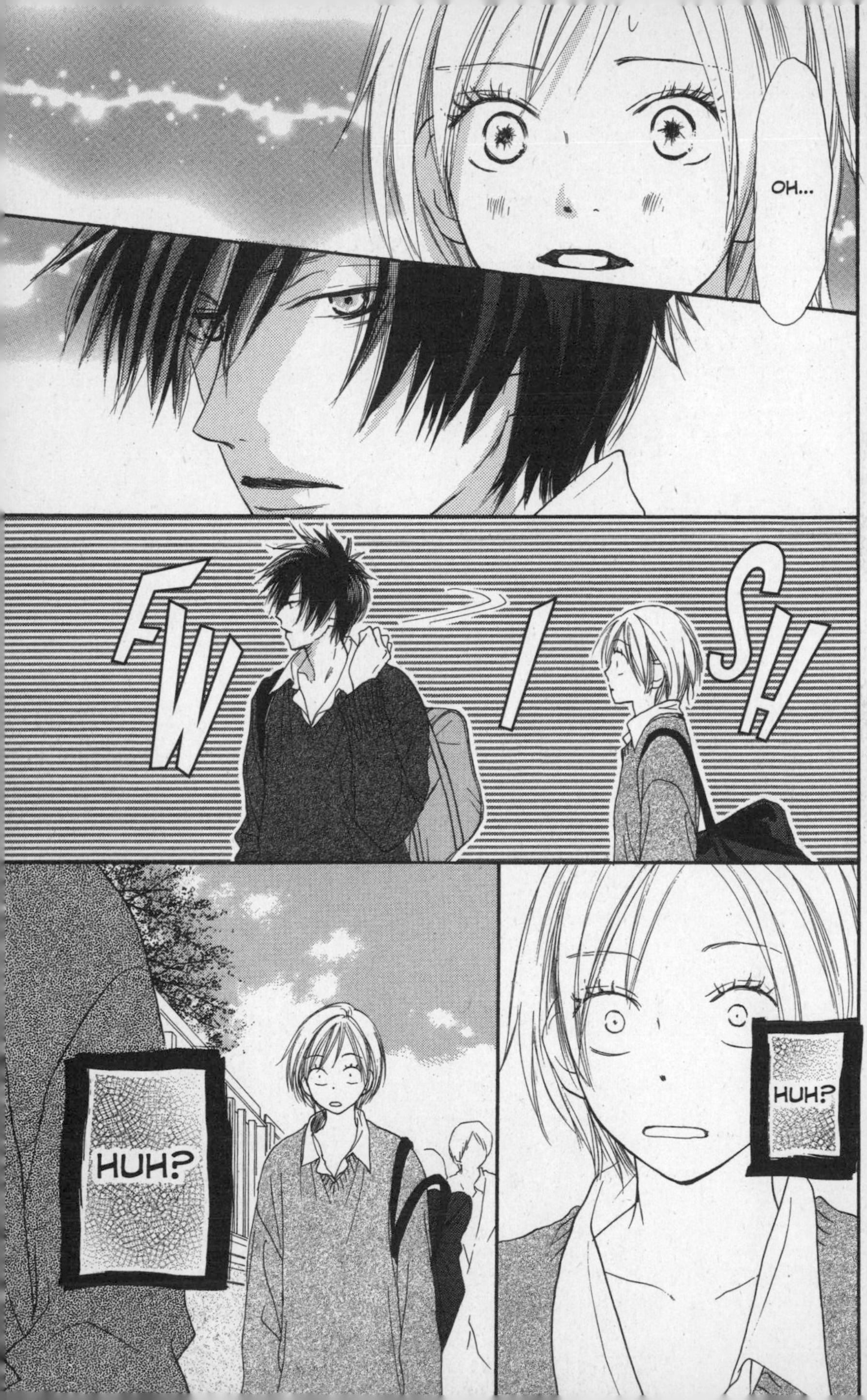
OH...
FWISH
HUH?
HUH?

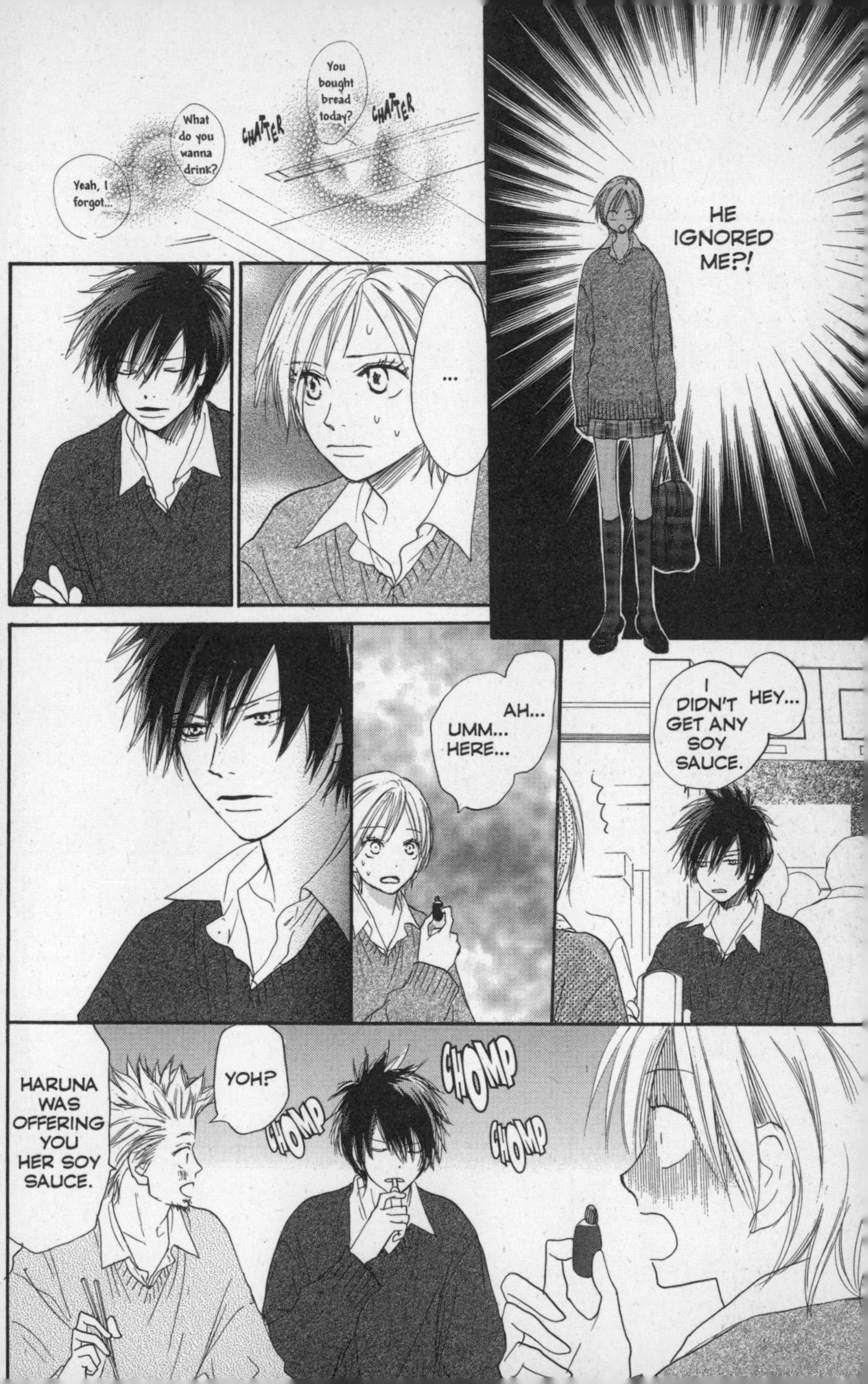
HE IGNORED ME?!
CHATTER
You bought bread today?
CHATTER
What do you wanna drink?
Yeah, I forgot...
...
HEY...
I DIDN'T GET ANY SOY SAUCE.
AH... UMM... HERE...
CHOMP
CHOMP
YOH?
CHOMP
HARUNA WAS OFFERING YOU HER SOY SAUCE.

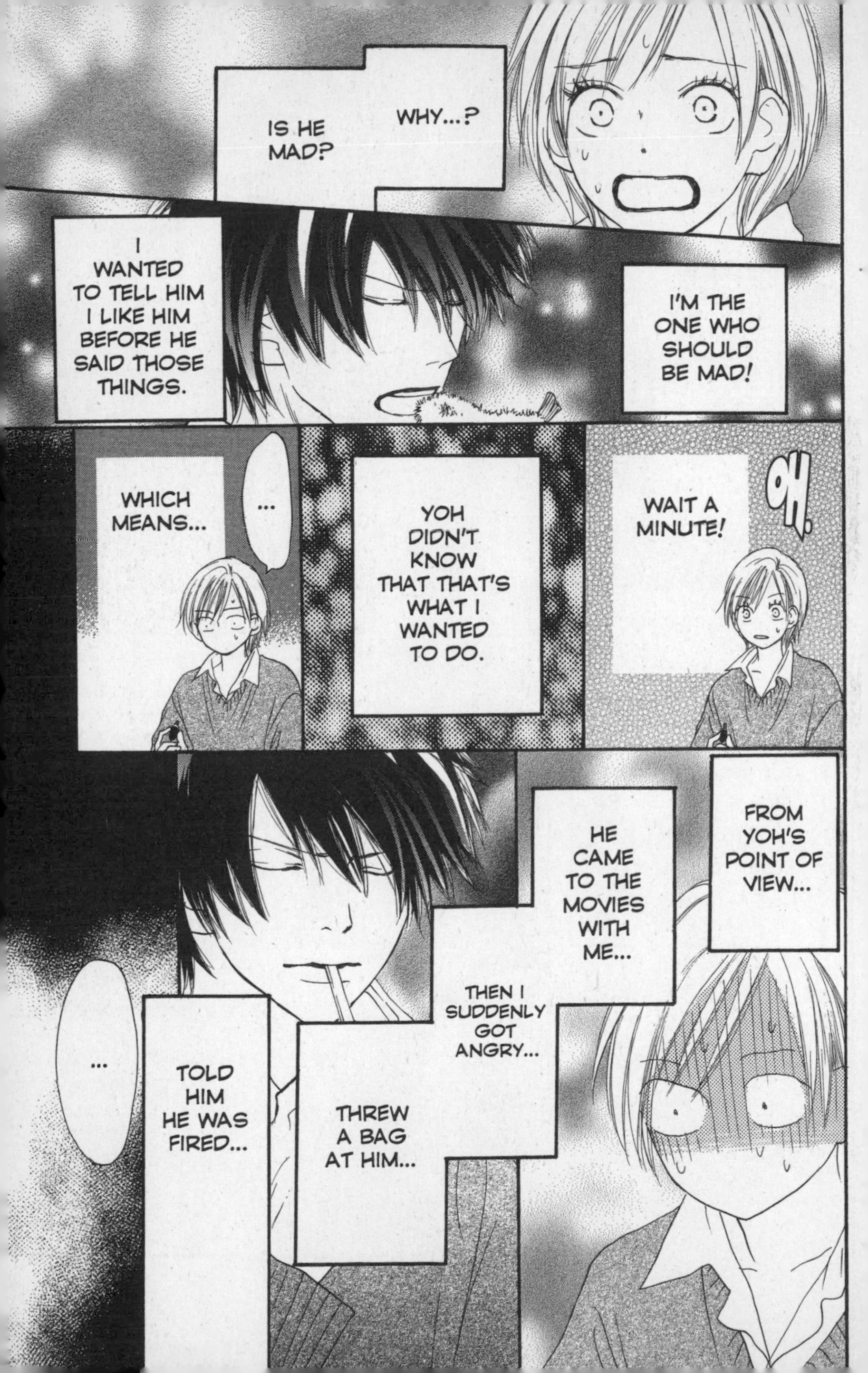
WHY...?
IS HE MAD?
I'M THE ONE WHO SHOULD BE MAD!
I WANTED TO TELL HIM I LIKE HIM BEFORE HE SAID THOSE THINGS.
OH.
WAIT A MINUTE!
YOH DIDN'T KNOW THAT THAT'S WHAT I WANTED TO DO.
...
WHICH MEANS...
FROM YOH'S POINT OF VIEW...
HE CAME TO THE MOVIES WITH ME...
THEN I SUDDENLY GOT ANGRY...
THREW A BAG AT HIM...
TOLD HIM HE WAS FIRED...
...

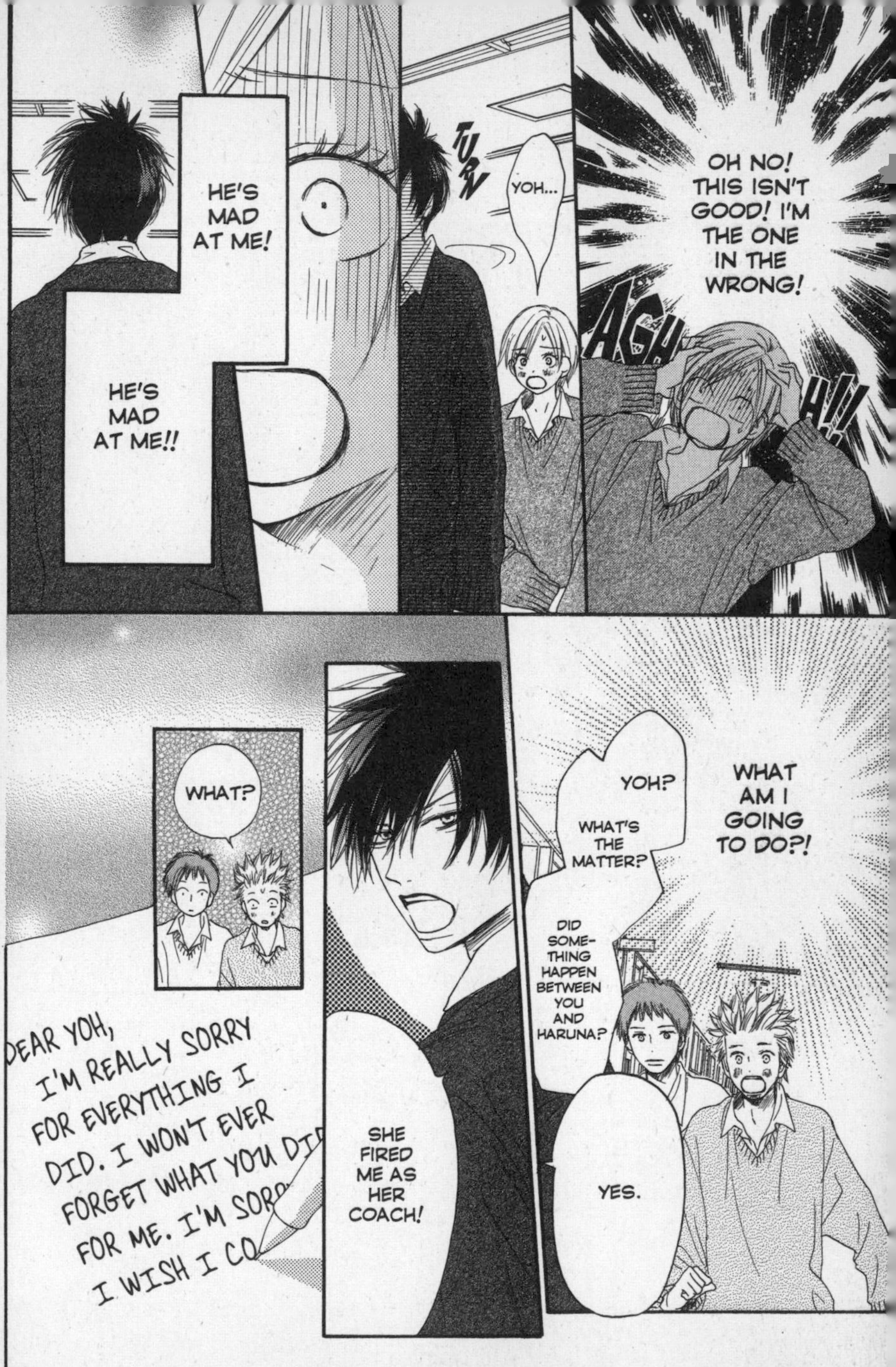
OH NO! THIS ISN'T GOOD! I'M THE ONE IN THE WRONG!
AGH
H!!
TURN
YOH...
HE'S MAD AT ME!
HE'S MAD AT ME!!
WHAT AM I GOING TO DO?!
YOH?
WHAT'S THE MATTER?
DID SOMETHING HAPPEN BETWEEN YOU AND HARUNA?
YES.
SHE FIRED ME AS HER COACH!
WHAT?
DEAR YOH,
I'M REALLY SORRY
FOR EVERYTHING I
DID. I WON'T EVER
FORGET WHAT YOU DI
FOR ME. I'M SOR
I WISH I CO

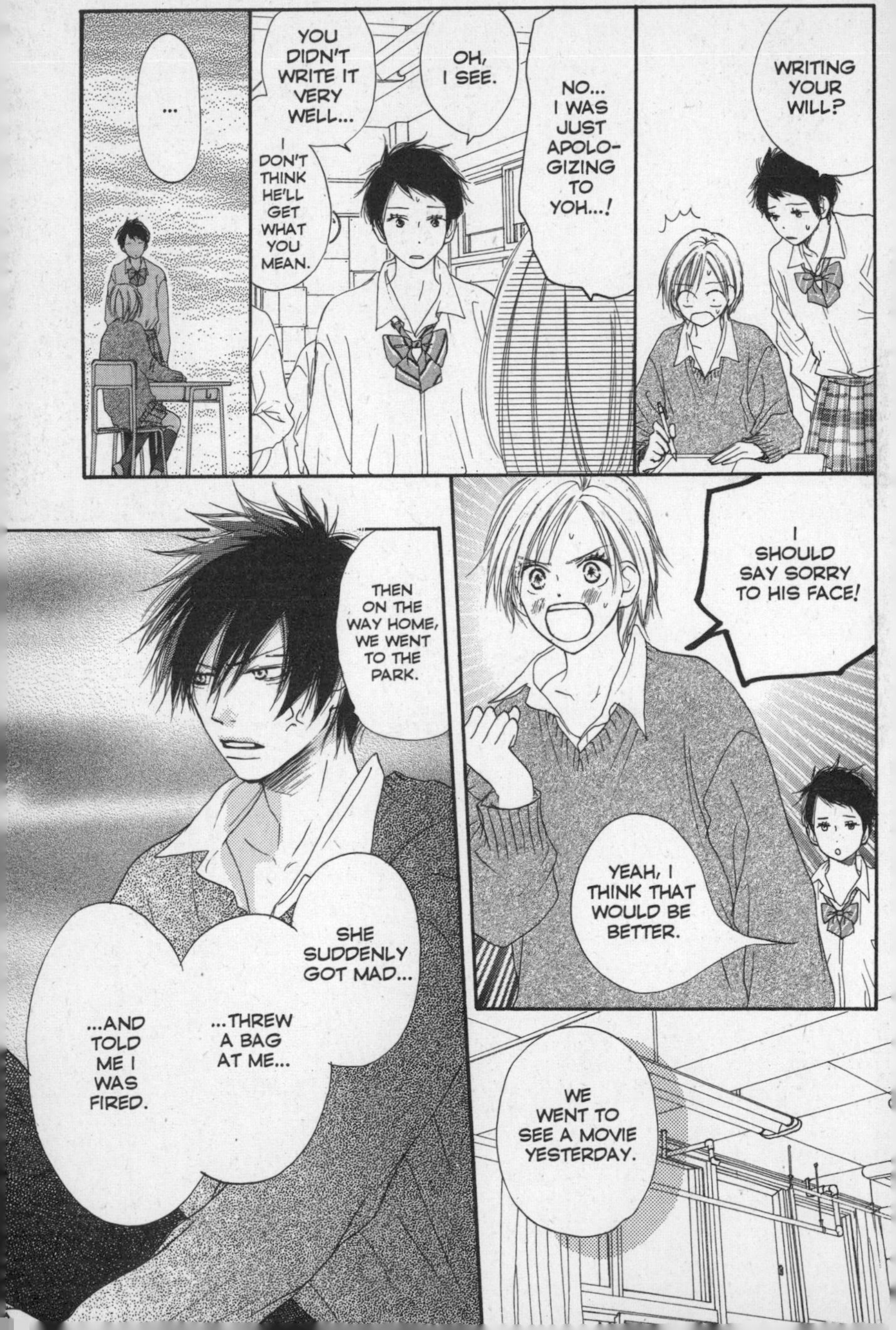
WRITING YOUR WILL?
NO... I WAS JUST APOLOGIZING TO YOH...!
OH, I SEE.
YOU DIDN'T WRITE IT VERY WELL...
I DON'T THINK HE'LL GET WHAT YOU MEAN.
...
I SHOULD SAY SORRY TO HIS FACE!
YEAH, I THINK THAT WOULD BE BETTER.
WE WENT TO SEE A MOVIE YESTERDAY.
THEN ON THE WAY HOME, WE WENT TO THE PARK.
SHE SUDDENLY GOT MAD...
...THREW A BAG AT ME...
...AND TOLD ME I WAS FIRED.

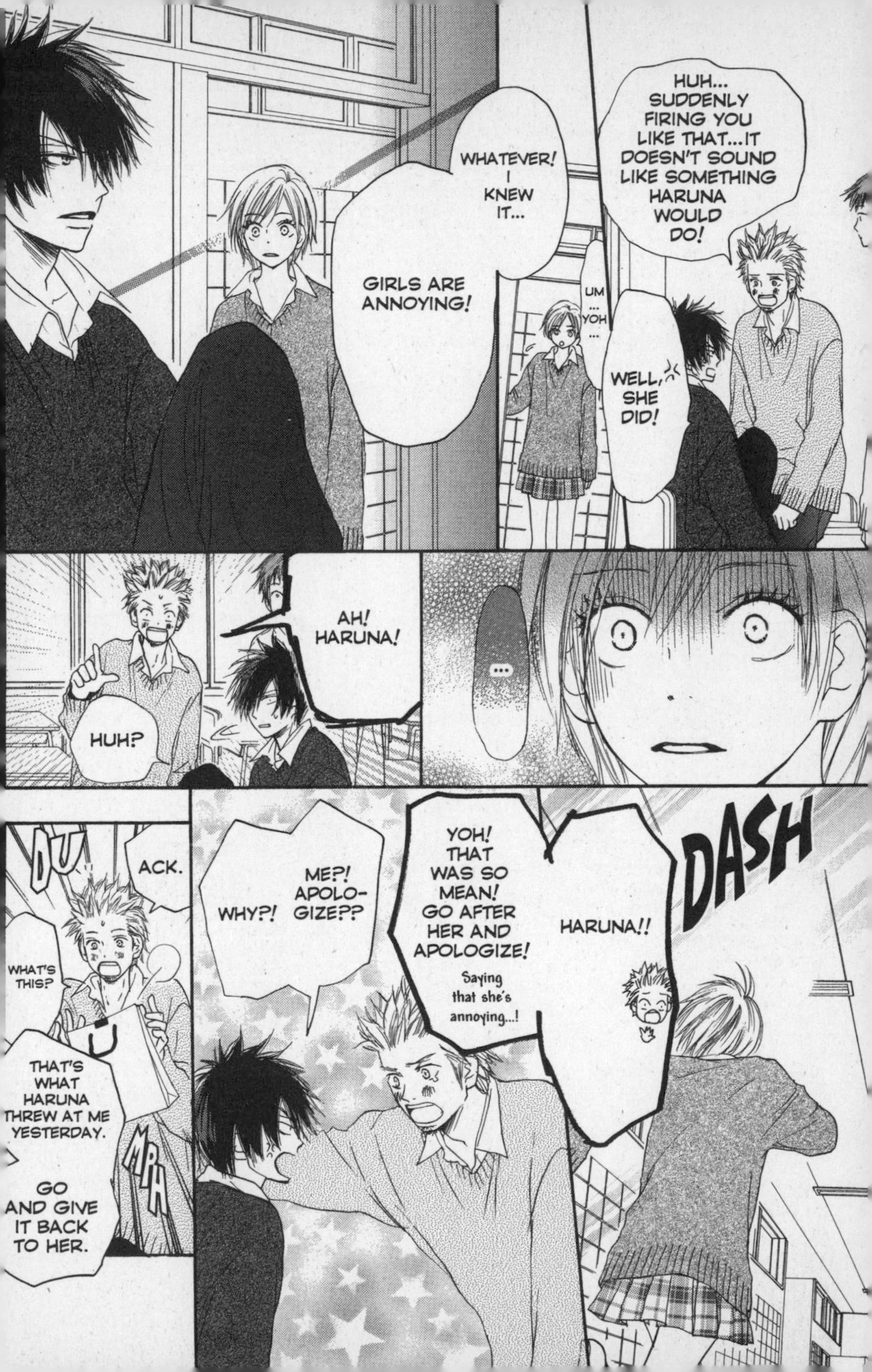
HUH... SUDDENLY FIRING YOU LIKE THAT...IT DOESN'T SOUND LIKE SOMETHING HARUNA WOULD DO!
WELL, SHE DID!
UM ... YOH ...
WHATEVER! I KNEW IT...
GIRLS ARE ANNOYING!
...
AH! HARUNA!
HUH?
DASH
HARUNA!!
YOH! THAT WAS SO MEAN! GO AFTER HER AND APOLOGIZE!
Saying that she's annoying...!
ME?! APOLOGIZE??
WHY?!
ACK.
DU
WHAT'S THIS?
THAT'S WHAT HARUNA THREW AT ME YESTERDAY.
MPH
GO AND GIVE IT BACK TO HER.

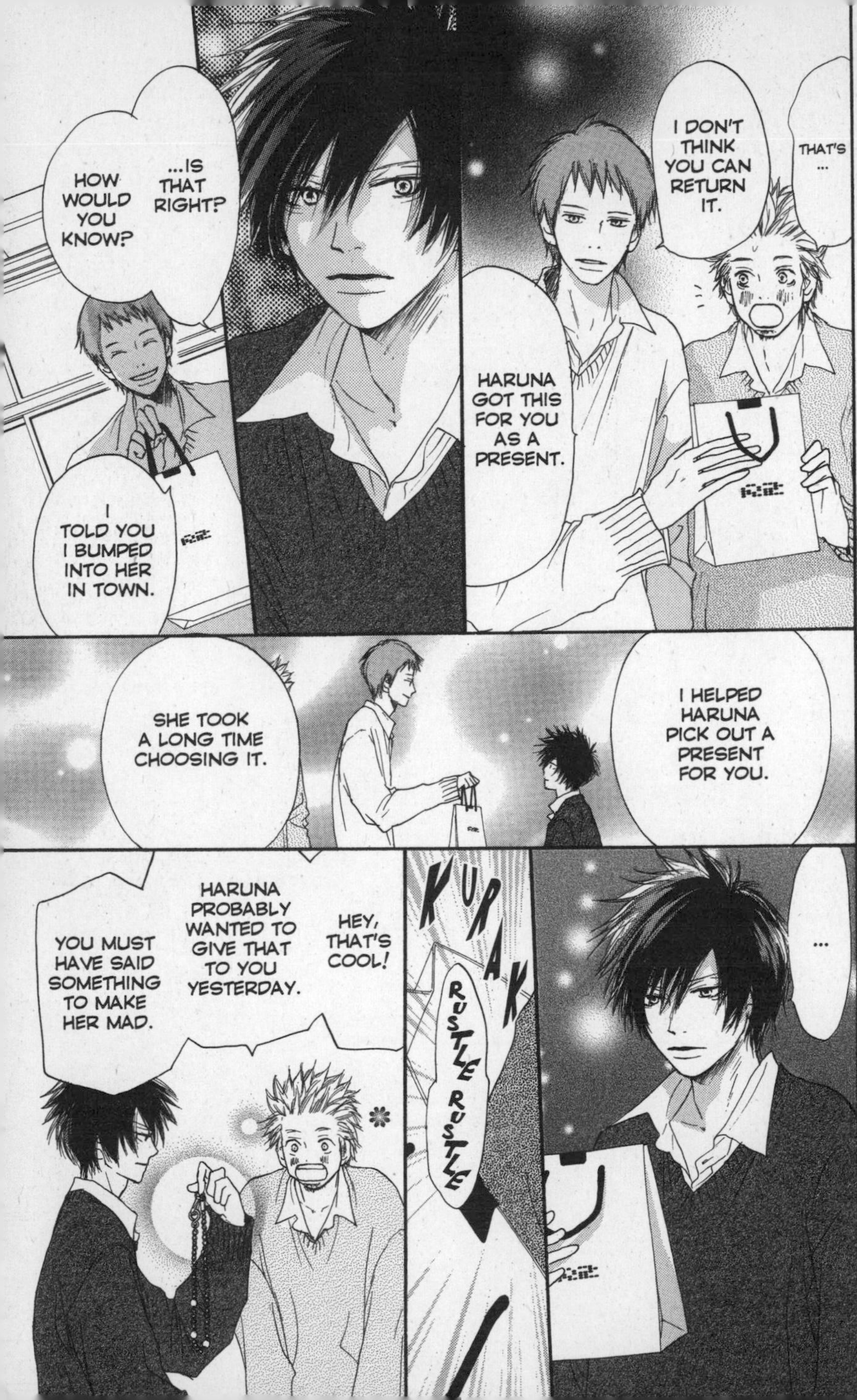
THAT'S ...
I DON'T THINK YOU CAN RETURN IT.
HARUNA GOT THIS FOR YOU AS A PRESENT.
...IS THAT RIGHT?
HOW WOULD YOU KNOW?
I TOLD YOU I BUMPED INTO HER IN TOWN.
I HELPED HARUNA PICK OUT A PRESENT FOR YOU.
SHE TOOK A LONG TIME CHOOSING IT.
...
KURAK
RUSTLE RUSTLE
HEY, THAT'S COOL!
HARUNA PROBABLY WANTED TO GIVE THAT TO YOU YESTERDAY.
YOU MUST HAVE SAID SOMETHING TO MAKE HER MAD.

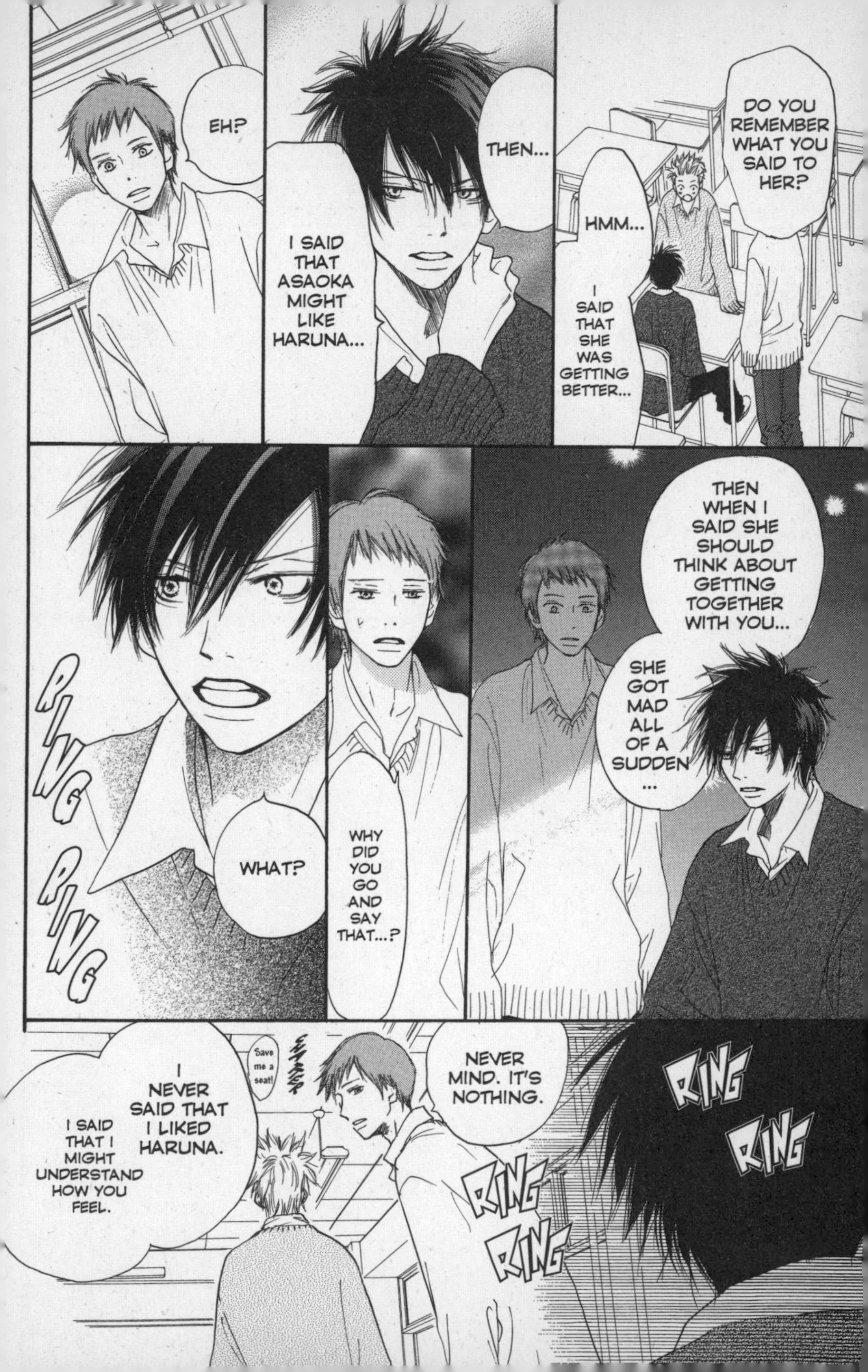
DO YOU REMEMBER WHAT YOU SAID TO HER?
HMM...
I SAID THAT SHE WAS GETTING BETTER...
THEN...
I SAID THAT ASAOKA MIGHT LIKE HARUNA...
EH?
THEN WHEN I SAID SHE SHOULD THINK ABOUT GETTING TOGETHER WITH YOU...
SHE GOT MAD ALL OF A SUDDEN ...
WHY DID YOU GO AND SAY THAT...?
WHAT?
RING RING RING
RING RING
RING RING
NEVER MIND. IT'S NOTHING.
Save me a seat!
I NEVER SAID THAT I LIKED HARUNA.
I SAID THAT I MIGHT UNDERSTAND HOW YOU FEEL.

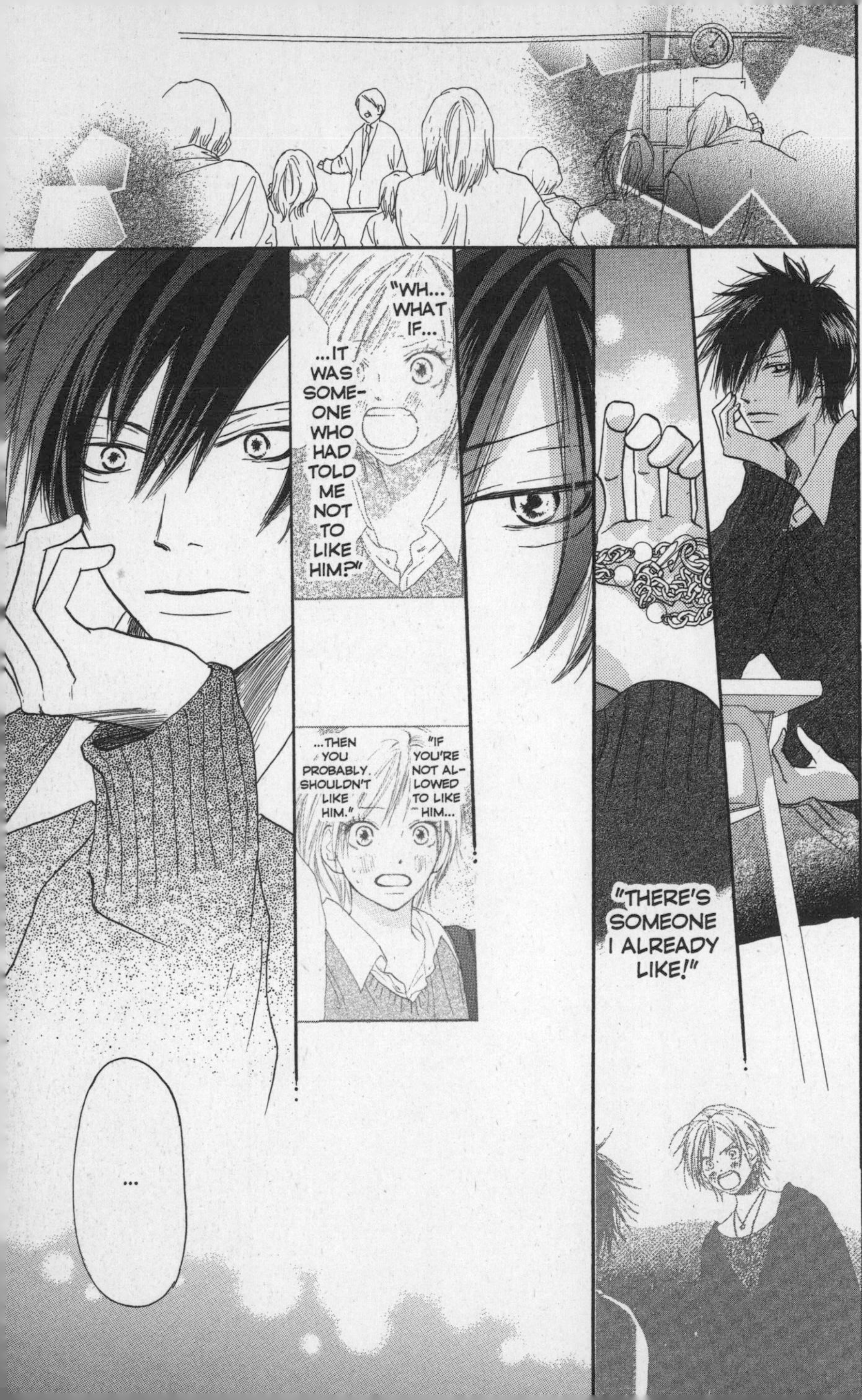
"THERE'S SOMEONE I ALREADY LIKE!"
"WH... WHAT IF... ...IT WAS SOMEONE WHO HAD TOLD ME NOT TO LIKE HIM?"
"IF YOU'RE NOT AL-LOWED TO LIKE HIM...
...THEN YOU PROBABLY SHOULDN'T LIKE HIM."
...

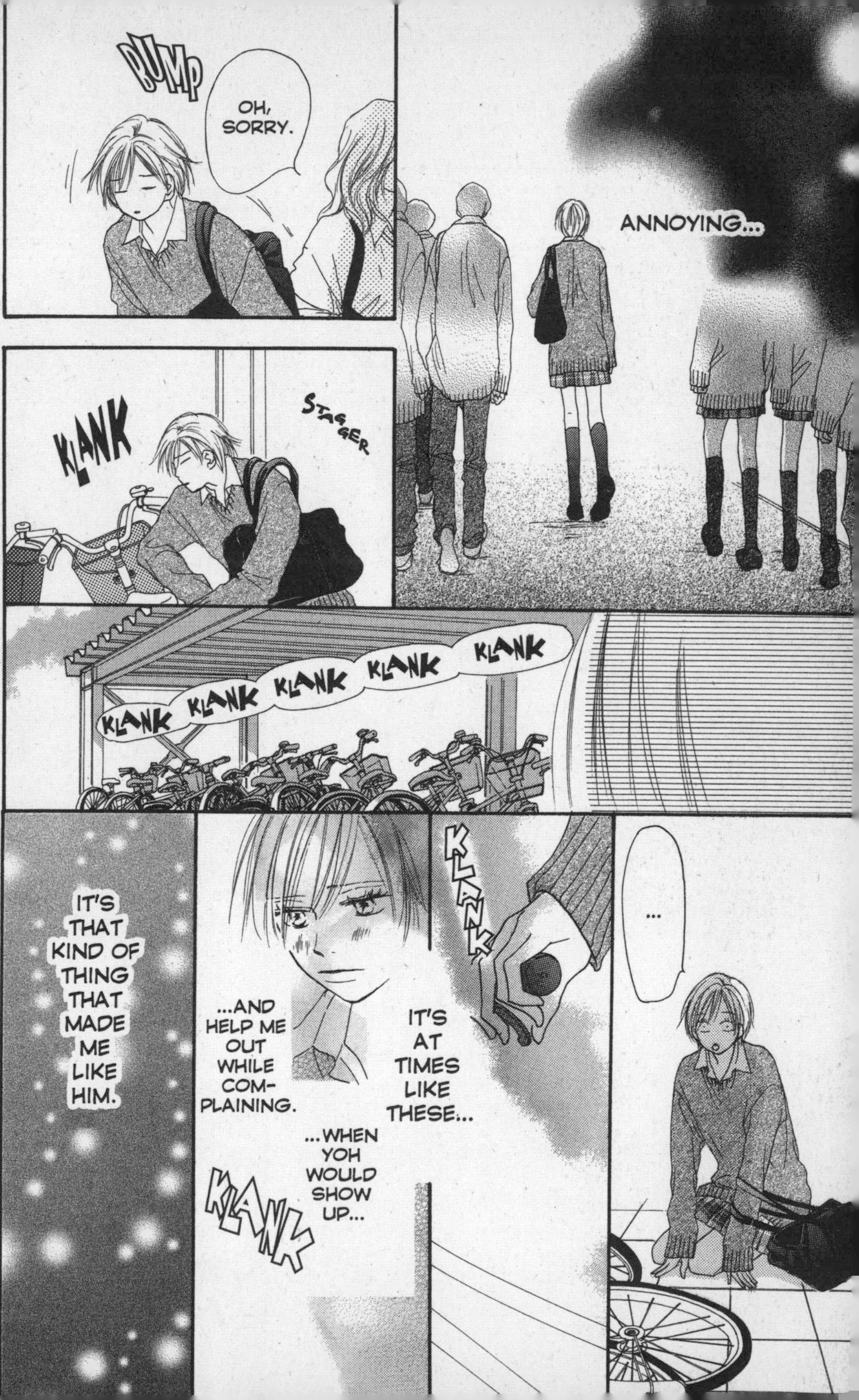
ANNOYING...
BUMP
OH, SORRY.
STAGGER
KLANK
KLANK
KLANK
KLANK
KLANK
KLANK
...
KLANK
IT'S AT TIMES LIKE THESE...
...WHEN YOH WOULD SHOW UP...
...AND HELP ME OUT WHILE COMPLAINING.
KLANK
IT'S THAT KIND OF THING THAT MADE ME LIKE HIM.

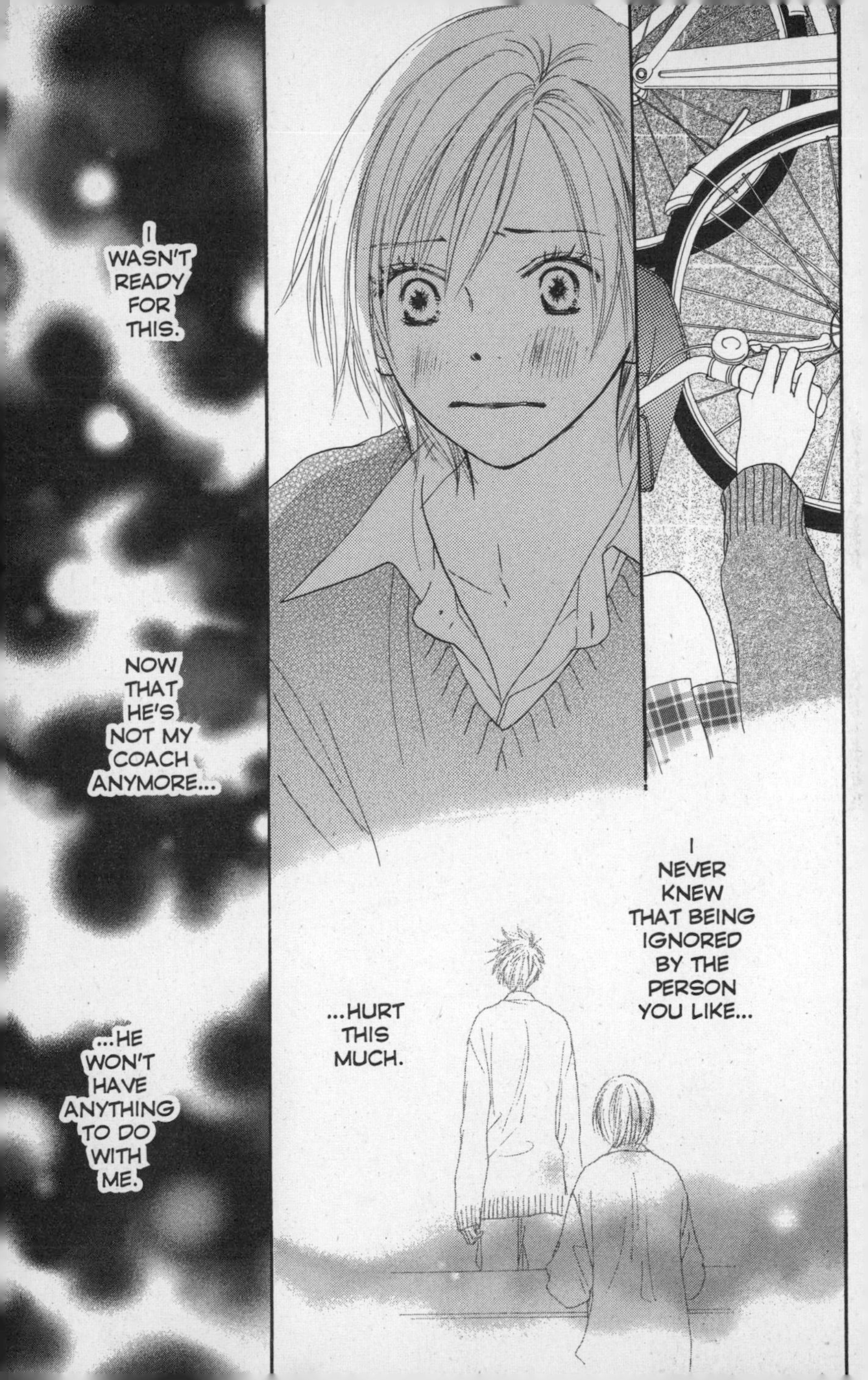
I NEVER KNEW THAT BEING IGNORED BY THE PERSON YOU LIKE...
...HURT THIS MUCH.
I WASN'T READY FOR THIS.
NOW THAT HE'S NOT MY COACH ANYMORE...
...HE WON'T HAVE ANYTHING TO DO WITH ME.

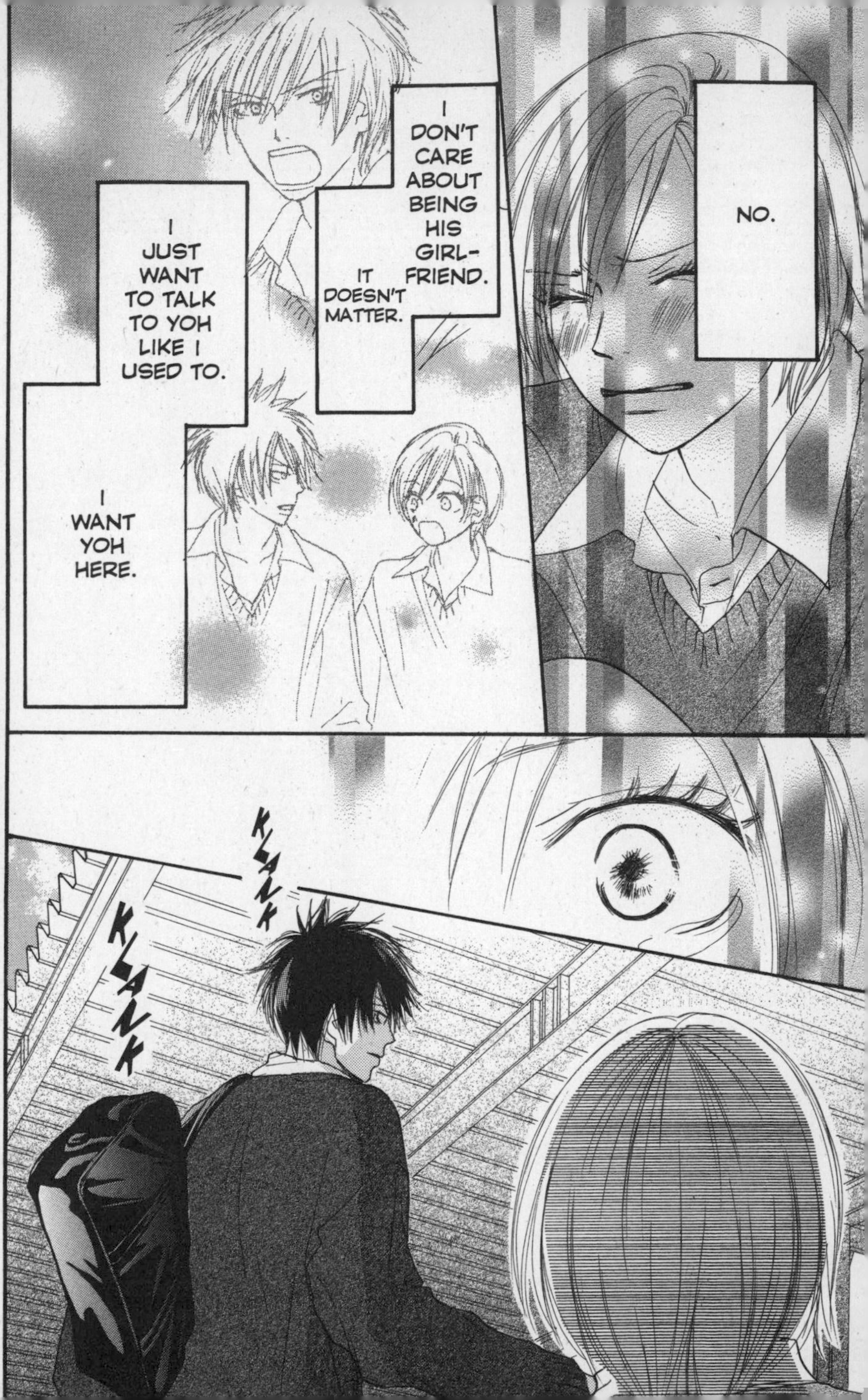
NO.
I DON'T CARE ABOUT BEING HIS GIRL-FRIEND.
IT DOESN'T MATTER.
I JUST WANT TO TALK TO YOH LIKE I USED TO.
I WANT YOH HERE.
KLANK
KLANK

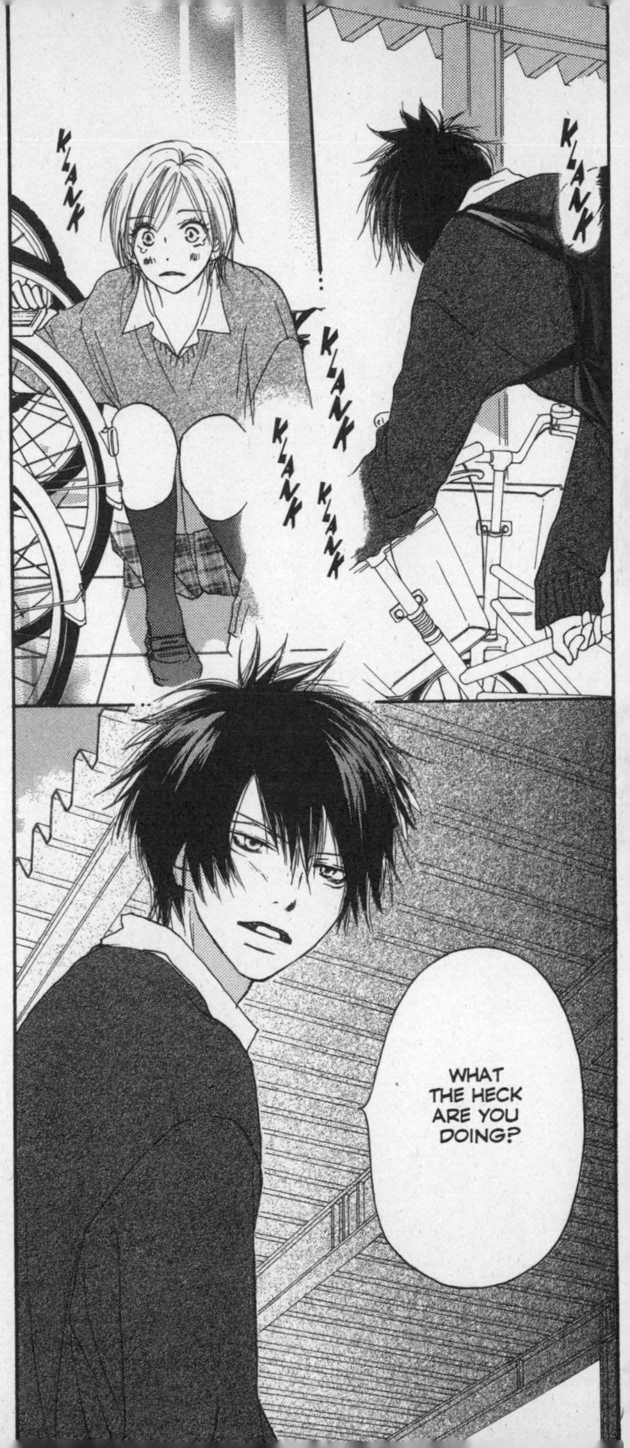
KLANK
KLANK
KLANK
KLANK
KLANK
WHAT THE HECK ARE YOU DOING?

2

I'm sorry, but I'm going to write about my relatives again. My nieces are pretty cute now that they've turned three and one. The younger ones cries like this:

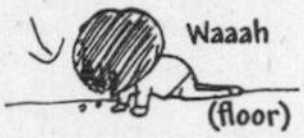
Waaah
(floor)

Also, recently, she surprised me by saying this...

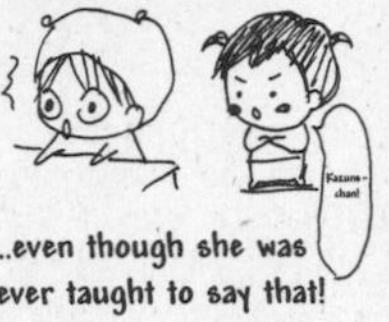
Kazune-chan!

...even though she was never taught to say that!

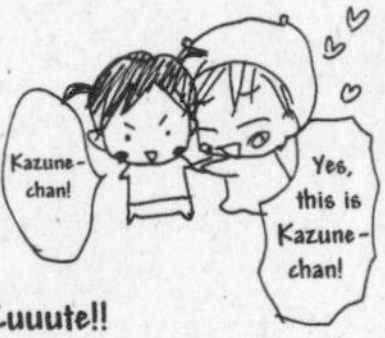
Kazune-chan!
Yes, this is Kazune-chan!

Cuuute!!

As for the older niece, when she tried to put something into a backpack and found that it was full of her little sister's toys, she said:

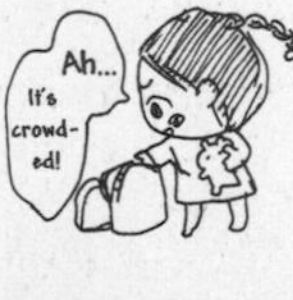
Ah...
It's crowded!

"It's crowded..." Sooo cute! I think I'll try saying that too. I wonder if someone will tell me I'm cute for saying it. Probably not.

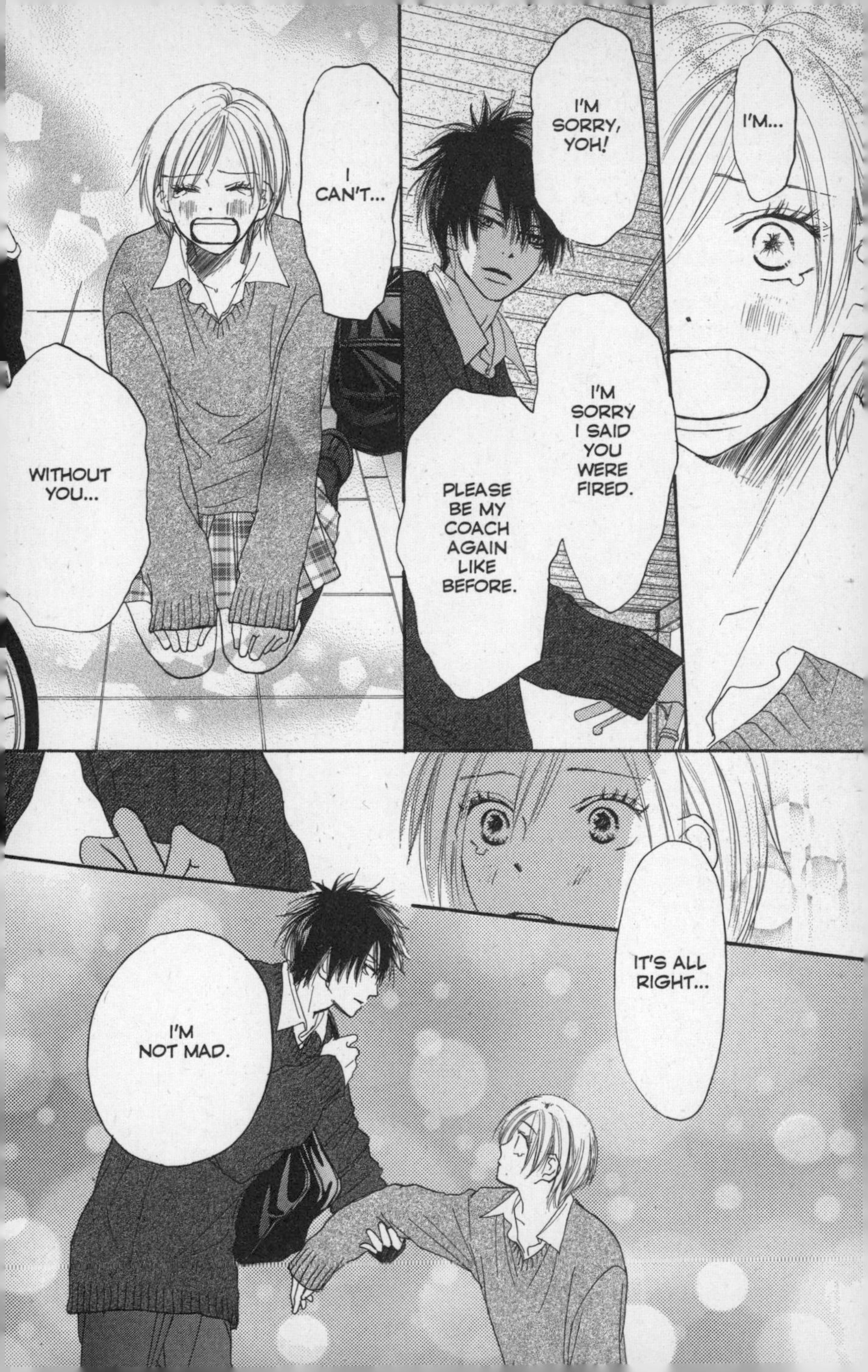
I'M...
I'M SORRY, YOH!
I'M SORRY I SAID YOU WERE FIRED.
PLEASE BE MY COACH AGAIN LIKE BEFORE.
I CAN'T...
WITHOUT YOU...
IT'S ALL RIGHT...
I'M NOT MAD.

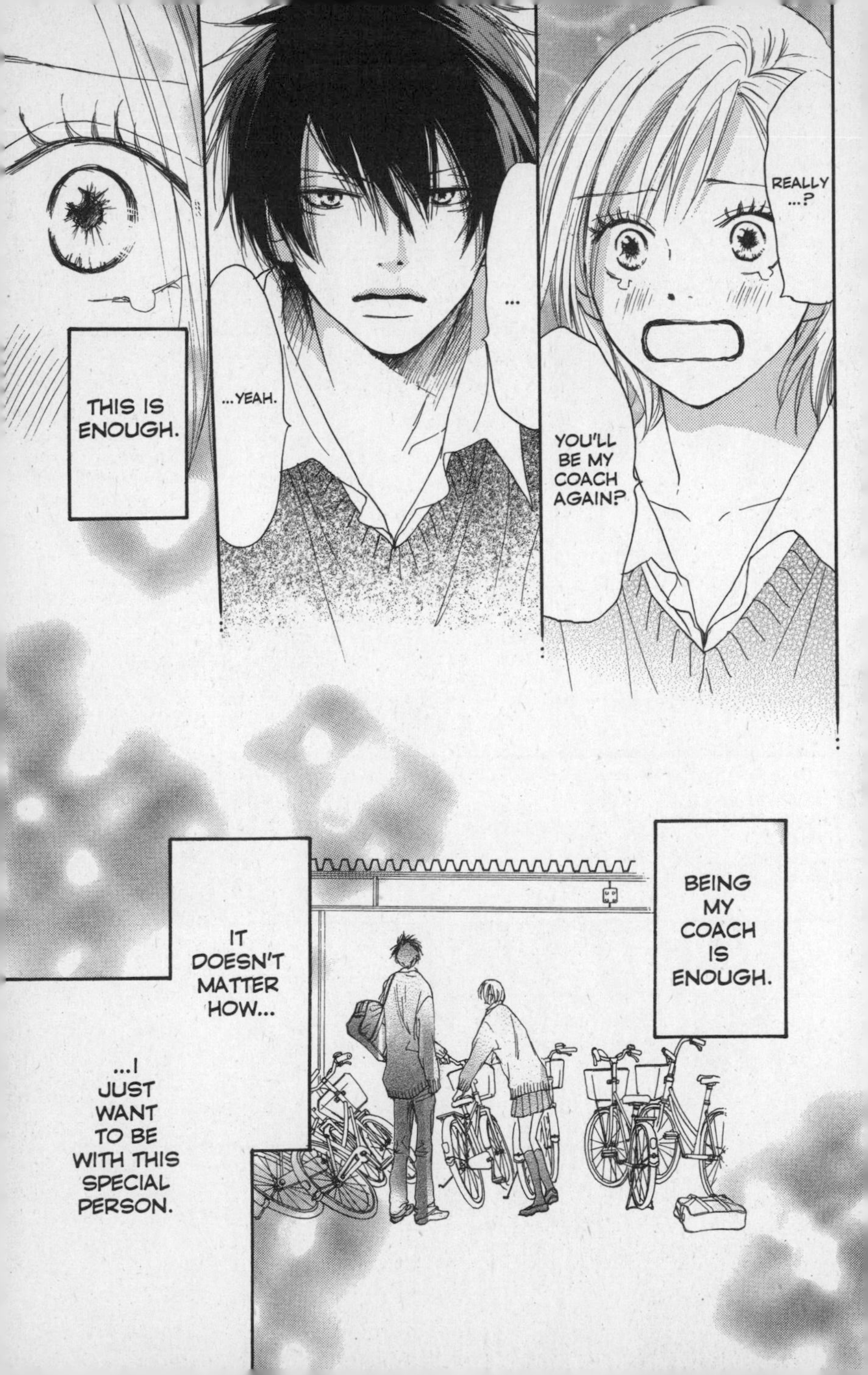
REALLY ...?
YOU'LL BE MY COACH AGAIN?
...
...YEAH.
THIS IS ENOUGH.
BEING MY COACH IS ENOUGH.
IT DOESN'T MATTER HOW...
...I JUST WANT TO BE WITH THIS SPECIAL PERSON.

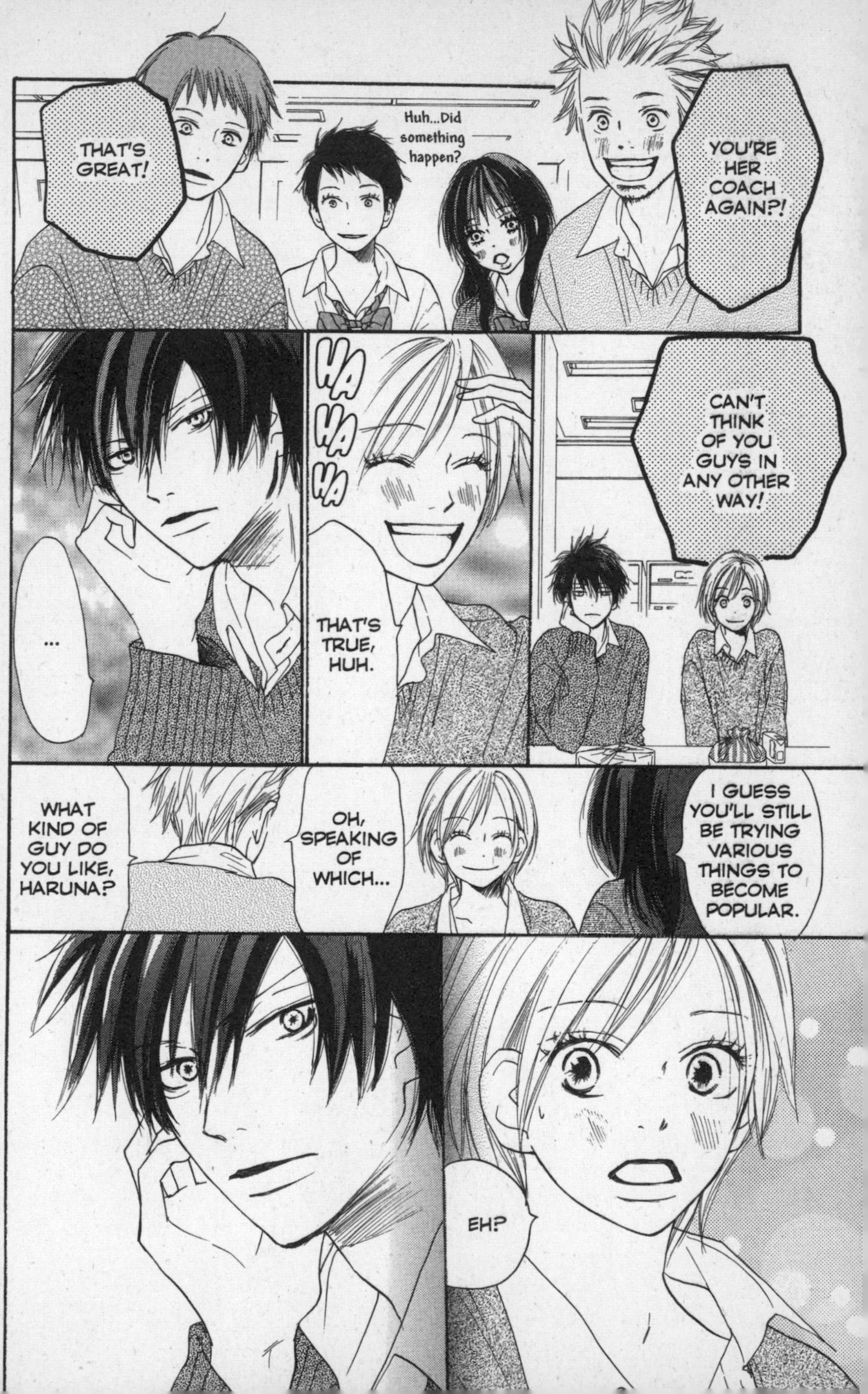
YOU'RE HER COACH AGAIN?!
Huh...Did something happen?
THAT'S GREAT!
CAN'T THINK OF YOU GUYS IN ANY OTHER WAY!
HA HA HA HA
THAT'S TRUE, HUH.
...
I GUESS YOU'LL STILL BE TRYING VARIOUS THINGS TO BECOME POPULAR.
OH, SPEAKING OF WHICH...
WHAT KIND OF GUY DO YOU LIKE, HARUNA?
EH?

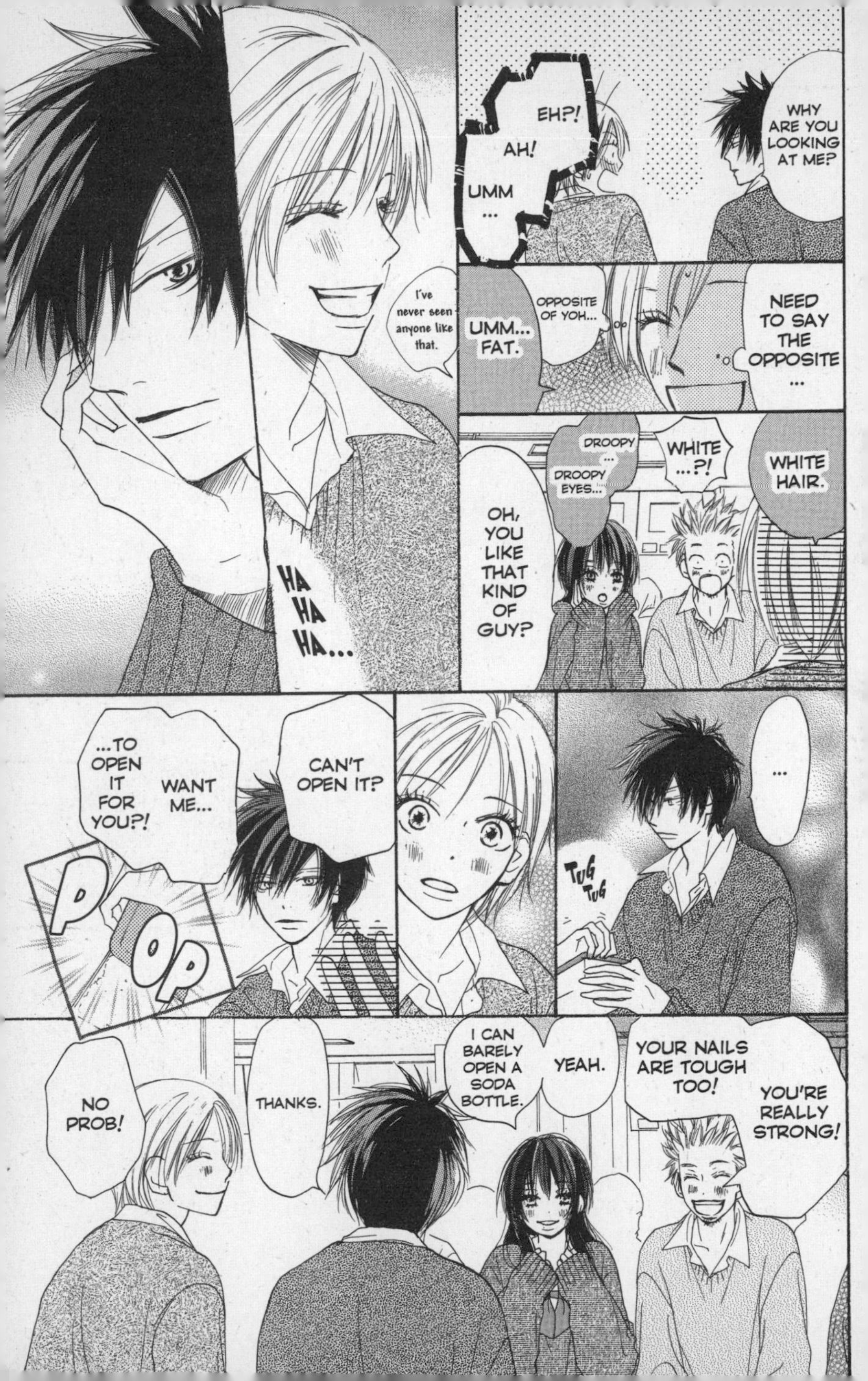

WHY ARE YOU LOOKING AT ME?
EH?!
AH!
UMM ...
NEED TO SAY THE OPPOSITE ...
OPPOSITE OF YOH...
UMM... FAT.
WHITE HAIR.
WHITE ...?!
DROOPY ... DROOPY EYES...
OH, YOU LIKE THAT KIND OF GUY?
I've never seen anyone like that.
HA HA HA...
...
TUG TUG
CAN'T OPEN IT?
WANT ME...
...TO OPEN IT FOR YOU?!
POP
YOU'RE REALLY STRONG!
YOUR NAILS ARE TOUGH TOO!
YEAH.
I CAN BARELY OPEN A SODA BOTTLE.
THANKS.
NO PROB!

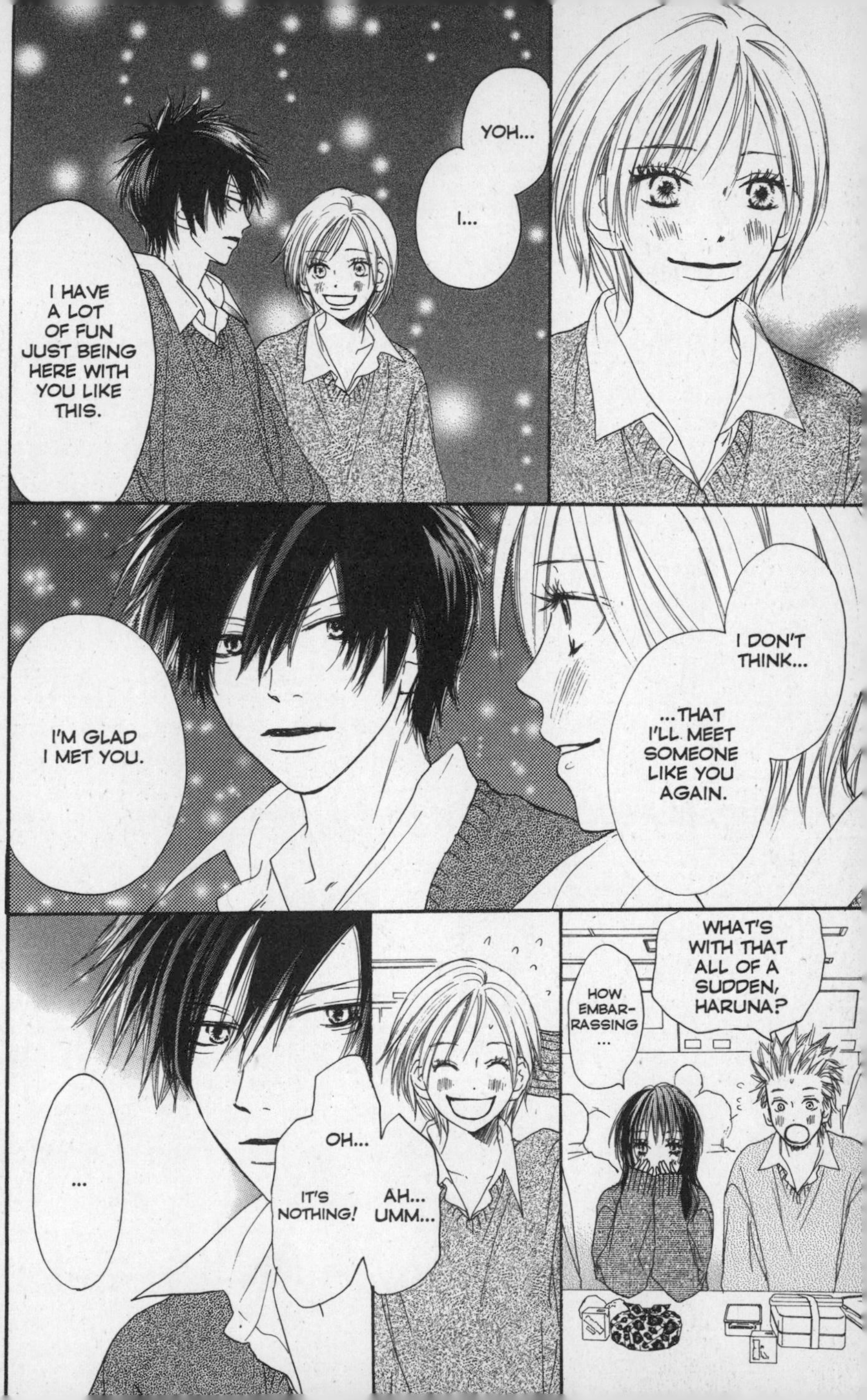
YOH...
I...
I HAVE A LOT OF FUN JUST BEING HERE WITH YOU LIKE THIS.
I DON'T THINK...
...THAT I'LL MEET SOMEONE LIKE YOU AGAIN.
I'M GLAD I MET YOU.
WHAT'S WITH THAT ALL OF A SUDDEN, HARUNA?
HOW EMBARRASSING...
OH...
AH... UMM...
IT'S NOTHING!
...

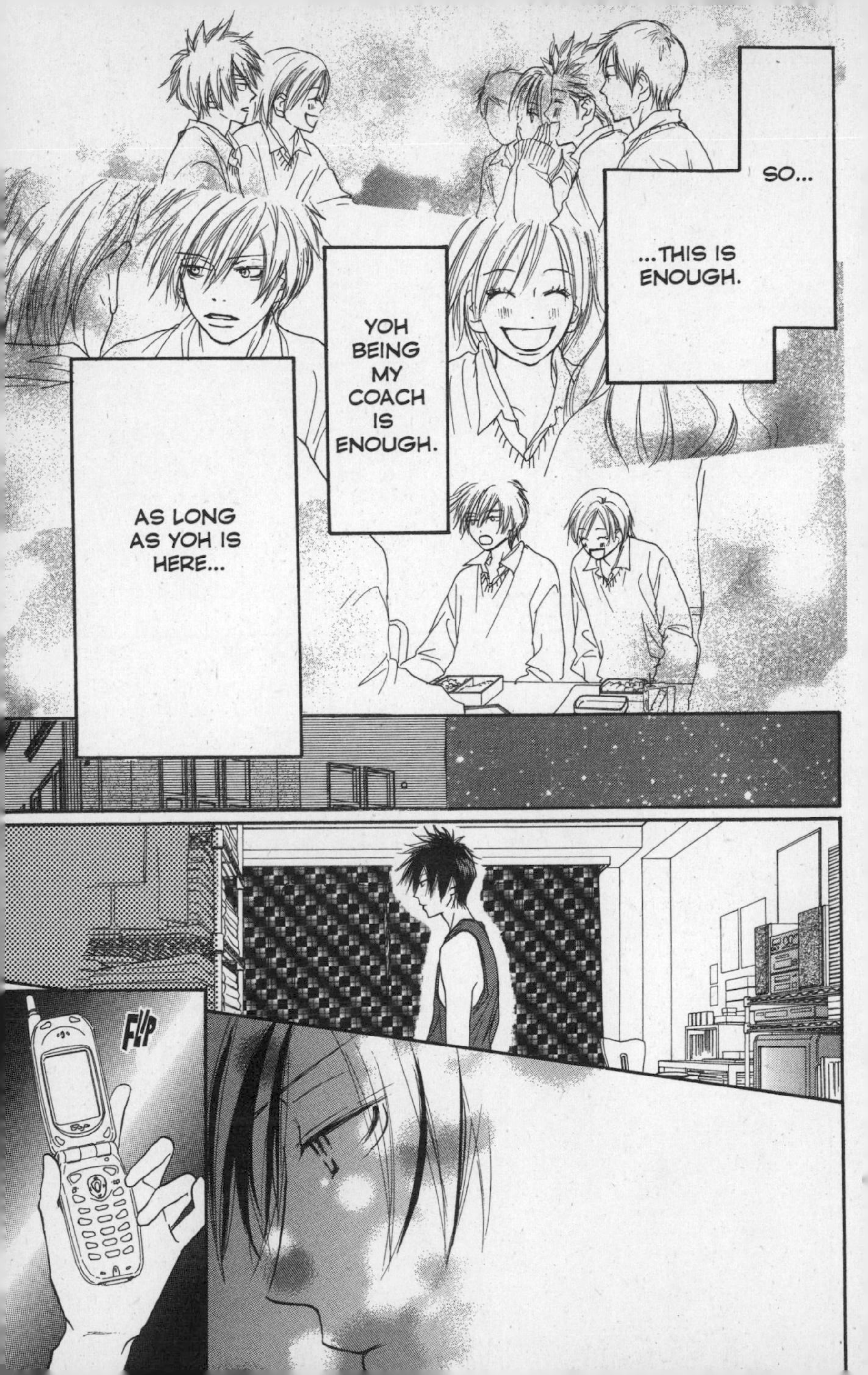
SO...
...THIS IS ENOUGH.
YOH BEING MY COACH IS ENOUGH.
AS LONG AS YOH IS HERE...
FLIP

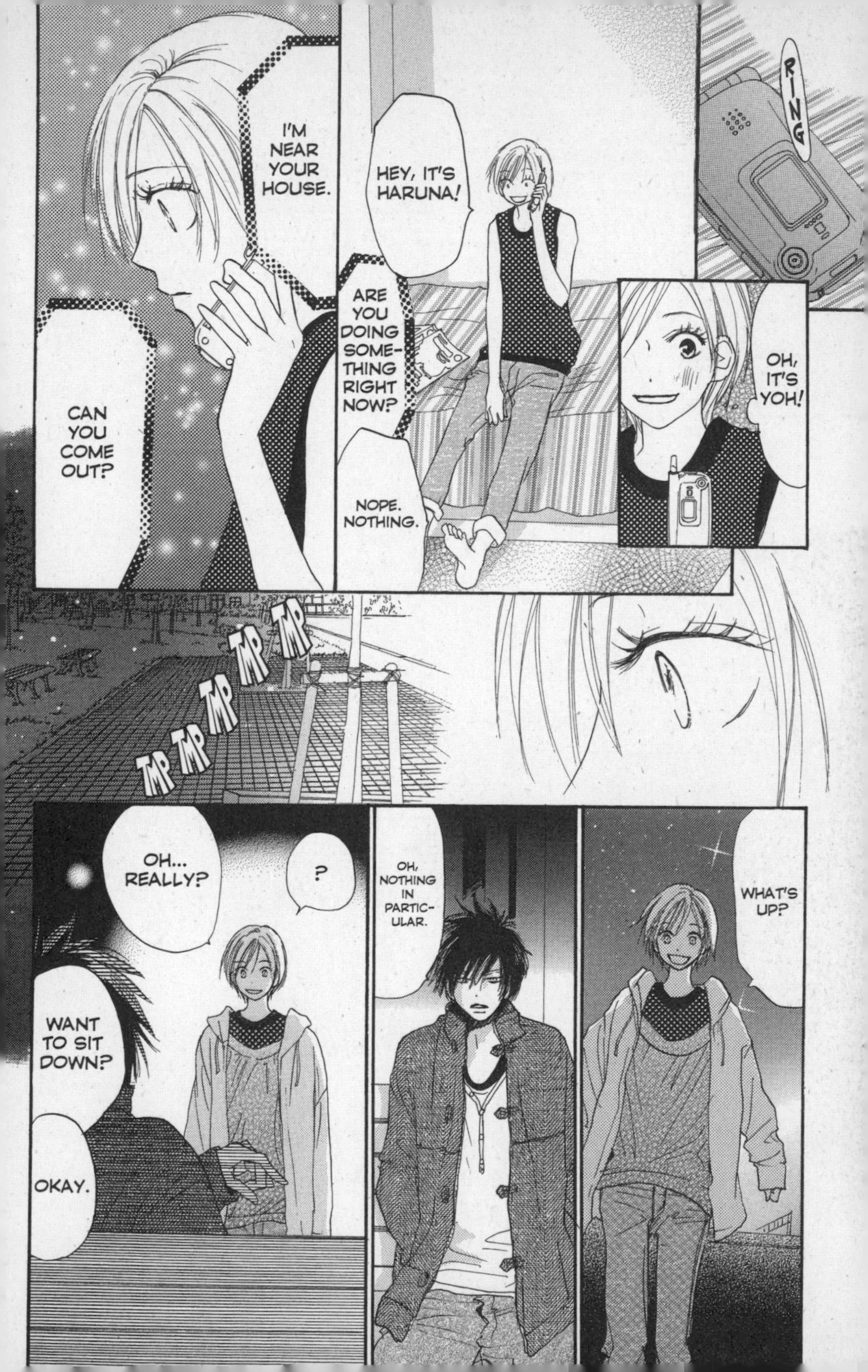
RING
OH, IT'S YOH!
HEY, IT'S HARUNA!
ARE YOU DOING SOMETHING RIGHT NOW?
NOPE. NOTHING.
I'M NEAR YOUR HOUSE.
CAN YOU COME OUT?
TMP TMP TMP TMP TMP TMP
WHAT'S UP?
OH, NOTHING IN PARTICULAR.
OH... REALLY?
?
WANT TO SIT DOWN?
OKAY.

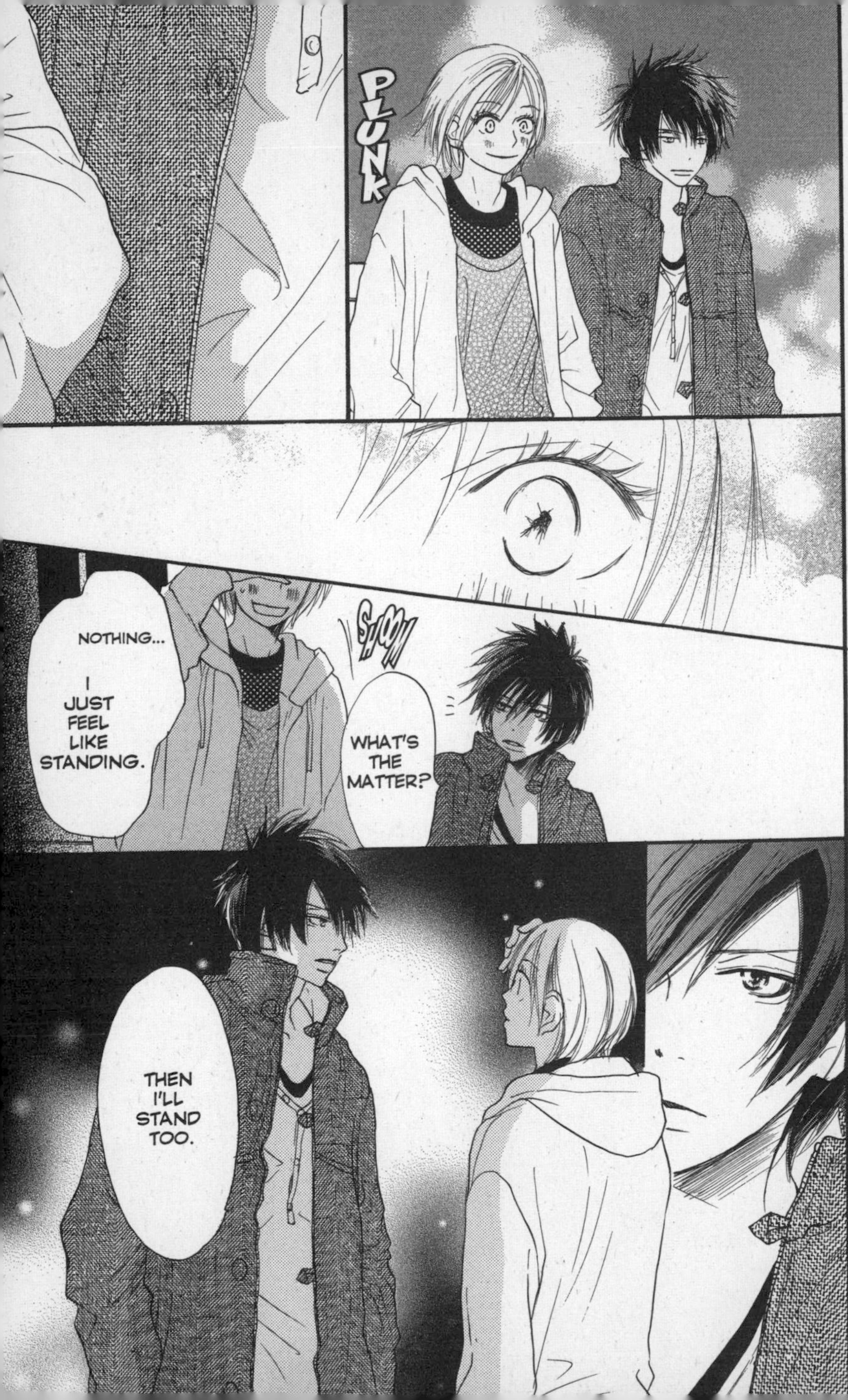
PLUNK
SHOOM
WHAT'S THE MATTER?
NOTHING...
I JUST FEEL LIKE STANDING.
THEN I'LL STAND TOO.

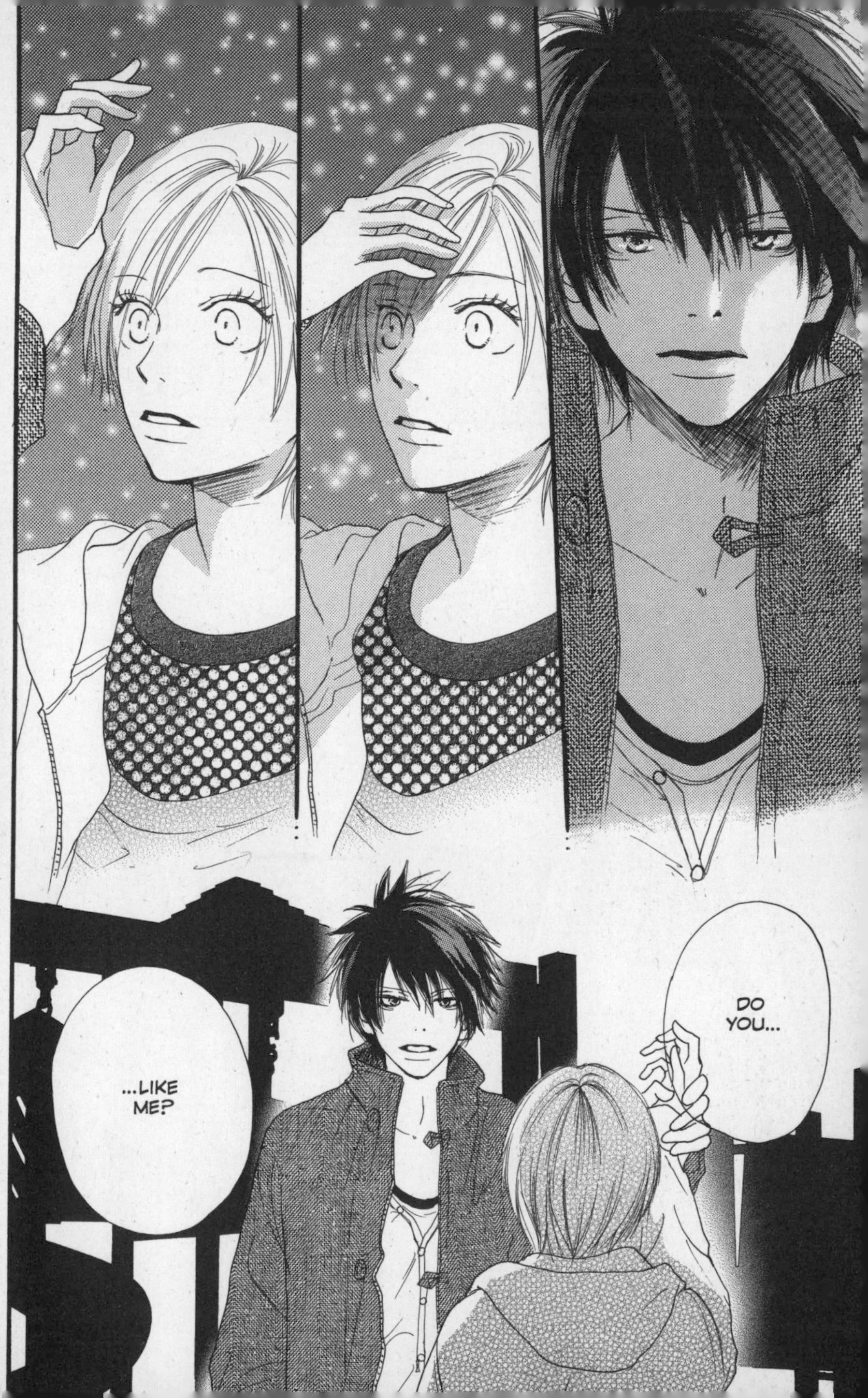
DO YOU...
...LIKE ME?

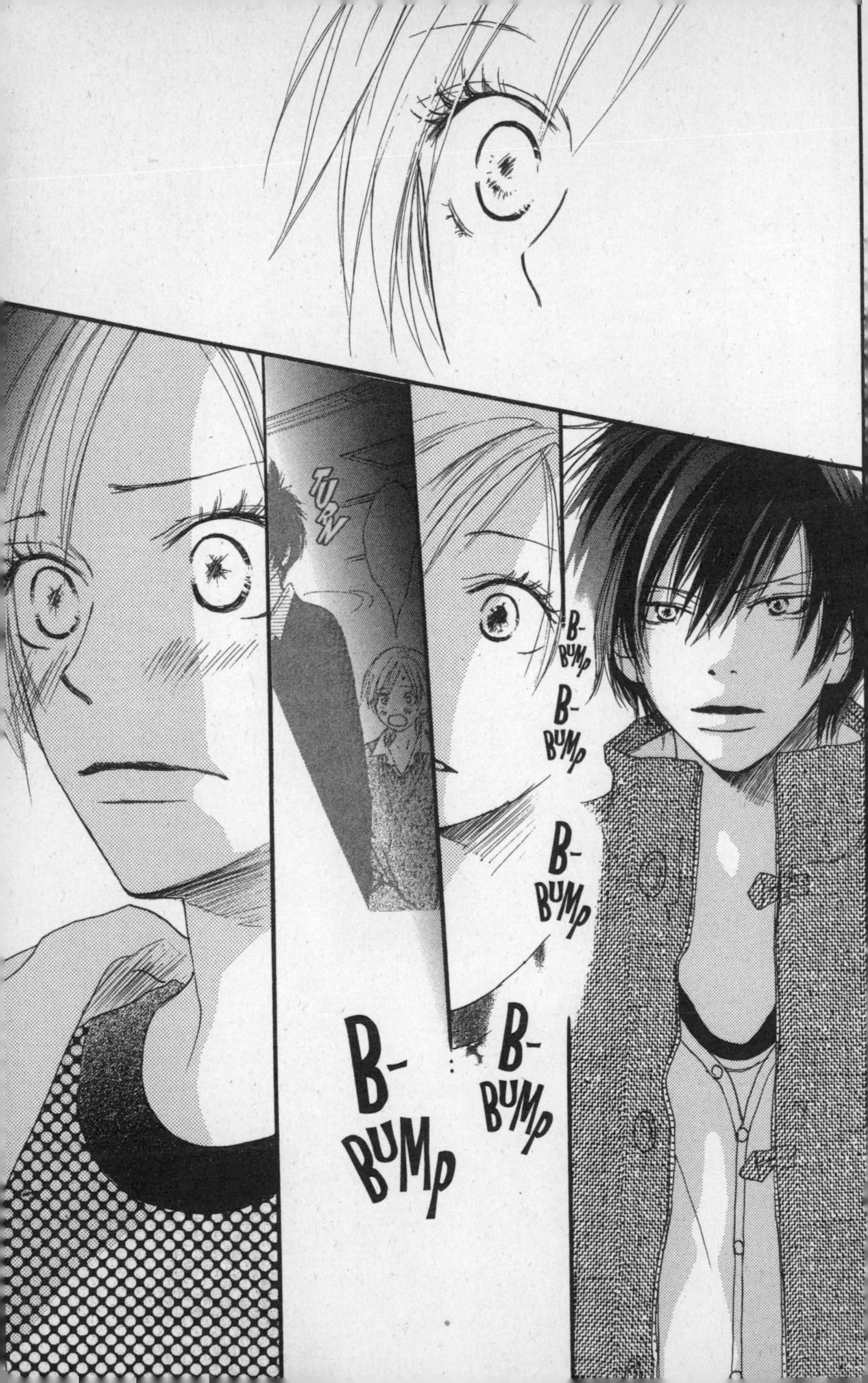
B-BUMP
B-BUMP
B-BUMP
B-BUMP
TURN
B-BUMP

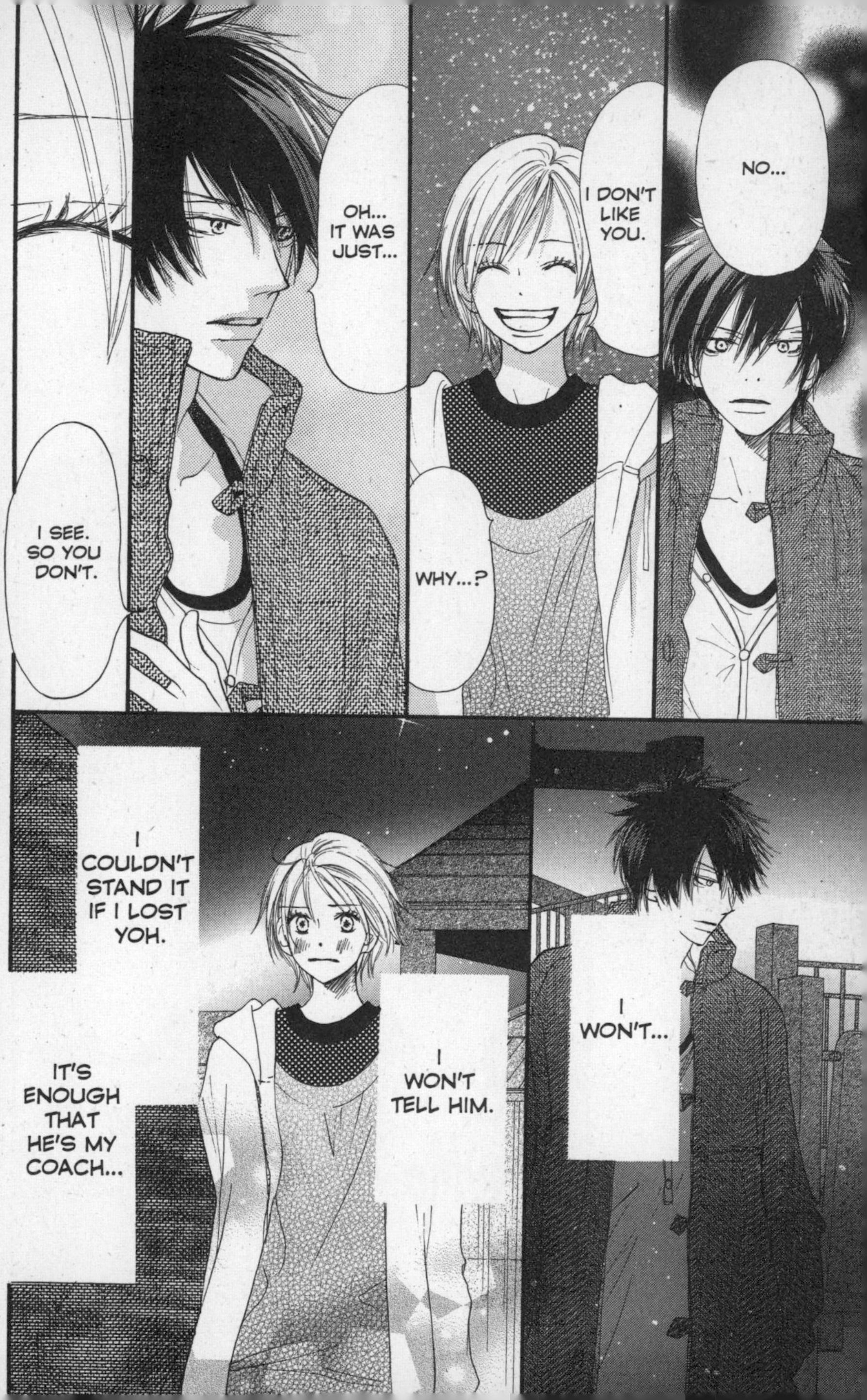
NO...
I DON'T LIKE YOU.
WHY...?
OH... IT WAS JUST...
I SEE. SO YOU DON'T.
I WON'T...
I WON'T TELL HIM.
I COULDN'T STAND IT IF I LOST YOH.
IT'S ENOUGH THAT HE'S MY COACH...

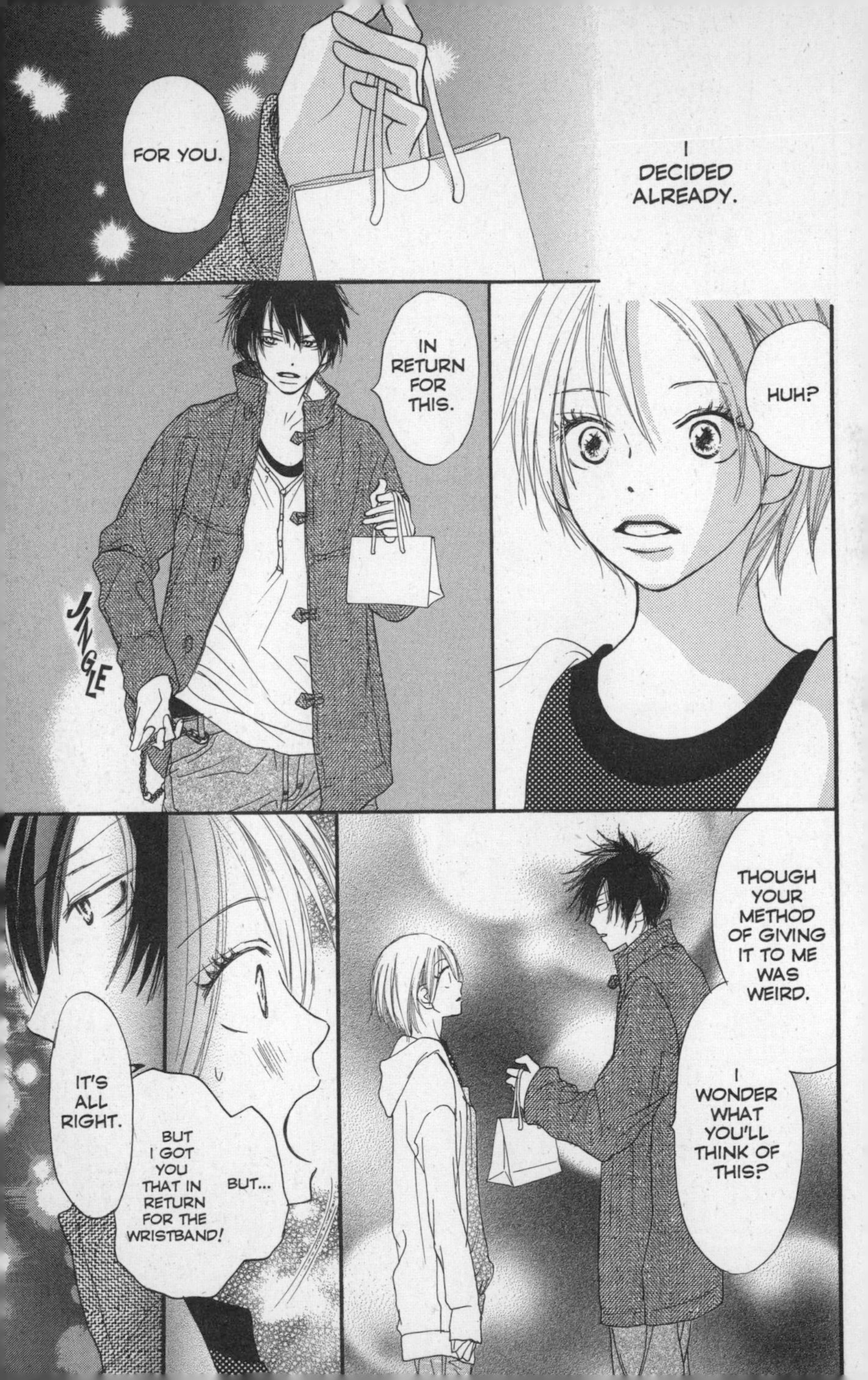
I DECIDED ALREADY.
FOR YOU.
HUH?
IN RETURN FOR THIS.
JINGLE
THOUGH YOUR METHOD OF GIVING IT TO ME WAS WEIRD.
I WONDER WHAT YOU'LL THINK OF THIS?
BUT I GOT YOU THAT IN RETURN FOR THE WRISTBAND!
BUT...
IT'S ALL RIGHT.

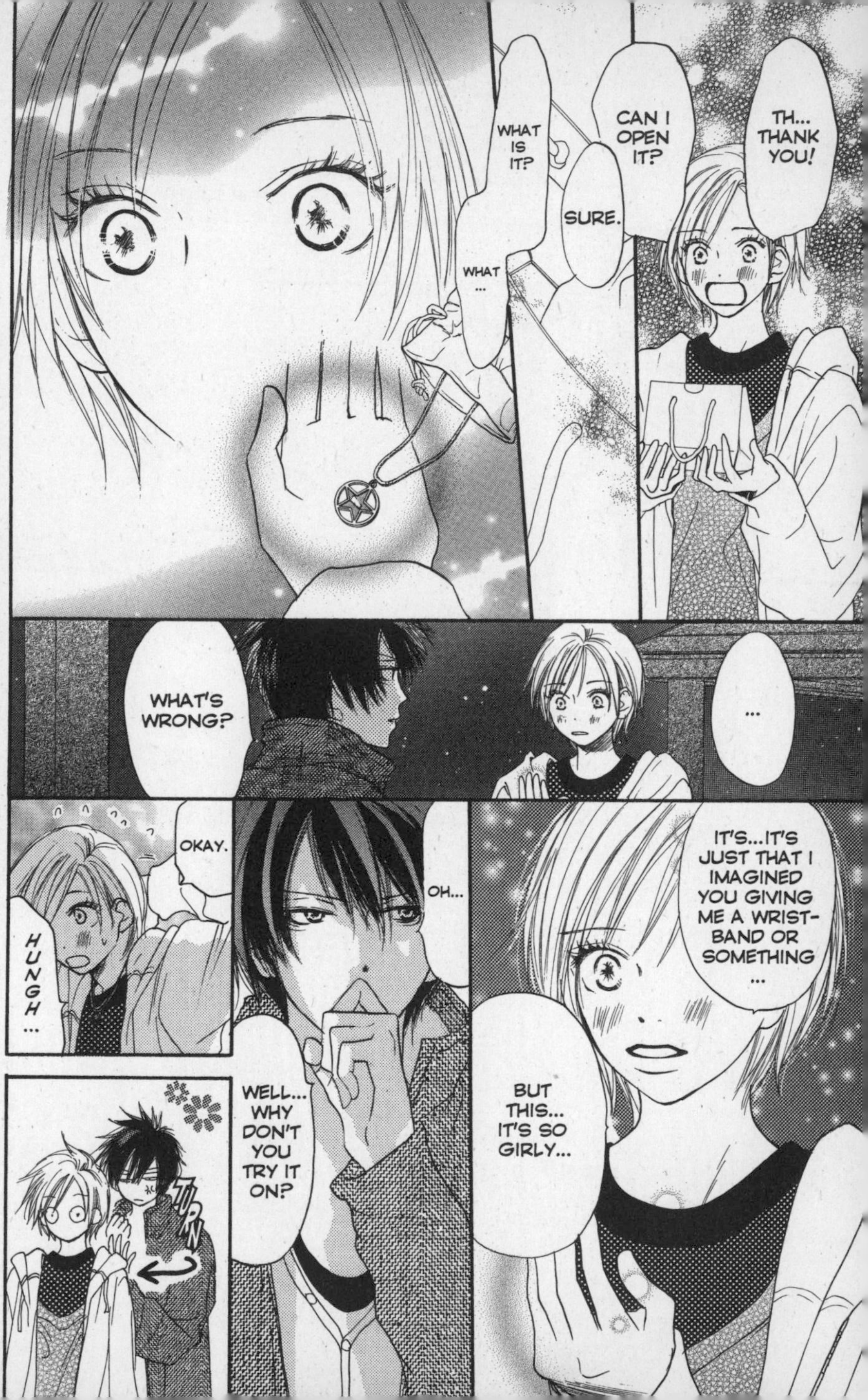
TH... THANK YOU!
CAN I OPEN IT?
SURE.
WHAT IS IT?
WHAT ...
...
WHAT'S WRONG?
IT'S...IT'S JUST THAT I IMAGINED YOU GIVING ME A WRIST-BAND OR SOMETHING ...
BUT THIS... IT'S SO GIRLY...
OH...
WELL... WHY DON'T YOU TRY IT ON?
OKAY.
HUNGH ...
TURN

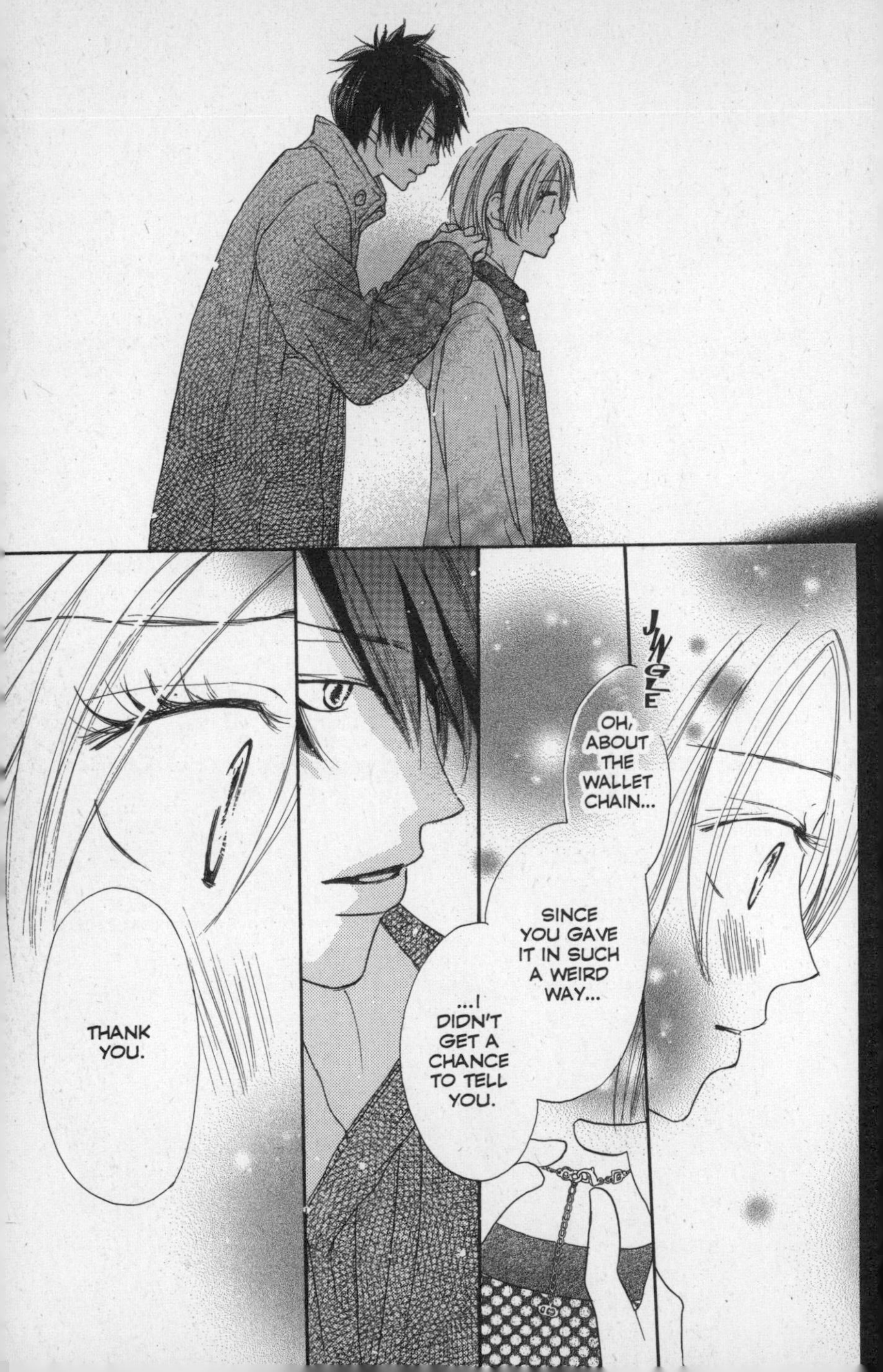
JINGLE
OH, ABOUT THE WALLET CHAIN...
SINCE YOU GAVE IT IN SUCH A WEIRD WAY...
...I DIDN'T GET A CHANCE TO TELL YOU.
THANK YOU.

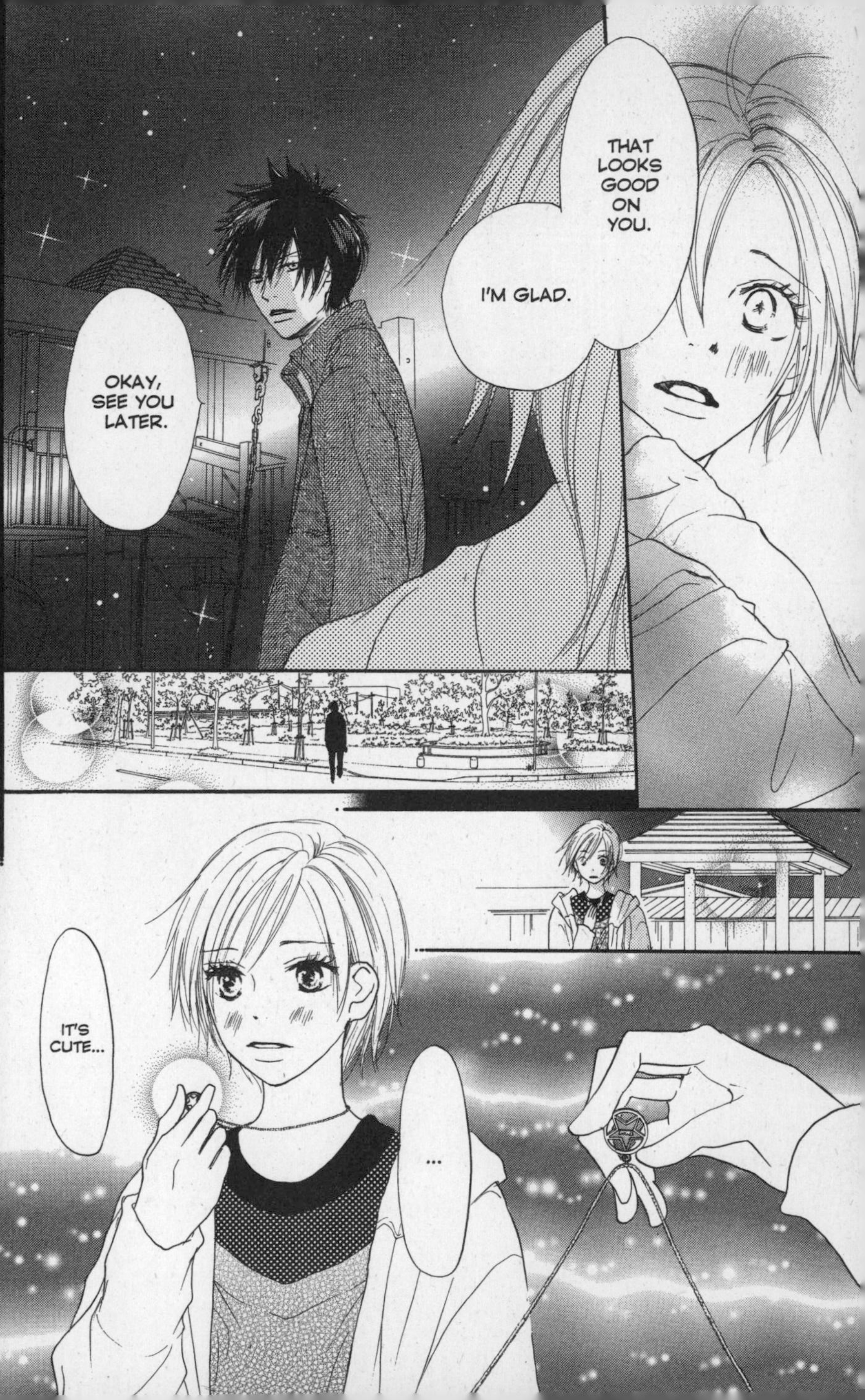
THAT LOOKS GOOD ON YOU.
I'M GLAD.
OKAY, SEE YOU LATER.
...
IT'S CUTE...

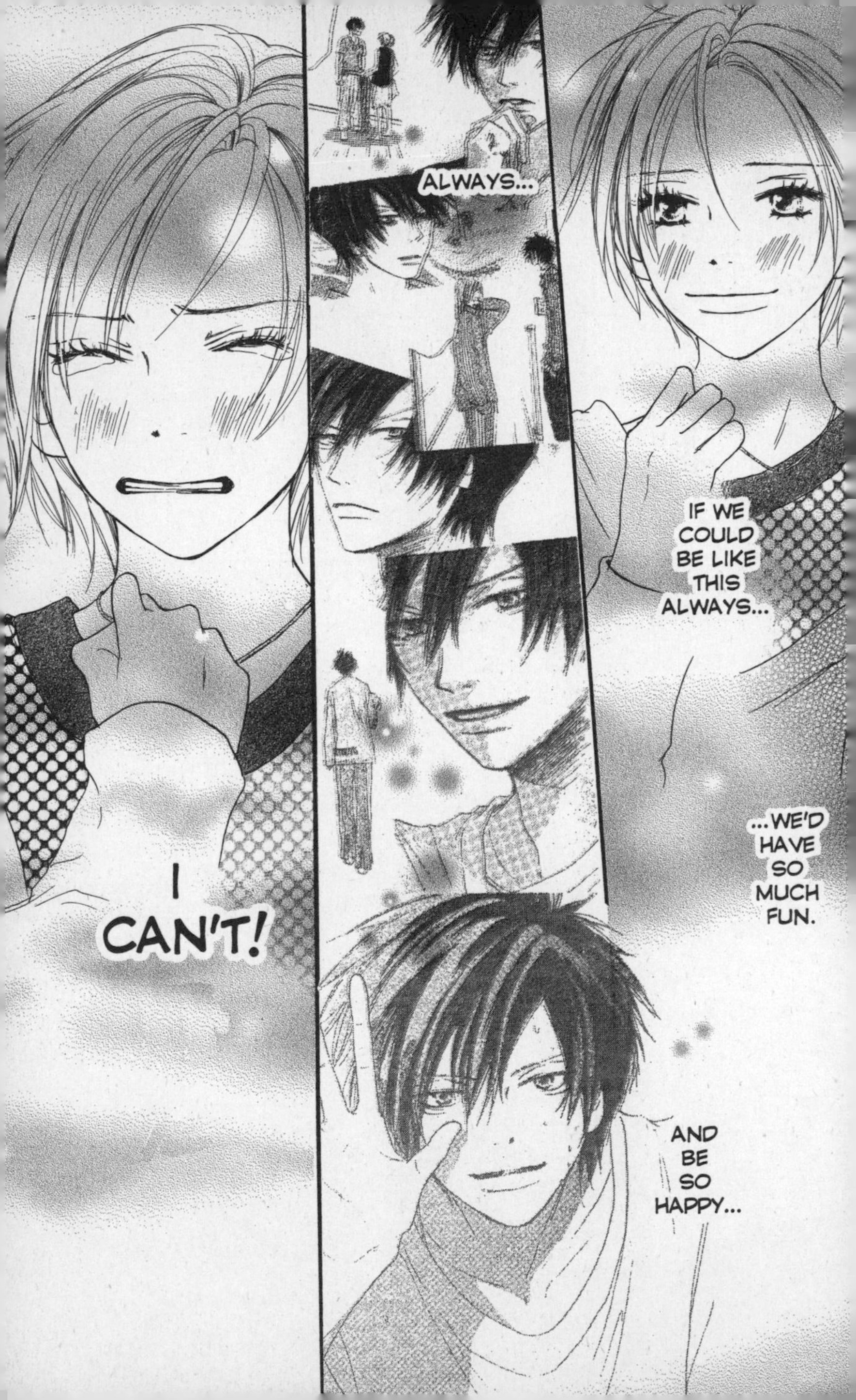
IF WE COULD BE LIKE THIS ALWAYS...
...WE'D HAVE SO MUCH FUN.
AND BE SO HAPPY...
ALWAYS...
I CAN'T!

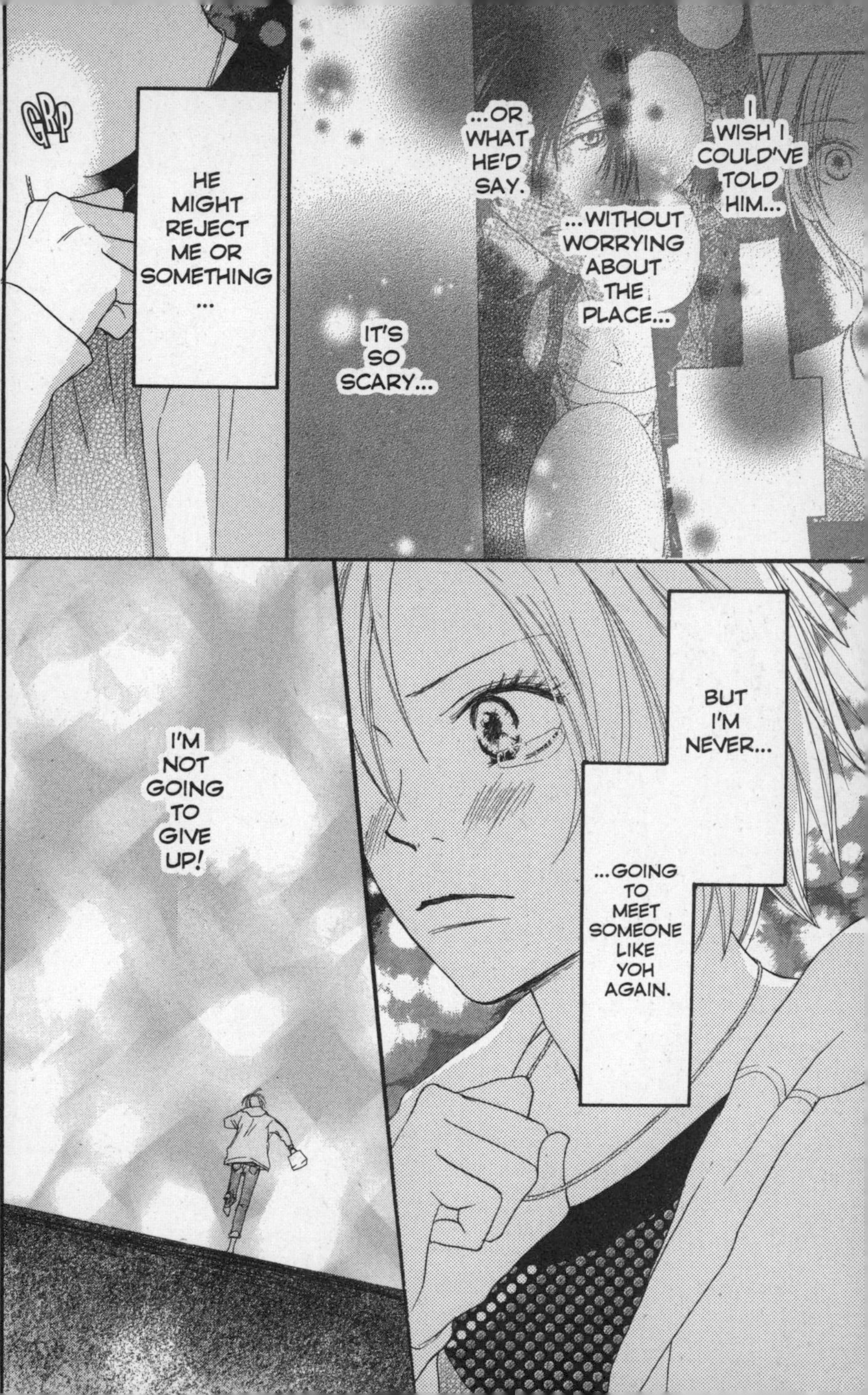
I WISH I COULD'VE TOLD HIM...
...WITHOUT WORRYING ABOUT THE PLACE...
...OR WHAT HE'D SAY.
IT'S SO SCARY...
GRP
HE MIGHT REJECT ME OR SOMETHING...
BUT I'M NEVER...
...GOING TO MEET SOMEONE LIKE YOH AGAIN.
I'M NOT GOING TO GIVE UP!

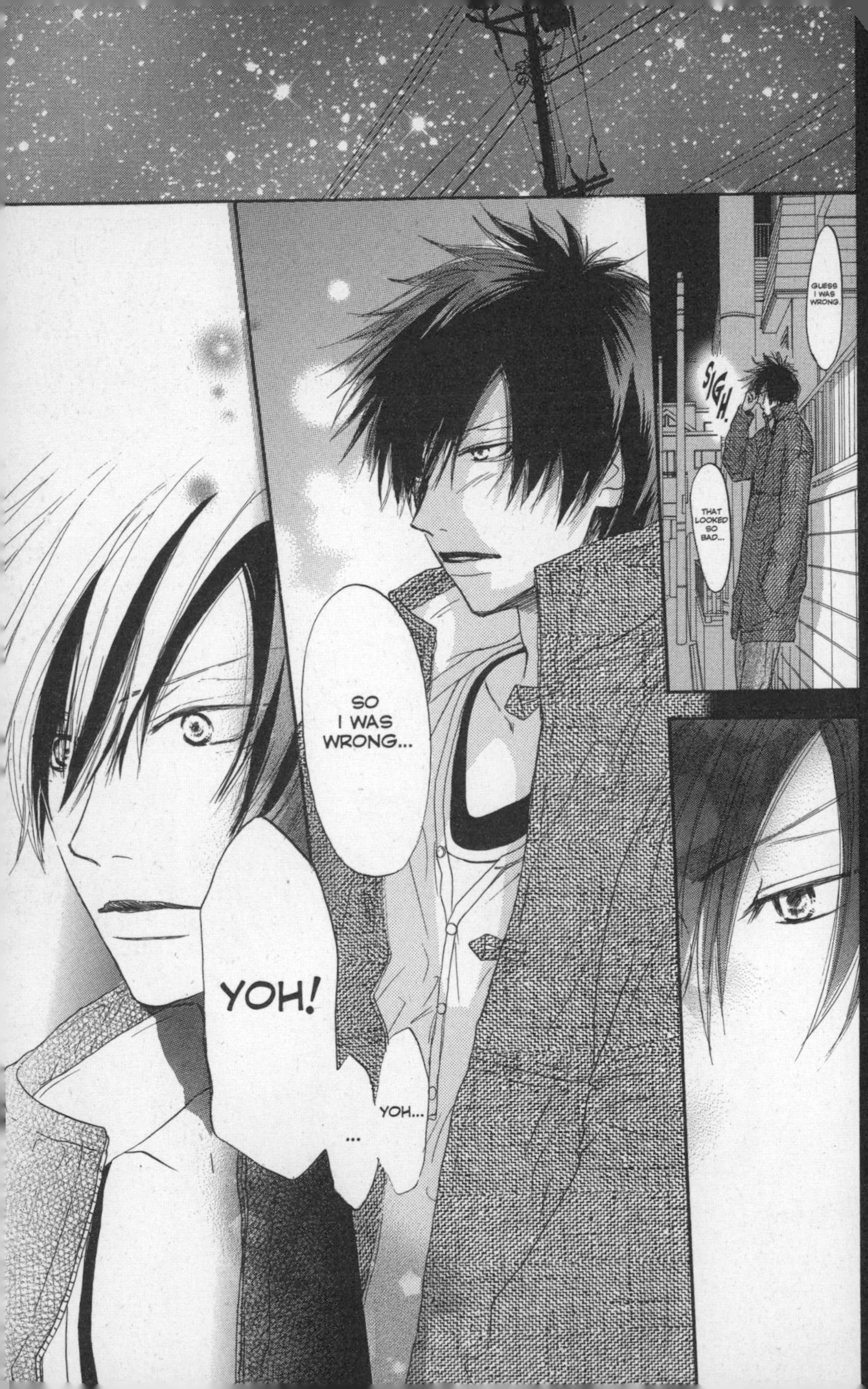
GUESS I WAS WRONG.
SIGH
THAT LOOKED SO BAD...
SO I WAS WRONG...
YOH!
YOH...
...

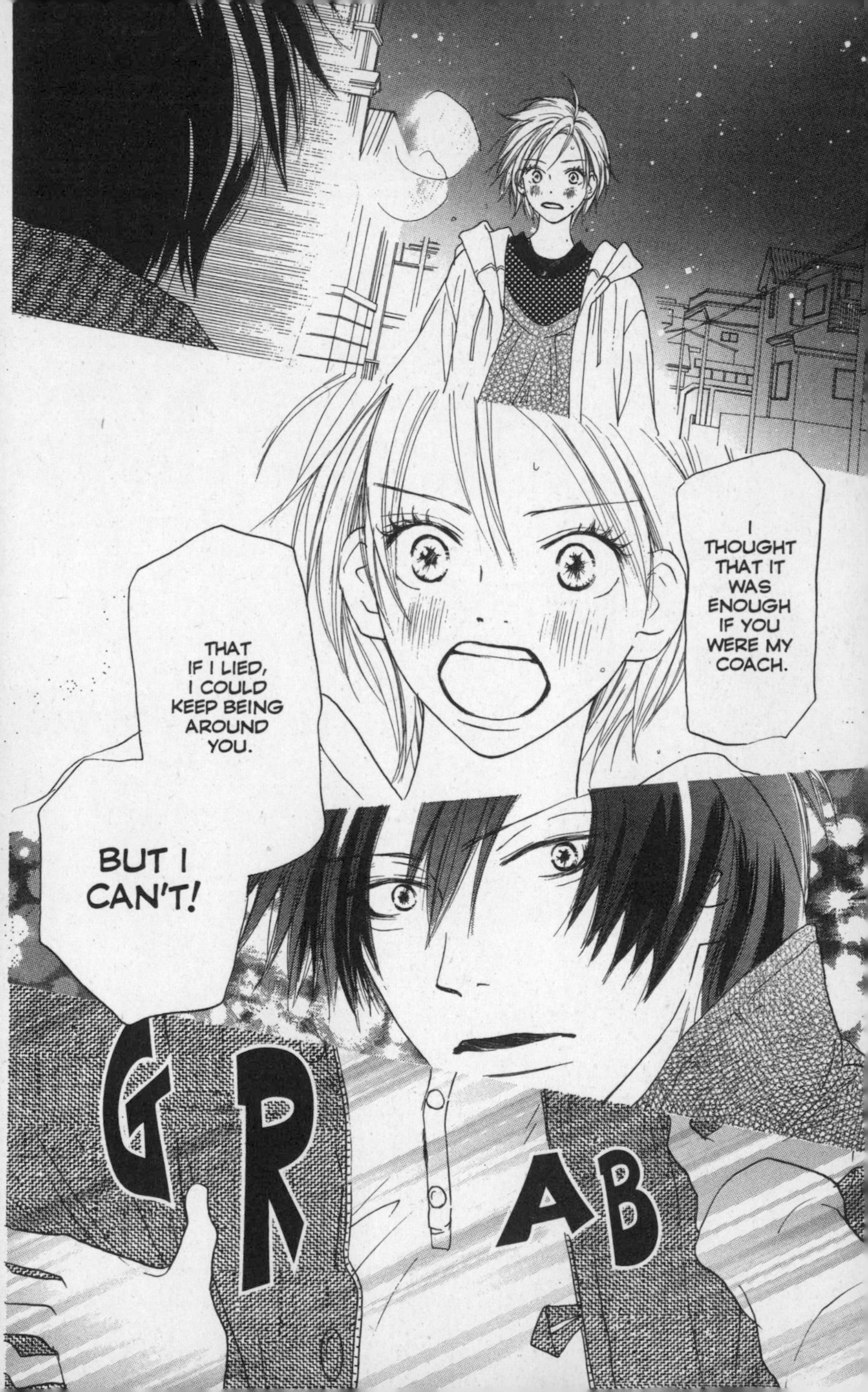
I THOUGHT THAT IT WAS ENOUGH IF YOU WERE MY COACH.
THAT IF I LIED, I COULD KEEP BEING AROUND YOU.
BUT I CAN'T!
GRAB

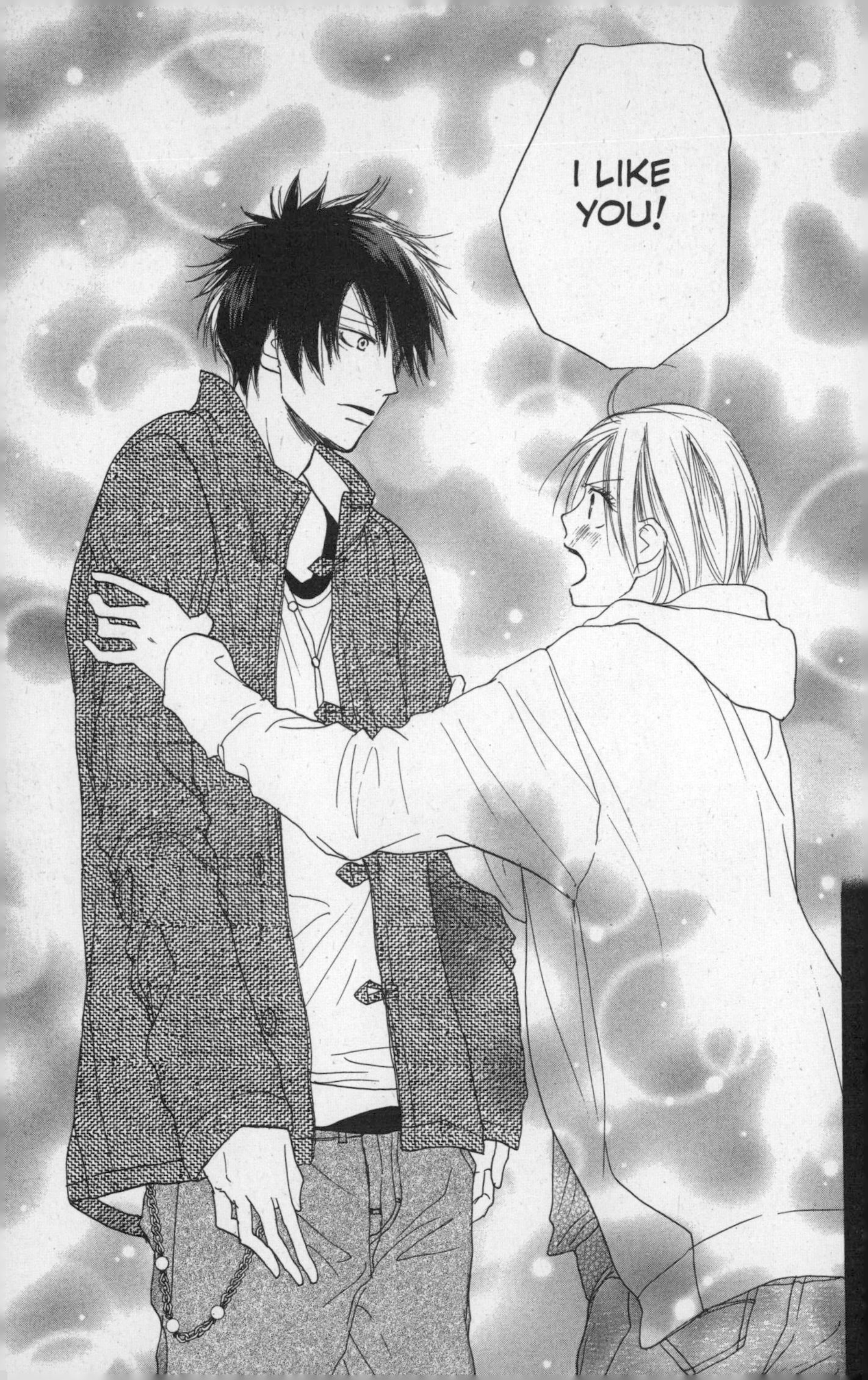
I LIKE YOU!

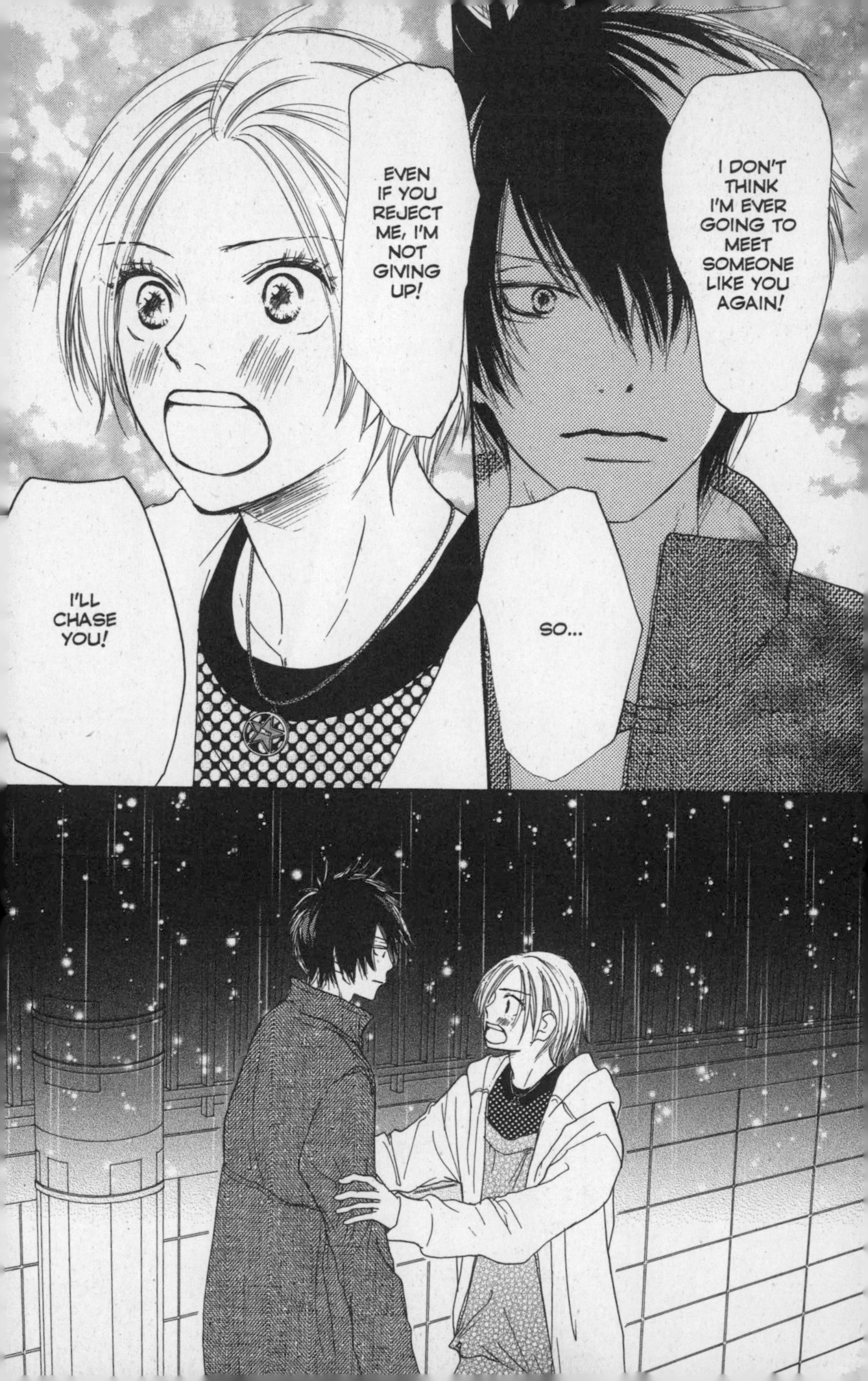
I DON'T THINK I'M EVER GOING TO MEET SOMEONE LIKE YOU AGAIN!
SO...
EVEN IF YOU REJECT ME, I'M NOT GIVING UP!
I'LL CHASE YOU!

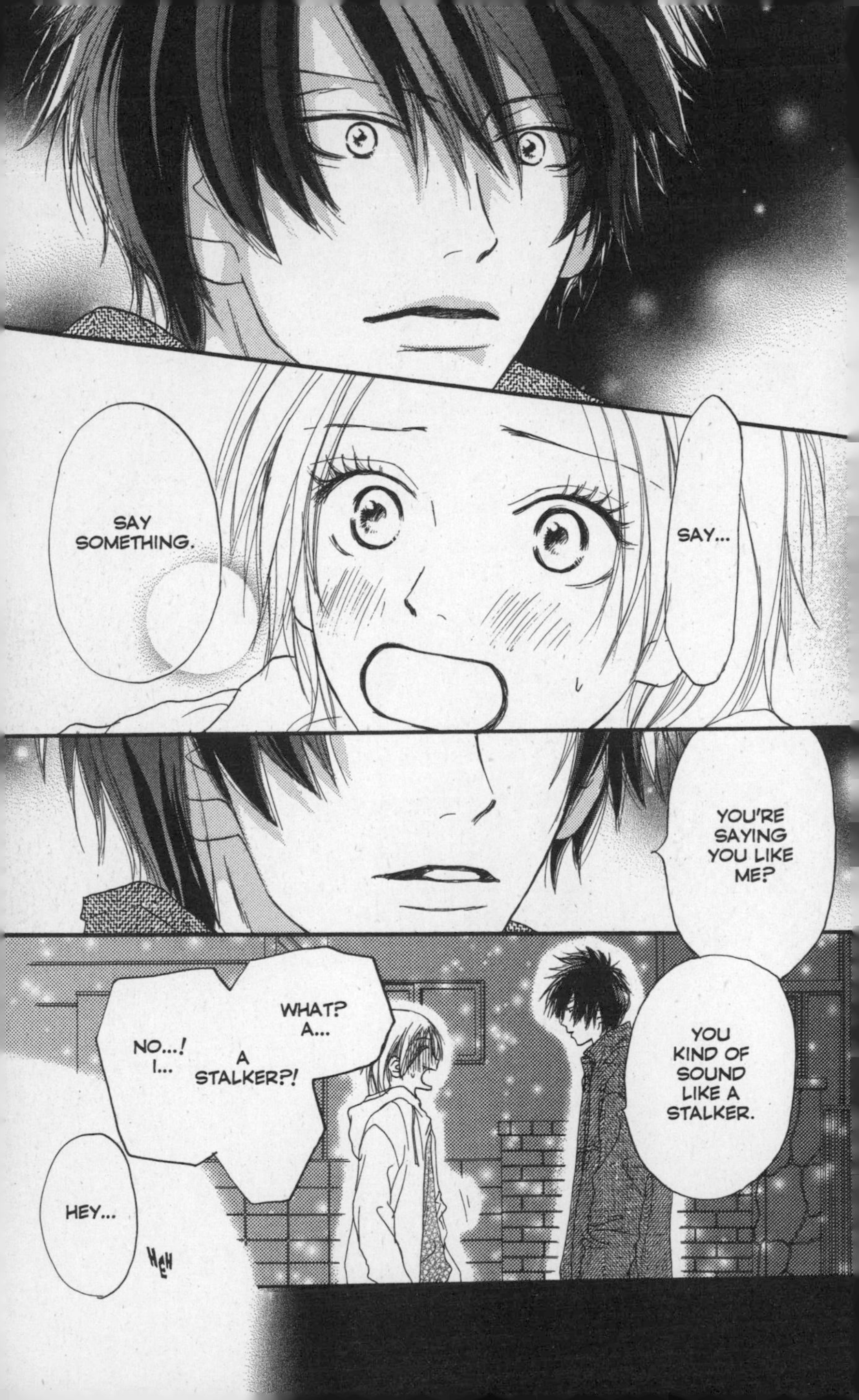
SAY...
SAY SOMETHING.
YOU'RE SAYING YOU LIKE ME?
YOU KIND OF SOUND LIKE A STALKER.
WHAT? A...
A STALKER?!
NO...! I...
HEY...
HEH

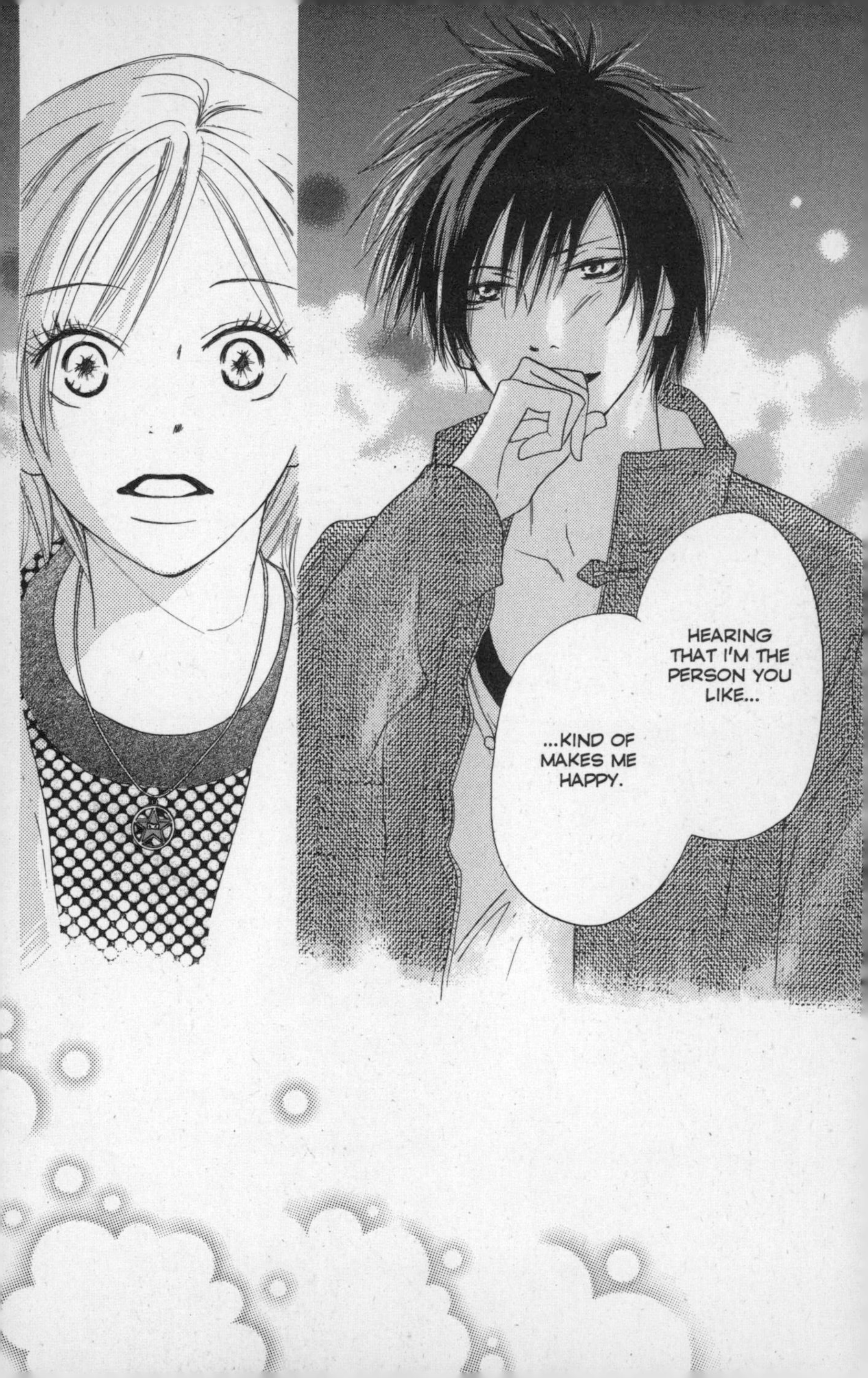
HEARING THAT I'M THE PERSON YOU LIKE...
...KIND OF MAKES ME HAPPY.

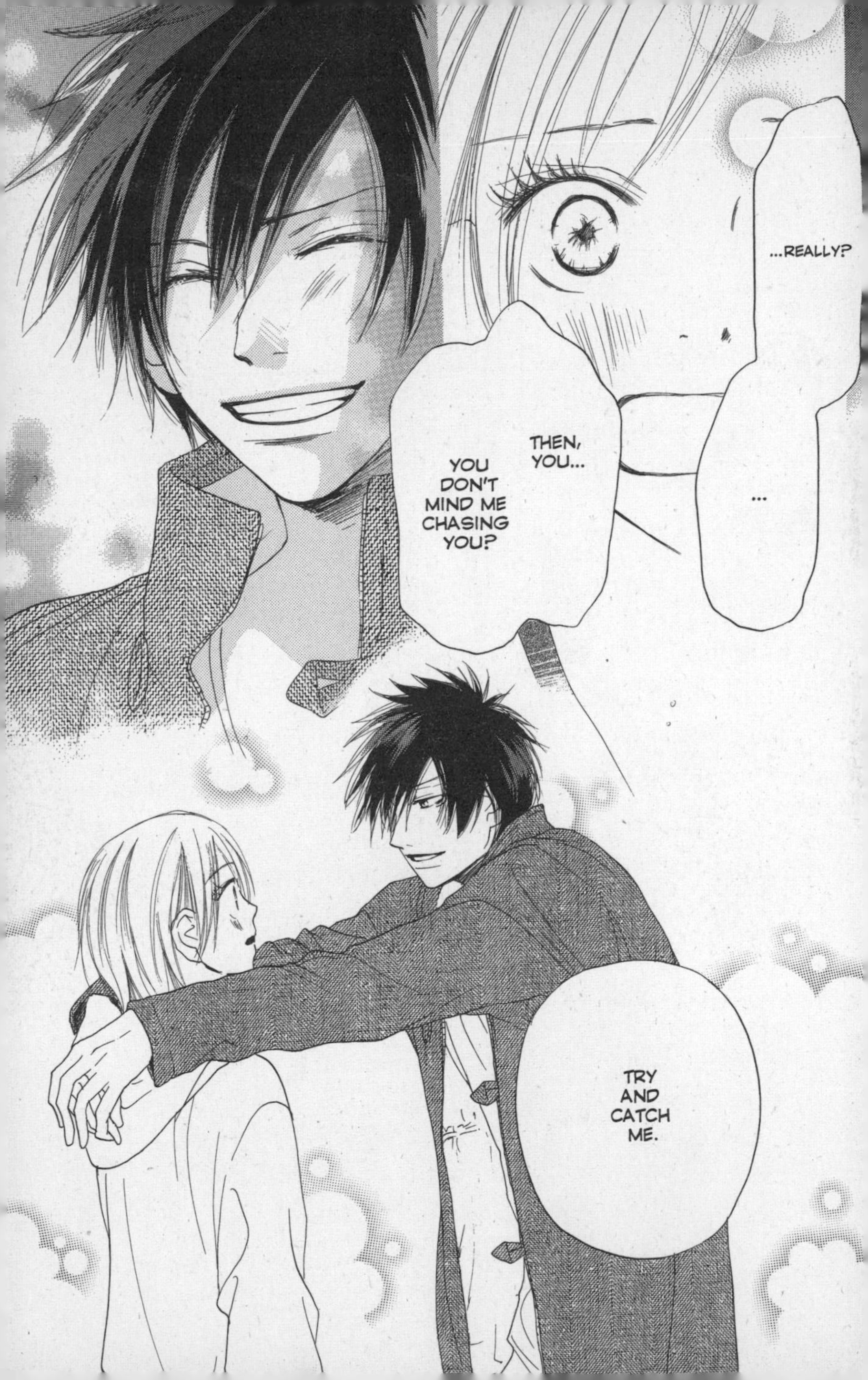
...REALLY?
...
THEN, YOU... YOU DON'T MIND ME CHASING YOU?
TRY AND CATCH ME.

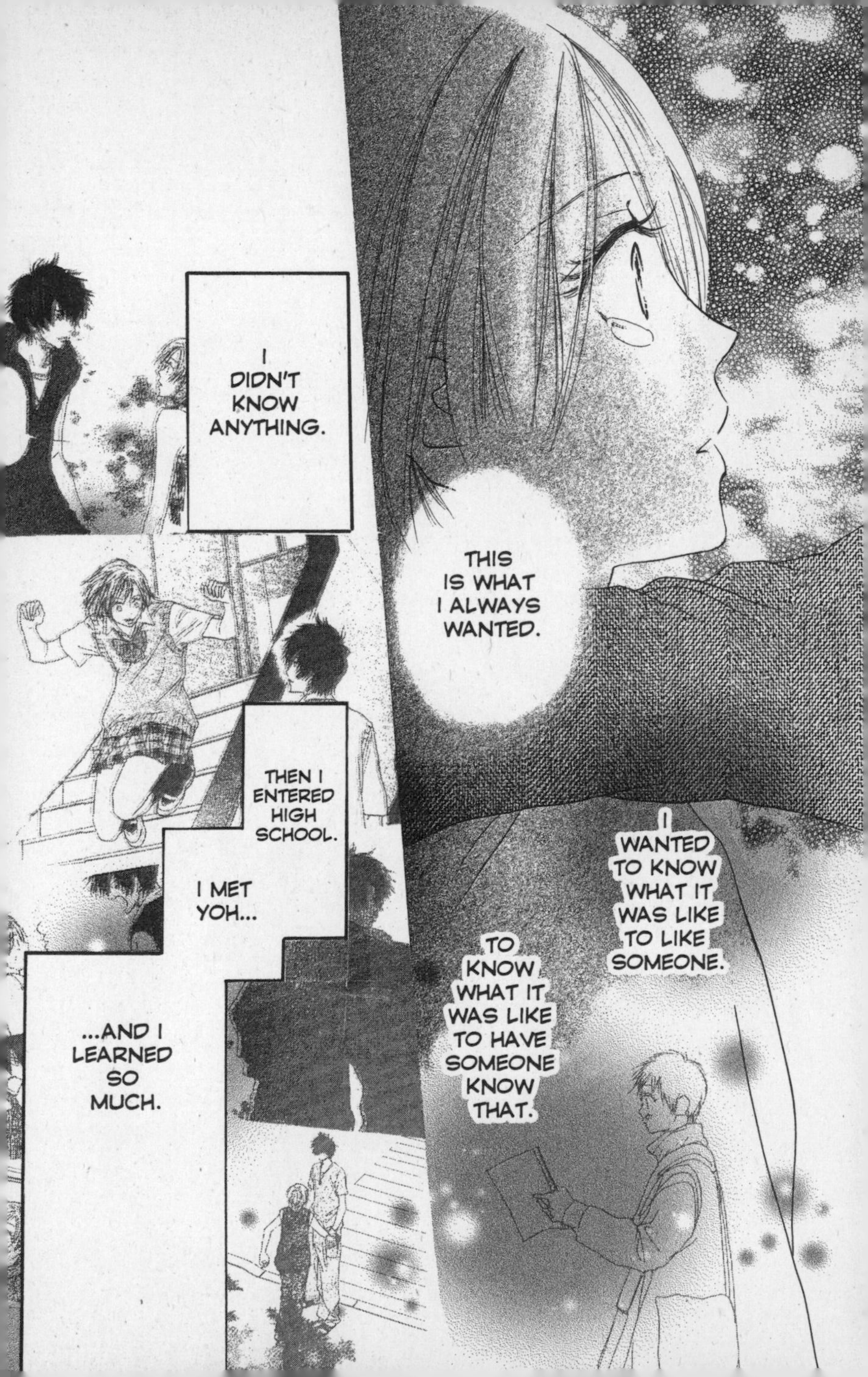
THIS IS WHAT I ALWAYS WANTED.
I WANTED TO KNOW WHAT IT WAS LIKE TO LIKE SOMEONE.
TO KNOW WHAT IT WAS LIKE TO HAVE SOMEONE KNOW THAT.
I DIDN'T KNOW ANYTHING.
THEN I ENTERED HIGH SCHOOL.
I MET YOH...
...AND I LEARNED SO MUCH.

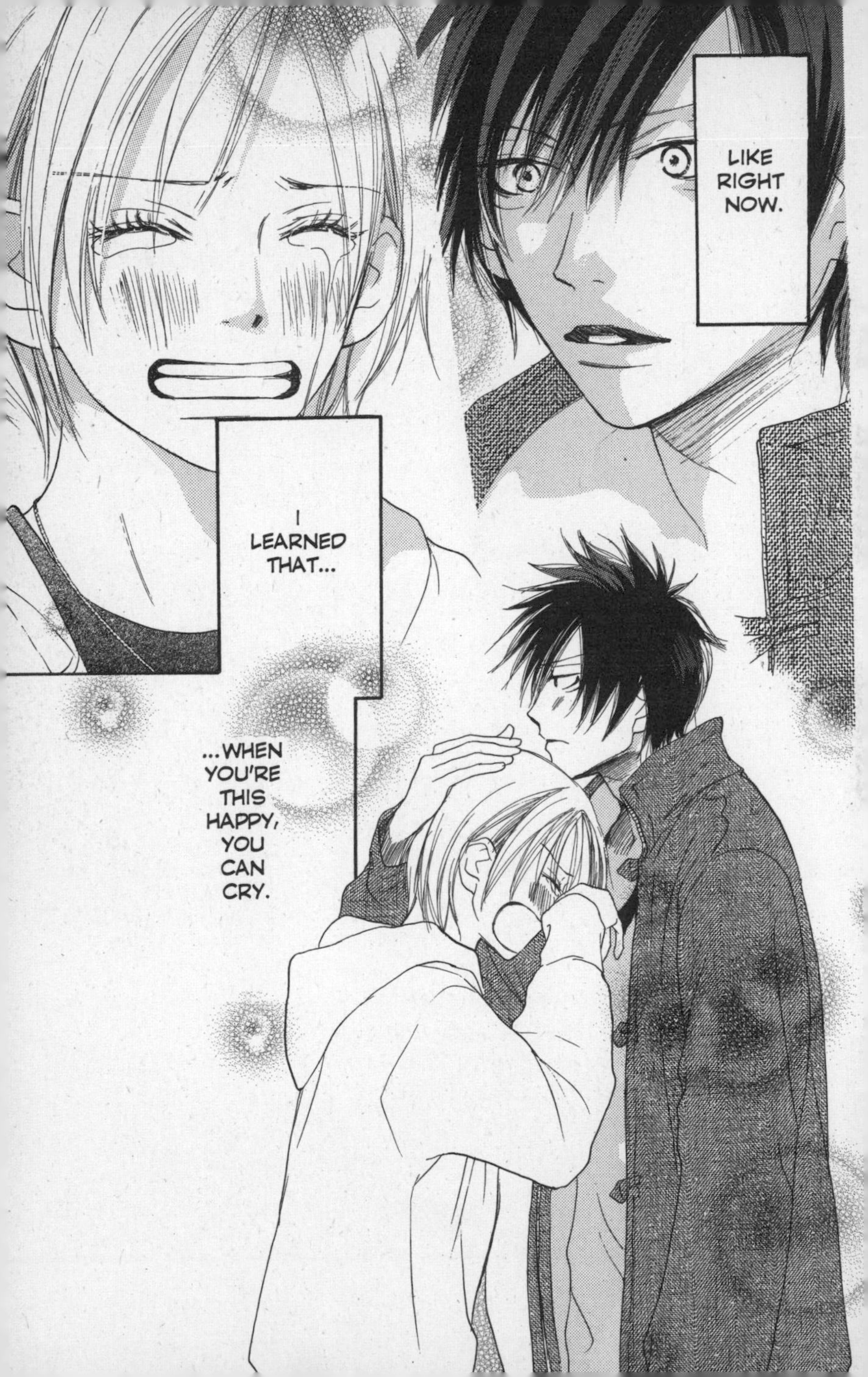
LIKE RIGHT NOW.
I LEARNED THAT...
...WHEN YOU'RE THIS HAPPY, YOU CAN CRY.

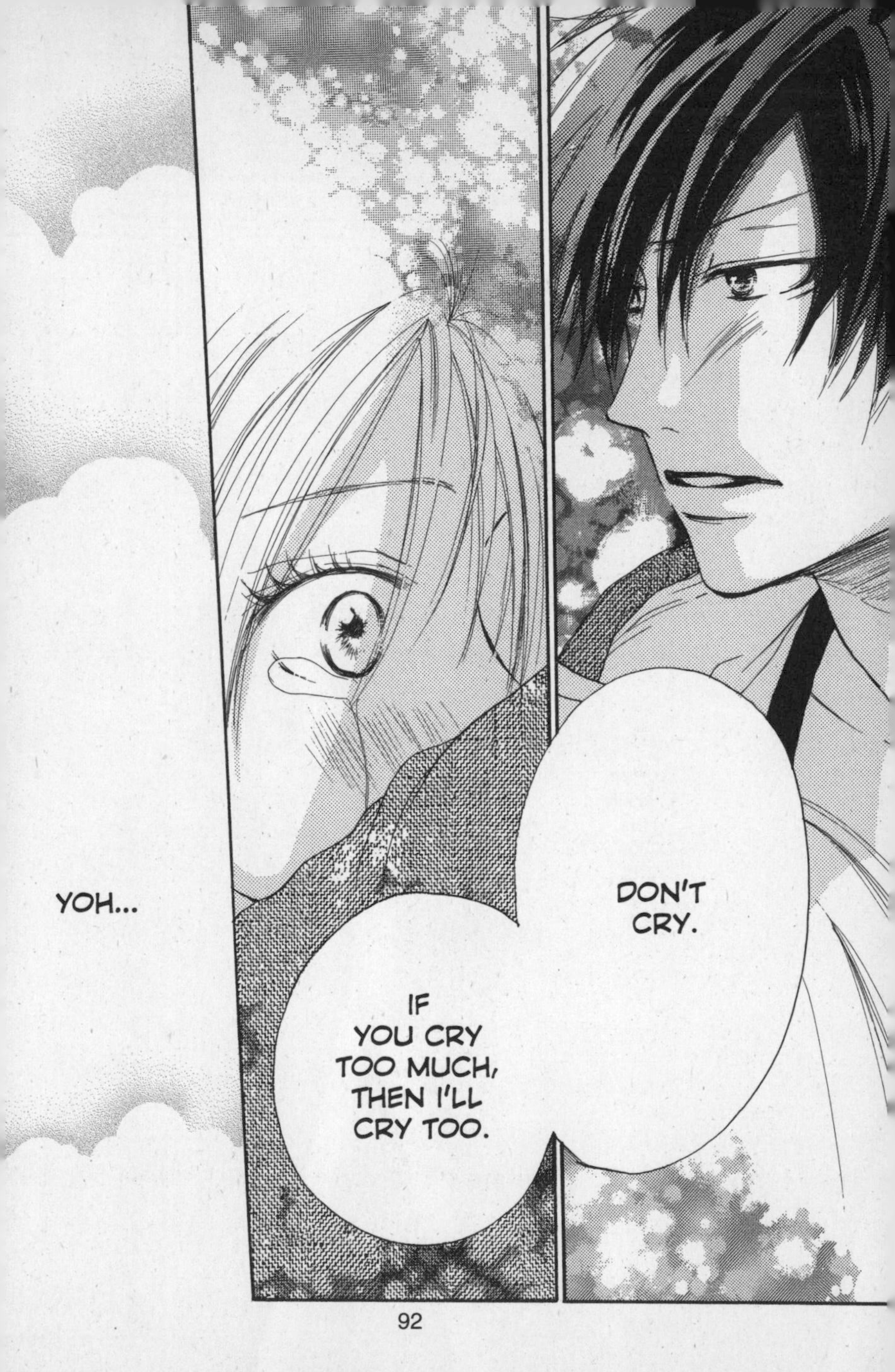
DON'T CRY.
IF YOU CRY TOO MUCH, THEN I'LL CRY TOO.
YOH...

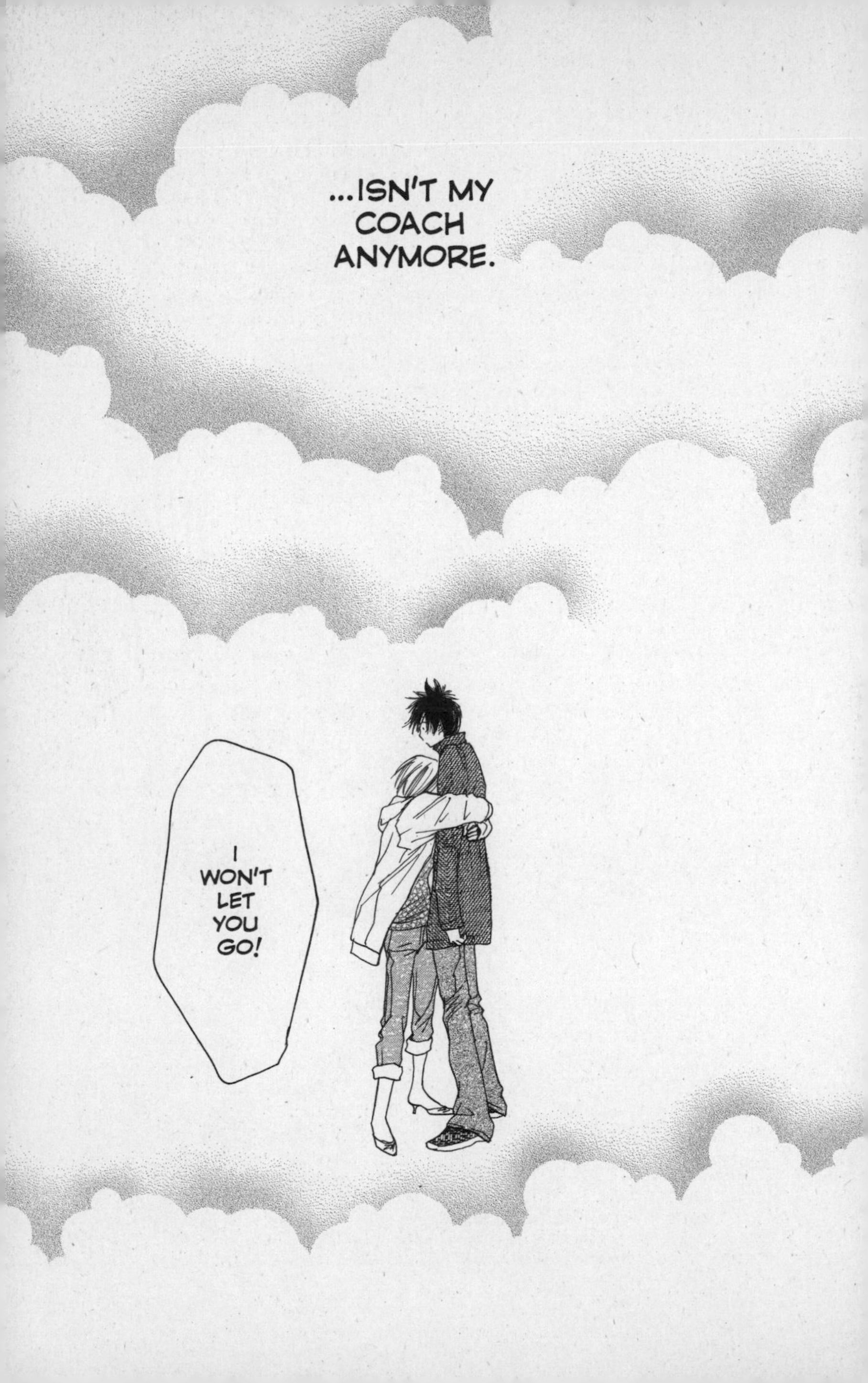
...ISN'T MY COACH ANYMORE.
I WON'T LET YOU GO!

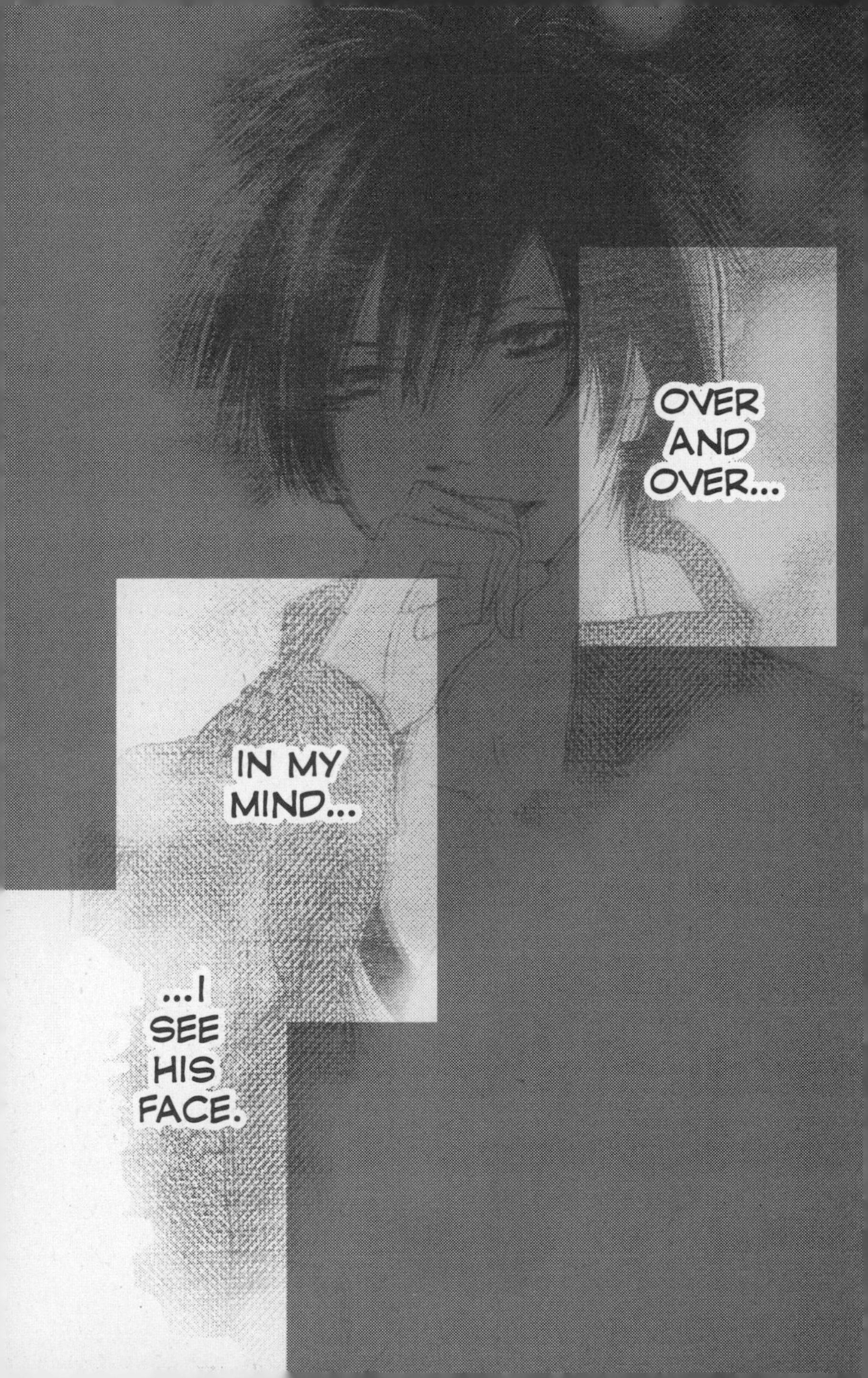
OVER AND OVER...
IN MY MIND...
...I SEE HIS FACE.

Haruna
and Mami

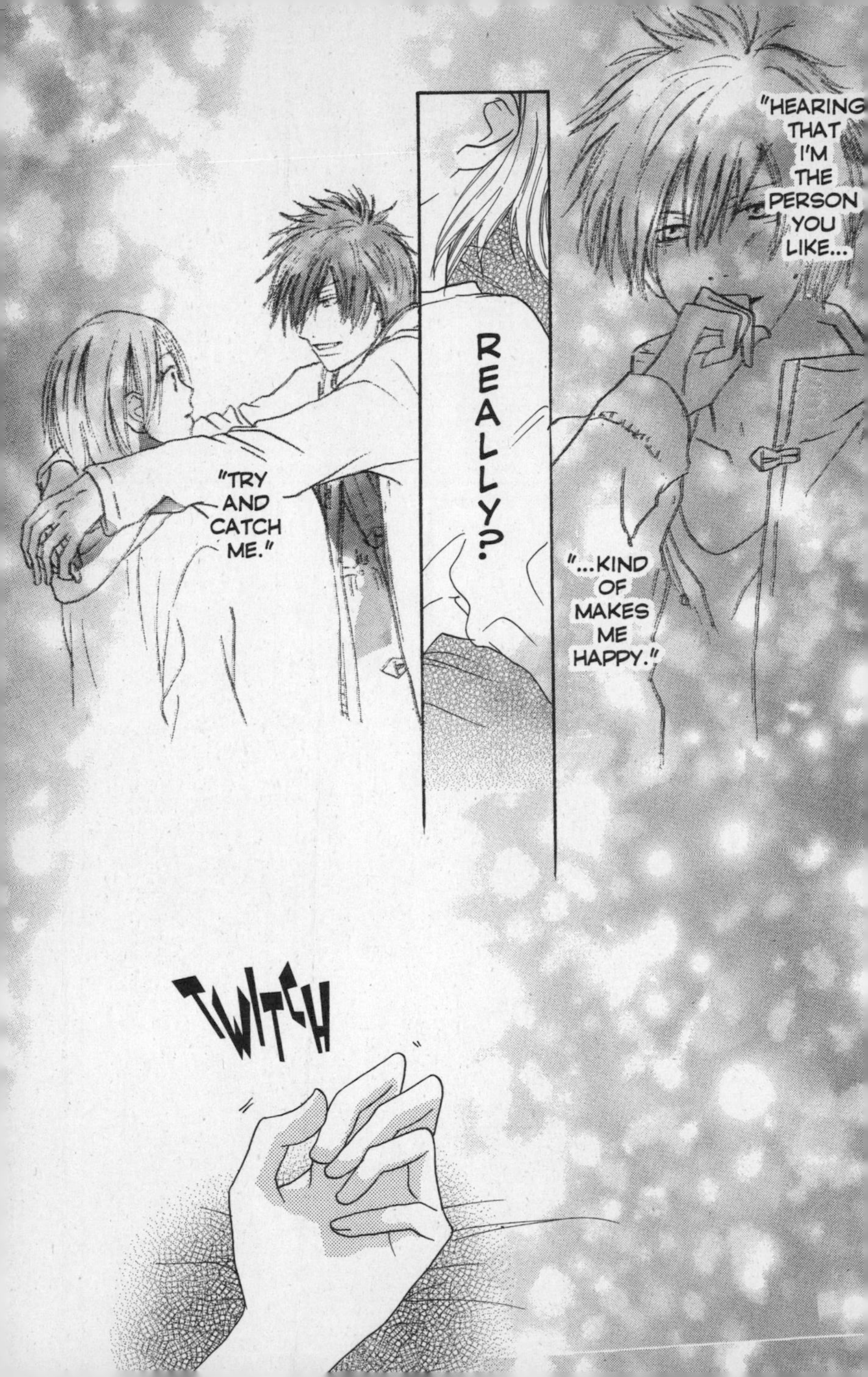
"HEARING THAT I'M THE PERSON YOU LIKE...
"...KIND OF MAKES ME HAPPY."
REALLY?
"TRY AND CATCH ME."
TWITCH

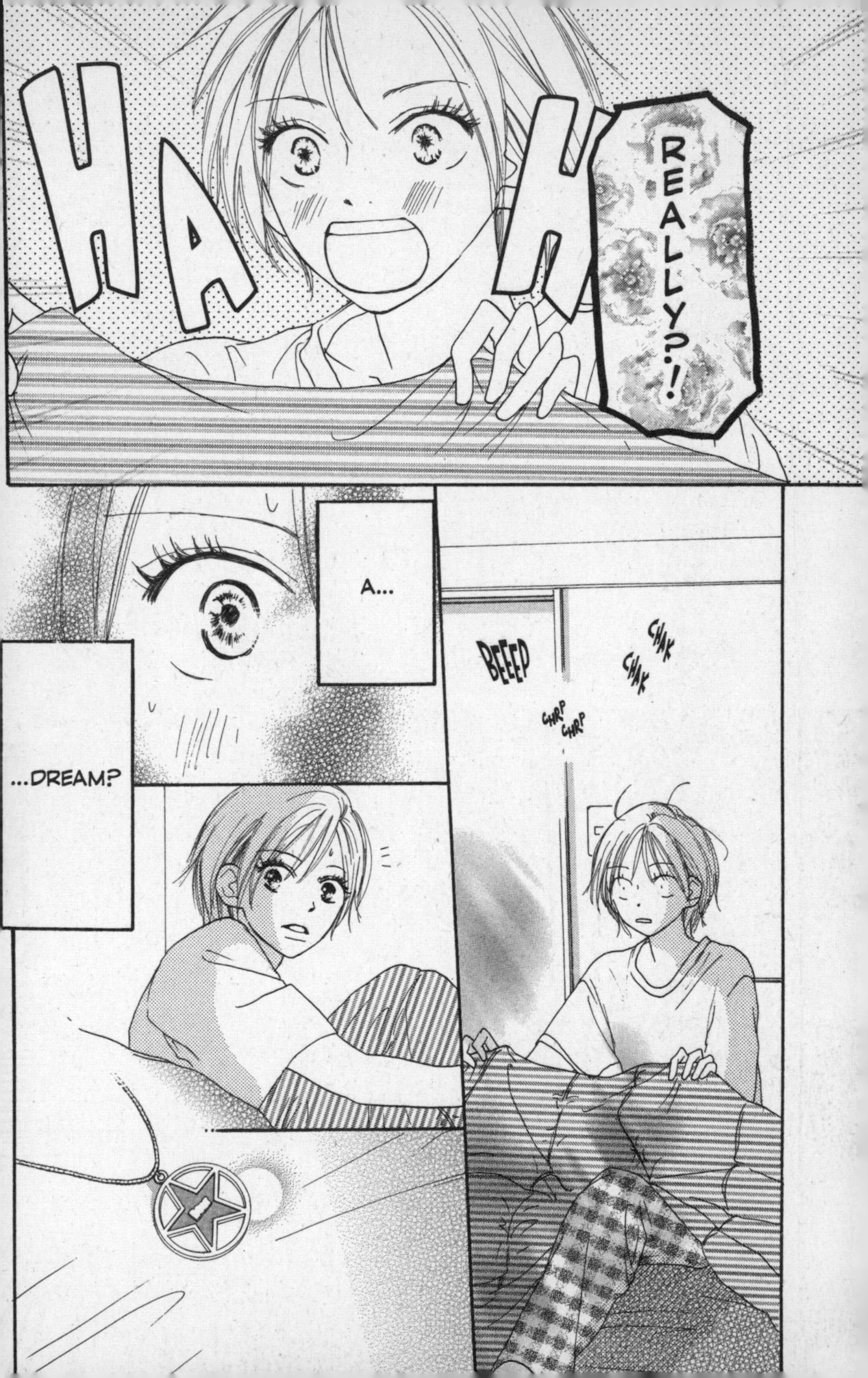
HAH
REALLY?!
CHAK
CHAK
BEEEP
CHRP
CHRP
A...
...DREAM?

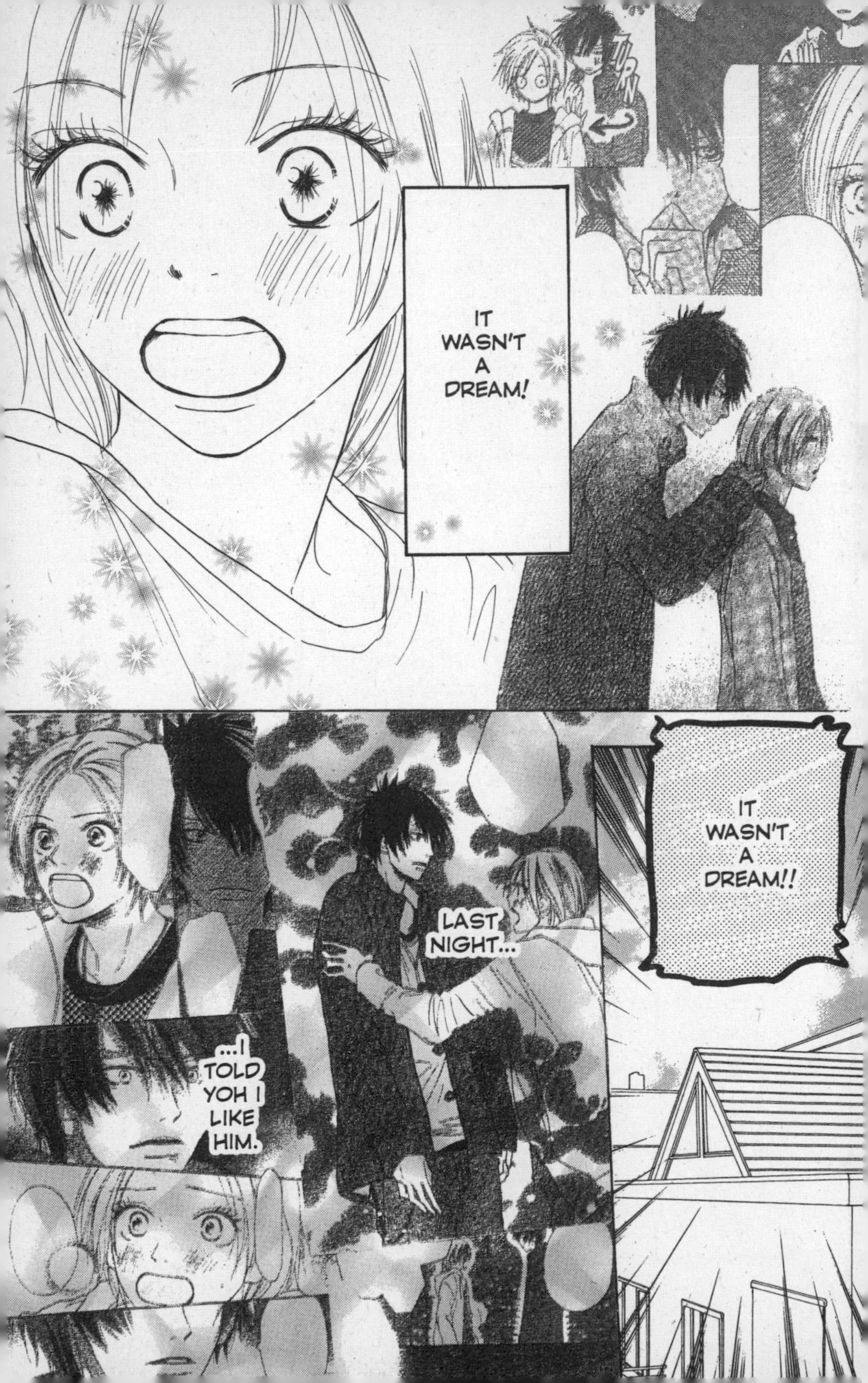
TURN
IT WASN'T A DREAM!
IT WASN'T A DREAM!!
LAST NIGHT...
...I TOLD YOH I LIKE HIM.

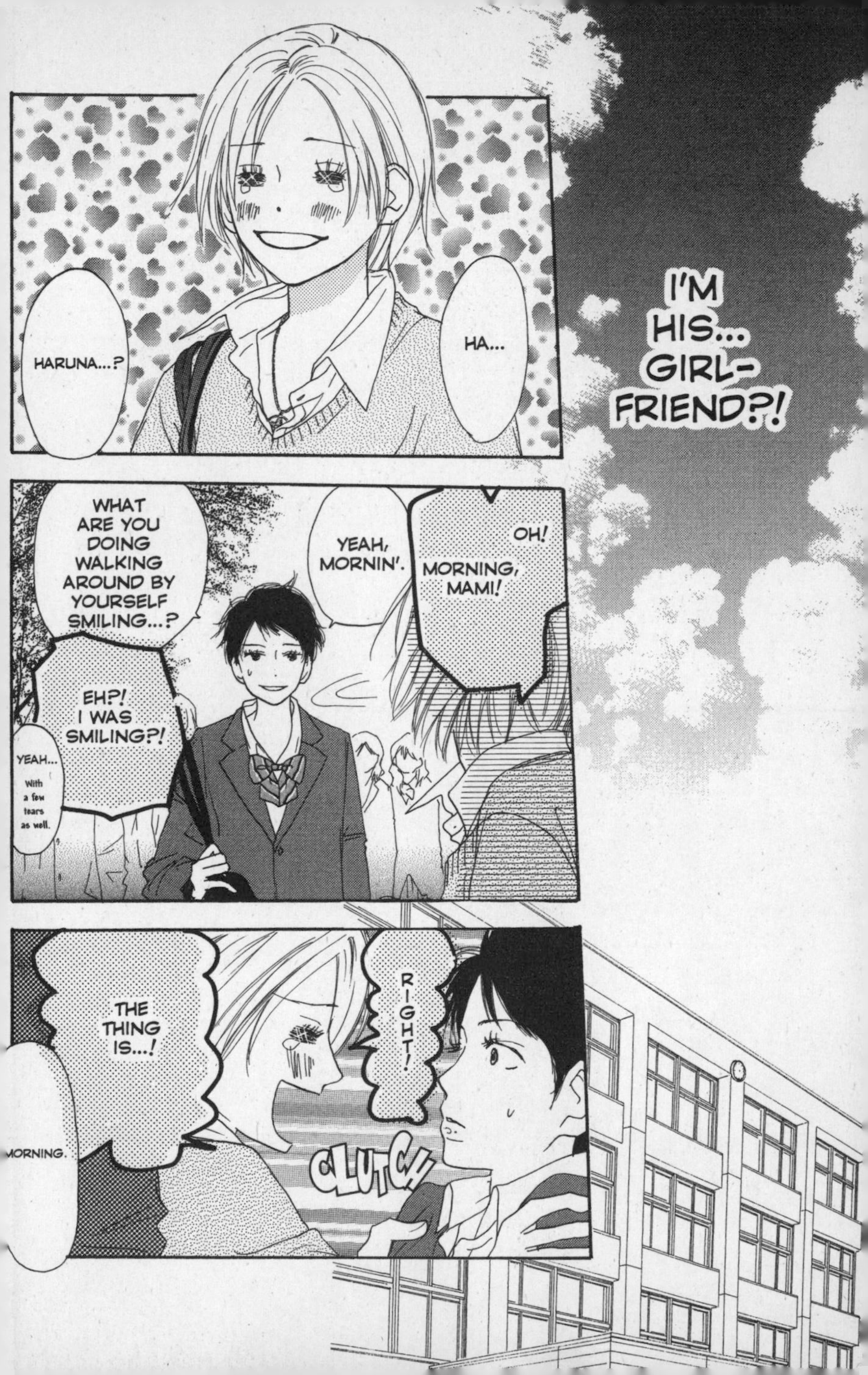
I'M HIS... GIRL-FRIEND?!
HA...
HARUNA...?
OH!
MORNING, MAMI!
YEAH, MORNIN'.
WHAT ARE YOU DOING WALKING AROUND BY YOURSELF SMILING...?
EH?! I WAS SMILING?!
YEAH...
With a few tears as well.
RIGHT!
THE THING IS...!
CLUTCH
MORNING.

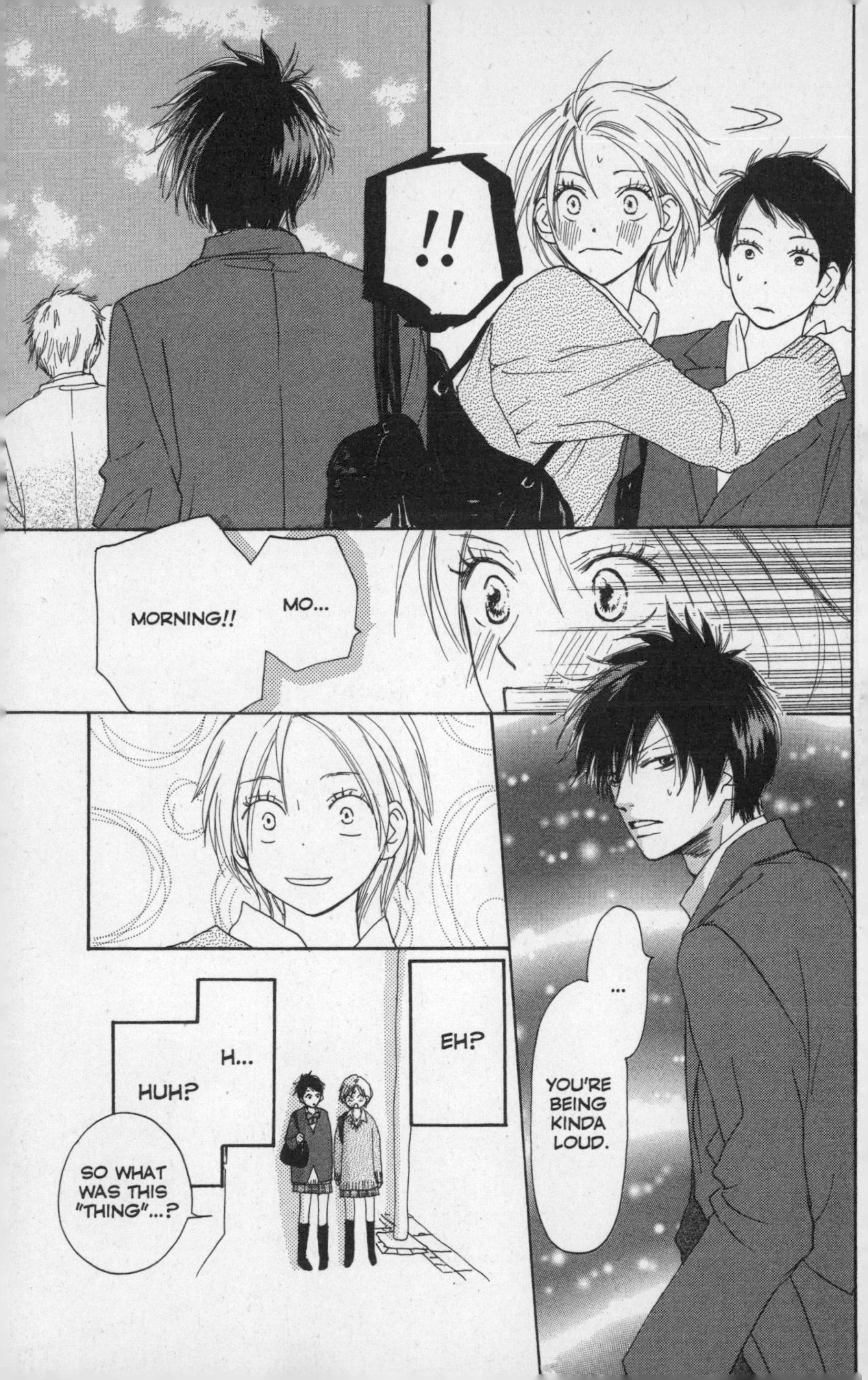
!!
MO...
MORNING!!
...
YOU'RE BEING KINDA LOUD.
EH?
H...
HUH?
SO WHAT WAS THIS "THING"...?

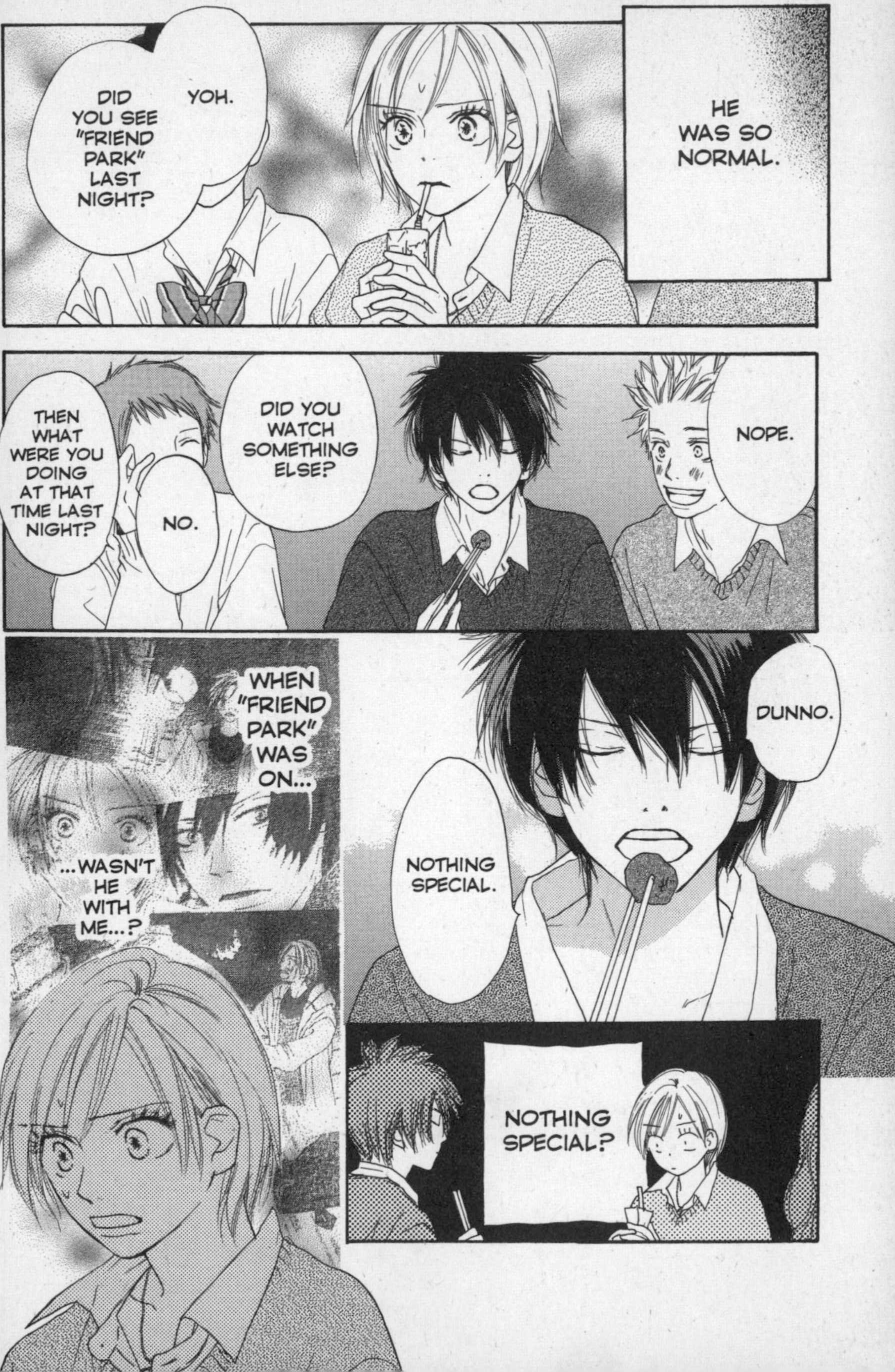
HE WAS SO NORMAL.
YOH.
DID YOU SEE "FRIEND PARK" LAST NIGHT?
NOPE.
DID YOU WATCH SOMETHING ELSE?
NO.
THEN WHAT WERE YOU DOING AT THAT TIME LAST NIGHT?
DUNNO.
NOTHING SPECIAL.
NOTHING SPECIAL?
WHEN "FRIEND PARK" WAS ON...
...WASN'T HE WITH ME...?

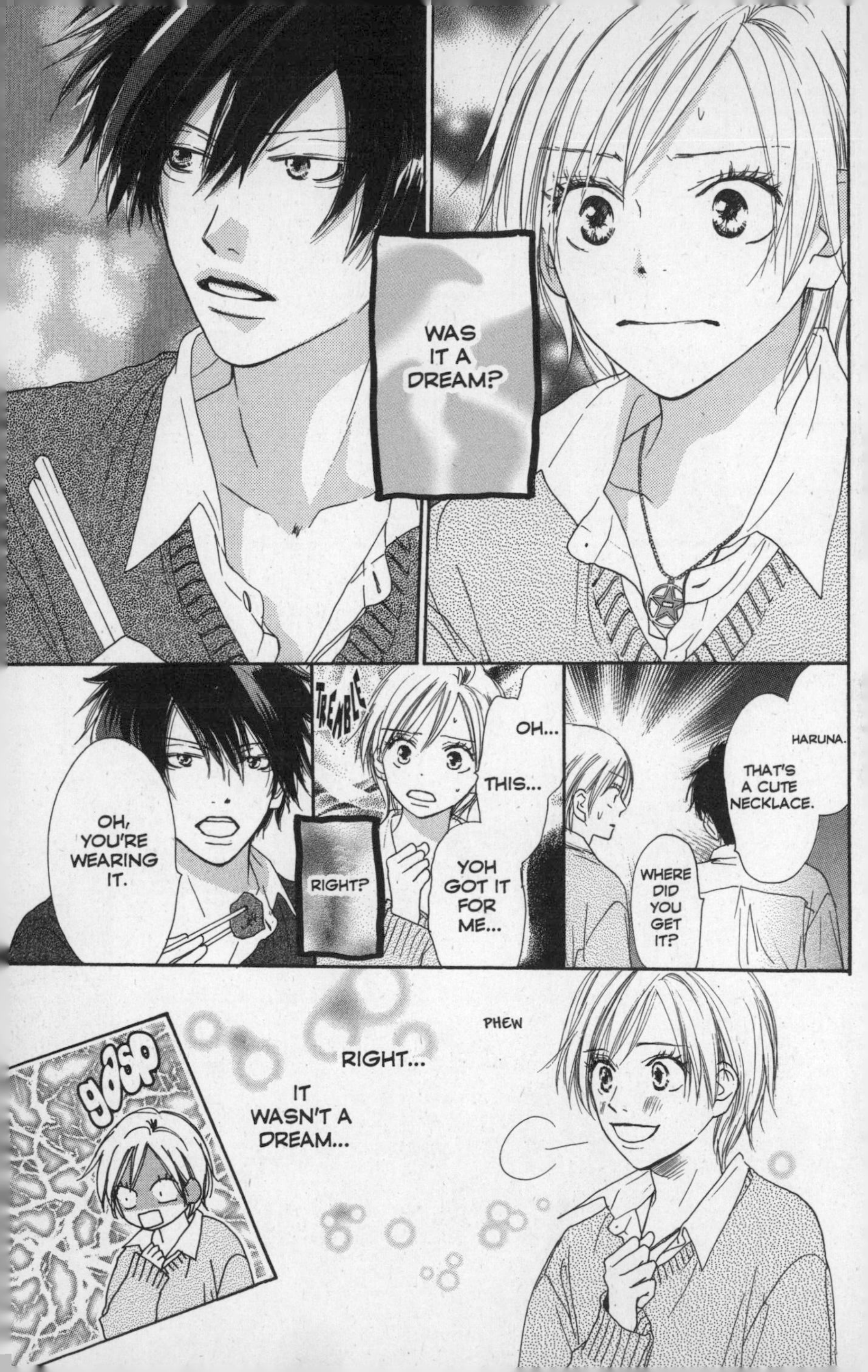
WAS IT A DREAM?
HARUNA.
THAT'S A CUTE NECKLACE.
WHERE DID YOU GET IT?
OH... THIS...
YOH GOT IT FOR ME...
TREMBLE
RIGHT?
OH, YOU'RE WEARING IT.
PHEW
RIGHT...
IT WASN'T A DREAM...
GASP

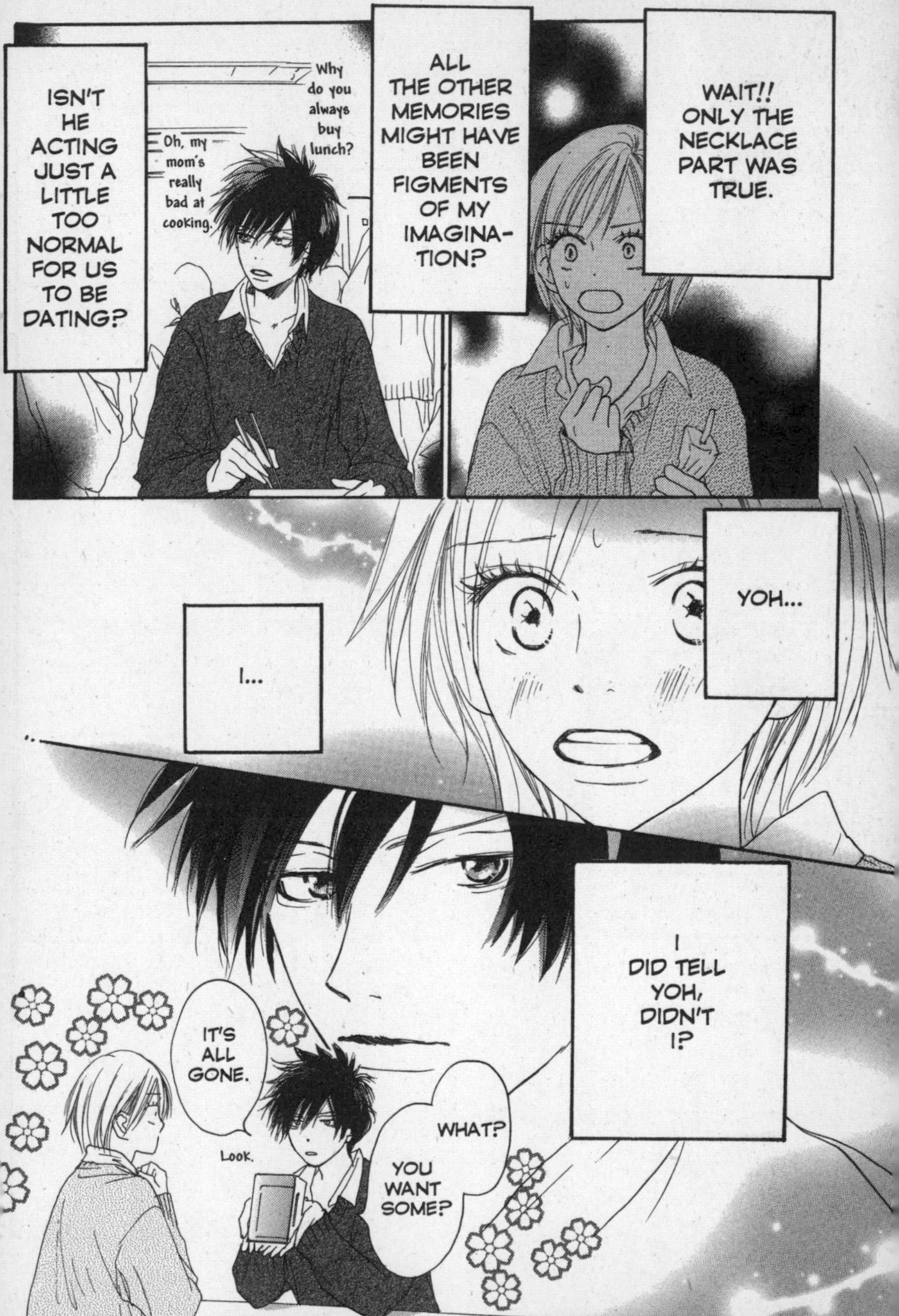
WAIT!! ONLY THE NECKLACE PART WAS TRUE.
ALL THE OTHER MEMORIES MIGHT HAVE BEEN FIGMENTS OF MY IMAGINATION?
Why do you always buy lunch?
Oh, my mom's really bad at cooking.
ISN'T HE ACTING JUST A LITTLE TOO NORMAL FOR US TO BE DATING?
YOH...
I...
I DID TELL YOH, DIDN'T I?
WHAT? YOU WANT SOME?
IT'S ALL GONE.
Look.

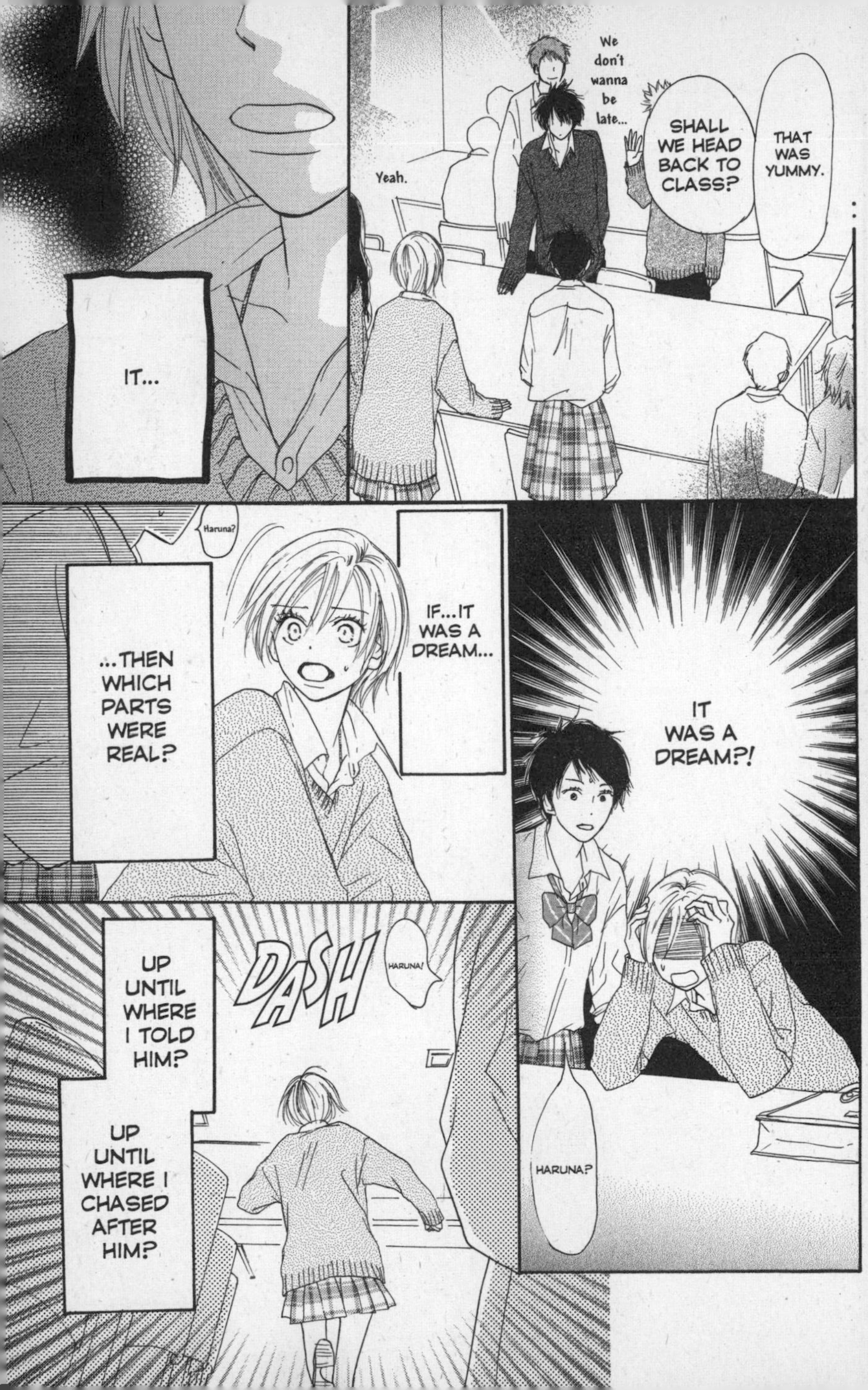
THAT WAS YUMMY.
SHALL WE HEAD BACK TO CLASS?
We don't wanna be late...
Yeah.
IT...
IT WAS A DREAM?!
HARUNA?
IF...IT WAS A DREAM...
Haruna?
...THEN WHICH PARTS WERE REAL?
HARUNA!
DASH
UP UNTIL WHERE I TOLD HIM?
UP UNTIL WHERE I CHASED AFTER HIM?

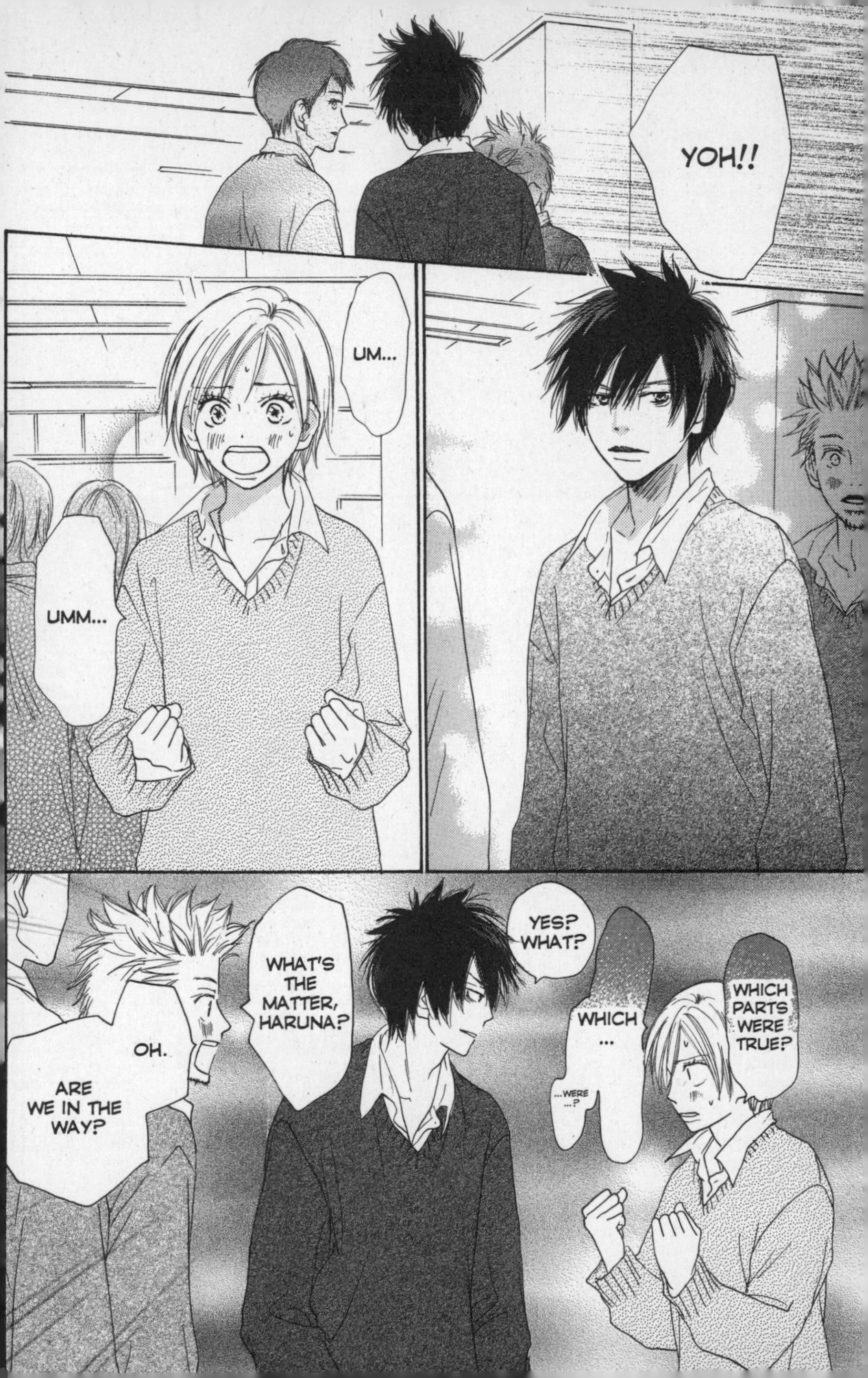
YOH!!
UM...
UMM...
WHICH PARTS WERE TRUE?
WHICH ...
...WERE ...?
YES? WHAT?
WHAT'S THE MATTER, HARUNA?
OH.
ARE WE IN THE WAY?

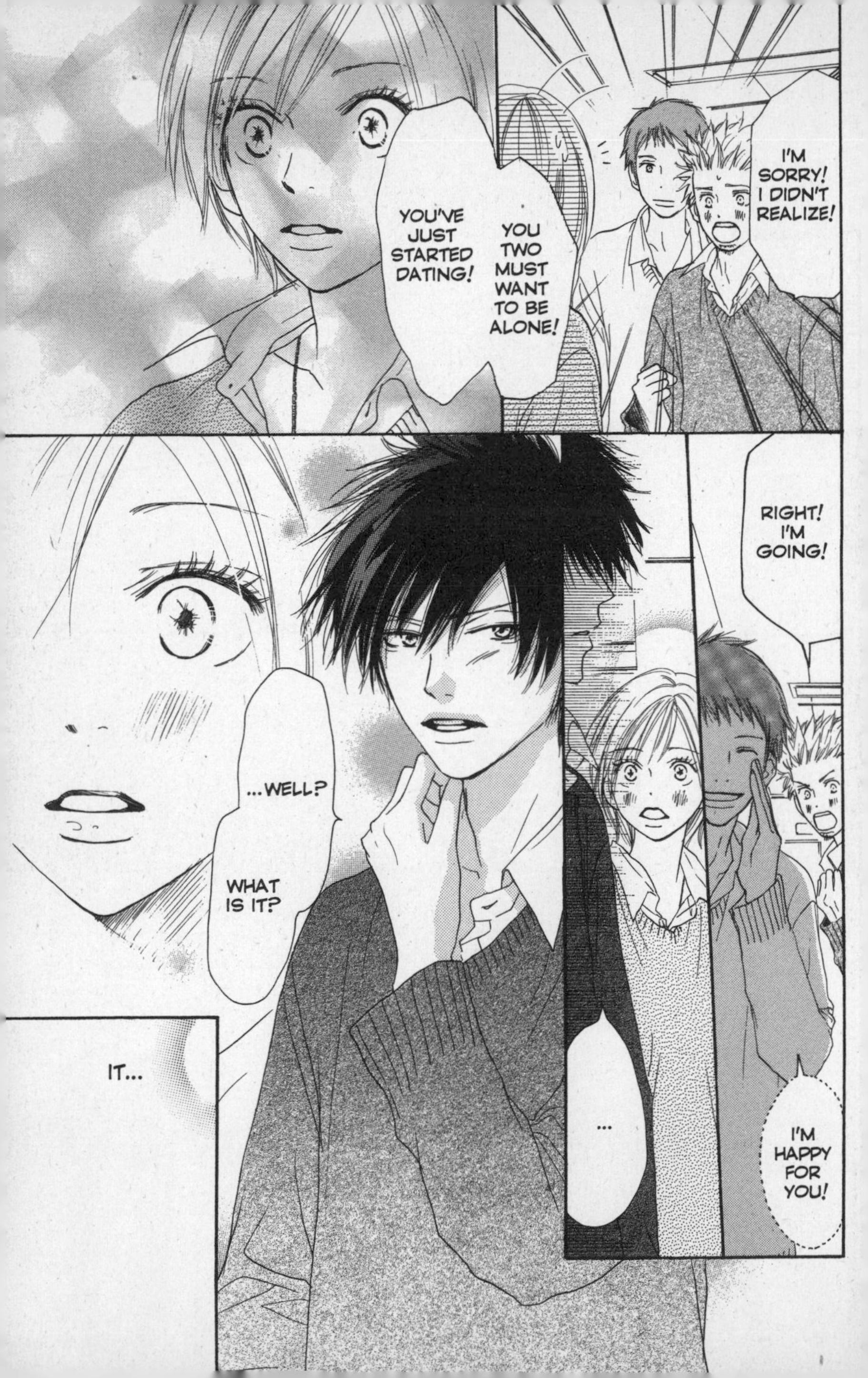
I'M SORRY! I DIDN'T REALIZE!
YOU'VE JUST STARTED DATING! YOU TWO MUST WANT TO BE ALONE!
RIGHT! I'M GOING!
I'M HAPPY FOR YOU!
...
...WELL?
WHAT IS IT?
IT...

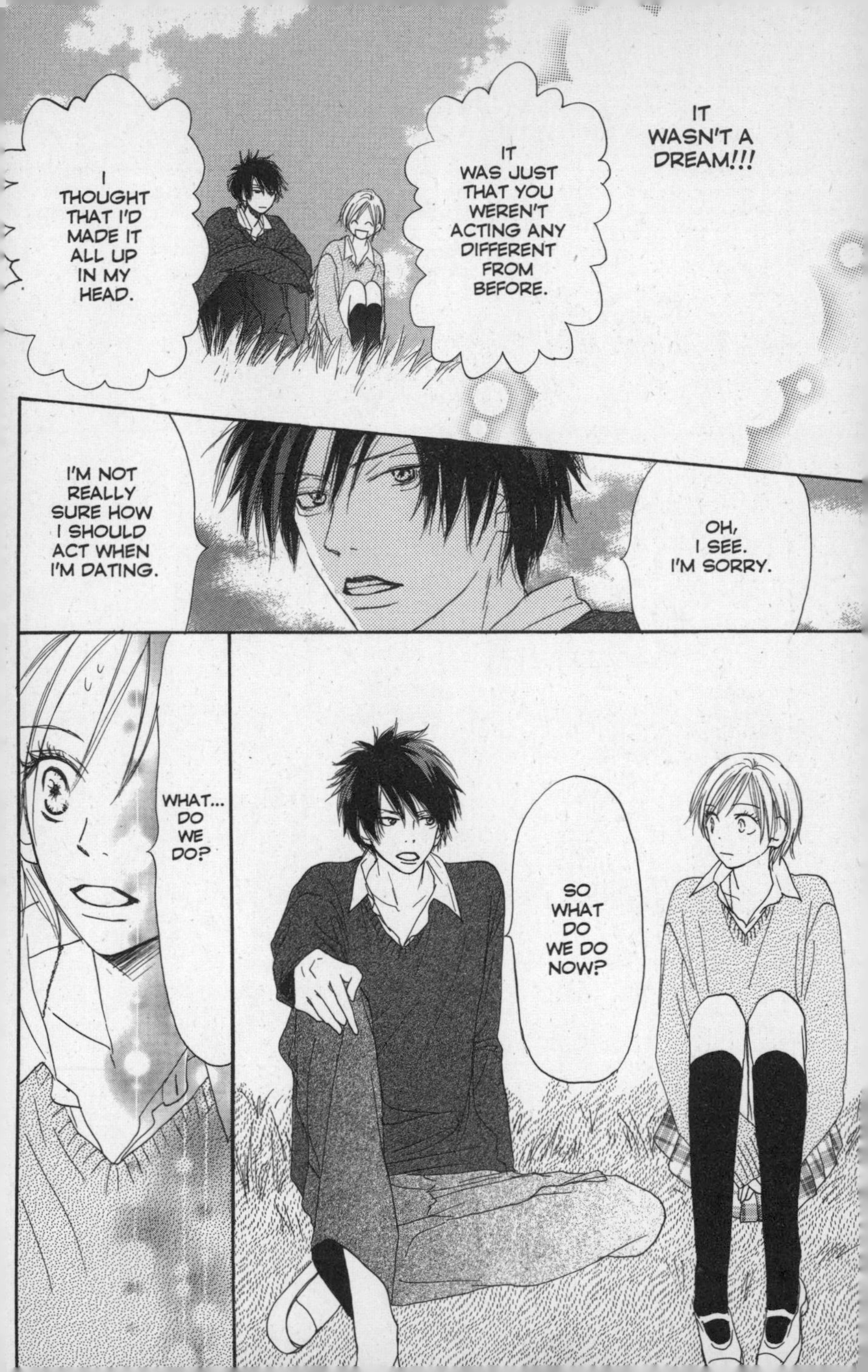
IT WASN'T A DREAM!!!
IT WAS JUST THAT YOU WEREN'T ACTING ANY DIFFERENT FROM BEFORE.
I THOUGHT THAT I'D MADE IT ALL UP IN MY HEAD.
OH, I SEE. I'M SORRY.
I'M NOT REALLY SURE HOW I SHOULD ACT WHEN I'M DATING.
SO WHAT DO WE DO NOW?
WHAT... DO WE DO?

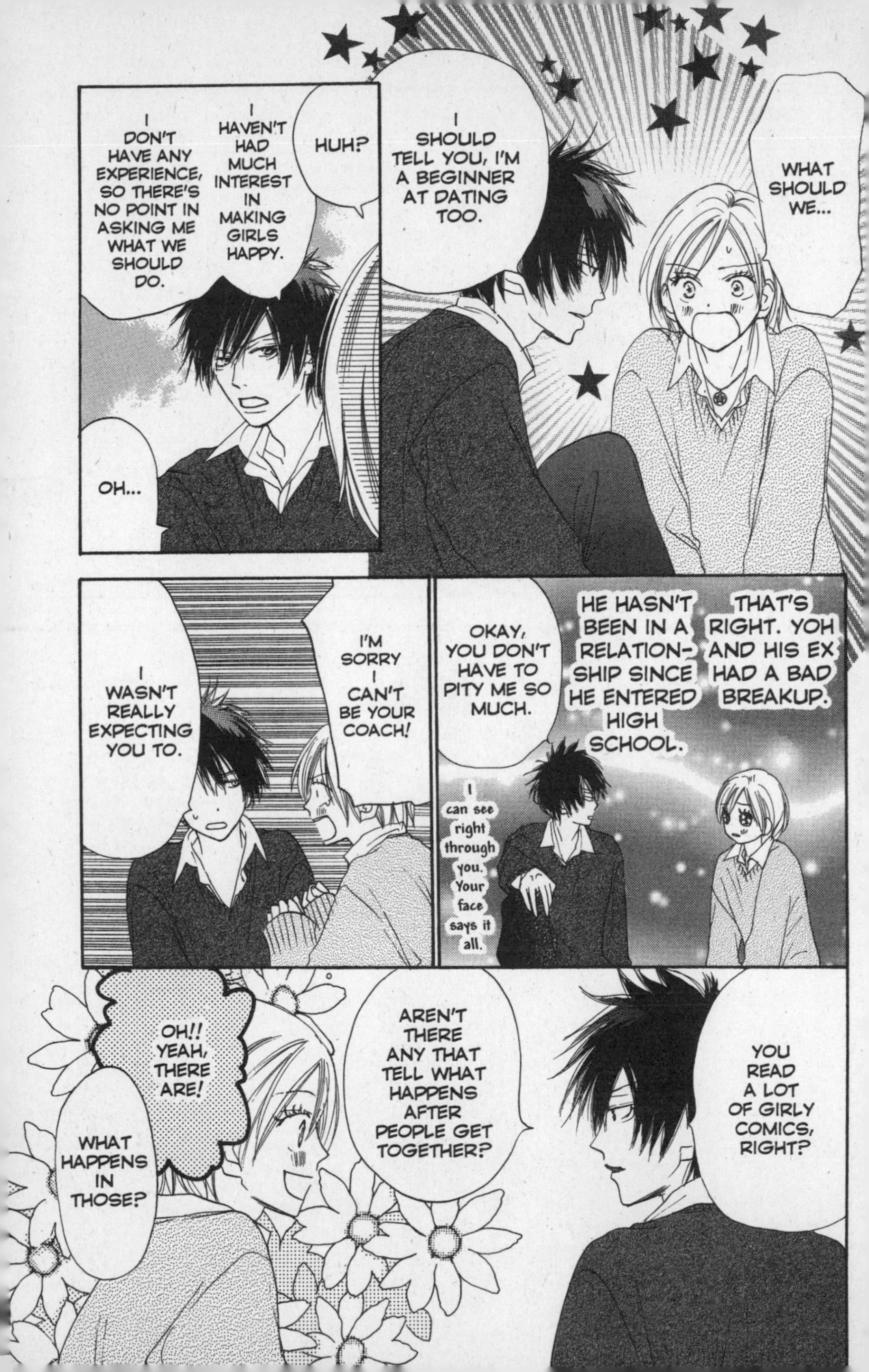
WHAT SHOULD WE...
I SHOULD TELL YOU, I'M A BEGINNER AT DATING TOO.
HUH?
I HAVEN'T HAD MUCH INTEREST IN MAKING GIRLS HAPPY.
I DON'T HAVE ANY EXPERIENCE, SO THERE'S NO POINT IN ASKING ME WHAT WE SHOULD DO.
OH...
THAT'S RIGHT. YOH AND HIS EX HAD A BAD BREAKUP.
HE HASN'T BEEN IN A RELATION-SHIP SINCE HE ENTERED HIGH SCHOOL.
OKAY, YOU DON'T HAVE TO PITY ME SO MUCH.
I can see right through you. Your face says it all.
I'M SORRY I CAN'T BE YOUR COACH!
I WASN'T REALLY EXPECTING YOU TO.
YOU READ A LOT OF GIRLY COMICS, RIGHT?
AREN'T THERE ANY THAT TELL WHAT HAPPENS AFTER PEOPLE GET TOGETHER?
OH!! YEAH, THERE ARE!
WHAT HAPPENS IN THOSE?

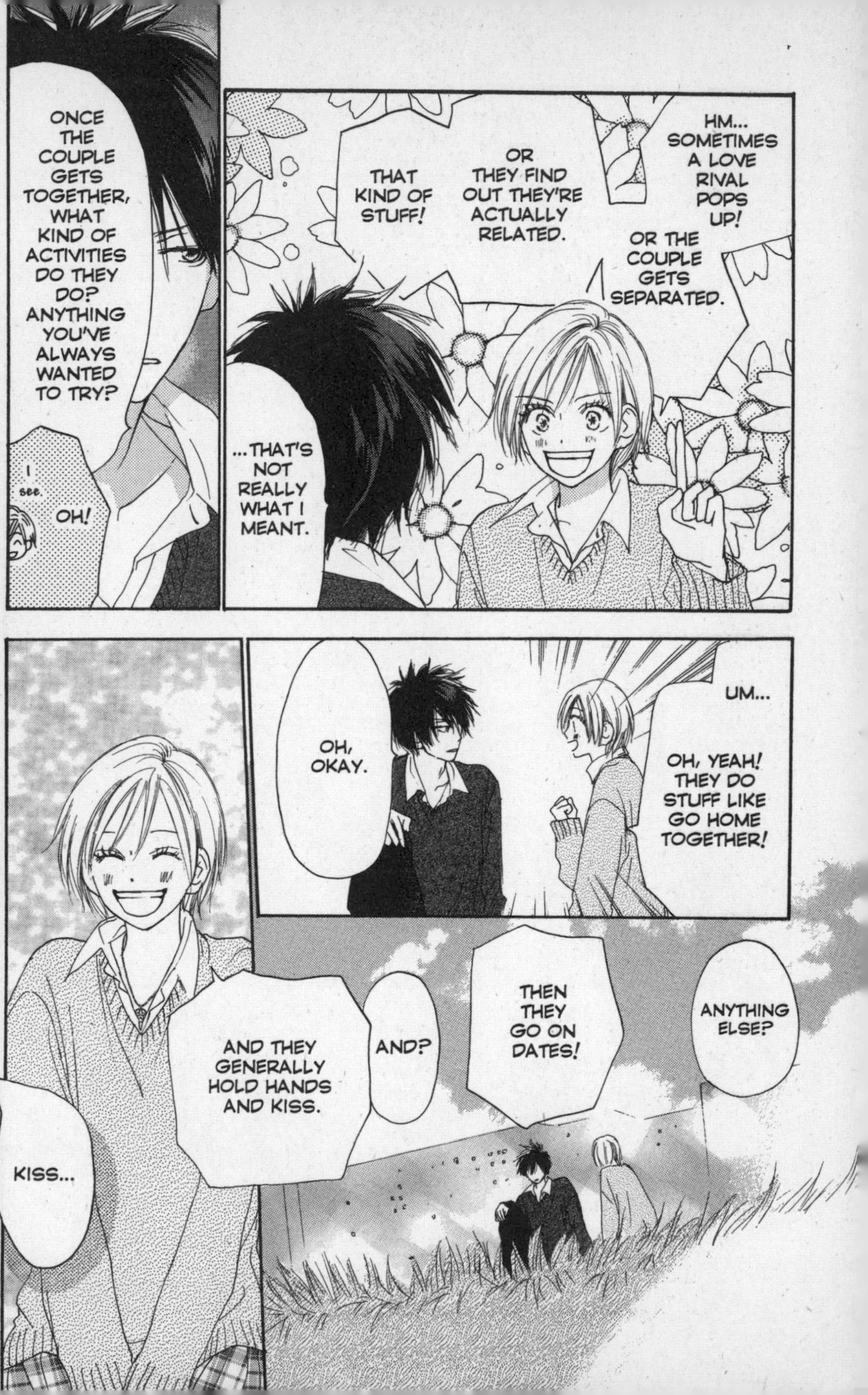
HM... SOMETIMES A LOVE RIVAL POPS UP!
OR THE COUPLE GETS SEPARATED.
OR THEY FIND OUT THEY'RE ACTUALLY RELATED.
THAT KIND OF STUFF!
...THAT'S NOT REALLY WHAT I MEANT.
ONCE THE COUPLE GETS TOGETHER, WHAT KIND OF ACTIVITIES DO THEY DO? ANYTHING YOU'VE ALWAYS WANTED TO TRY?
I see.
OH!
UM...
OH, YEAH! THEY DO STUFF LIKE GO HOME TOGETHER!
OH, OKAY.
ANYTHING ELSE?
THEN THEY GO ON DATES!
AND?
AND THEY GENERALLY HOLD HANDS AND KISS.
KISS...

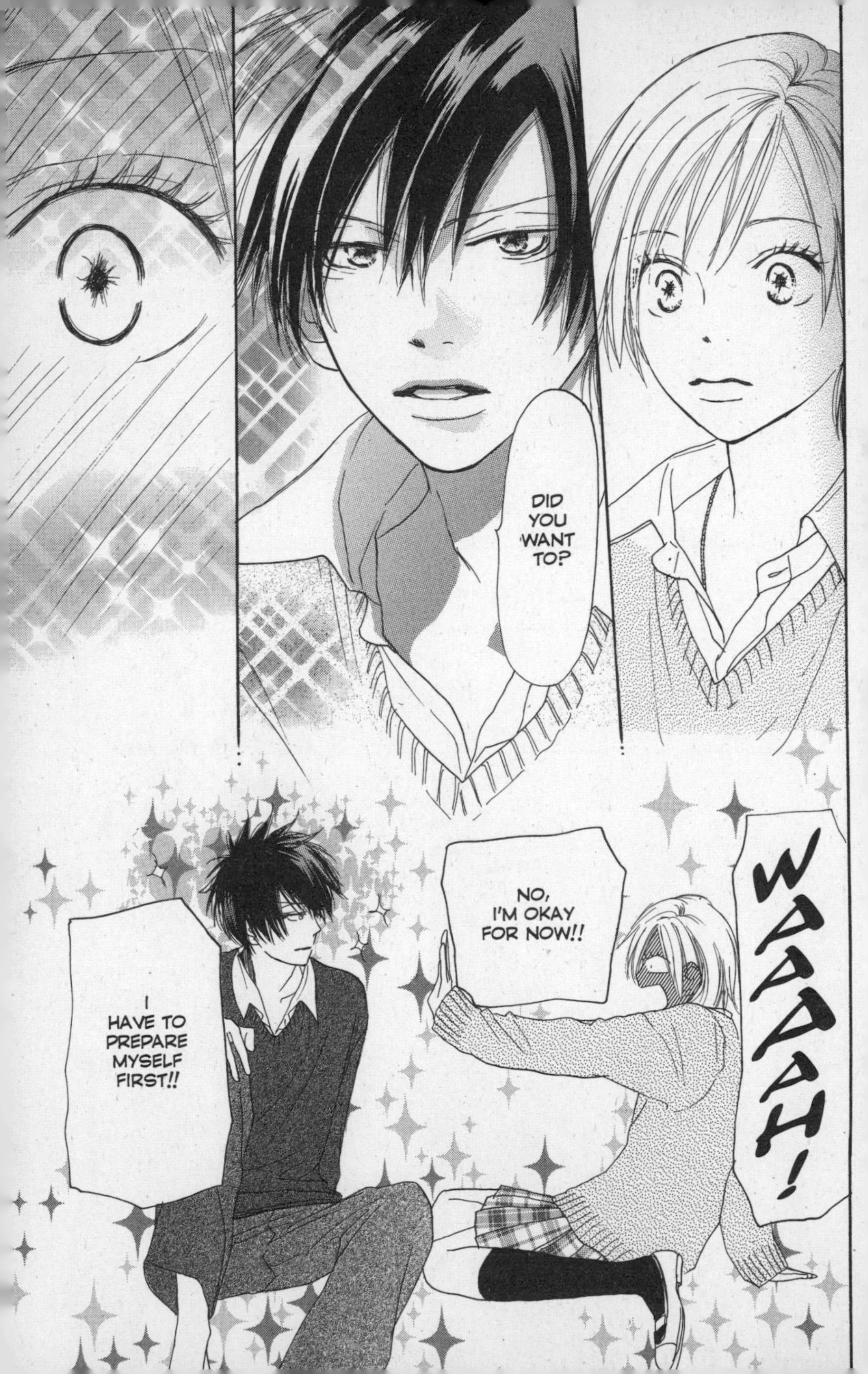
DID YOU WANT TO?
WAAAAH!
NO, I'M OKAY FOR NOW!!
I HAVE TO PREPARE MYSELF FIRST!!

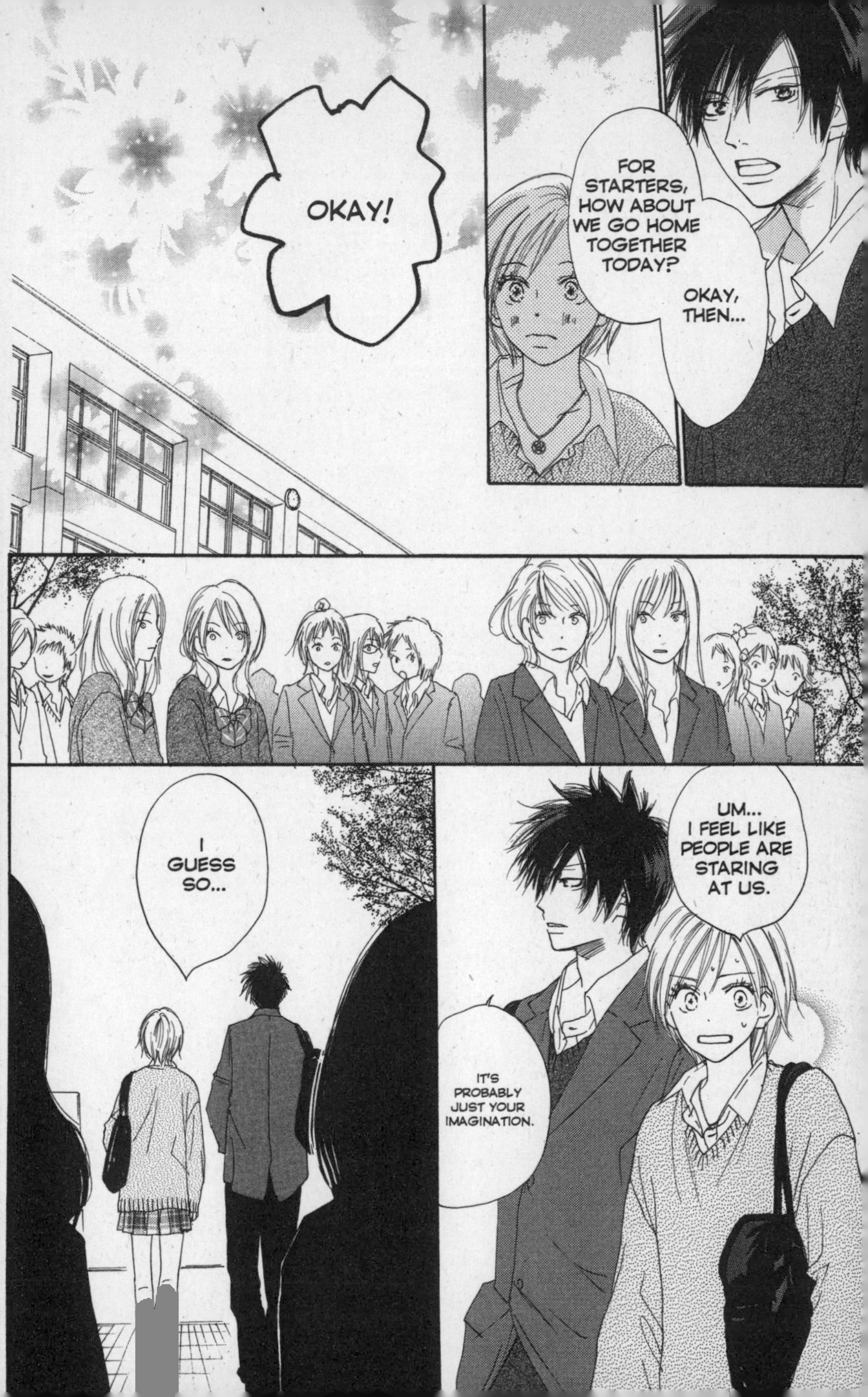
OKAY, THEN...
FOR STARTERS, HOW ABOUT WE GO HOME TOGETHER TODAY?
OKAY!
UM... I FEEL LIKE PEOPLE ARE STARING AT US.
IT'S PROBABLY JUST YOUR IMAGINATION.
I GUESS SO...

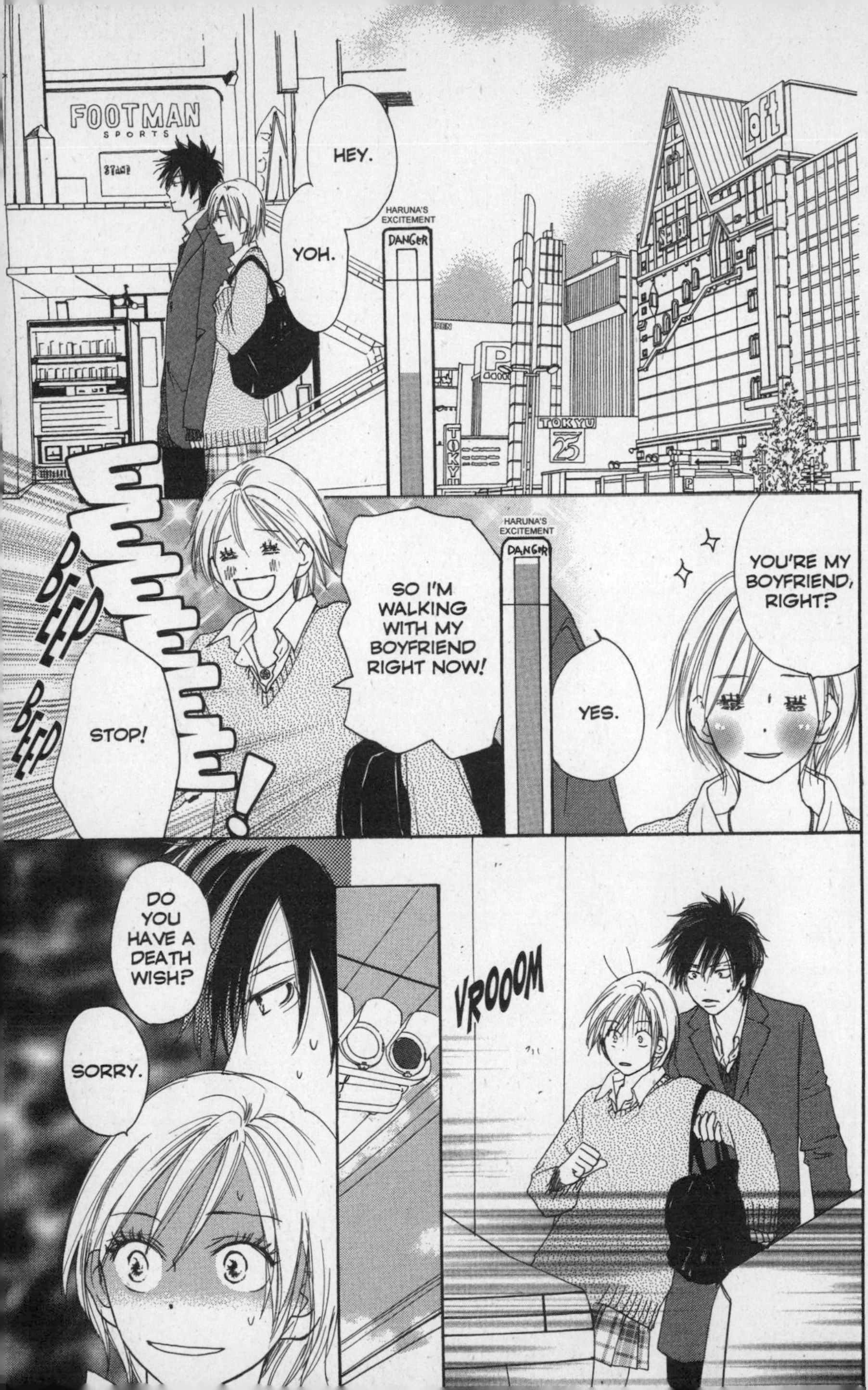
FOOTMAN SPORTS
Loft
HEY.
YOH.
HARUNA'S EXCITEMENT
DANGER
TOKYU
YOU'RE MY BOYFRIEND, RIGHT?
YES.
HARUNA'S EXCITEMENT
DANGER
SO I'M WALKING WITH MY BOYFRIEND RIGHT NOW!
STOP!
BEEP BEEP
VROOOM
DO YOU HAVE A DEATH WISH?
SORRY.

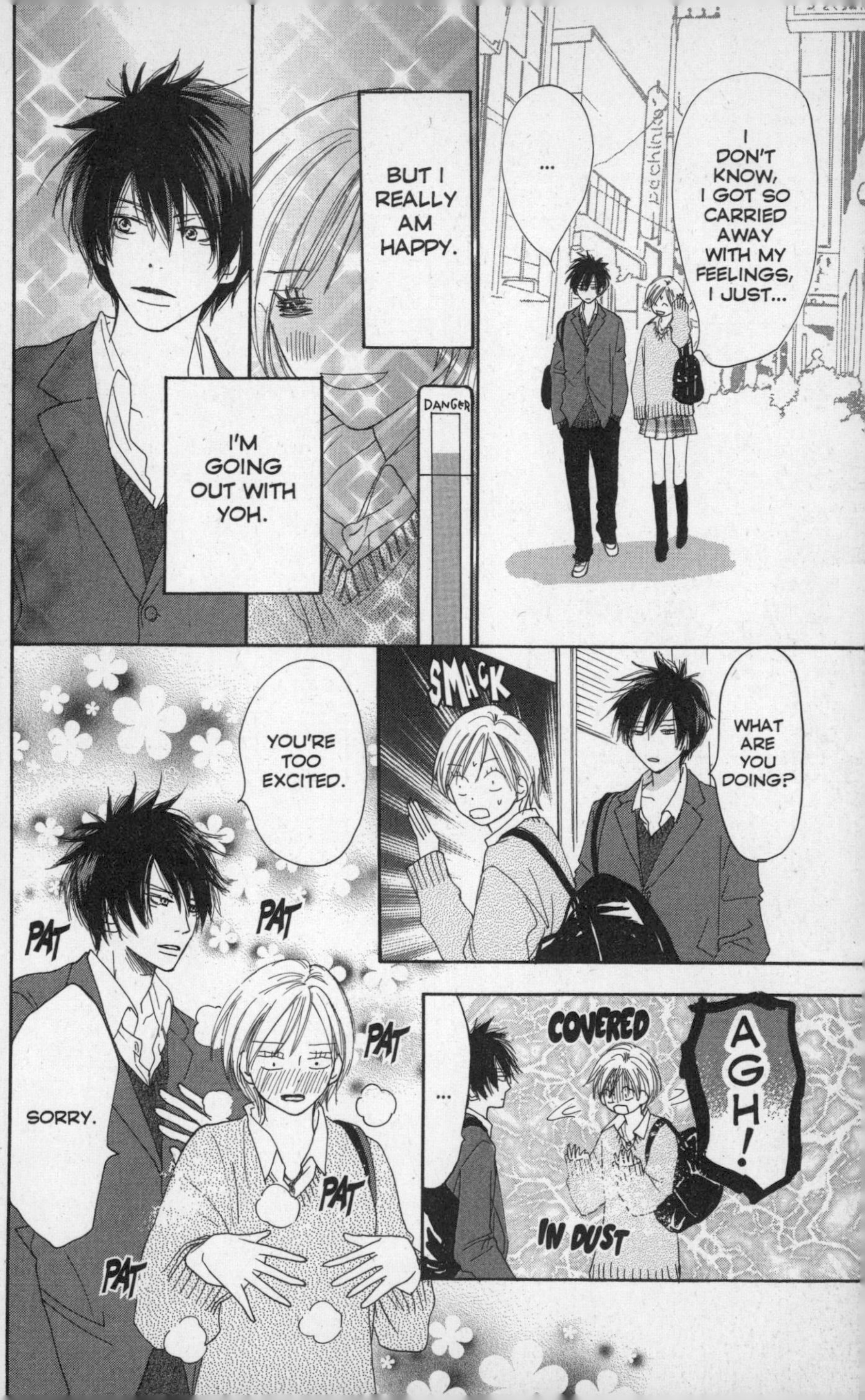
I DON'T KNOW, I GOT SO CARRIED AWAY WITH MY FEELINGS, I JUST...
...
BUT I REALLY AM HAPPY.
DANGER
I'M GOING OUT WITH YOH.
WHAT ARE YOU DOING?
SMACK
AGH!
COVERED
IN DUST
...
YOU'RE TOO EXCITED.
PAT
PAT
PAT
PAT
PAT
SORRY.

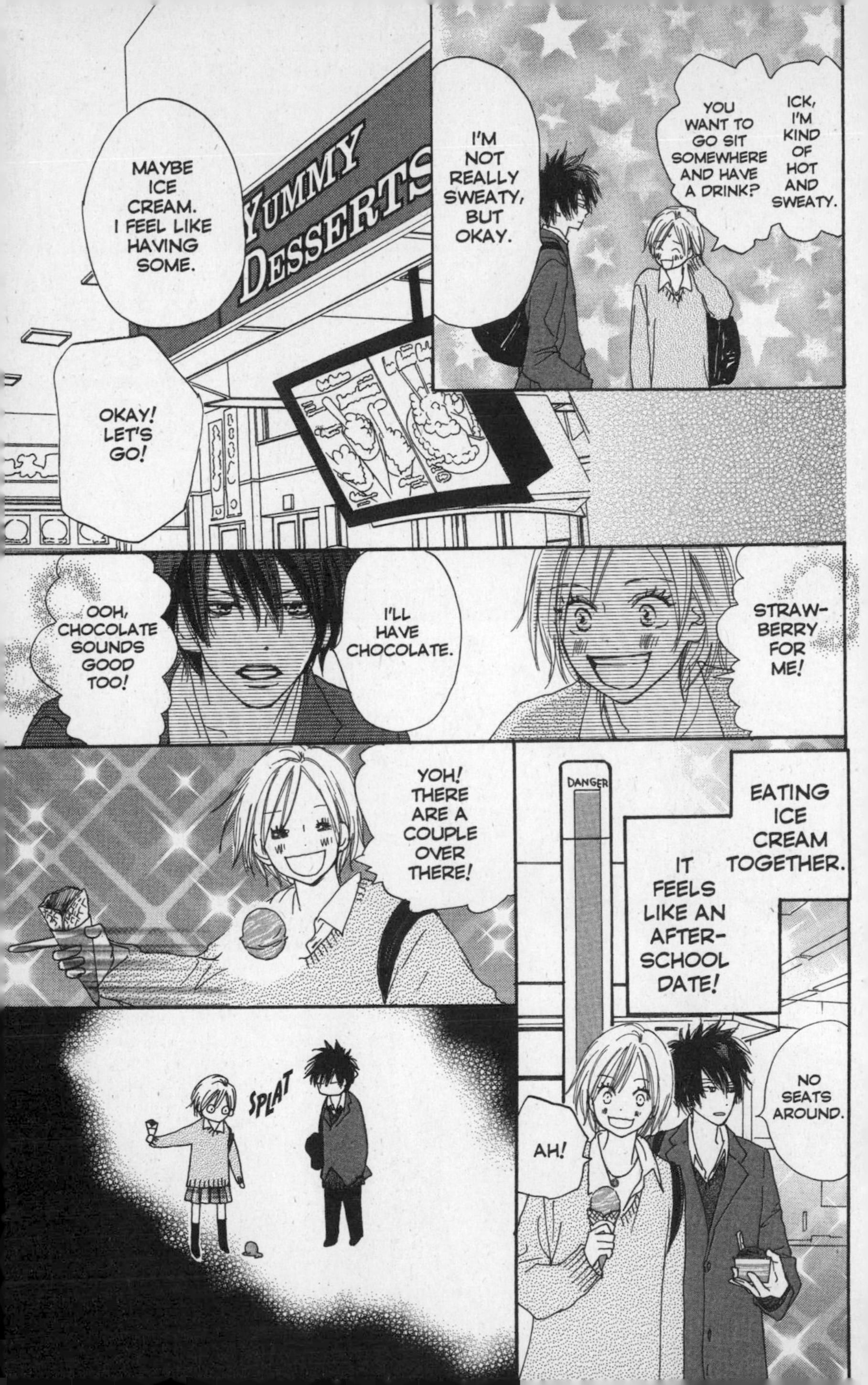
ICK, I'M KIND OF HOT AND SWEATY.
YOU WANT TO GO SIT SOMEWHERE AND HAVE A DRINK?
I'M NOT REALLY SWEATY, BUT OKAY.
YUMMY DESSERTS
MAYBE ICE CREAM. I FEEL LIKE HAVING SOME.
OKAY! LET'S GO!
STRAW-BERRY FOR ME!
I'LL HAVE CHOCOLATE.
OOH, CHOCOLATE SOUNDS GOOD TOO!
EATING ICE CREAM TOGETHER.
IT FEELS LIKE AN AFTER-SCHOOL DATE!
DANGER
NO SEATS AROUND.
AH!
YOH! THERE ARE A COUPLE OVER THERE!
SPLAT

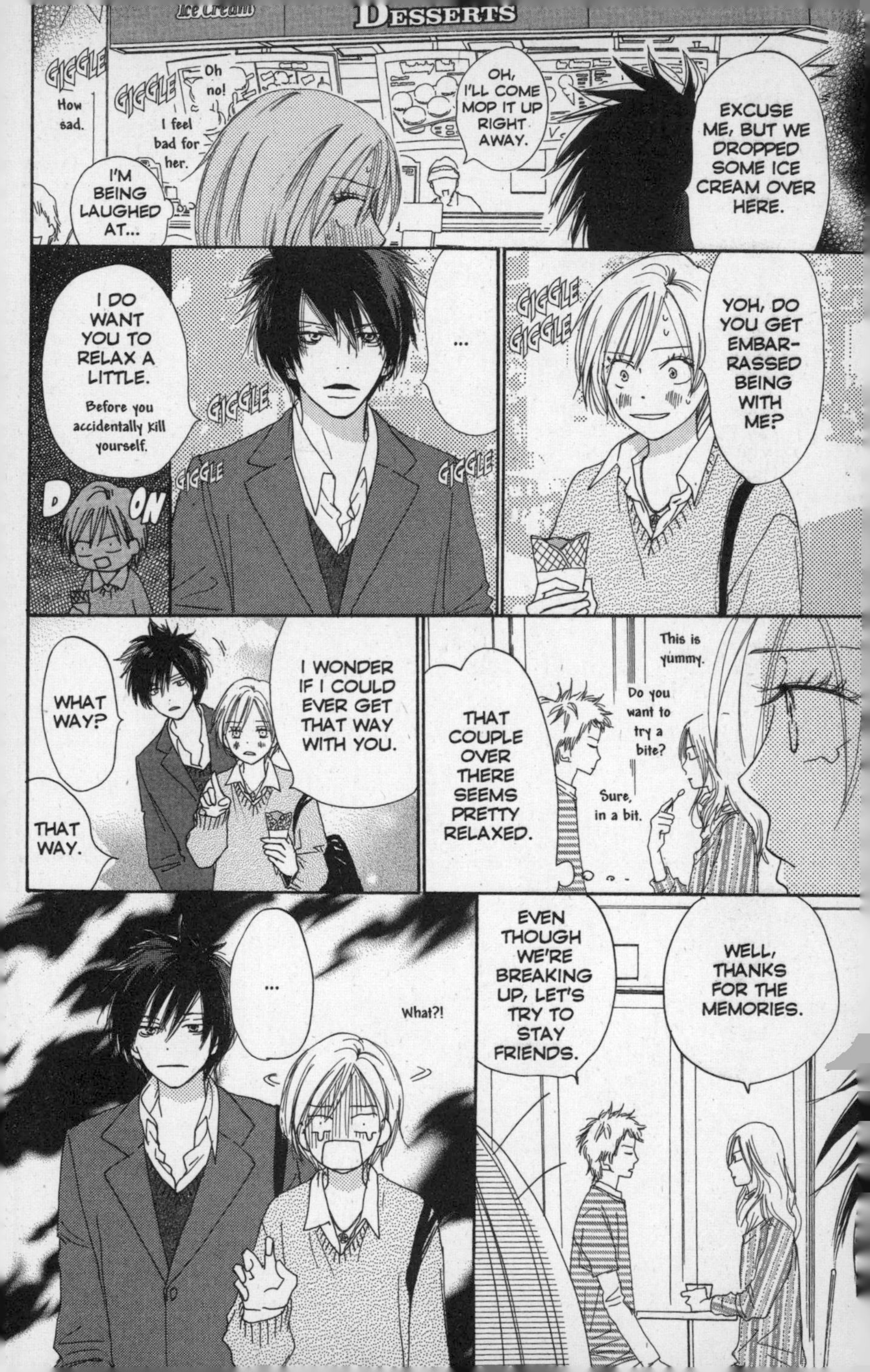
Ice Cream
DESSERTS
EXCUSE ME, BUT WE DROPPED SOME ICE CREAM OVER HERE.
OH, I'LL COME MOP IT UP RIGHT AWAY.
Oh no!
I feel bad for her.
GIGGLE
GIGGLE
How sad.
I'M BEING LAUGHED AT...
YOH, DO YOU GET EMBARRASSED BEING WITH ME?
GIGGLE GIGGLE
...
GIGGLE
GIGGLE
GIGGLE
I DO WANT YOU TO RELAX A LITTLE.
Before you accidentally kill yourself.
DON
This is yummy.
Do you want to try a bite?
Sure, in a bit.
THAT COUPLE OVER THERE SEEMS PRETTY RELAXED.
I WONDER IF I COULD EVER GET THAT WAY WITH YOU.
WHAT WAY?
THAT WAY.
WELL, THANKS FOR THE MEMORIES.
EVEN THOUGH WE'RE BREAKING UP, LET'S TRY TO STAY FRIENDS.
What?!
...

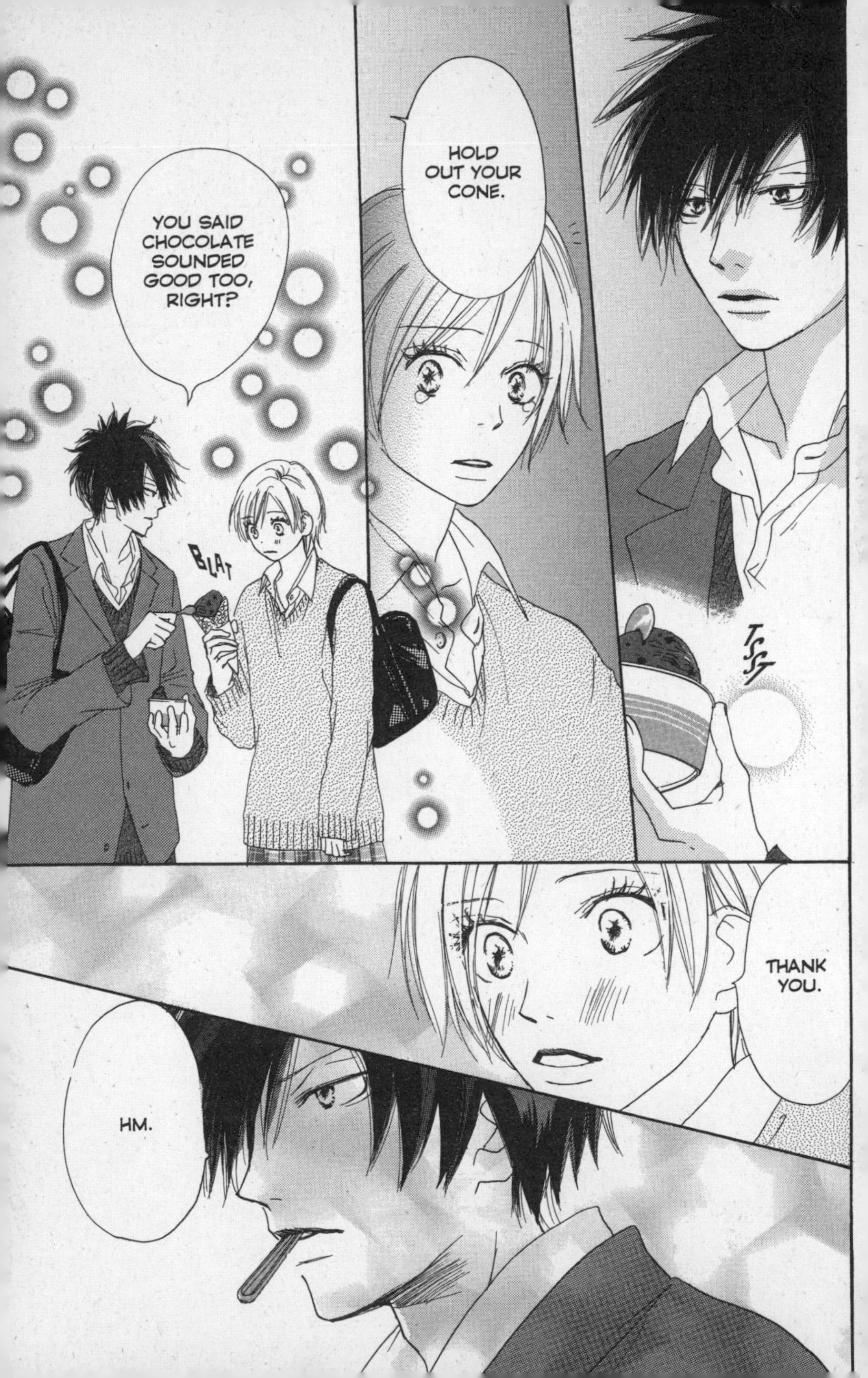
TSST
HOLD OUT YOUR CONE.
YOU SAID CHOCOLATE SOUNDED GOOD TOO, RIGHT?
BLAT
THANK YOU.
HM.

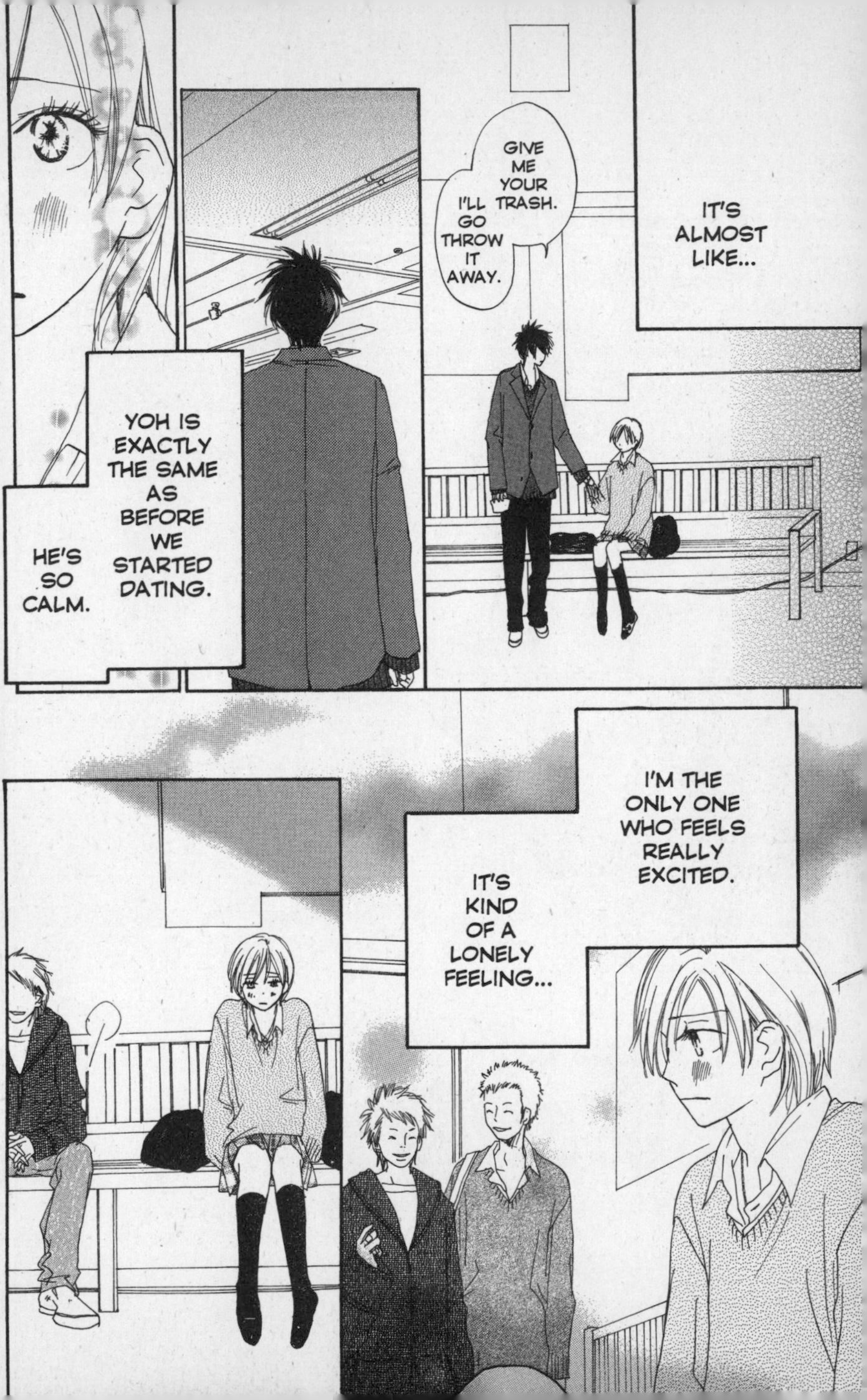
IT'S ALMOST LIKE...
GIVE ME YOUR TRASH. I'LL GO THROW IT AWAY.
YOH IS EXACTLY THE SAME AS BEFORE WE STARTED DATING.
HE'S SO CALM.
I'M THE ONLY ONE WHO FEELS REALLY EXCITED.
IT'S KIND OF A LONELY FEELING...

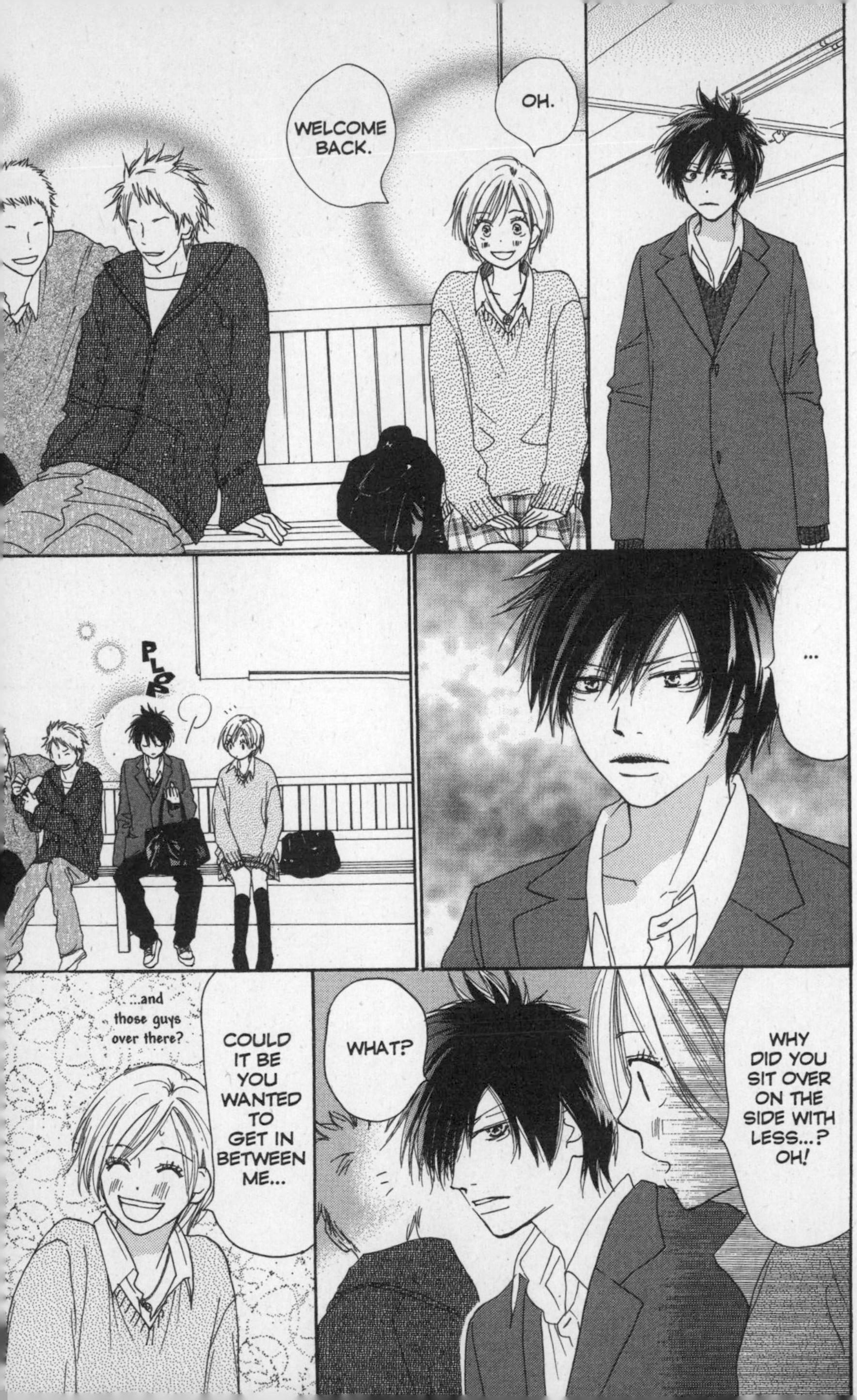
OH.
WELCOME BACK.
...
PLOP
WHY DID YOU SIT OVER ON THE SIDE WITH LESS...? OH!
WHAT?
COULD IT BE YOU WANTED TO GET IN BETWEEN ME...
...and those guys over there?

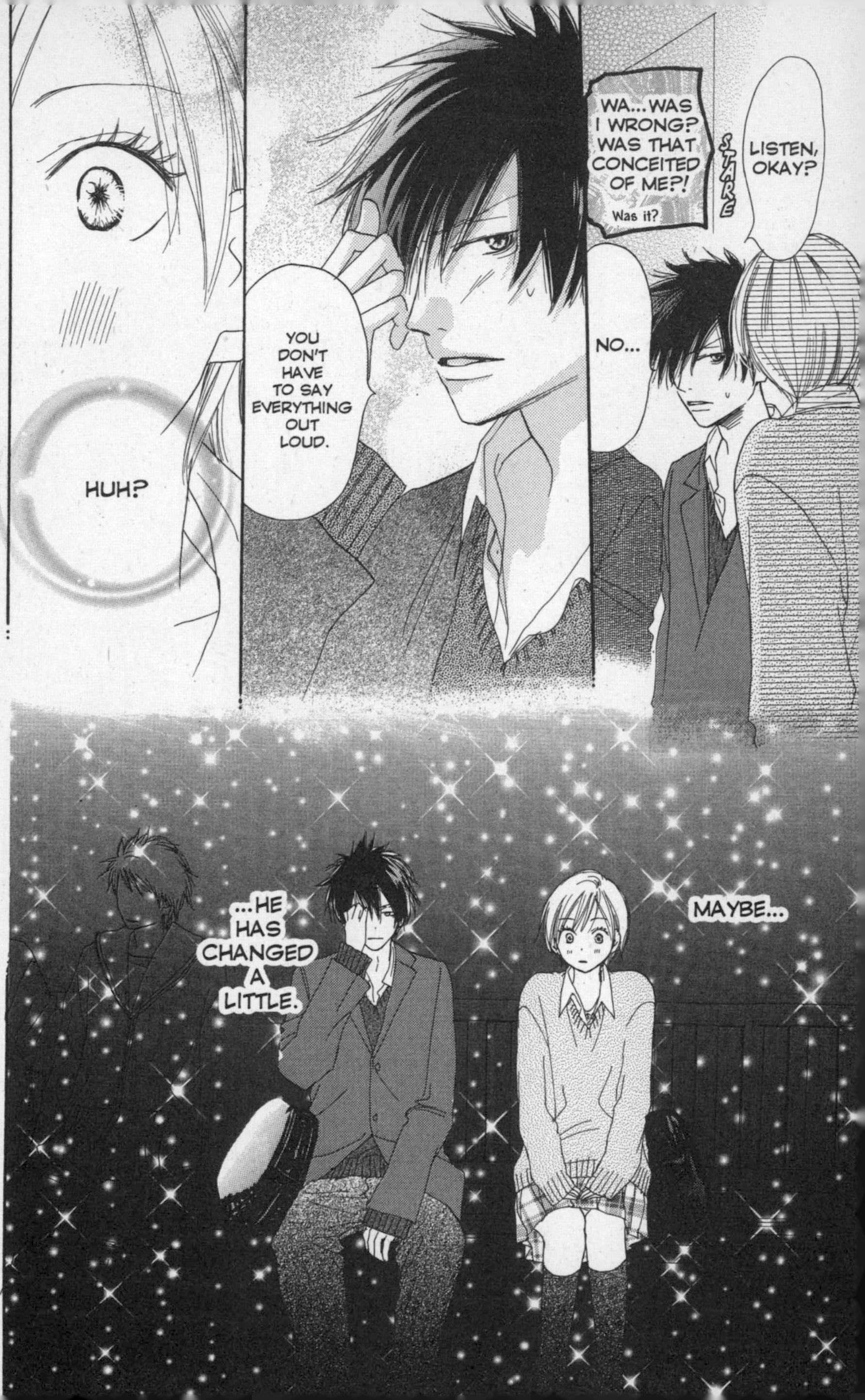
LISTEN, OKAY?
STARE
WA...WAS I WRONG? WAS THAT CONCEITED OF ME?!
Was it?
NO...
YOU DON'T HAVE TO SAY EVERYTHING OUT LOUD.
HUH?
MAYBE...
...HE HAS CHANGED A LITTLE.

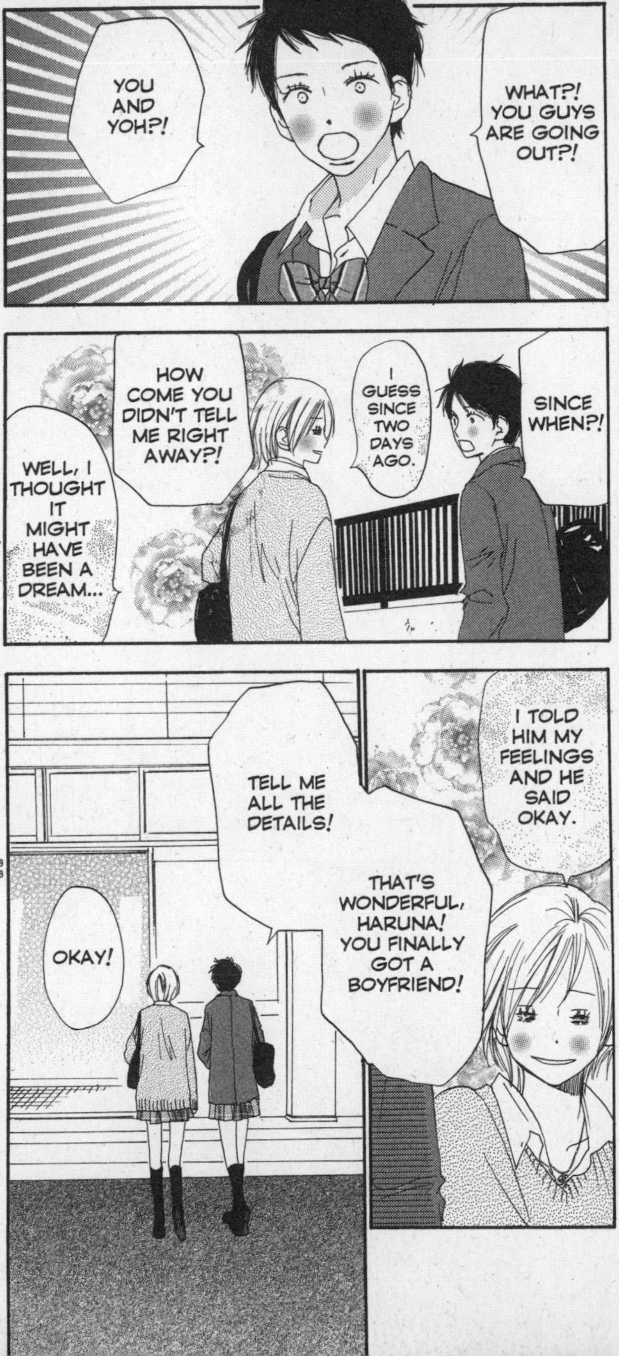
WHAT?! YOU GUYS ARE GOING OUT?!
YOU AND YOH?!
SINCE WHEN?!
I GUESS SINCE TWO DAYS AGO.
HOW COME YOU DIDN'T TELL ME RIGHT AWAY?!
WELL, I THOUGHT IT MIGHT HAVE BEEN A DREAM...
I TOLD HIM MY FEELINGS AND HE SAID OKAY.
THAT'S WONDERFUL, HARUNA! YOU FINALLY GOT A BOYFRIEND!
TELL ME ALL THE DETAILS!
OKAY!

3

Recently, I've been getting into children's books and end up crying when I read them. I mean, I've always liked children's literature... They're just right. They're not very difficult... But unlike when I was a child, now that I'm an adult, I tend to go...

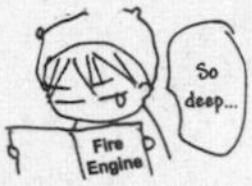
So deep...
Fire Engine

Or I read some sort of meaning into them even though I'm not sure whether the writer originally intended to have that meaning or not.

When I rent children's videos and watch them with my nieces, I usually end up crying.

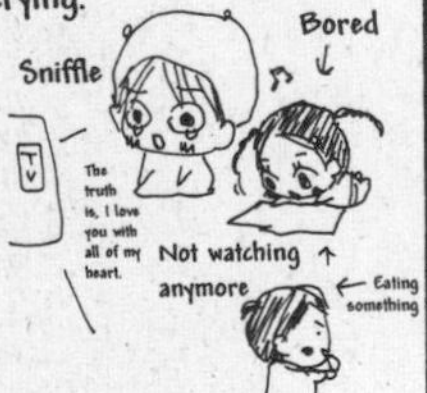
Sniffle
Bored
TV
The truth is, I love you with all of my heart.
Not watching anymore
Eating something

I think you're meant to cry during those times. Little things are very moving. Children's stuff is jam-packed with emotion.

Well anyway, I'd be happy if you join us for the next volume. This has been the very adult Kazune.

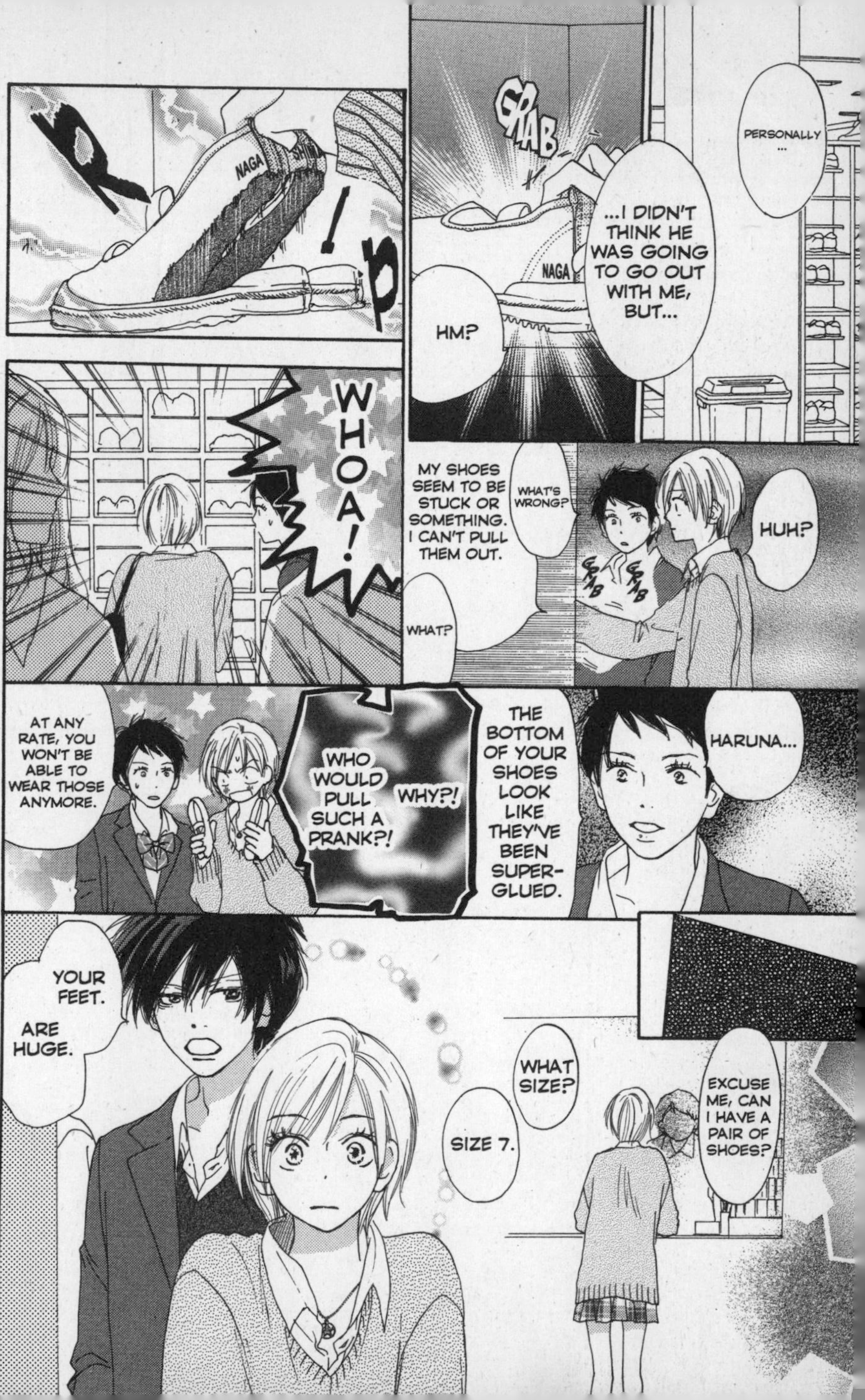
PERSONALLY...
...I DIDN'T THINK HE WAS GOING TO GO OUT WITH ME, BUT...
GRAB
NAGA
HM?
NAGA SHIMA
HUH?
WHAT'S WRONG?
MY SHOES SEEM TO BE STUCK OR SOMETHING. I CAN'T PULL THEM OUT.
WHAT?
GRAB GRAB
WHOA!
HARUNA...
THE BOTTOM OF YOUR SHOES LOOK LIKE THEY'VE BEEN SUPER-GLUED.
WHY?!
WHO WOULD PULL SUCH A PRANK?!
AT ANY RATE, YOU WON'T BE ABLE TO WEAR THOSE ANYMORE.
EXCUSE ME, CAN I HAVE A PAIR OF SHOES?
WHAT SIZE?
SIZE 7.
YOUR FEET.
ARE HUGE.

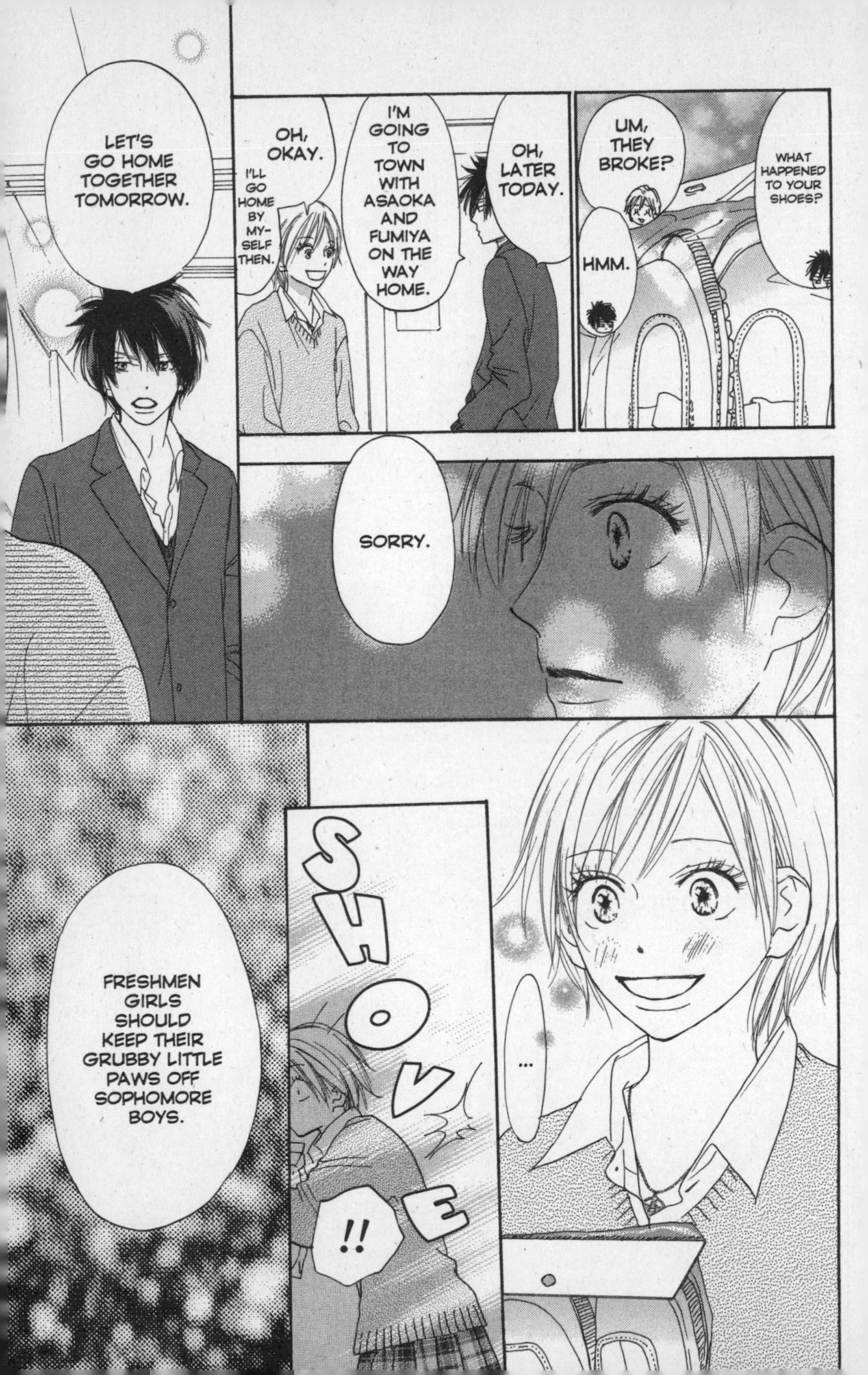
WHAT HAPPENED TO YOUR SHOES?
UM, THEY BROKE?
HMM.
OH, LATER TODAY.
I'M GOING TO TOWN WITH ASAOKA AND FUMIYA ON THE WAY HOME.
OH, OKAY.
I'LL GO HOME BY MY-SELF THEN.
SORRY.
LET'S GO HOME TOGETHER TOMORROW.
...
SHOVE
!!
FRESHMEN GIRLS SHOULD KEEP THEIR GRUBBY LITTLE PAWS OFF SOPHOMORE BOYS.

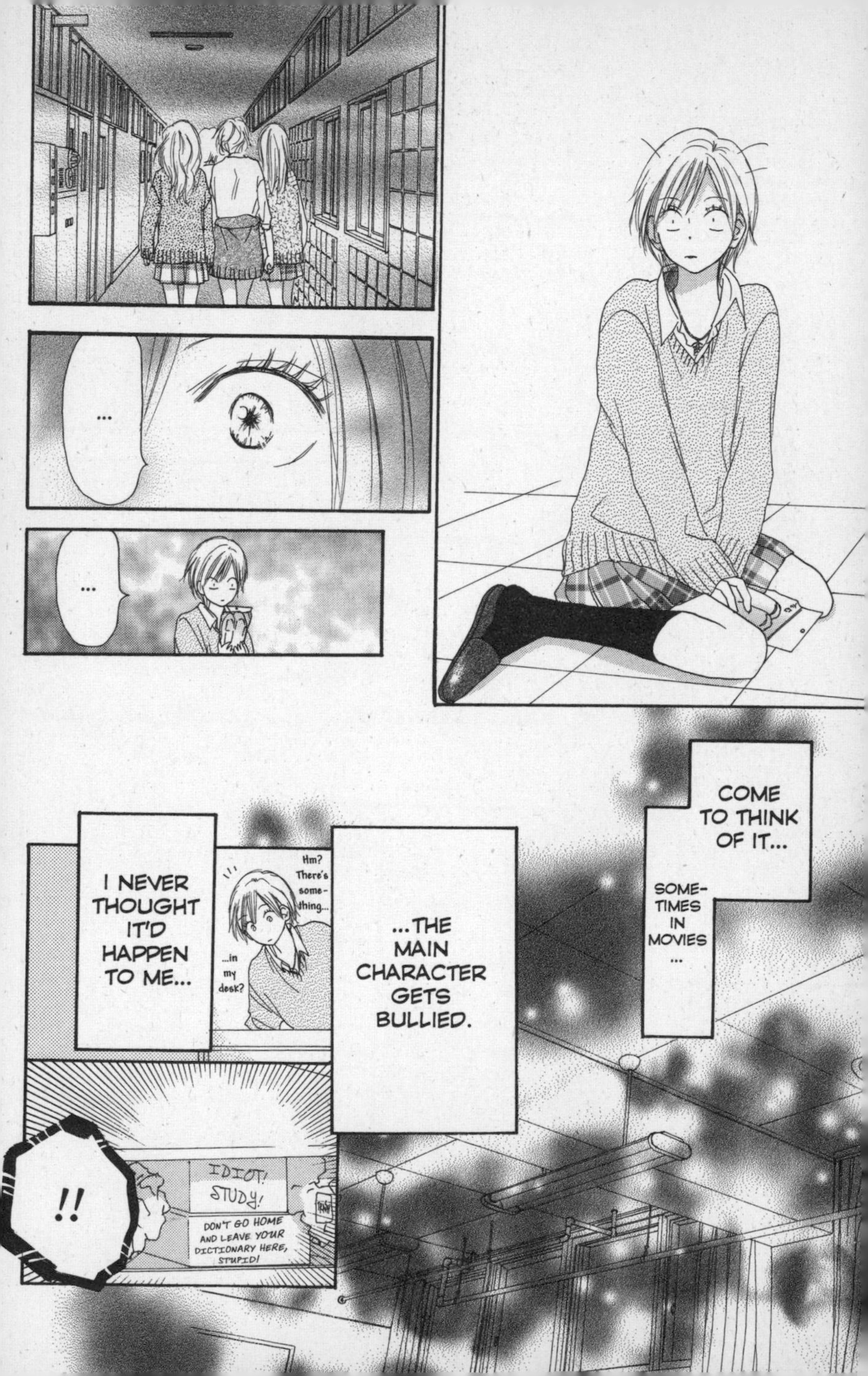
...
...
COME TO THINK OF IT...
SOME-TIMES IN MOVIES...
...THE MAIN CHARACTER GETS BULLIED.
Hm? There's some-thing...
...in my desk?
I NEVER THOUGHT IT'D HAPPEN TO ME...
!!
IDIOT! STUDY!
DON'T GO HOME AND LEAVE YOUR DICTIONARY HERE, STUPID!

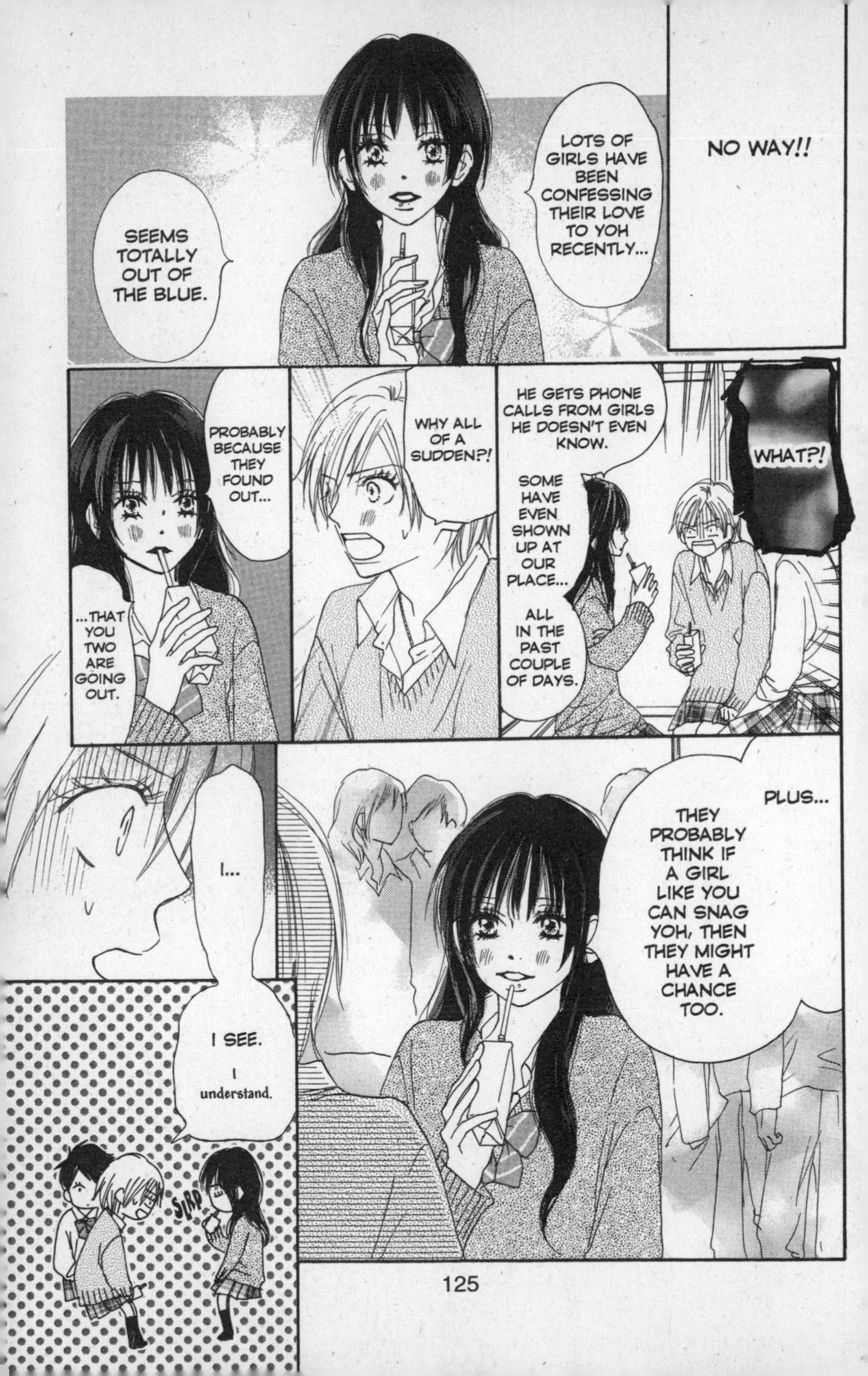
NO WAY!!
LOTS OF GIRLS HAVE BEEN CONFESSING THEIR LOVE TO YOH RECENTLY...
SEEMS TOTALLY OUT OF THE BLUE.
WHAT?!
HE GETS PHONE CALLS FROM GIRLS HE DOESN'T EVEN KNOW.
SOME HAVE EVEN SHOWN UP AT OUR PLACE...
ALL IN THE PAST COUPLE OF DAYS.
WHY ALL OF A SUDDEN?!
PROBABLY BECAUSE THEY FOUND OUT...
...THAT YOU TWO ARE GOING OUT.
PLUS...
THEY PROBABLY THINK IF A GIRL LIKE YOU CAN SNAG YOH, THEN THEY MIGHT HAVE A CHANCE TOO.
I...
I SEE.
I understand.
SLRP

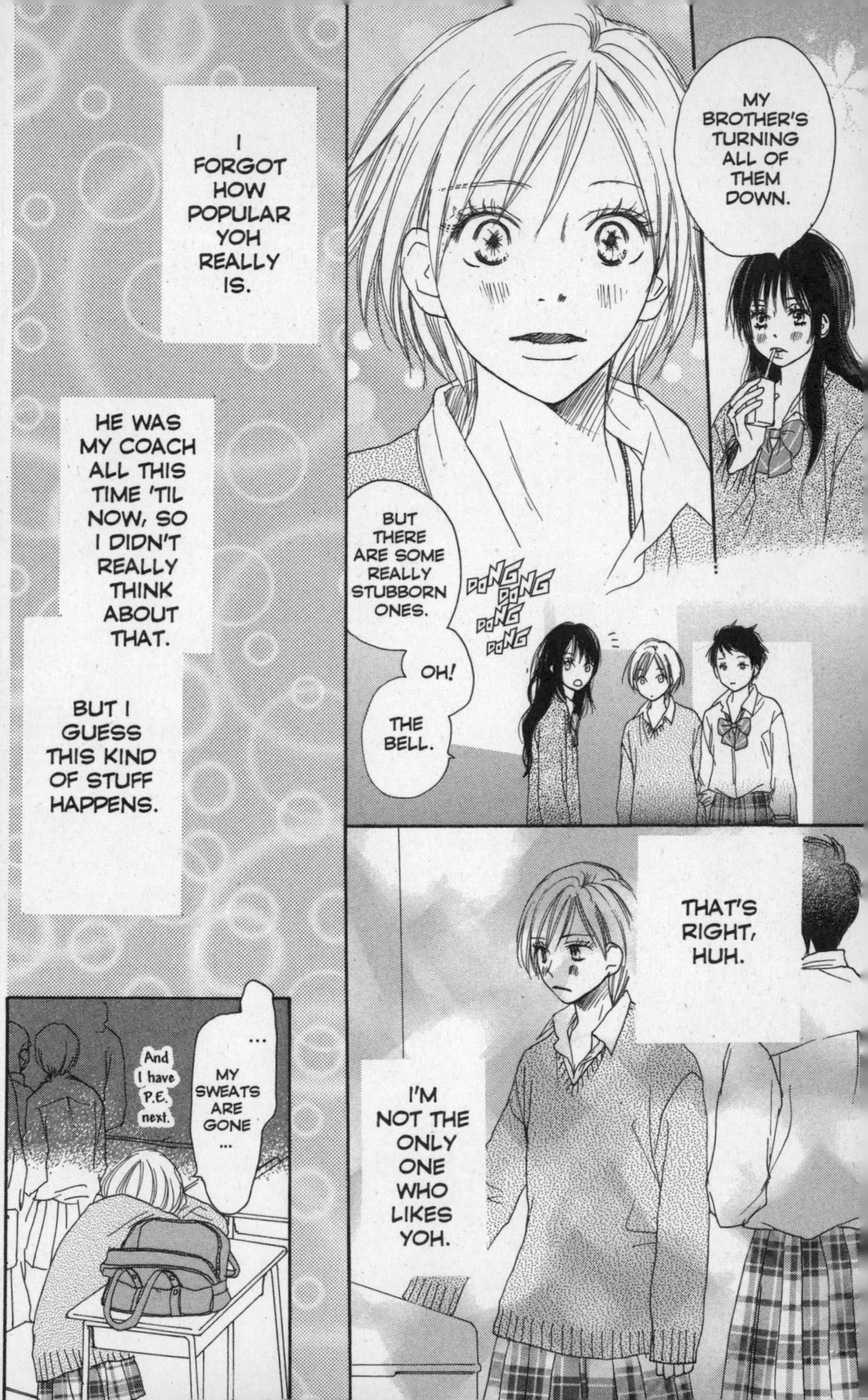
MY BROTHER'S TURNING ALL OF THEM DOWN.
BUT THERE ARE SOME REALLY STUBBORN ONES.
DONG DONG DONG DONG
OH!
THE BELL.
I FORGOT HOW POPULAR YOH REALLY IS.
HE WAS MY COACH ALL THIS TIME 'TIL NOW, SO I DIDN'T REALLY THINK ABOUT THAT.
BUT I GUESS THIS KIND OF STUFF HAPPENS.
THAT'S RIGHT, HUH.
I'M NOT THE ONLY ONE WHO LIKES YOH.
...
MY SWEATS ARE GONE ...
And I have P.E. next.

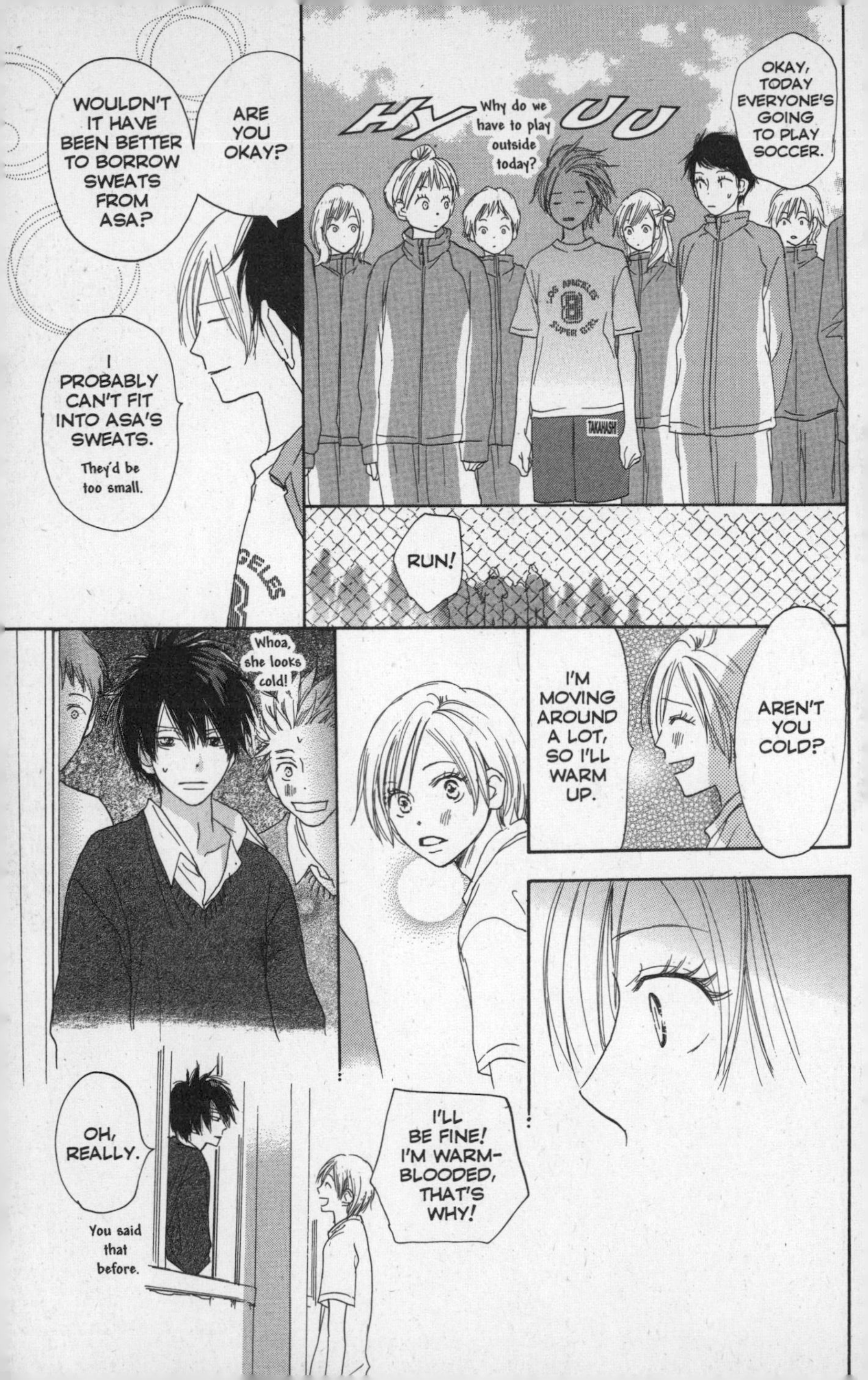
OKAY, TODAY EVERYONE'S GOING TO PLAY SOCCER.
HYUU
Why do we have to play outside today?
RUN!
ARE YOU OKAY?
WOULDN'T IT HAVE BEEN BETTER TO BORROW SWEATS FROM ASA?
I PROBABLY CAN'T FIT INTO ASA'S SWEATS.
They'd be too small.
AREN'T YOU COLD?
I'M MOVING AROUND A LOT, SO I'LL WARM UP.
Whoa, she looks cold!
I'LL BE FINE! I'M WARM-BLOODED, THAT'S WHY!
OH, REALLY.
You said that before.

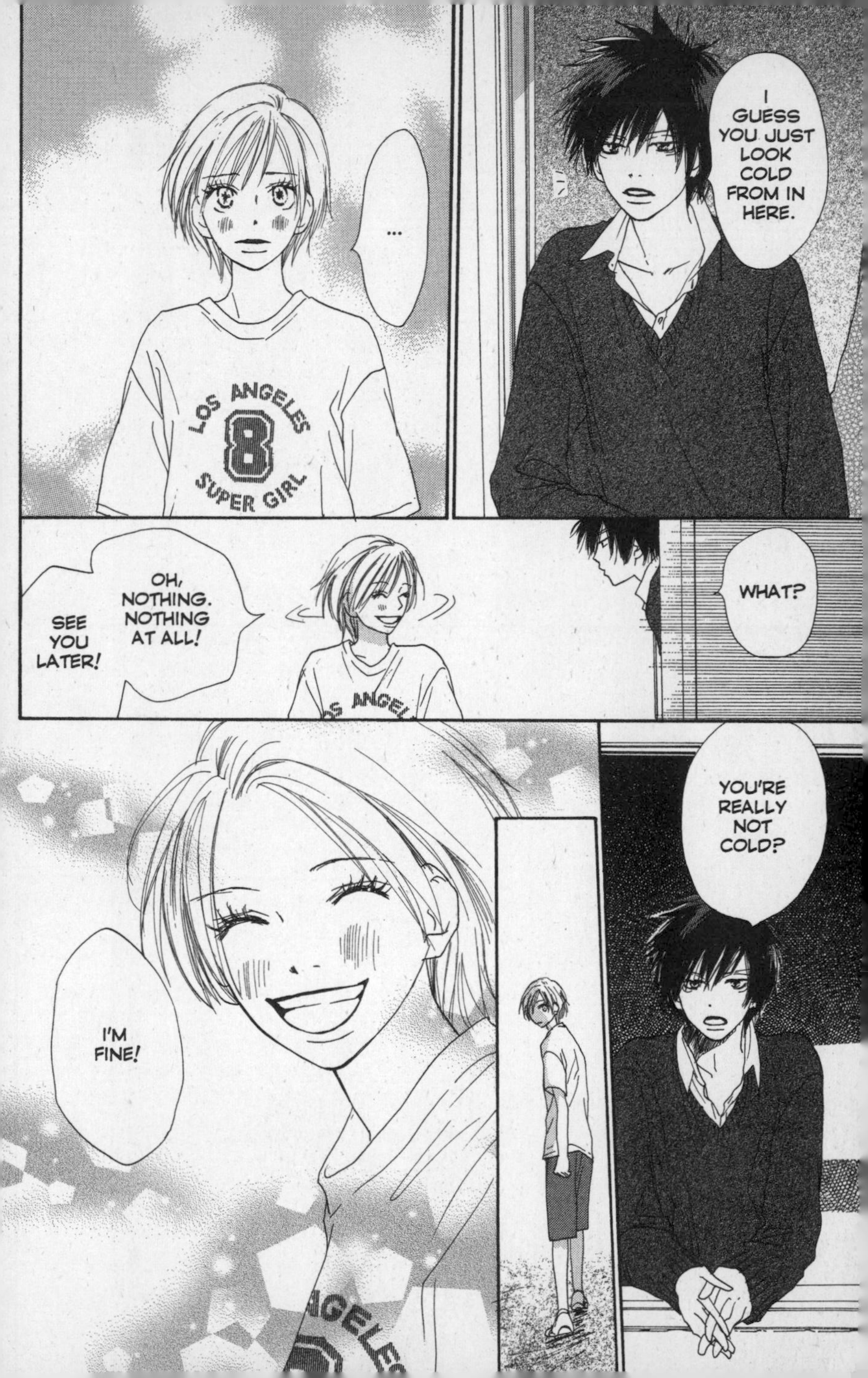
I GUESS YOU JUST LOOK COLD FROM IN HERE.
...
WHAT?
OH, NOTHING. NOTHING AT ALL!
SEE YOU LATER!
YOU'RE REALLY NOT COLD?
I'M FINE!

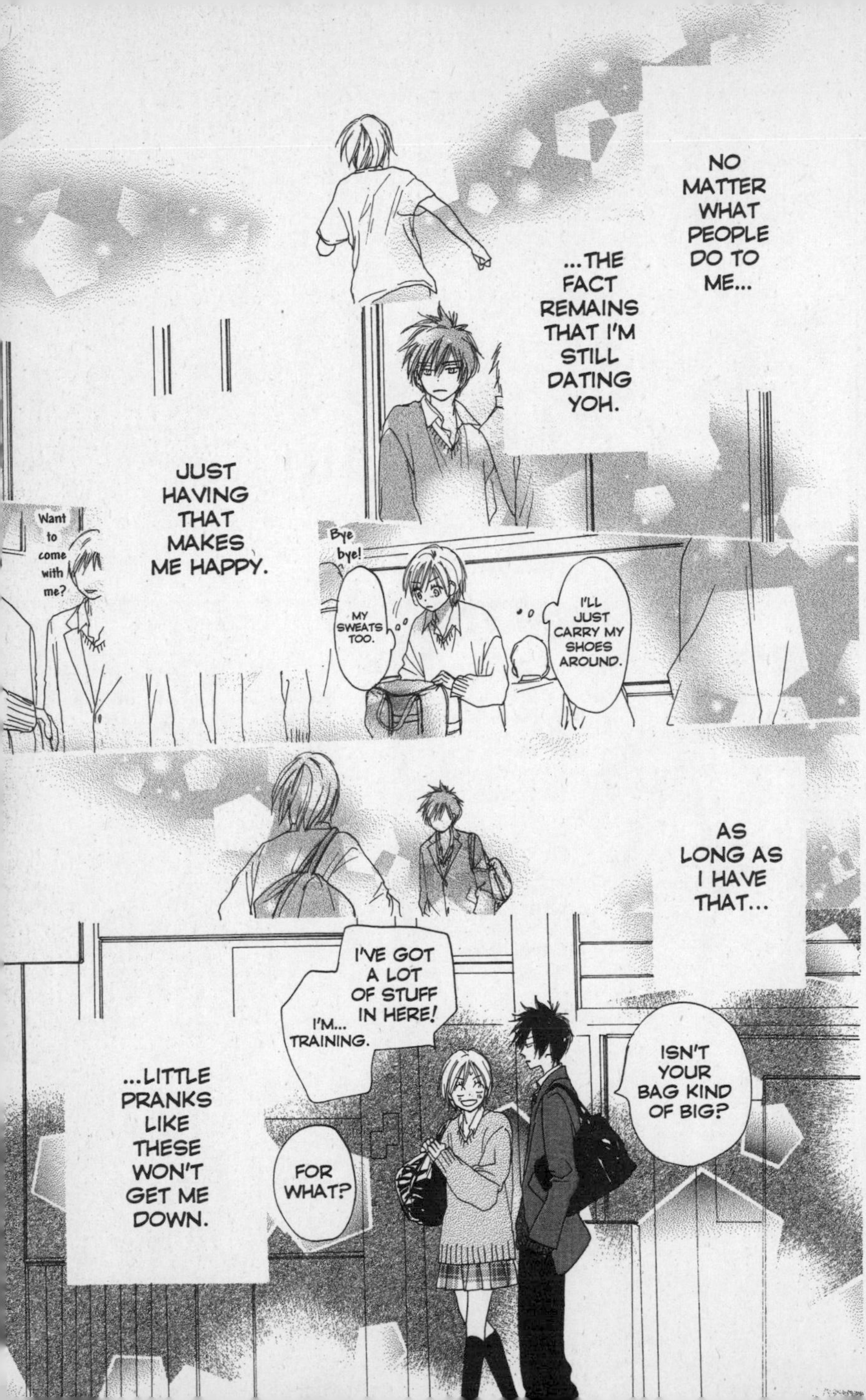
NO MATTER WHAT PEOPLE DO TO ME...
...THE FACT REMAINS THAT I'M STILL DATING YOH.
JUST HAVING THAT MAKES ME HAPPY.
Bye bye!
I'LL JUST CARRY MY SHOES AROUND.
MY SWEATS TOO.
Want to come with me?
AS LONG AS I HAVE THAT...
ISN'T YOUR BAG KIND OF BIG?
I'VE GOT A LOT OF STUFF IN HERE!
FOR WHAT?
I'M... TRAINING.
...LITTLE PRANKS LIKE THESE WON'T GET ME DOWN.

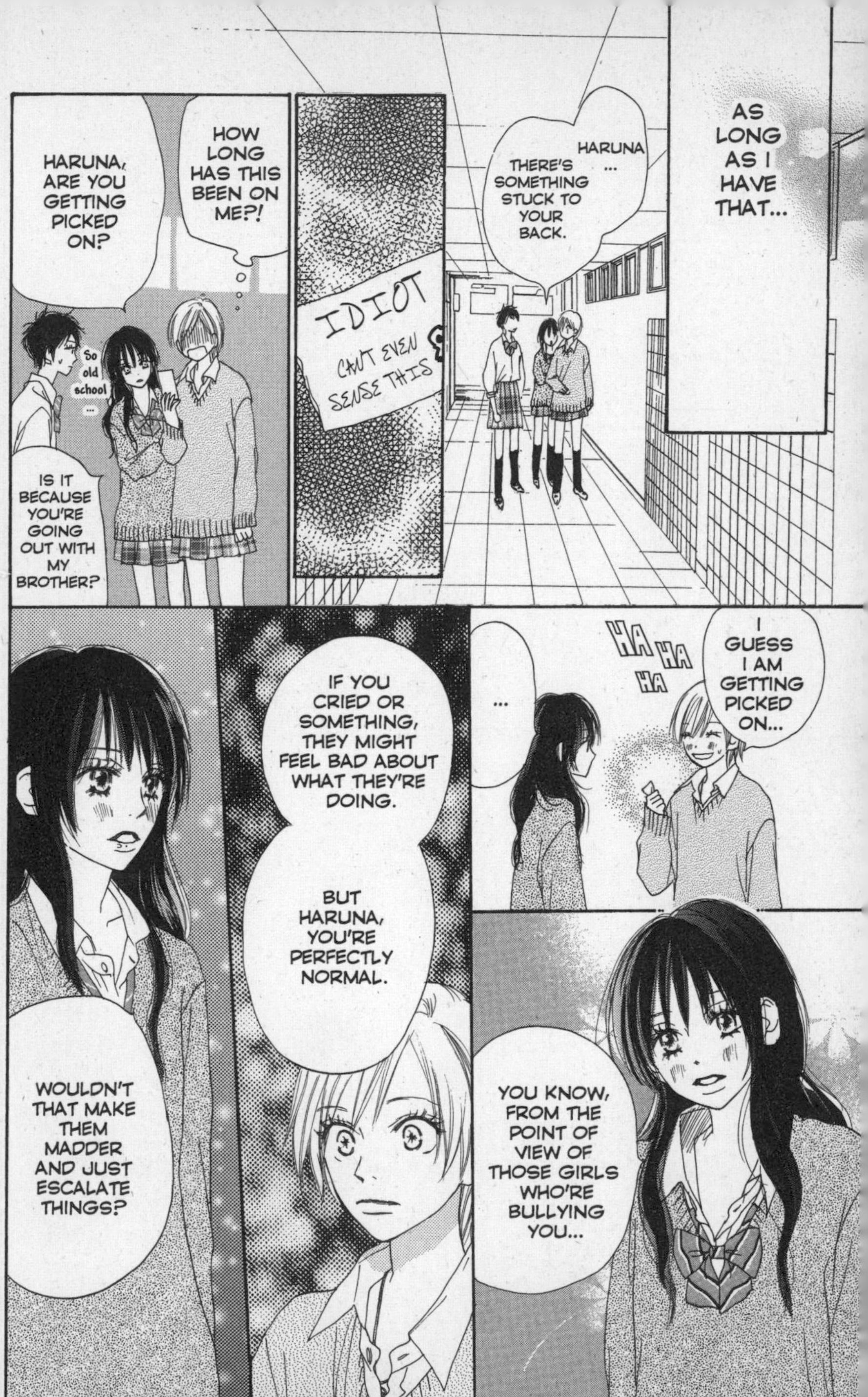
AS LONG AS I HAVE THAT...
HARUNA ... THERE'S SOMETHING STUCK TO YOUR BACK.
IDIOT
CAN'T EVEN SENSE THIS
HOW LONG HAS THIS BEEN ON ME?!
HARUNA, ARE YOU GETTING PICKED ON?
So old school ...
IS IT BECAUSE YOU'RE GOING OUT WITH MY BROTHER?
I GUESS I AM GETTING PICKED ON...
HA HA HA
...
YOU KNOW, FROM THE POINT OF VIEW OF THOSE GIRLS WHO'RE BULLYING YOU...
IF YOU CRIED OR SOMETHING, THEY MIGHT FEEL BAD ABOUT WHAT THEY'RE DOING.
BUT HARUNA, YOU'RE PERFECTLY NORMAL.
WOULDN'T THAT MAKE THEM MADDER AND JUST ESCALATE THINGS?

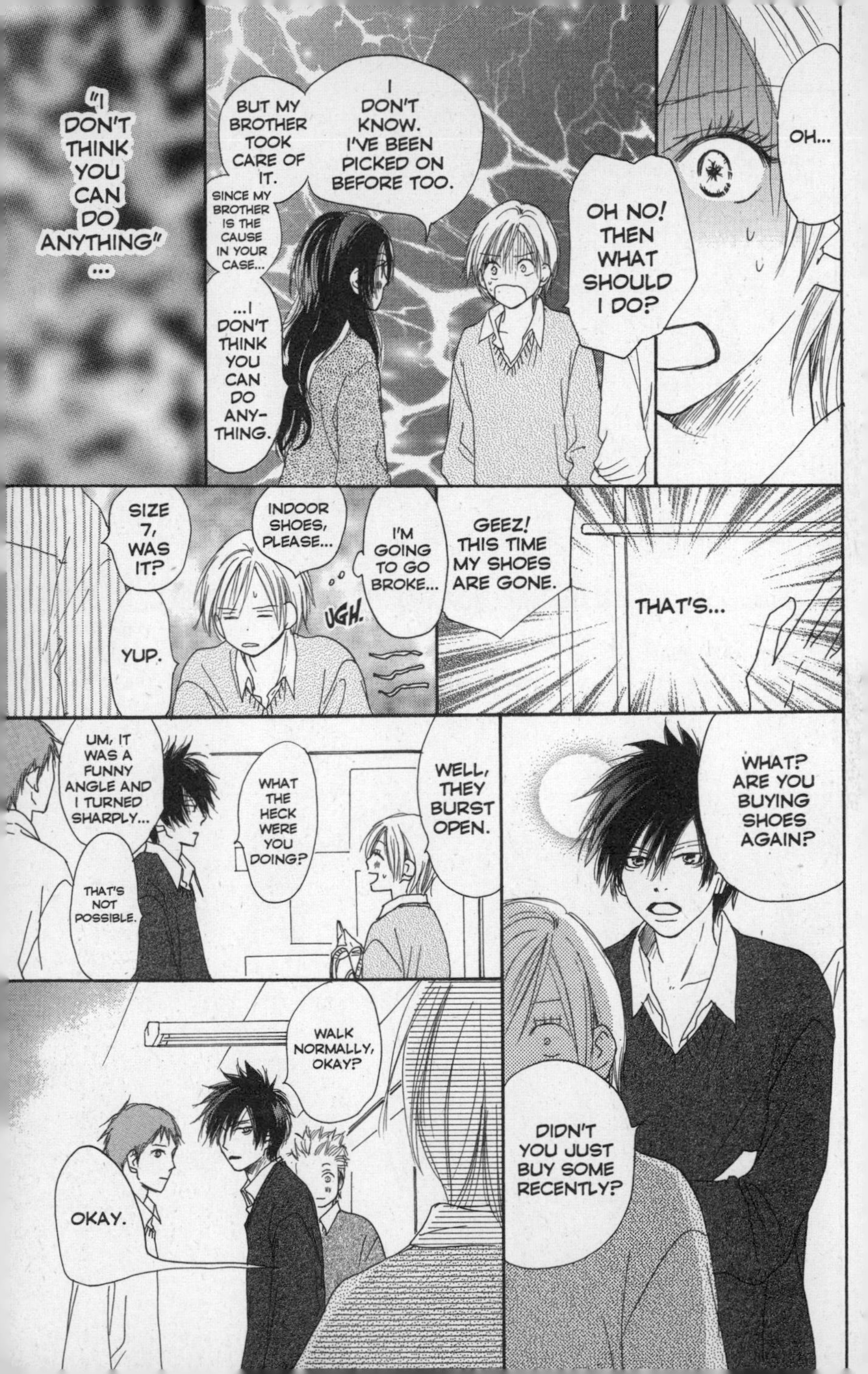
OH...
OH NO! THEN WHAT SHOULD I DO?
I DON'T KNOW. I'VE BEEN PICKED ON BEFORE TOO.
BUT MY BROTHER TOOK CARE OF IT.
SINCE MY BROTHER IS THE CAUSE IN YOUR CASE...
...I DON'T THINK YOU CAN DO ANY-THING.
"I DON'T THINK YOU CAN DO ANYTHING"...
THAT'S...
GEEZ! THIS TIME MY SHOES ARE GONE.
INDOOR SHOES, PLEASE...
I'M GOING TO GO BROKE...
UGH.
SIZE 7, WAS IT?
YUP.
WHAT? ARE YOU BUYING SHOES AGAIN?
DIDN'T YOU JUST BUY SOME RECENTLY?
WELL, THEY BURST OPEN.
WHAT THE HECK WERE YOU DOING?
UM, IT WAS A FUNNY ANGLE AND I TURNED SHARPLY...
THAT'S NOT POSSIBLE.
WALK NORMALLY, OKAY?
OKAY.

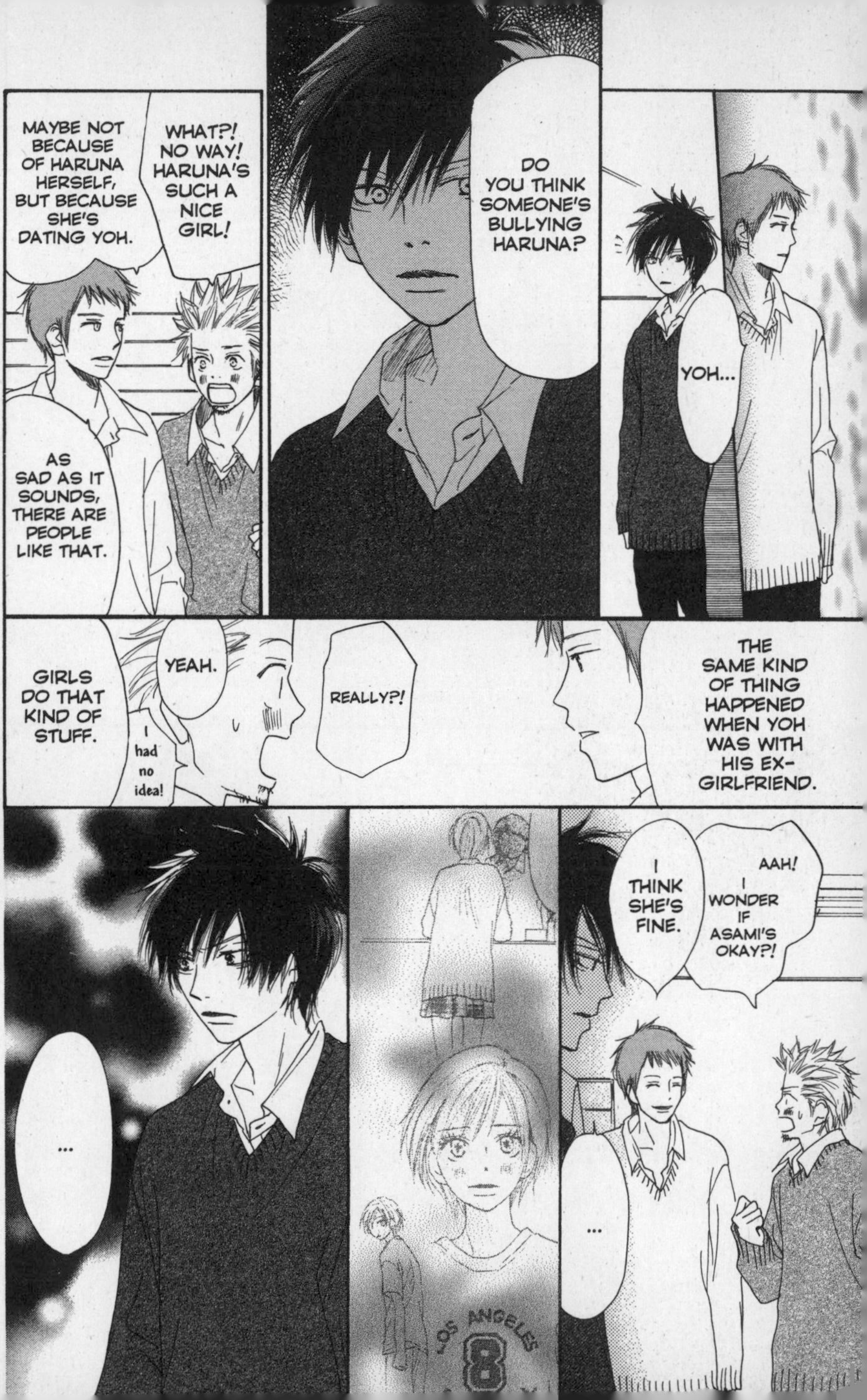
YOH...
DO YOU THINK SOMEONE'S BULLYING HARUNA?
WHAT?! NO WAY! HARUNA'S SUCH A NICE GIRL!
MAYBE NOT BECAUSE OF HARUNA HERSELF, BUT BECAUSE SHE'S DATING YOH.
AS SAD AS IT SOUNDS, THERE ARE PEOPLE LIKE THAT.
THE SAME KIND OF THING HAPPENED WHEN YOH WAS WITH HIS EX-GIRLFRIEND.
REALLY?!
YEAH.
GIRLS DO THAT KIND OF STUFF.
I had no idea!
AAH! I WONDER IF ASAMI'S OKAY?!
I THINK SHE'S FINE.
...
...

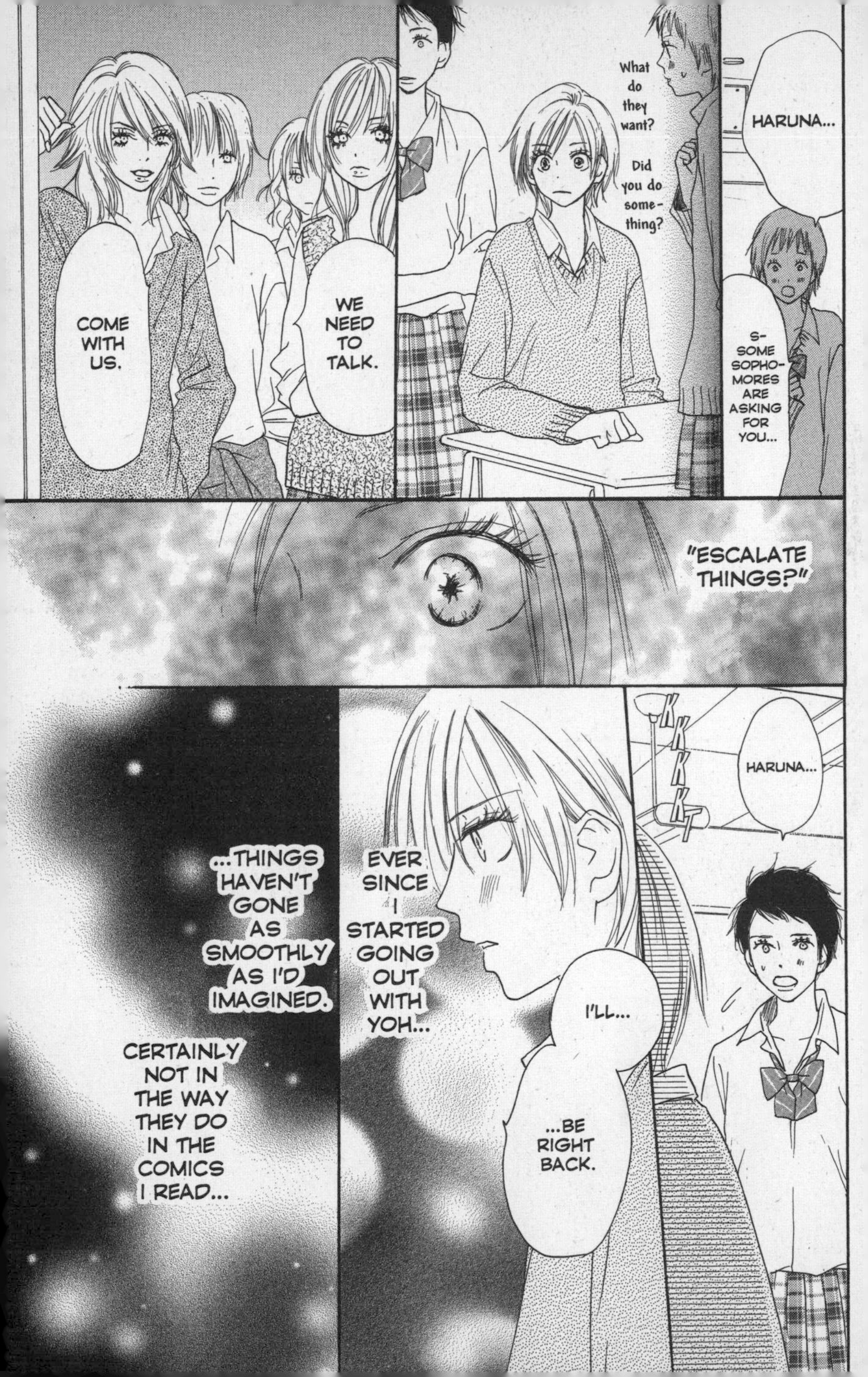
HARUNA...
S-SOME SOPHOMORES ARE ASKING FOR YOU...
What do they want?
Did you do some-thing?
WE NEED TO TALK.
COME WITH US.
"ESCALATE THINGS?"
KKKKT
HARUNA...
I'LL...
...BE RIGHT BACK.
EVER SINCE I STARTED GOING OUT WITH YOH...
...THINGS HAVEN'T GONE AS SMOOTHLY AS I'D IMAGINED.
CERTAINLY NOT IN THE WAY THEY DO IN THE COMICS I READ...

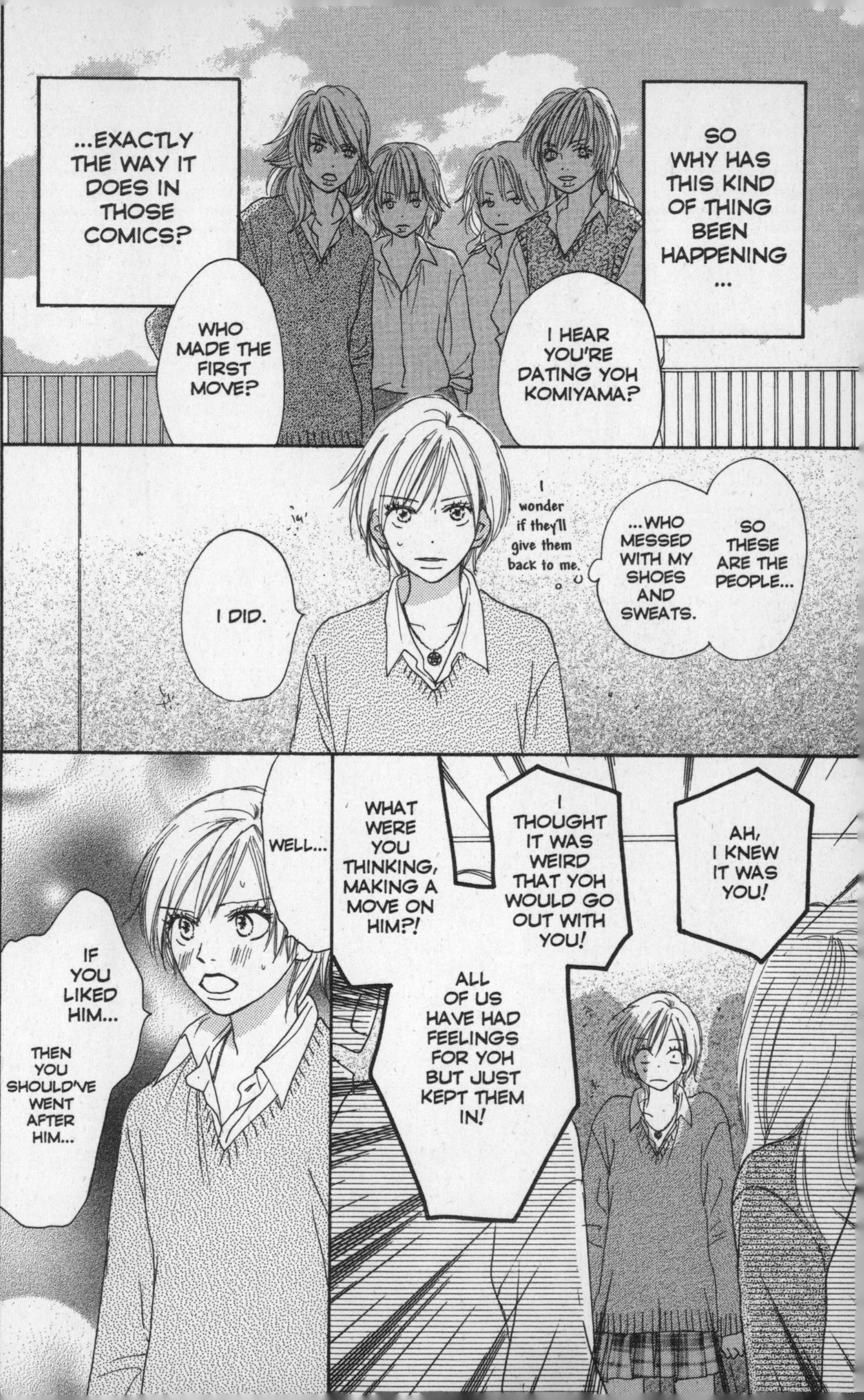
SO WHY HAS THIS KIND OF THING BEEN HAPPENING...
...EXACTLY THE WAY IT DOES IN THOSE COMICS?
I HEAR YOU'RE DATING YOH KOMIYAMA?
WHO MADE THE FIRST MOVE?
SO THESE ARE THE PEOPLE...
...WHO MESSED WITH MY SHOES AND SWEATS.
I wonder if they'll give them back to me.
I DID.
AH, I KNEW IT WAS YOU!
I THOUGHT IT WAS WEIRD THAT YOH WOULD GO OUT WITH YOU!
WHAT WERE YOU THINKING, MAKING A MOVE ON HIM?!
ALL OF US HAVE HAD FEELINGS FOR YOH BUT JUST KEPT THEM IN!
WELL...
IF YOU LIKED HIM...
THEN YOU SHOULD'VE WENT AFTER HIM...

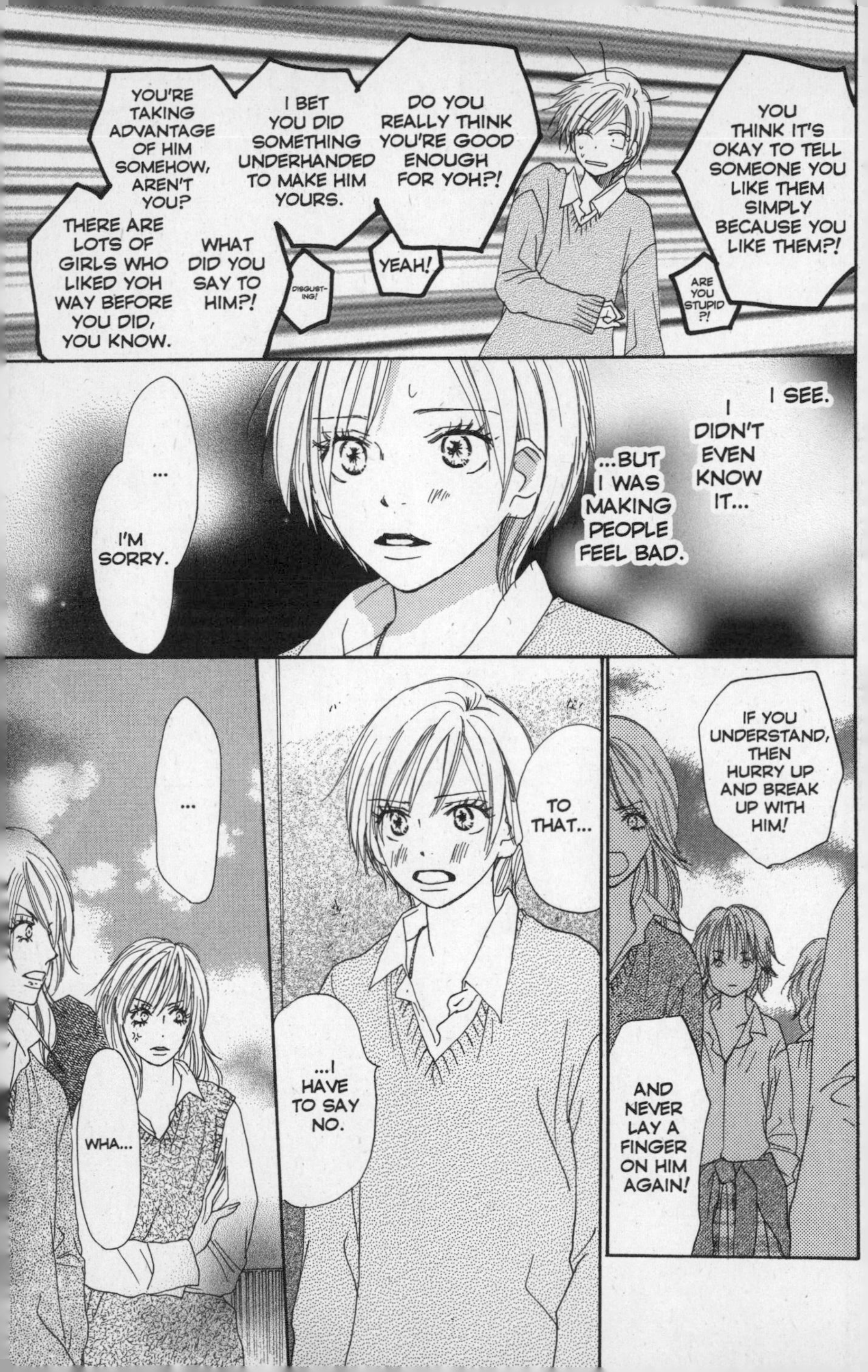
YOU THINK IT'S OKAY TO TELL SOMEONE YOU LIKE THEM SIMPLY BECAUSE YOU LIKE THEM?!
ARE YOU STUPID?!
DO YOU REALLY THINK YOU'RE GOOD ENOUGH FOR YOH?!
I BET YOU DID SOMETHING UNDERHANDED TO MAKE HIM YOURS.
YOU'RE TAKING ADVANTAGE OF HIM SOMEHOW, AREN'T YOU?
YEAH!
DISGUSTING!
WHAT DID YOU SAY TO HIM?!
THERE ARE LOTS OF GIRLS WHO LIKED YOH WAY BEFORE YOU DID, YOU KNOW.
I SEE.
I DIDN'T EVEN KNOW IT...
...BUT I WAS MAKING PEOPLE FEEL BAD.
...
I'M SORRY.
IF YOU UNDERSTAND, THEN HURRY UP AND BREAK UP WITH HIM!
AND NEVER LAY A FINGER ON HIM AGAIN!
TO THAT...
...I HAVE TO SAY NO.
...
WHA...

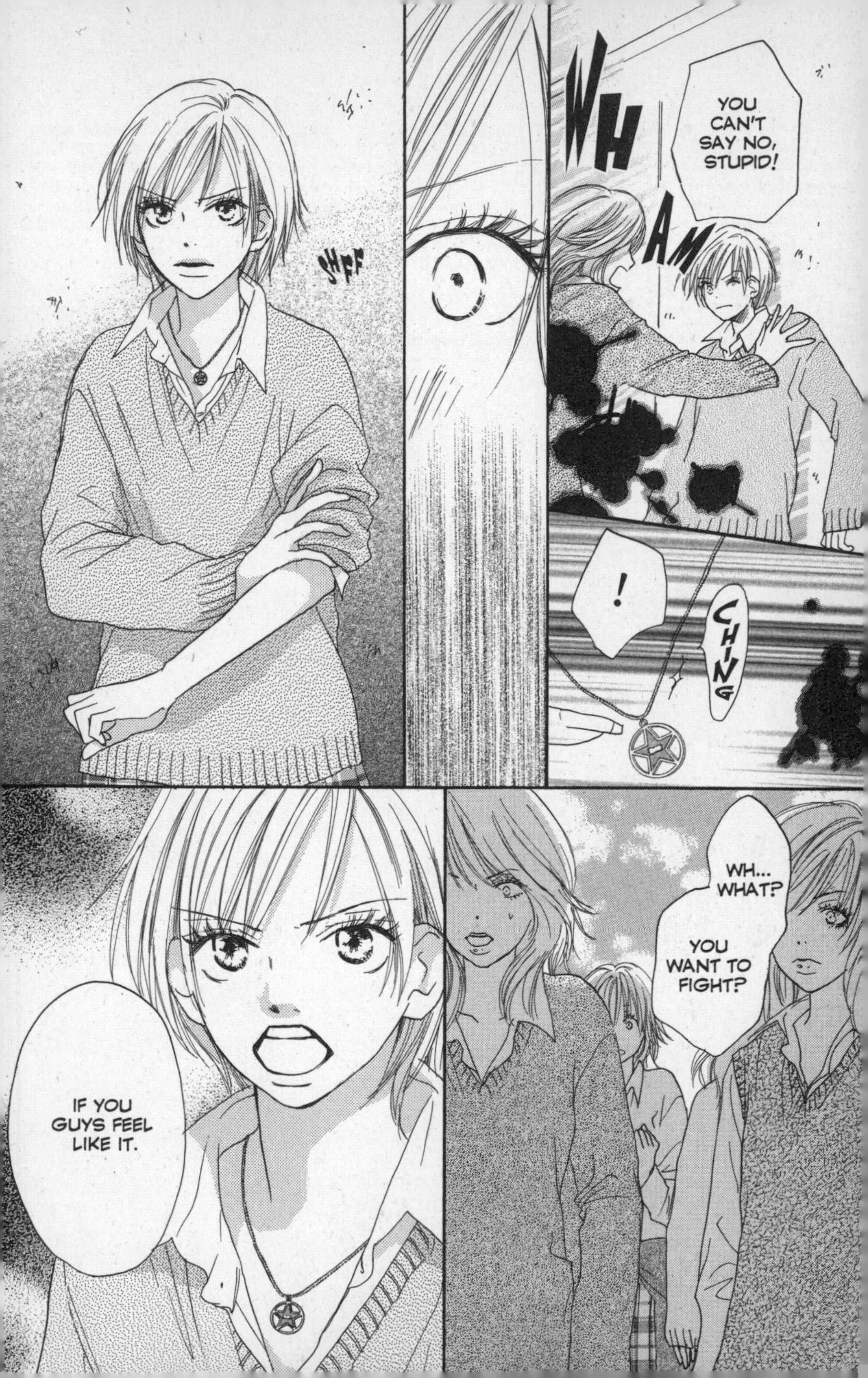
WHAM
YOU CAN'T SAY NO, STUPID!
!
CHING
SHFF
WH... WHAT?
YOU WANT TO FIGHT?
IF YOU GUYS FEEL LIKE IT.

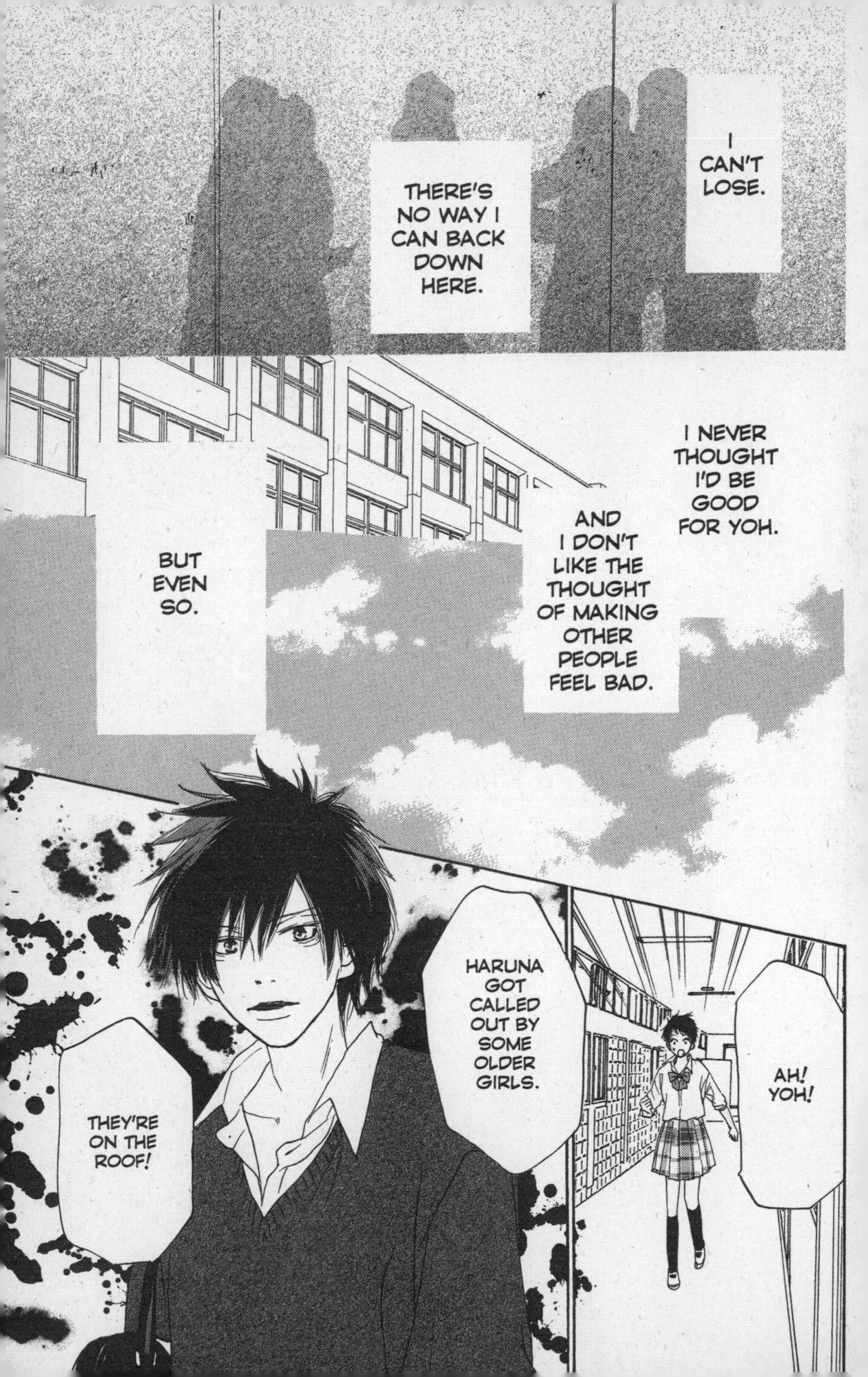
I CAN'T LOSE.
THERE'S NO WAY I CAN BACK DOWN HERE.
I NEVER THOUGHT I'D BE GOOD FOR YOH.
AND I DON'T LIKE THE THOUGHT OF MAKING OTHER PEOPLE FEEL BAD.
BUT EVEN SO.
AH! YOH!
HARUNA GOT CALLED OUT BY SOME OLDER GIRLS.
THEY'RE ON THE ROOF!

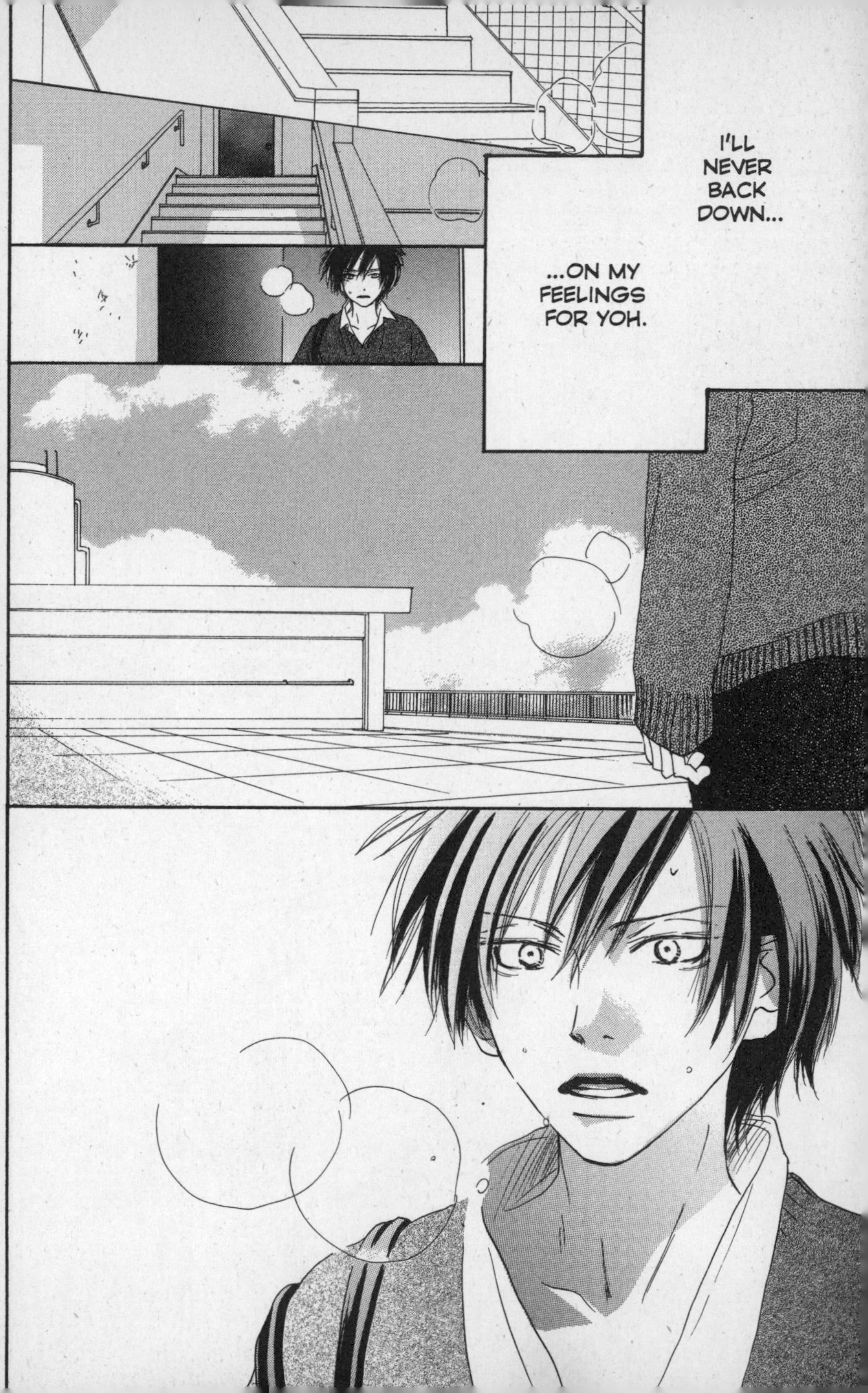
I'LL NEVER BACK DOWN...
...ON MY FEELINGS FOR YOH.

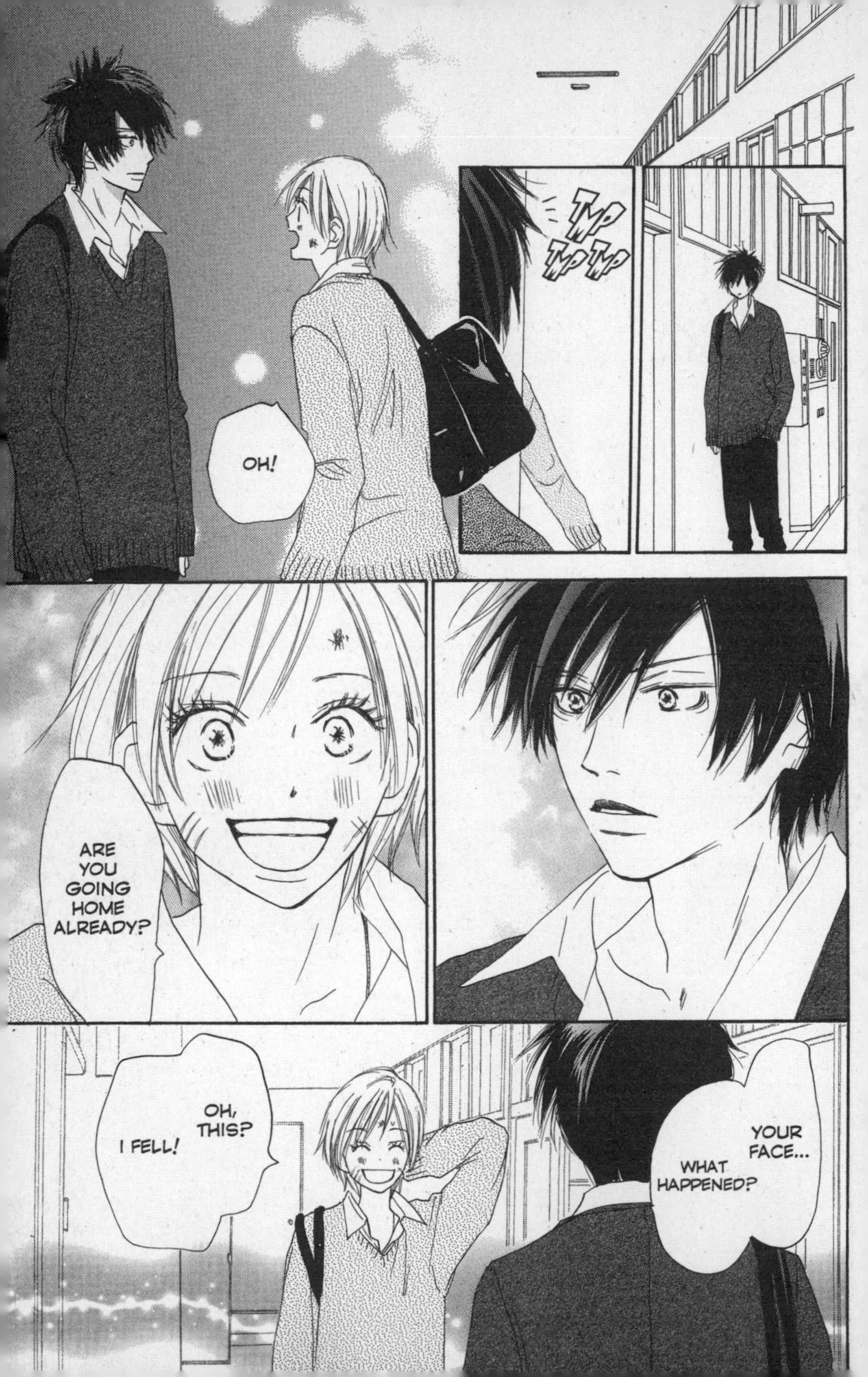
TMP TMP TMP
OH!
ARE YOU GOING HOME ALREADY?
YOUR FACE... WHAT HAPPENED?
OH, THIS? I FELL!

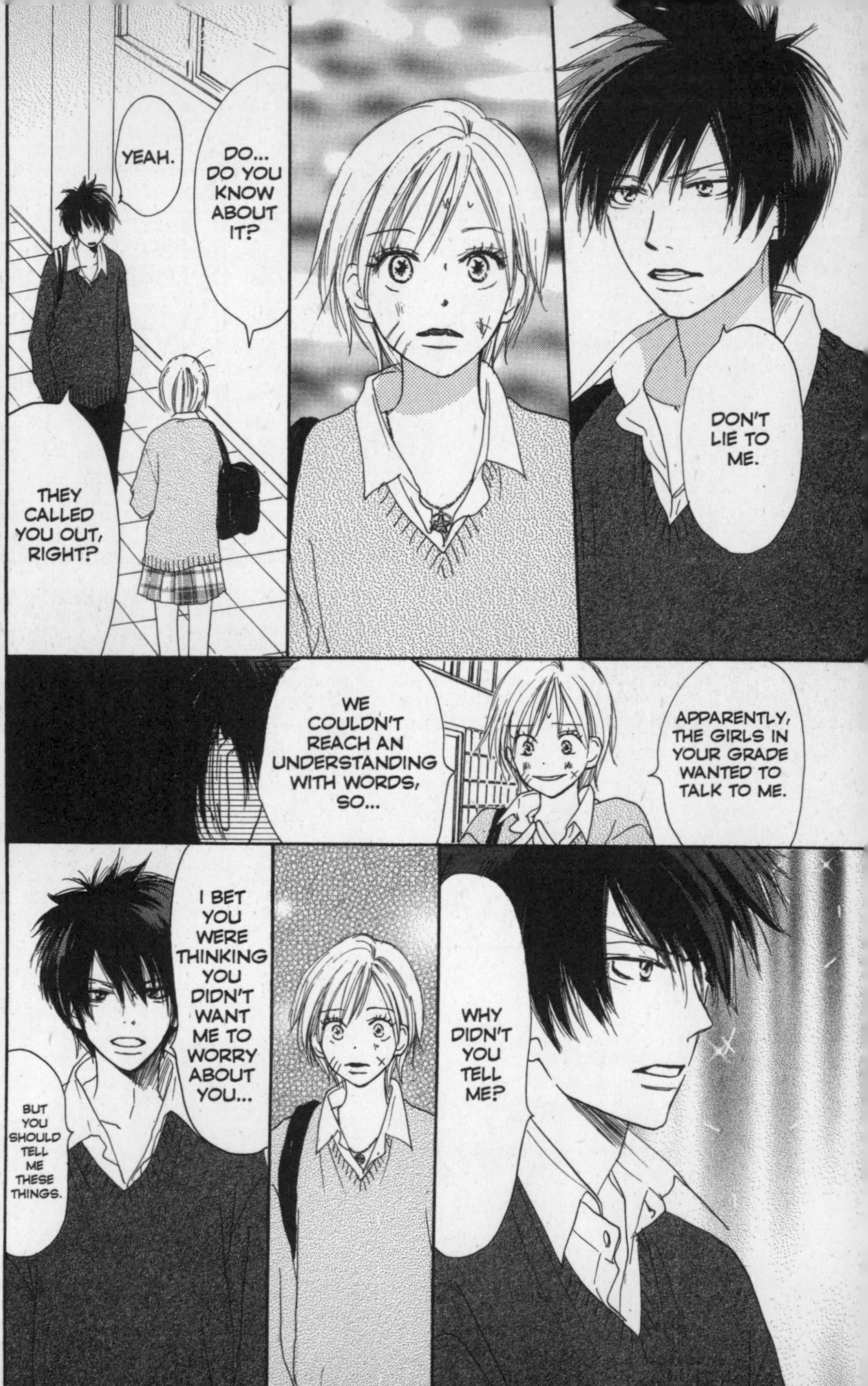
DON'T LIE TO ME.
DO... DO YOU KNOW ABOUT IT?
YEAH.
THEY CALLED YOU OUT, RIGHT?
APPARENTLY, THE GIRLS IN YOUR GRADE WANTED TO TALK TO ME.
WE COULDN'T REACH AN UNDERSTANDING WITH WORDS, SO...
WHY DIDN'T YOU TELL ME?
I BET YOU WERE THINKING YOU DIDN'T WANT ME TO WORRY ABOUT YOU...
BUT YOU SHOULD TELL ME THESE THINGS.

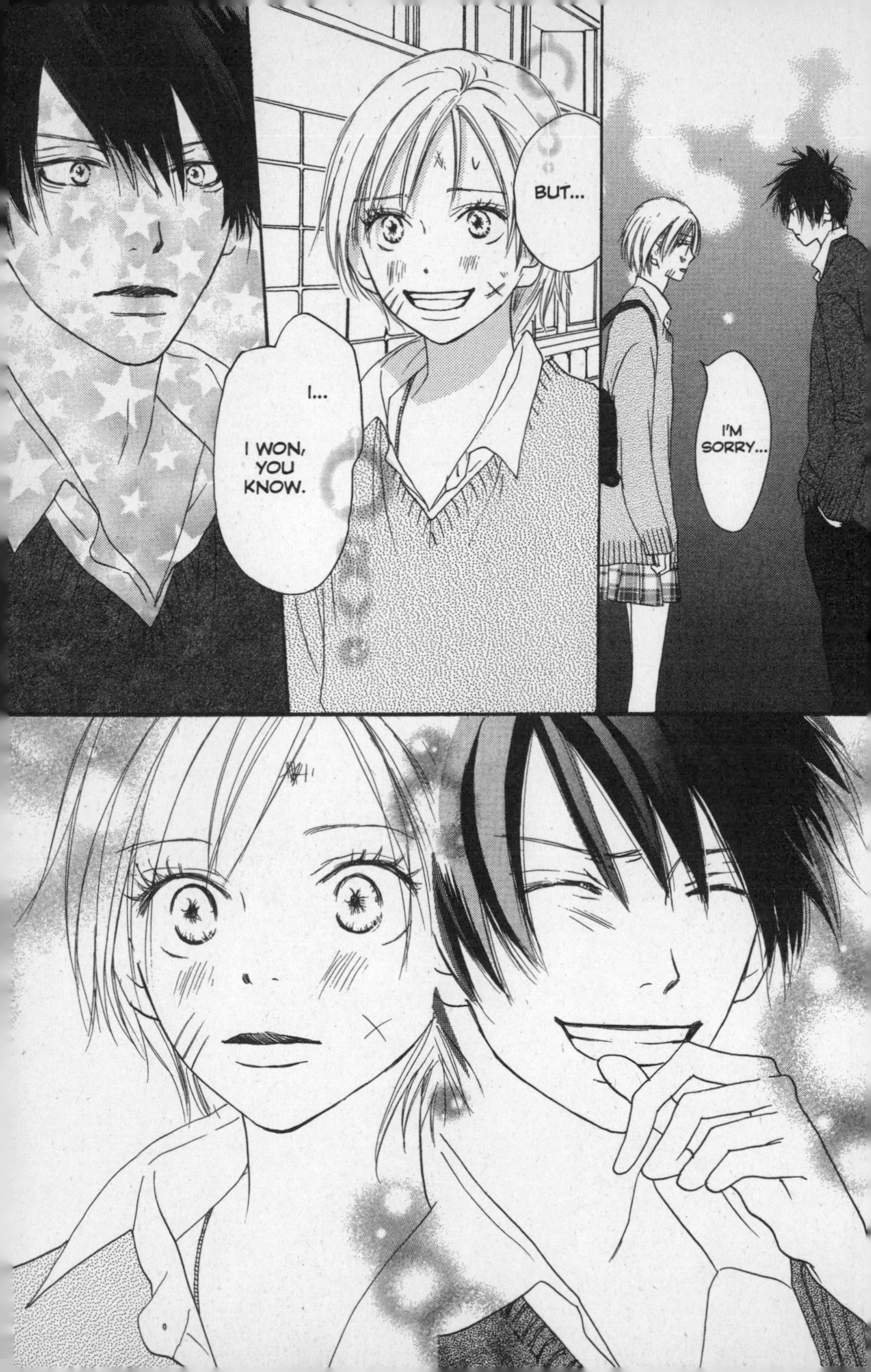
I'M SORRY...
BUT...
I...
I WON, YOU KNOW.

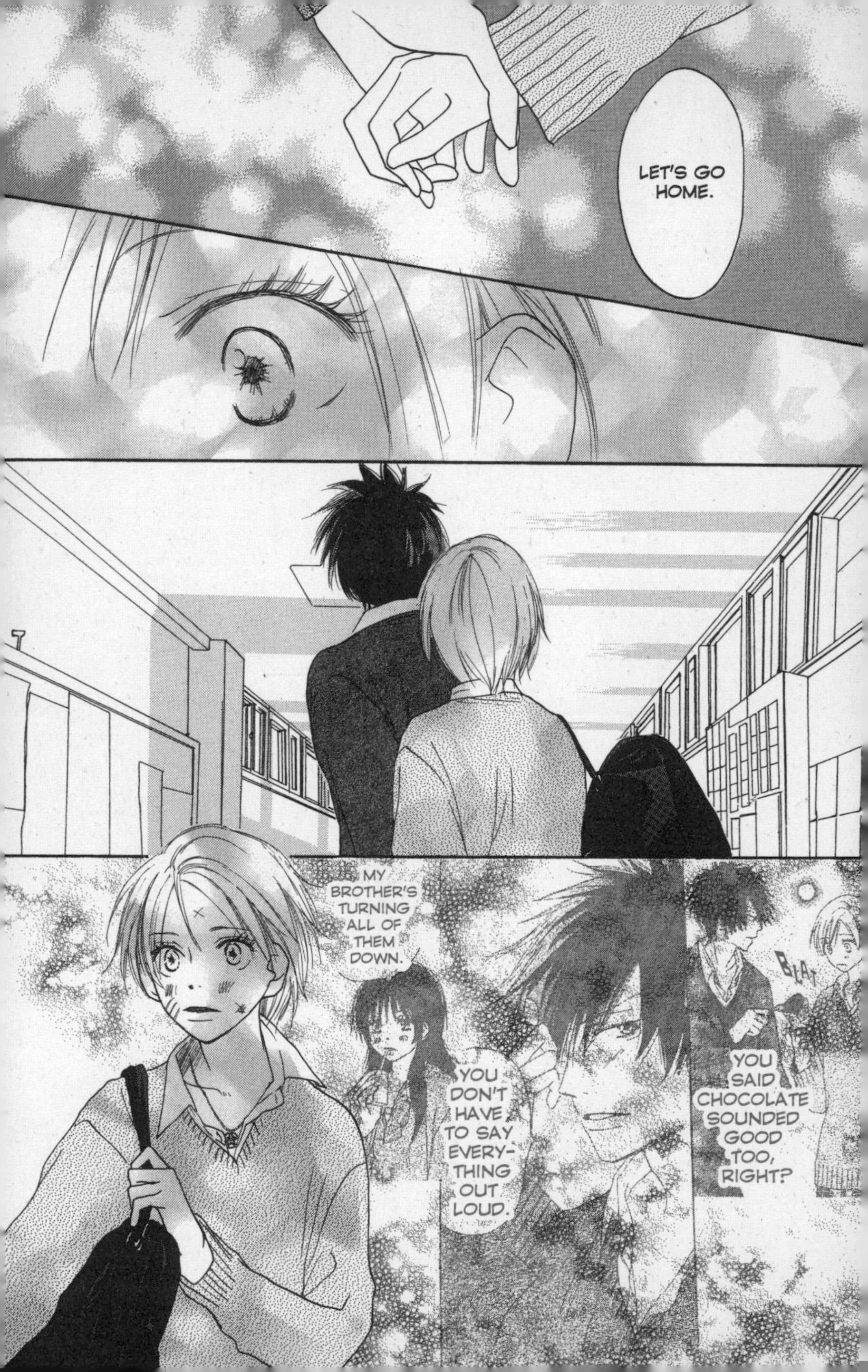
LET'S GO HOME.
YOU SAID CHOCOLATE SOUNDED GOOD TOO, RIGHT?
BLAT
YOU DON'T HAVE TO SAY EVERY-THING OUT LOUD.
MY BROTHER'S TURNING ALL OF THEM DOWN.

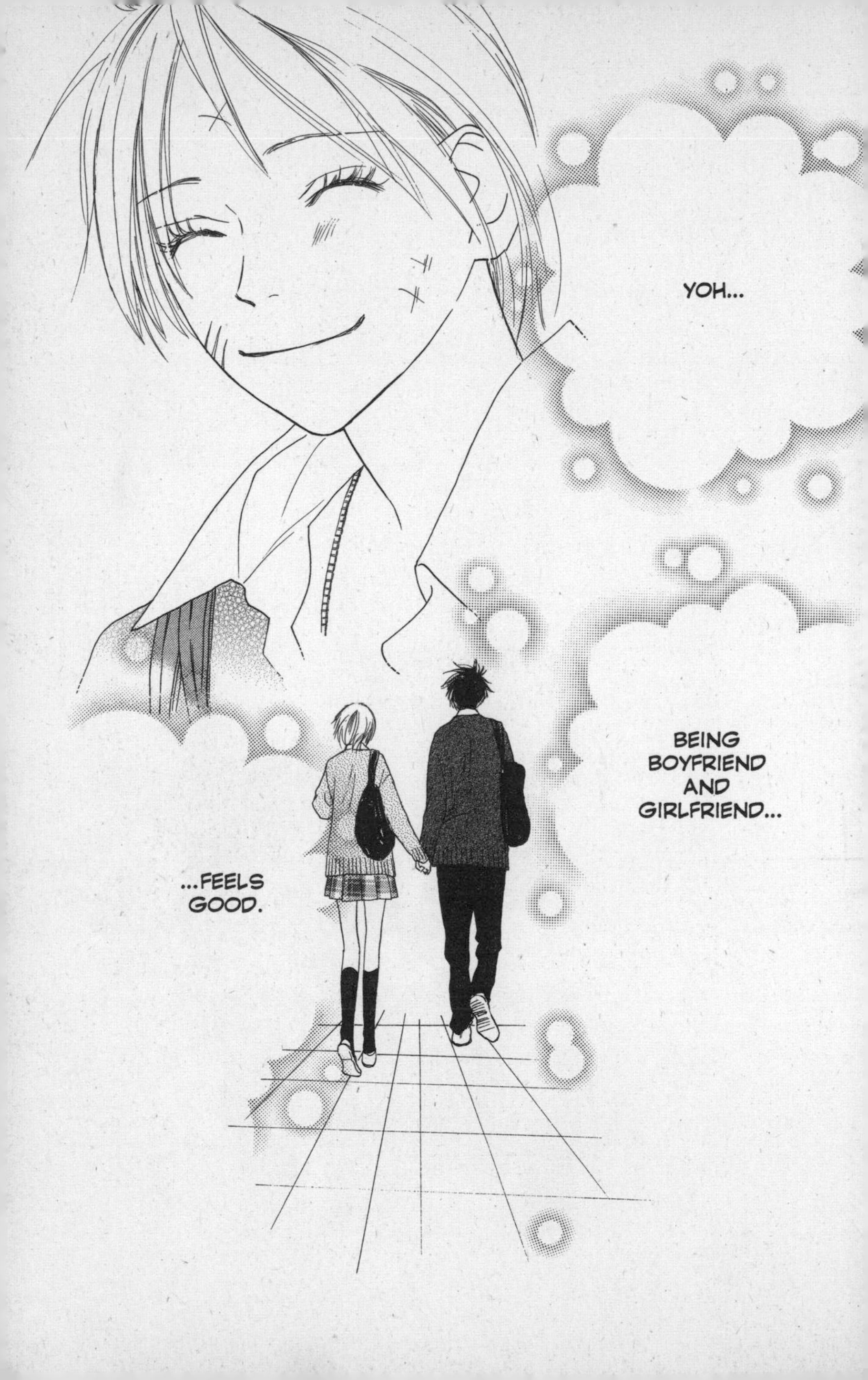
YOH...
BEING BOYFRIEND AND GIRLFRIEND...
...FEELS GOOD.

Yoh
and
Asami

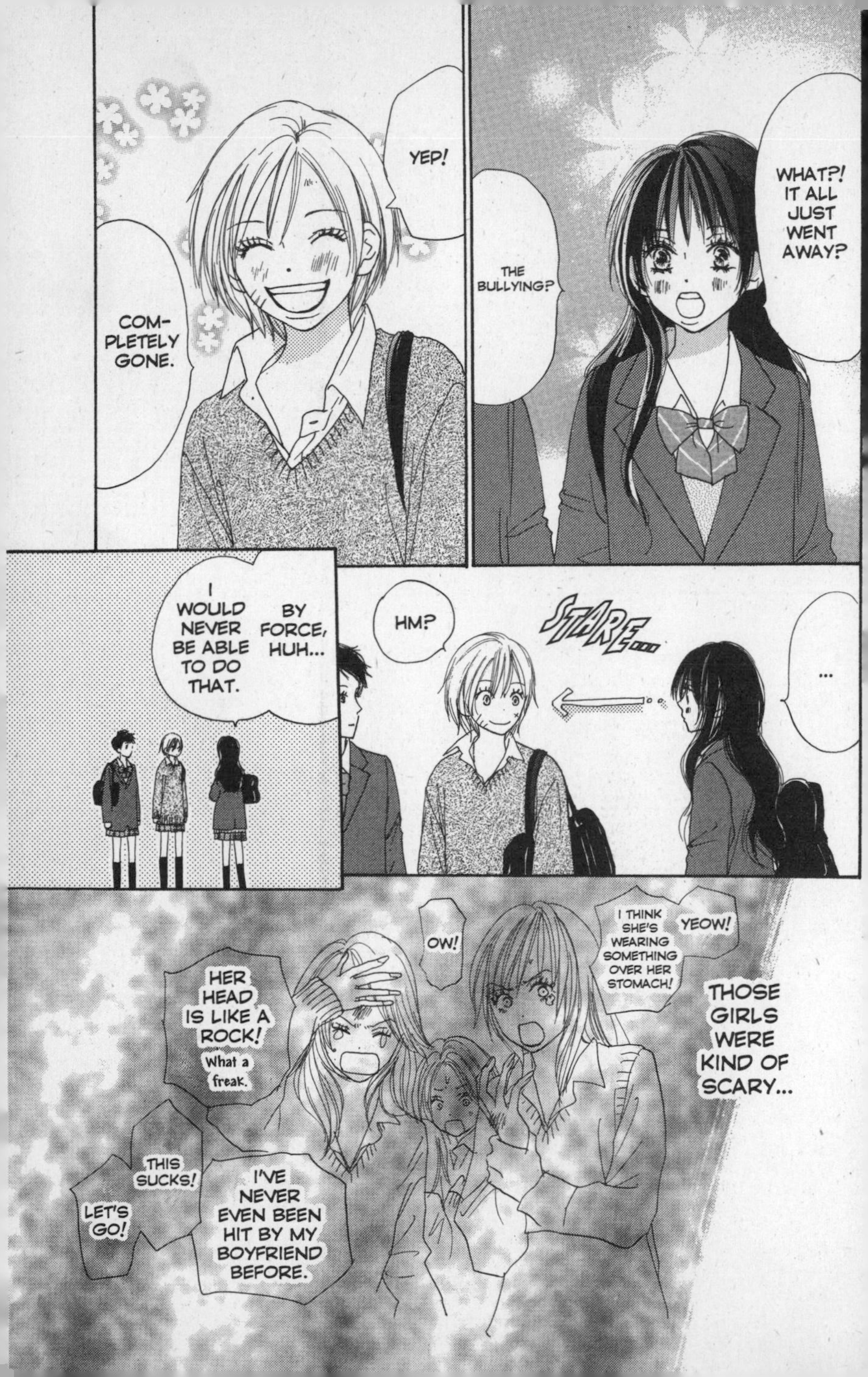
WHAT?! IT ALL JUST WENT AWAY?
THE BULLYING?
YEP!
COMPLETELY GONE.
...
STARE...
HM?
BY FORCE, HUH...
I WOULD NEVER BE ABLE TO DO THAT.
THOSE GIRLS WERE KIND OF SCARY...
YEOW!
I THINK SHE'S WEARING SOMETHING OVER HER STOMACH!
OW!
HER HEAD IS LIKE A ROCK!
What a freak.
I'VE NEVER EVEN BEEN HIT BY MY BOYFRIEND BEFORE.
THIS SUCKS!
LET'S GO!

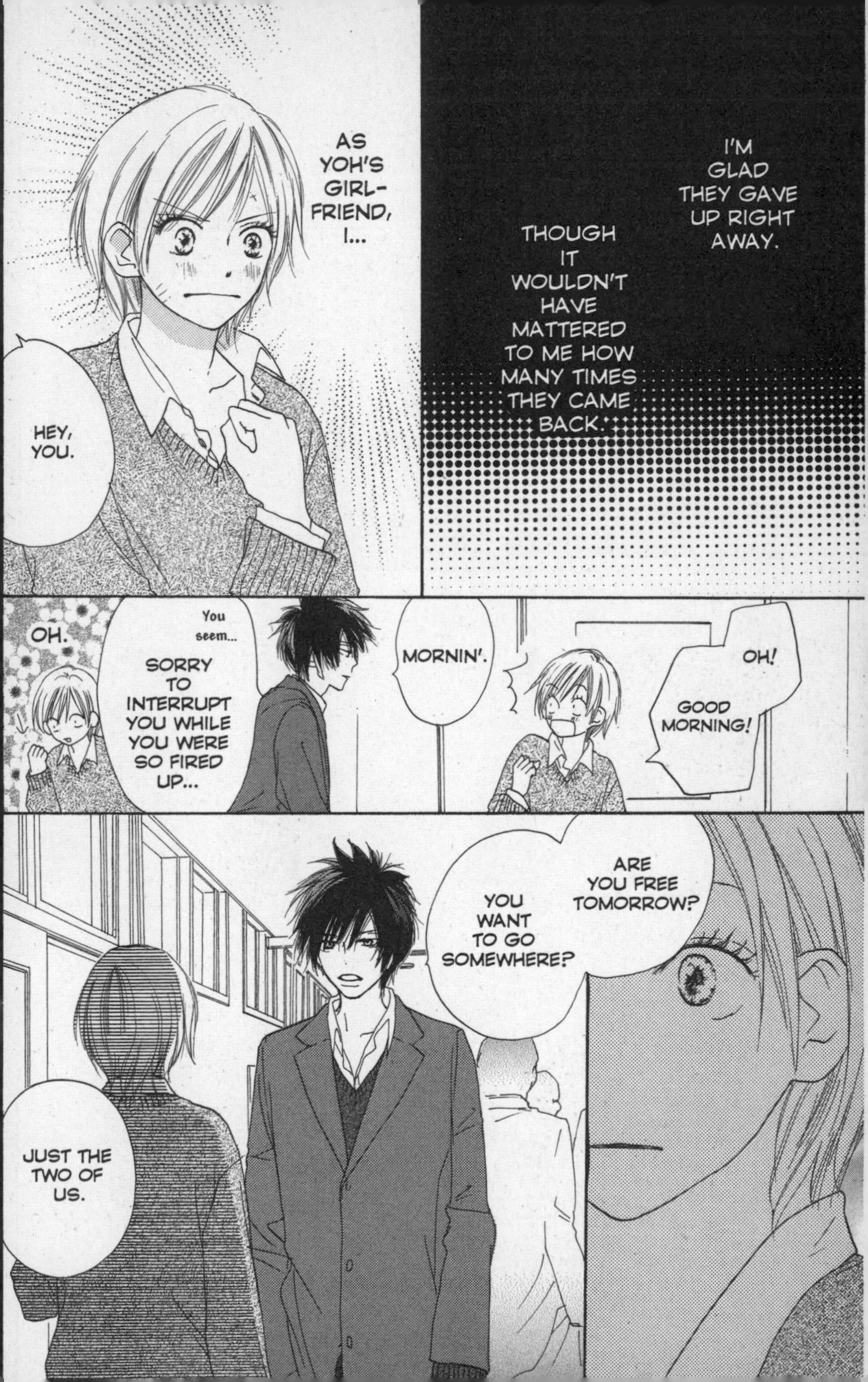
I'M GLAD THEY GAVE UP RIGHT AWAY.
THOUGH IT WOULDN'T HAVE MATTERED TO ME HOW MANY TIMES THEY CAME BACK.
AS YOH'S GIRL-FRIEND, I...
HEY, YOU.
OH!
GOOD MORNING!
MORNIN'.
You seem...
SORRY TO INTERRUPT YOU WHILE YOU WERE SO FIRED UP...
OH.
ARE YOU FREE TOMORROW?
YOU WANT TO GO SOMEWHERE?
JUST THE TWO OF US.

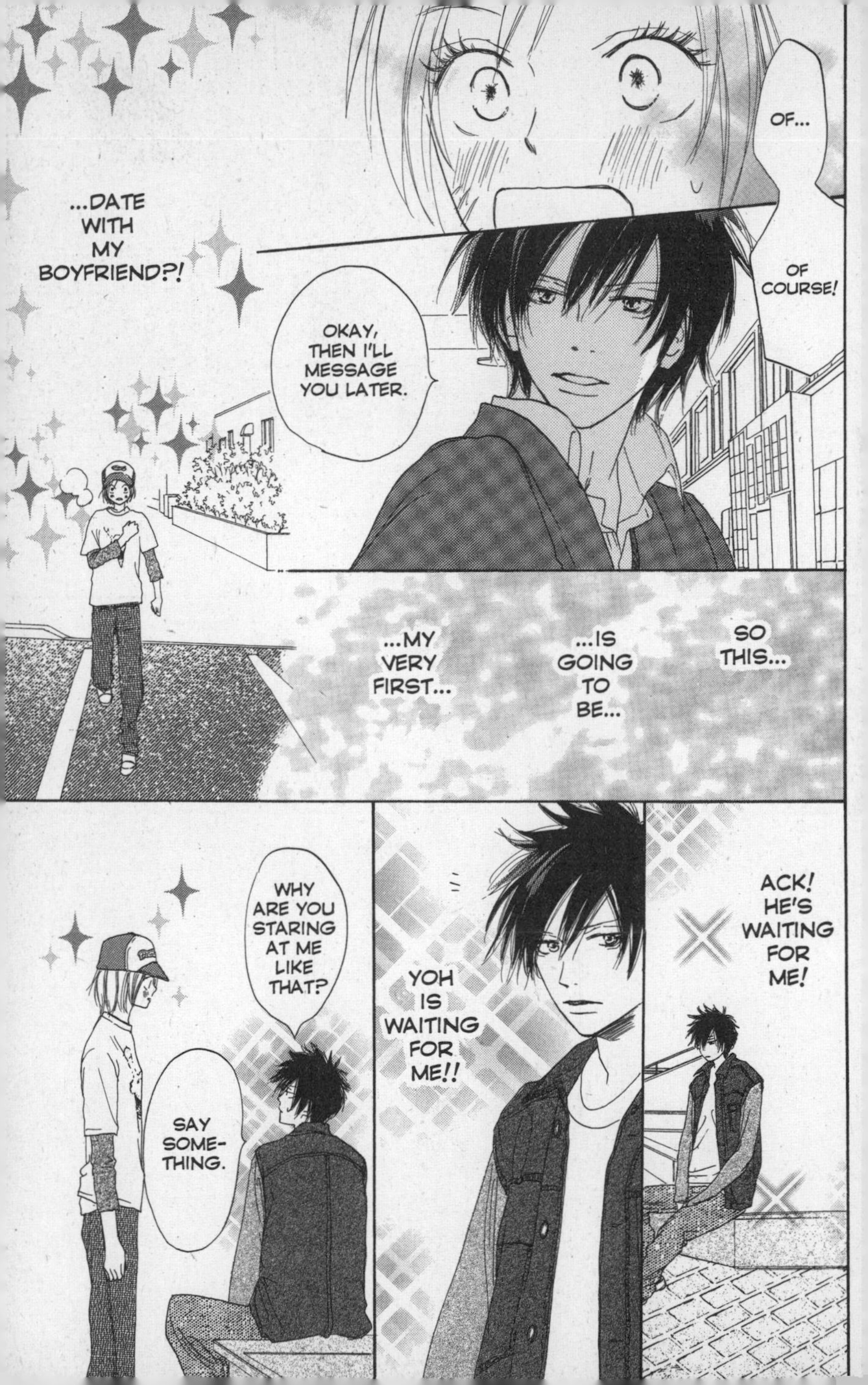
OF...
OF COURSE!
OKAY, THEN I'LL MESSAGE YOU LATER.
SO THIS...
...IS GOING TO BE...
...MY VERY FIRST...
...DATE WITH MY BOYFRIEND?!
ACK! HE'S WAITING FOR ME!
YOH IS WAITING FOR ME!!
WHY ARE YOU STARING AT ME LIKE THAT?
SAY SOME-THING.

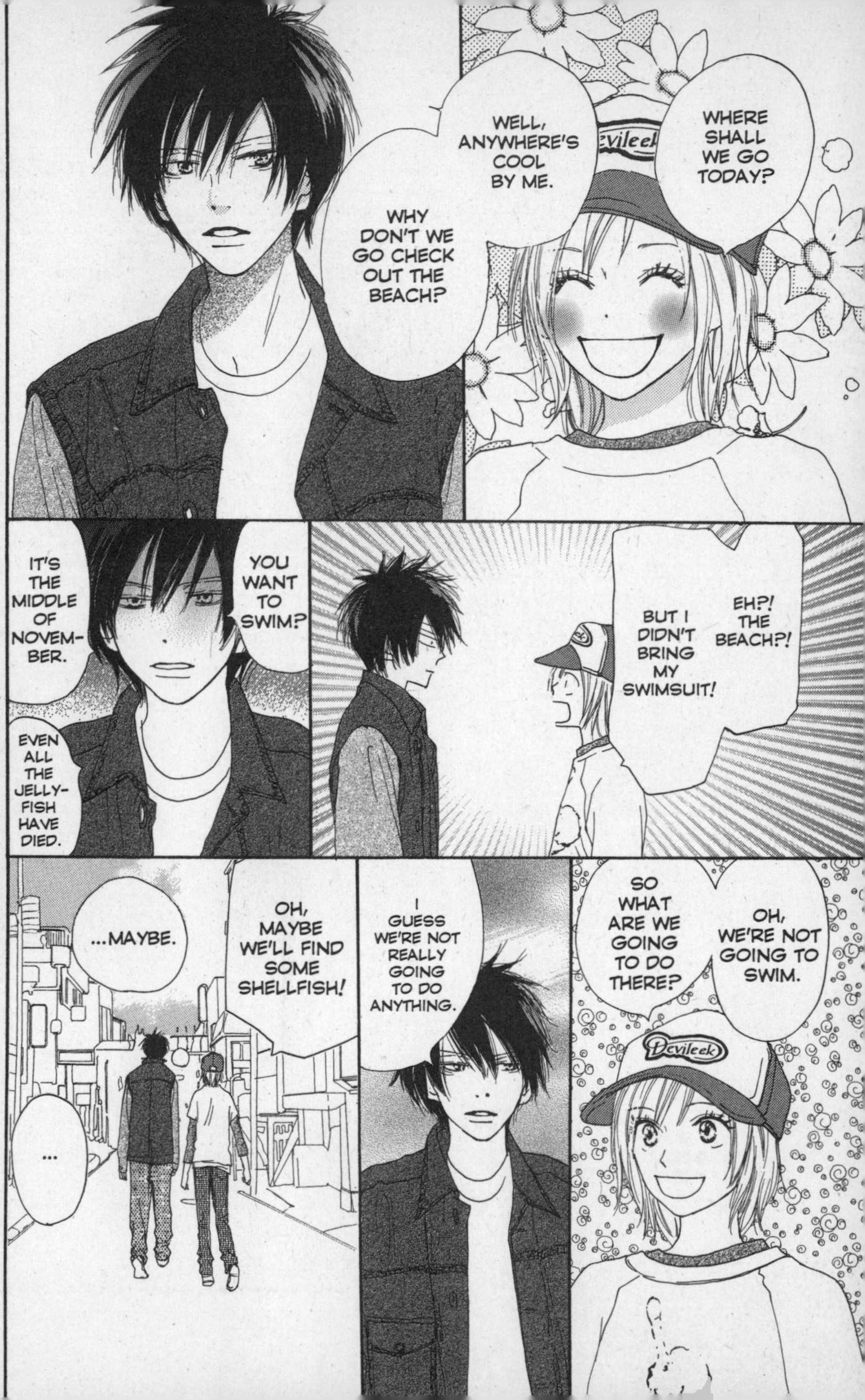
WHERE SHALL WE GO TODAY?
WELL, ANYWHERE'S COOL BY ME.
WHY DON'T WE GO CHECK OUT THE BEACH?
EH?! THE BEACH?!
BUT I DIDN'T BRING MY SWIMSUIT!
YOU WANT TO SWIM?
IT'S THE MIDDLE OF NOVEMBER.
EVEN ALL THE JELLYFISH HAVE DIED.
OH, WE'RE NOT GOING TO SWIM.
SO WHAT ARE WE GOING TO DO THERE?
Devileek
I GUESS WE'RE NOT REALLY GOING TO DO ANYTHING.
OH, MAYBE WE'LL FIND SOME SHELLFISH!
...MAYBE.
...

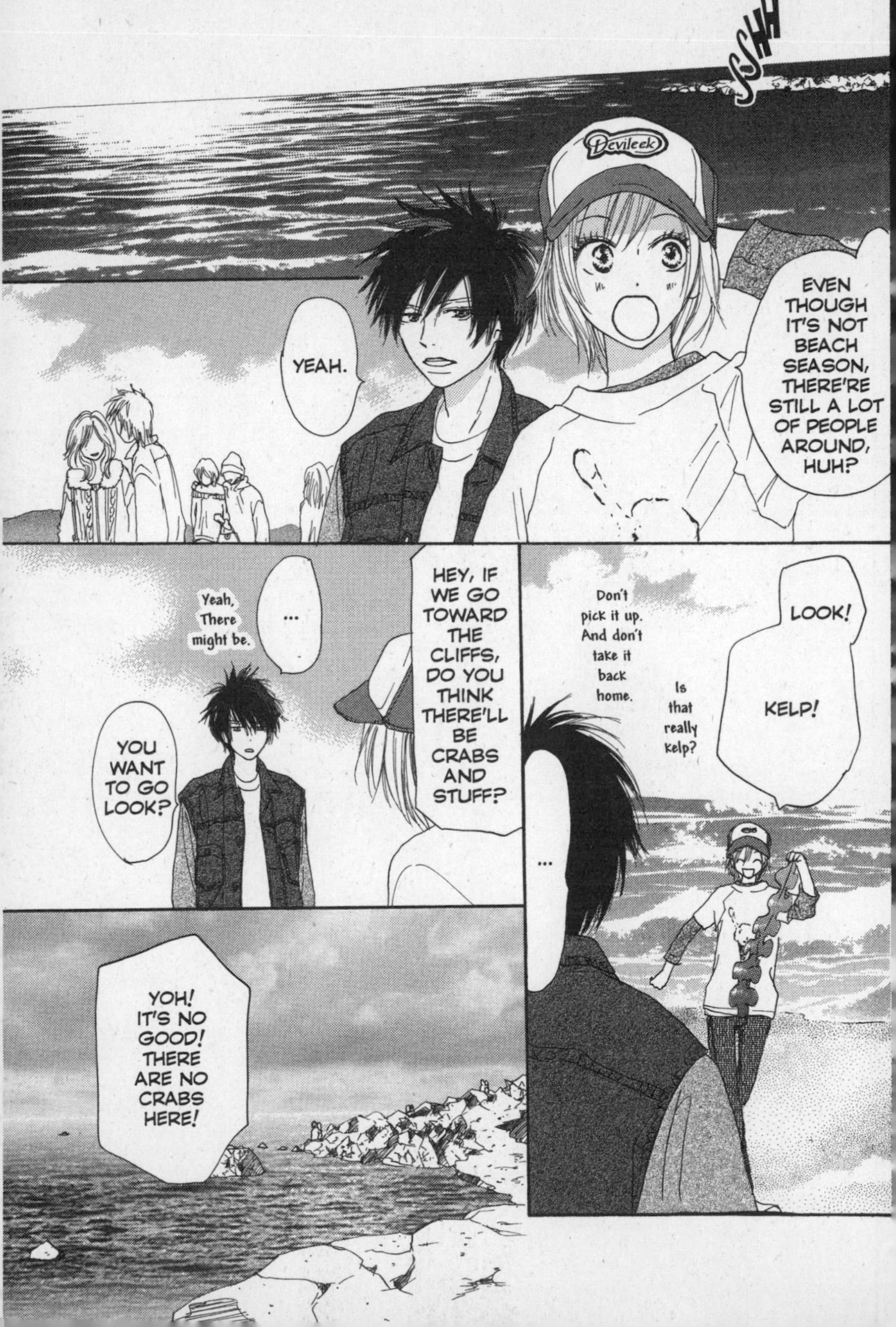
SHH
Devileek
EVEN THOUGH IT'S NOT BEACH SEASON, THERE'RE STILL A LOT OF PEOPLE AROUND, HUH?
YEAH.
LOOK! KELP!
Is that really kelp?
Don't pick it up. And don't take it back home.
...
HEY, IF WE GO TOWARD THE CLIFFS, DO YOU THINK THERE'LL BE CRABS AND STUFF?
...
Yeah, There might be.
YOU WANT TO GO LOOK?
YOH! IT'S NO GOOD! THERE ARE NO CRABS HERE!

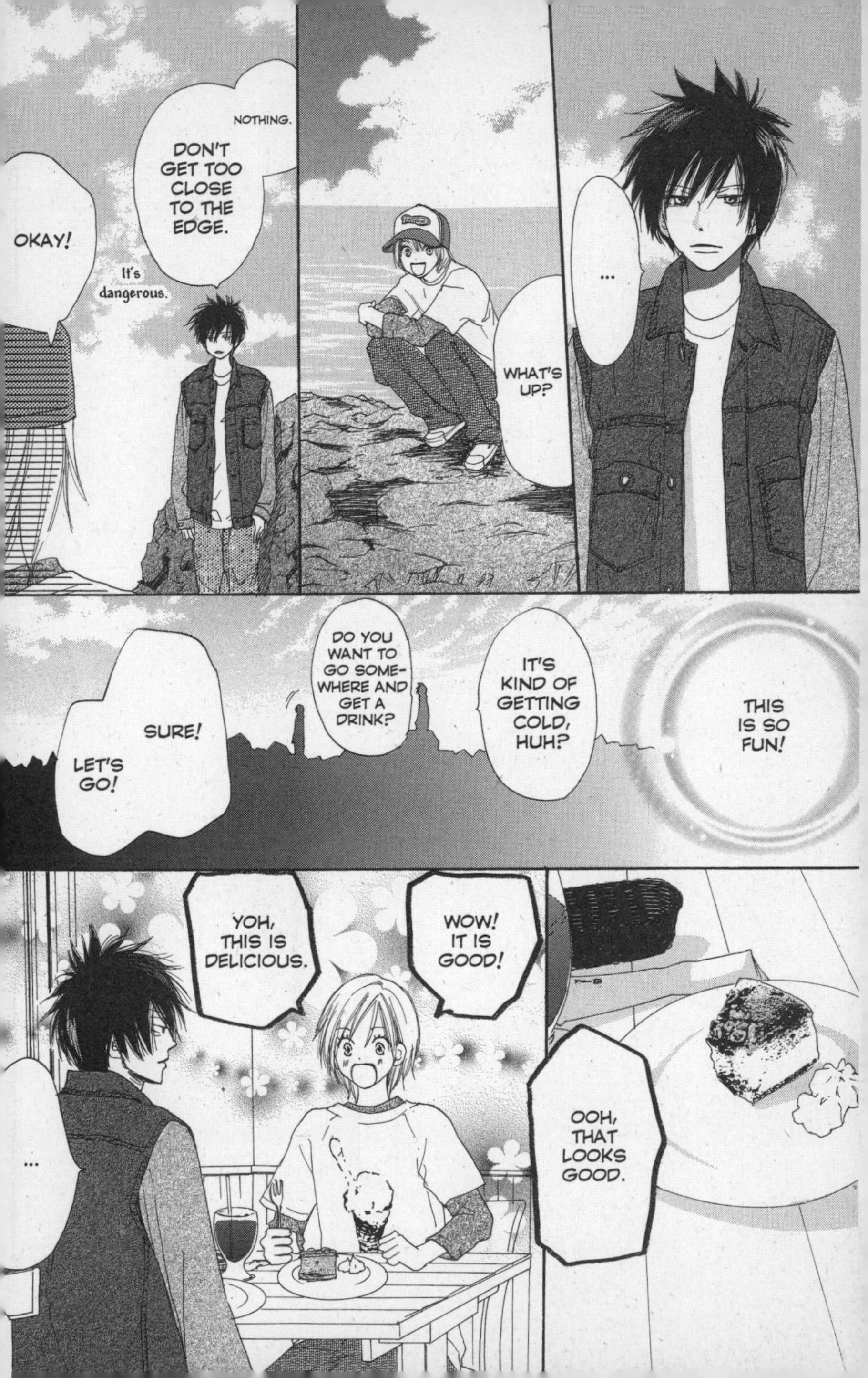
...
WHAT'S UP?
NOTHING.
DON'T GET TOO CLOSE TO THE EDGE.
It's dangerous.
OKAY!
THIS IS SO FUN!
IT'S KIND OF GETTING COLD, HUH?
DO YOU WANT TO GO SOME-WHERE AND GET A DRINK?
SURE!
LET'S GO!
OOH, THAT LOOKS GOOD.
WOW! IT IS GOOD!
YOH, THIS IS DELICIOUS.
...

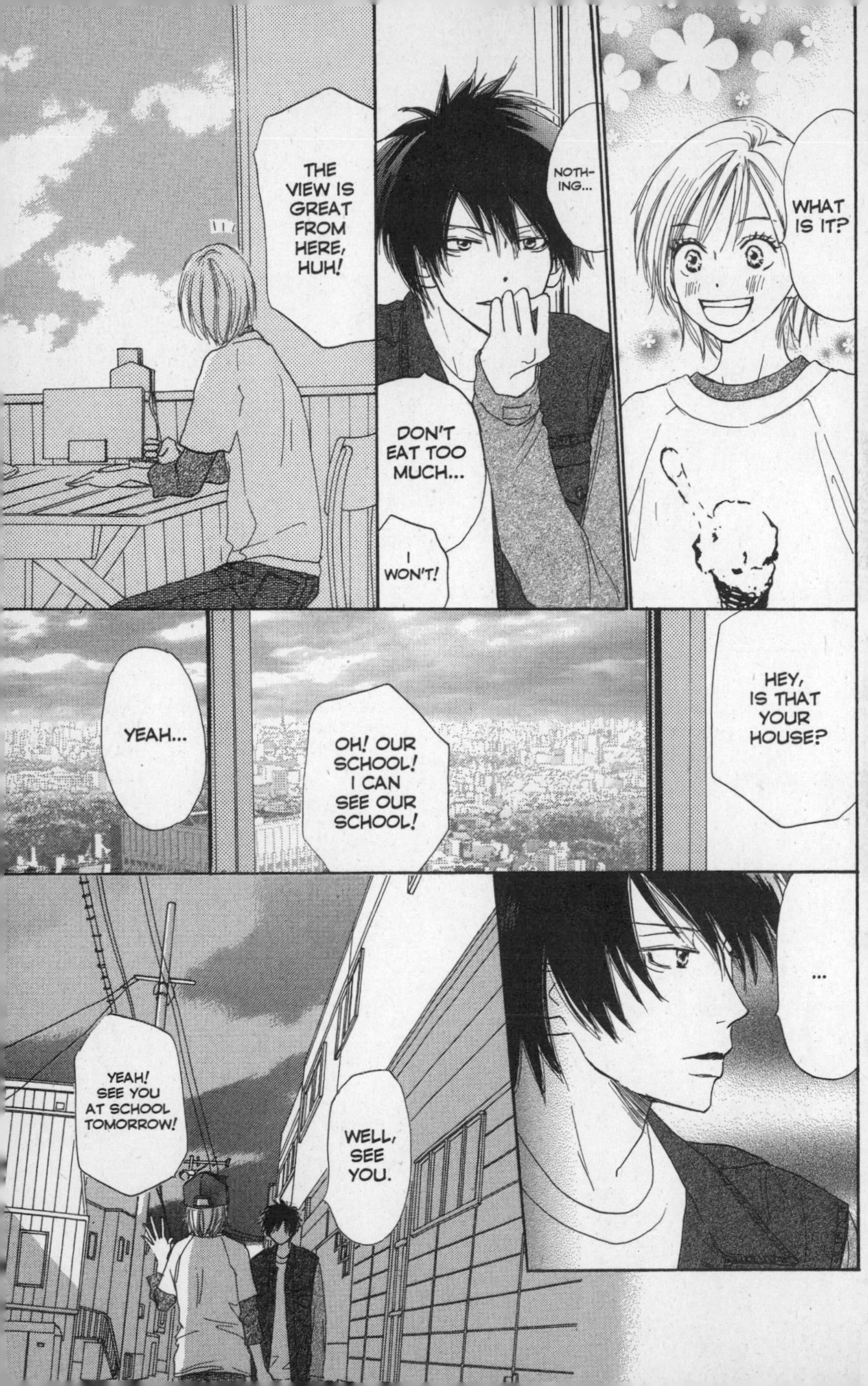
WHAT IS IT?
NOTH-ING...
DON'T EAT TOO MUCH...
I WON'T!
THE VIEW IS GREAT FROM HERE, HUH!
HEY, IS THAT YOUR HOUSE?
OH! OUR SCHOOL! I CAN SEE OUR SCHOOL!
YEAH...
...
WELL, SEE YOU.
YEAH! SEE YOU AT SCHOOL TOMORROW!

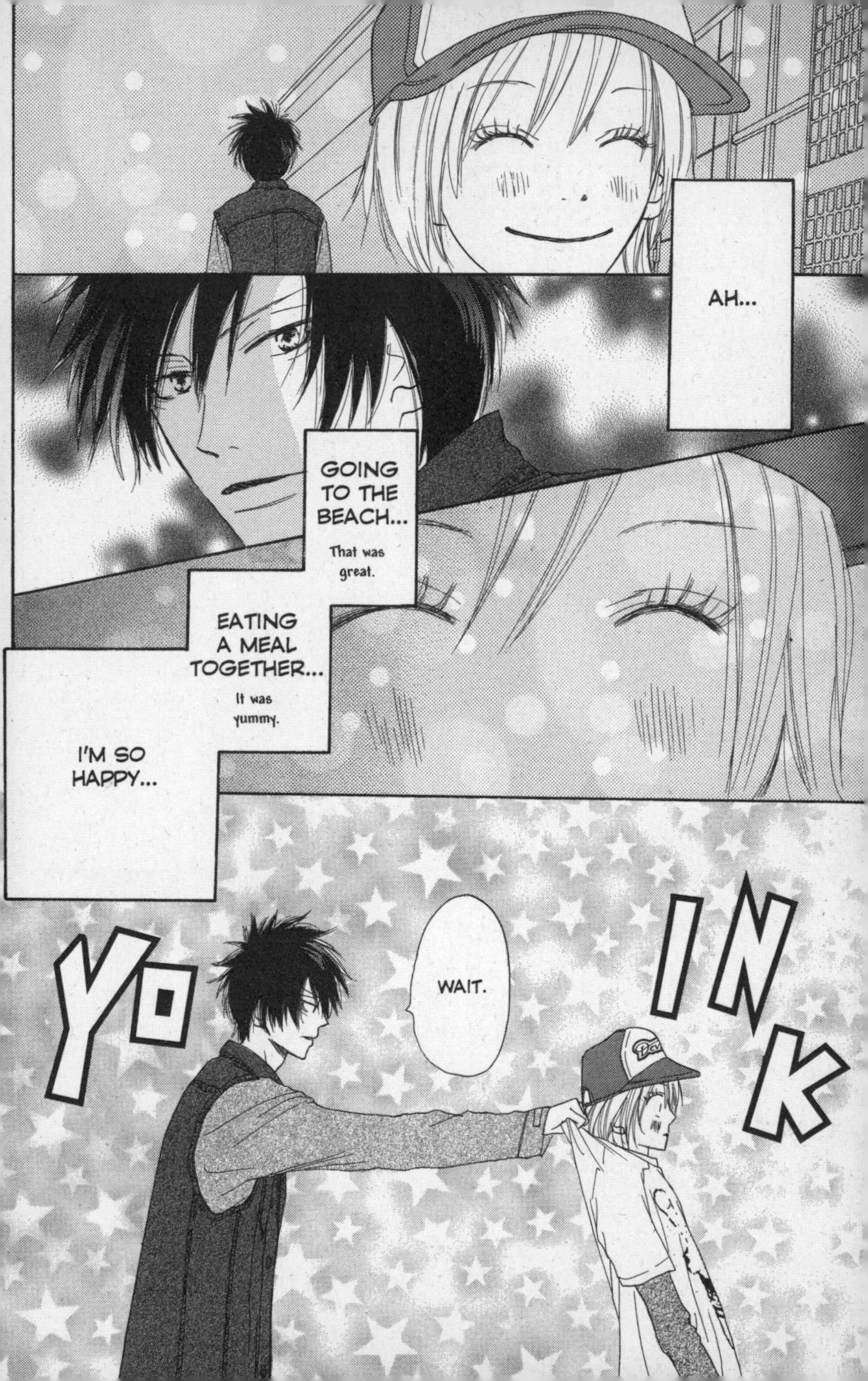
AH...
GOING TO THE BEACH...
That was great.
EATING A MEAL TOGETHER...
It was yummy.
I'M SO HAPPY...
YOINK
WAIT.

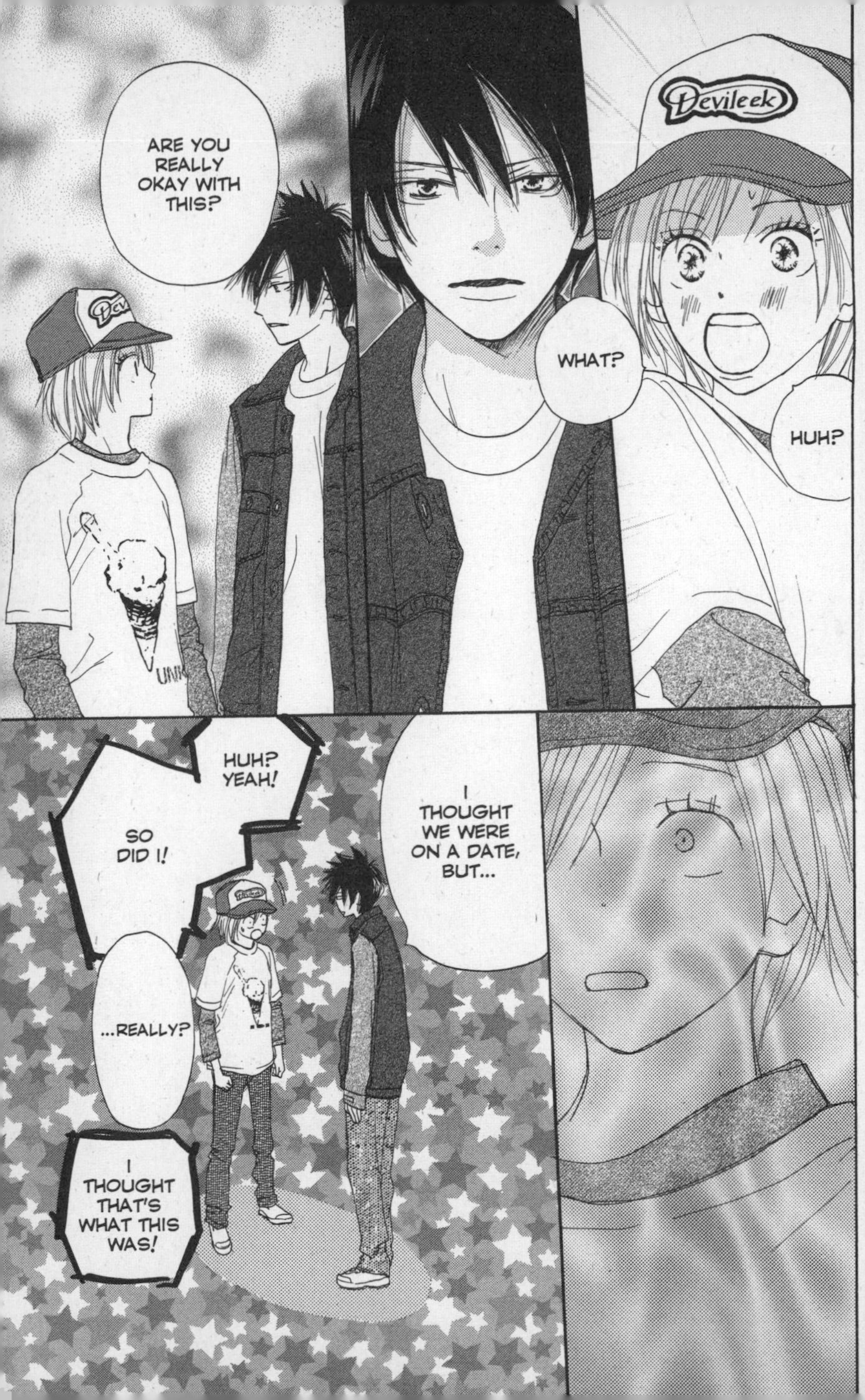
WHAT?
HUH?
ARE YOU REALLY OKAY WITH THIS?
I THOUGHT WE WERE ON A DATE, BUT...
HUH? YEAH!
SO DID I!
...REALLY?
I THOUGHT THAT'S WHAT THIS WAS!

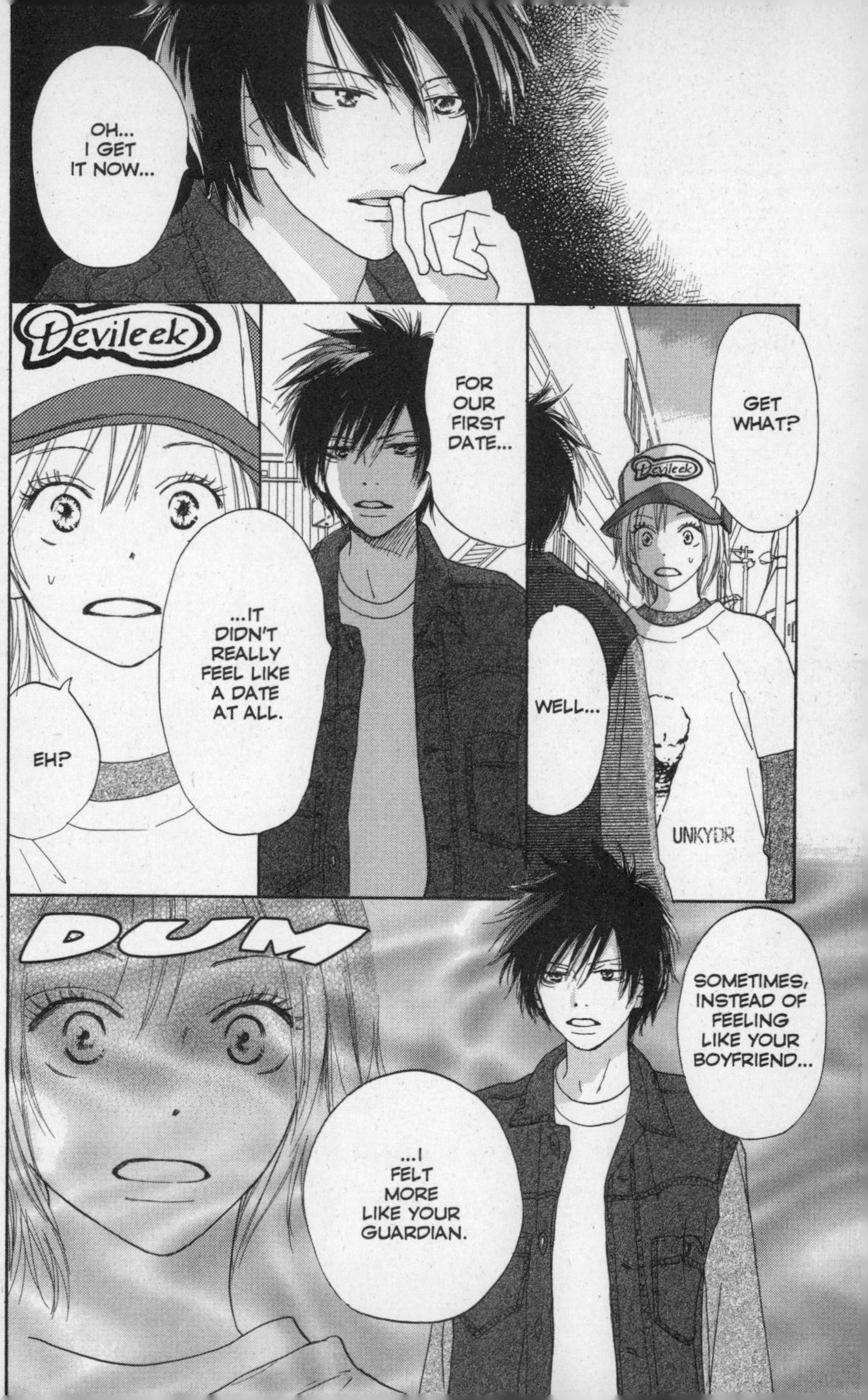
OH... I GET IT NOW...
GET WHAT?
WELL...
UNKYDR
FOR OUR FIRST DATE...
...IT DIDN'T REALLY FEEL LIKE A DATE AT ALL.
Devileek
EH?
SOMETIMES, INSTEAD OF FEELING LIKE YOUR BOYFRIEND...
DUM
...I FELT MORE LIKE YOUR GUARDIAN.

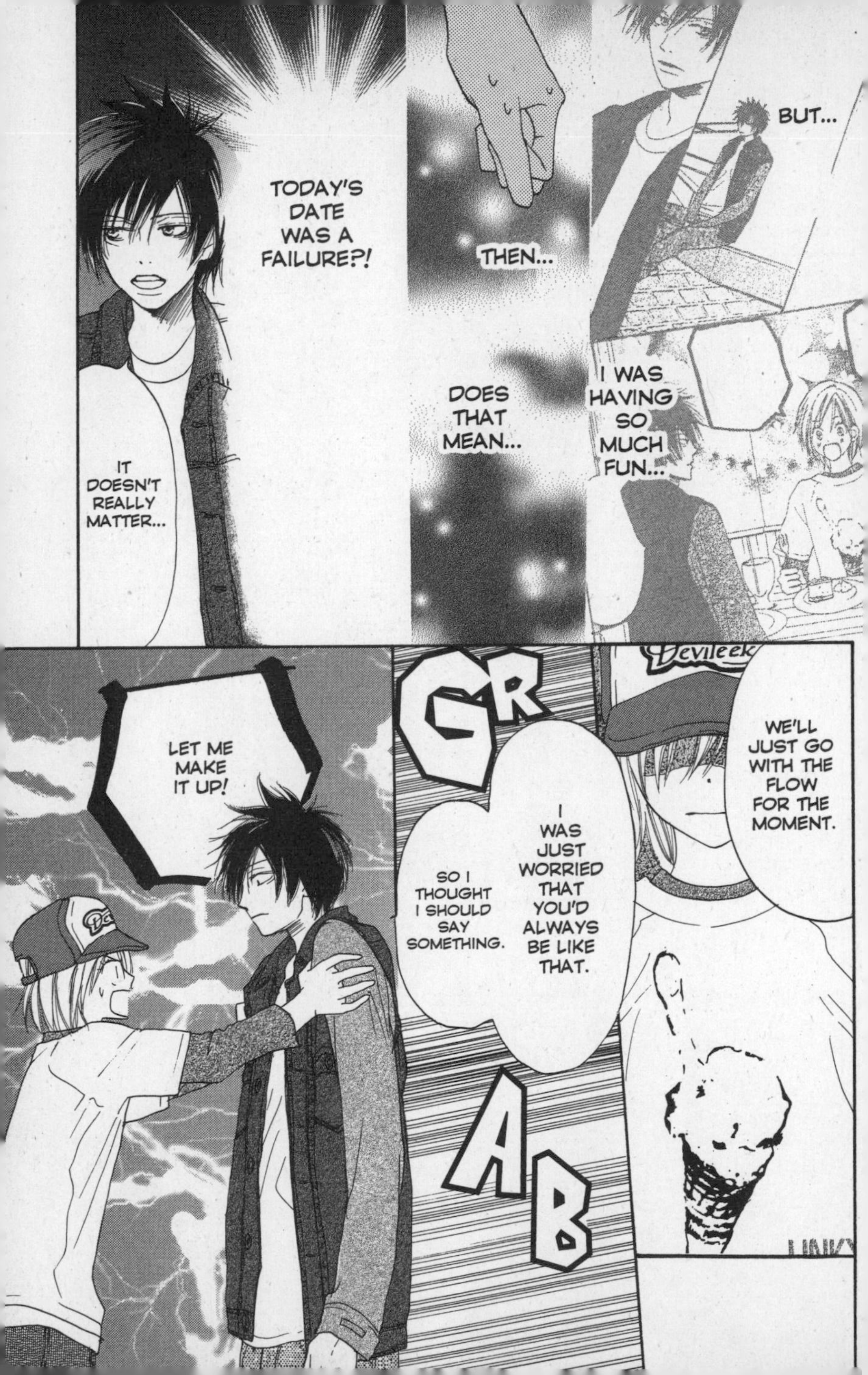
BUT...
I WAS HAVING SO MUCH FUN...
THEN...
DOES THAT MEAN...
TODAY'S DATE WAS A FAILURE?!
IT DOESN'T REALLY MATTER...
Devileek
WE'LL JUST GO WITH THE FLOW FOR THE MOMENT.
I WAS JUST WORRIED THAT YOU'D ALWAYS BE LIKE THAT.
SO I THOUGHT I SHOULD SAY SOMETHING.
GRAB
LET ME MAKE IT UP!

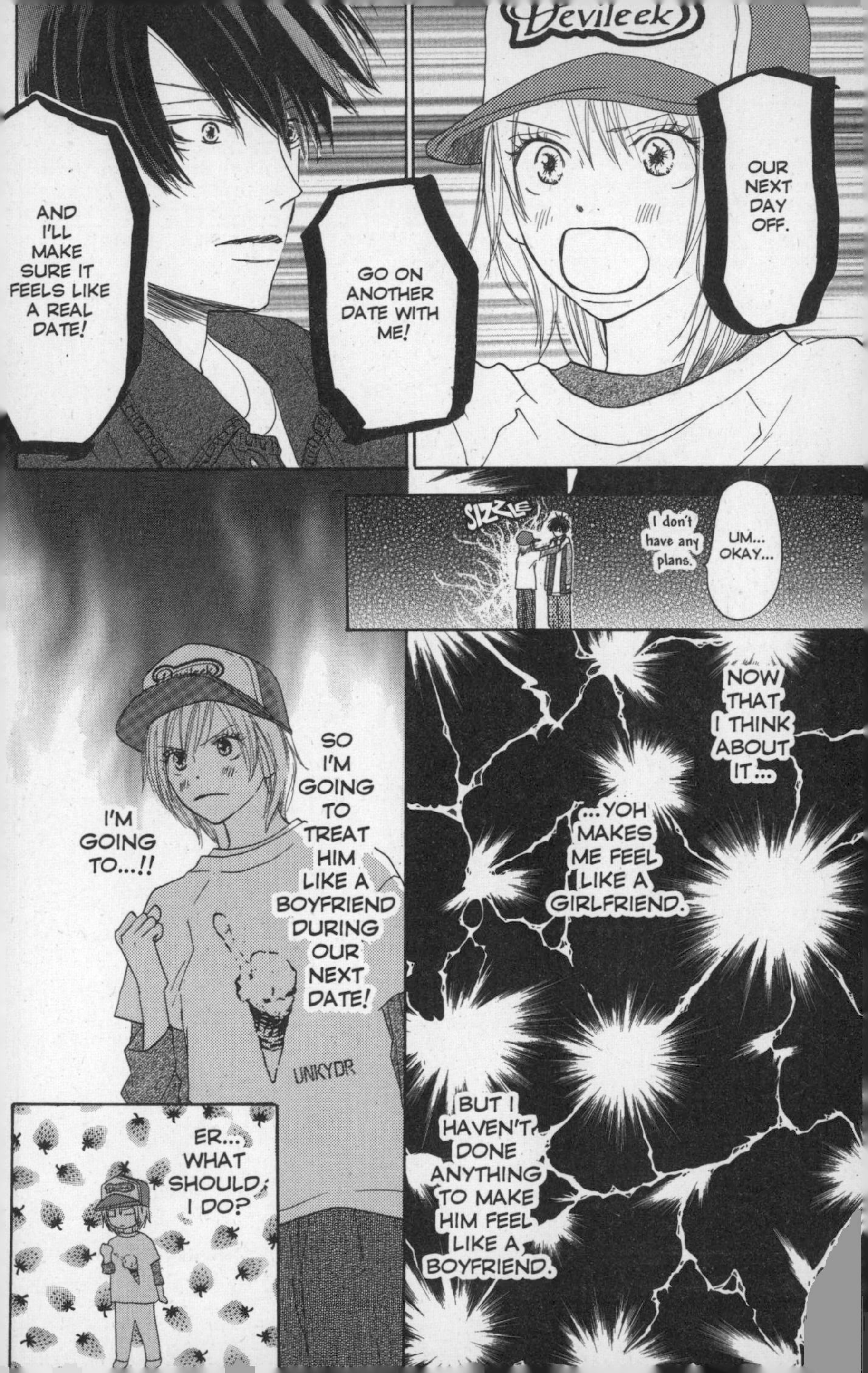
Devileek
OUR NEXT DAY OFF.
GO ON ANOTHER DATE WITH ME!
AND I'LL MAKE SURE IT FEELS LIKE A REAL DATE!
UM... OKAY...
I don't have any plans.
SIZZLE
NOW THAT I THINK ABOUT IT...
...YOH MAKES ME FEEL LIKE A GIRLFRIEND.
BUT I HAVEN'T DONE ANYTHING TO MAKE HIM FEEL LIKE A BOYFRIEND.
SO I'M GOING TO TREAT HIM LIKE A BOYFRIEND DURING OUR NEXT DATE!
I'M GOING TO...!!
UNKYDR
ER... WHAT SHOULD I DO?

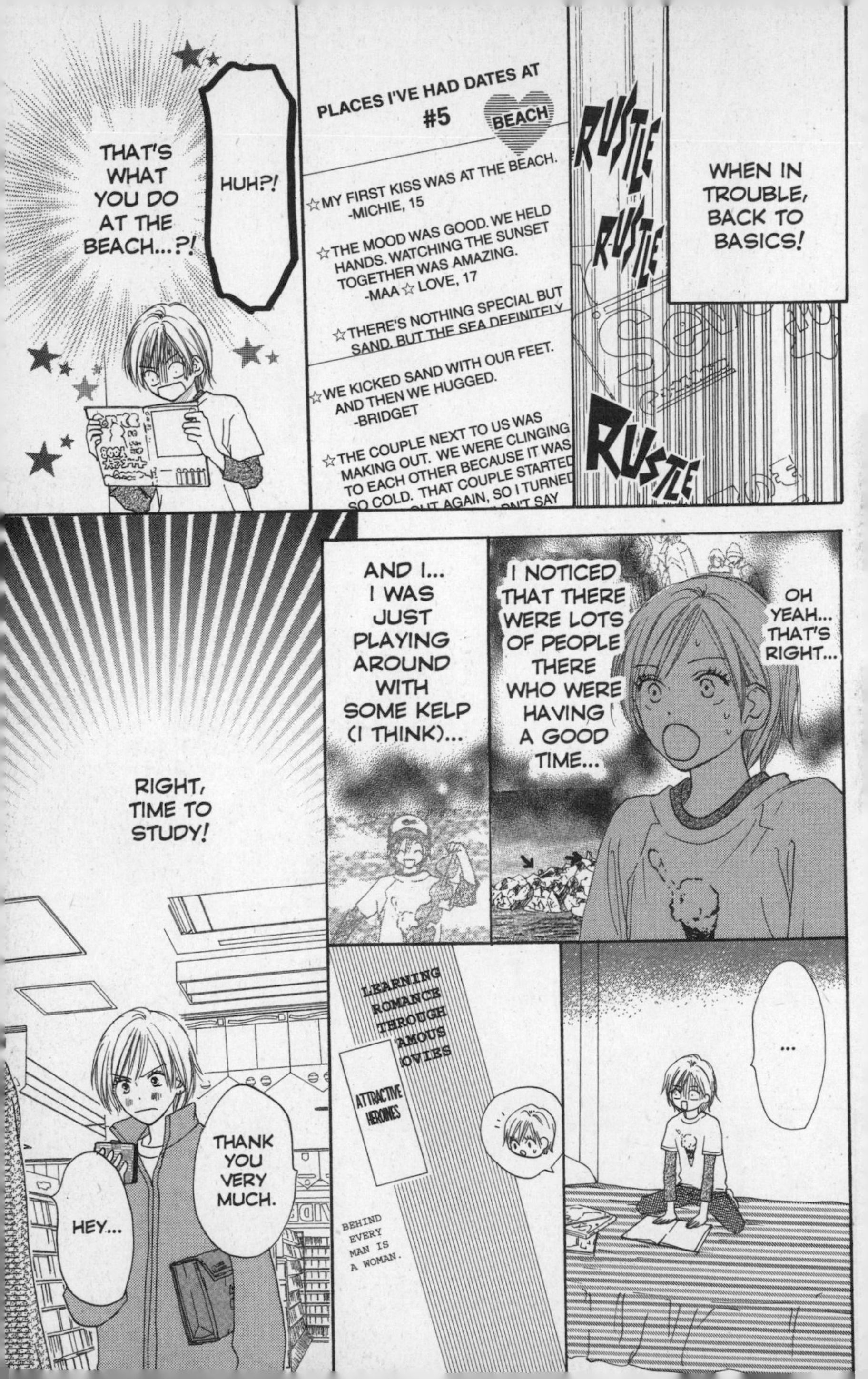
WHEN IN TROUBLE, BACK TO BASICS!
RUSTLE
RUSTLE
RUSTLE
PLACES I'VE HAD DATES AT
#5
BEACH
☆MY FIRST KISS WAS AT THE BEACH. -MICHIE, 15
☆THE MOOD WAS GOOD. WE HELD HANDS. WATCHING THE SUNSET TOGETHER WAS AMAZING. -MAA☆LOVE, 17
☆THERE'S NOTHING SPECIAL BUT SAND. BUT THE SEA DEFINITELY
☆WE KICKED SAND WITH OUR FEET. AND THEN WE HUGGED. -BRIDGET
☆THE COUPLE NEXT TO US WAS MAKING OUT. WE WERE CLINGING TO EACH OTHER BECAUSE IT WAS SO COLD. THAT COUPLE STARTED
HUH?!
THAT'S WHAT YOU DO AT THE BEACH...?!
OH YEAH... THAT'S RIGHT...
I NOTICED THAT THERE WERE LOTS OF PEOPLE THERE WHO WERE HAVING A GOOD TIME...
AND I... I WAS JUST PLAYING AROUND WITH SOME KELP (I THINK)...
...
LEARNING ROMANCE THROUGH FAMOUS MOVIES
ATTRACTIVE HEROINES
BEHIND EVERY MAN IS A WOMAN.
RIGHT, TIME TO STUDY!
THANK YOU VERY MUCH.
HEY...

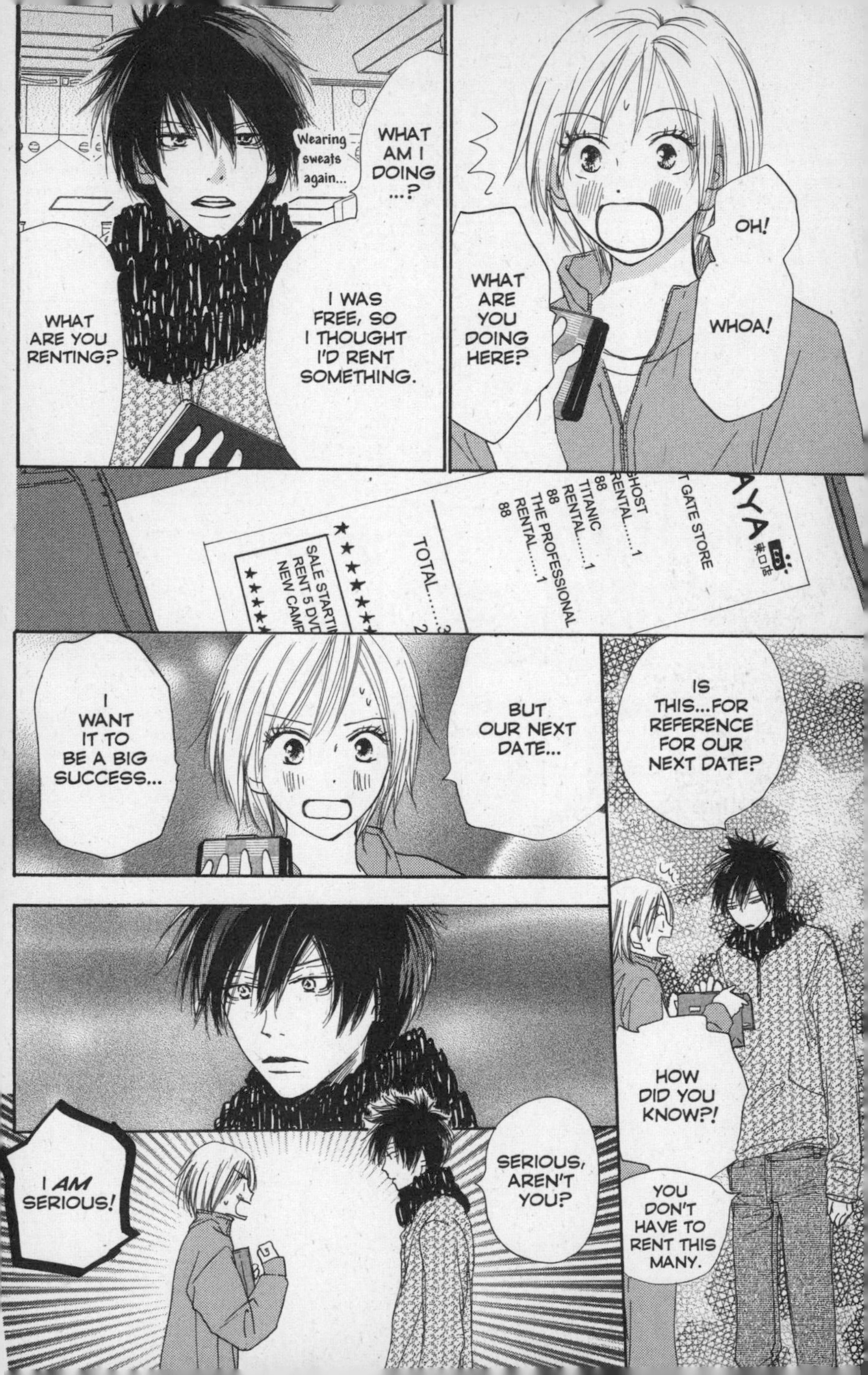
OH!
WHOA!
WHAT ARE YOU DOING HERE?
WHAT AM I DOING ...?
Wearing sweats again...
I WAS FREE, SO I THOUGHT I'D RENT SOMETHING.
WHAT ARE YOU RENTING?
東口店
GHOST
RENTAL.....1
88
TITANIC
RENTAL.....1
88
THE PROFESSIONAL
RENTAL.....1
88
IS THIS...FOR REFERENCE FOR OUR NEXT DATE?
HOW DID YOU KNOW?!
YOU DON'T HAVE TO RENT THIS MANY.
BUT OUR NEXT DATE...
I WANT IT TO BE A BIG SUCCESS...
SERIOUS, AREN'T YOU?
I *AM* SERIOUS!

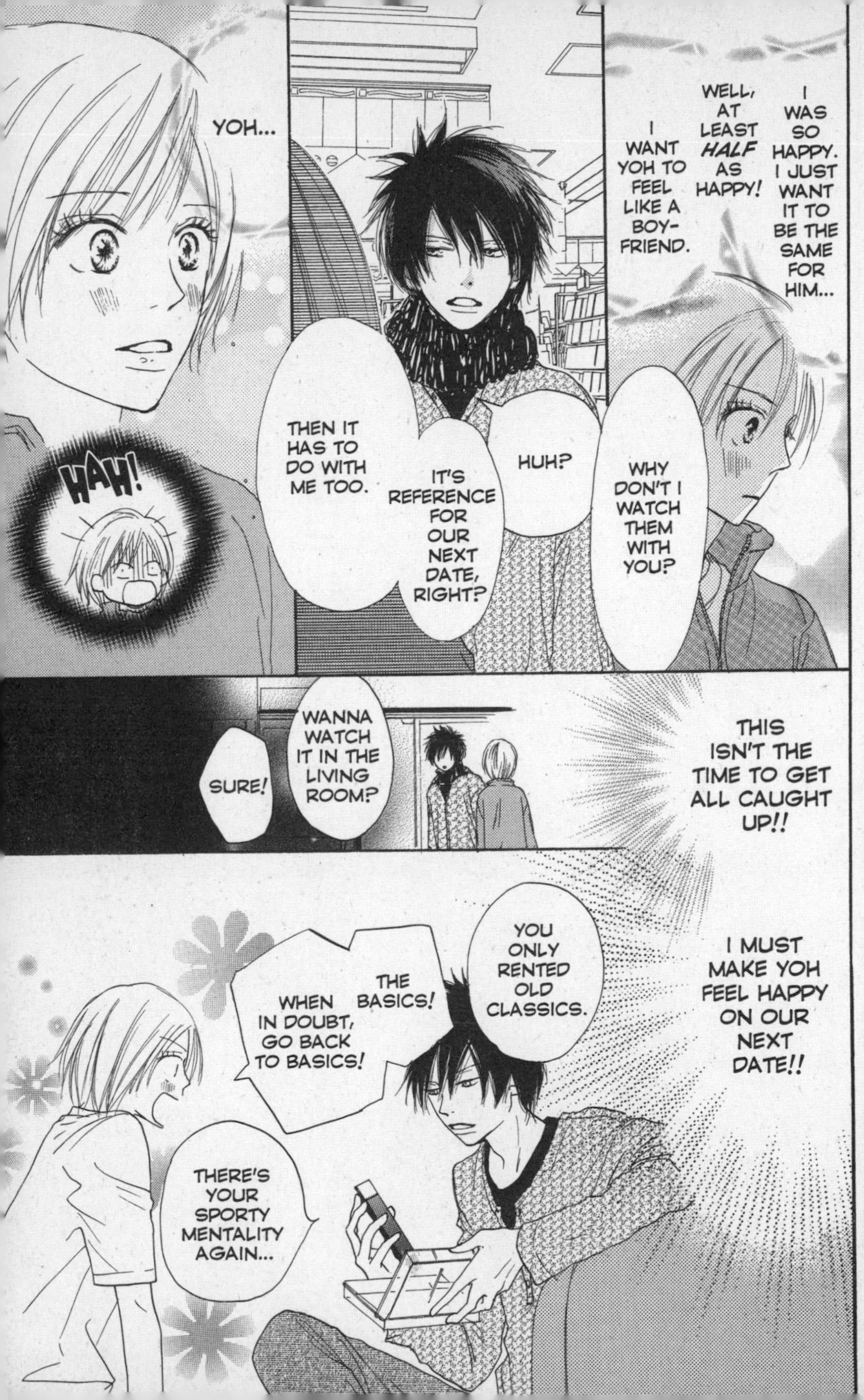
I WAS SO HAPPY. I JUST WANT IT TO BE THE SAME FOR HIM...
WELL, AT LEAST *HALF* AS HAPPY!
I WANT YOH TO FEEL LIKE A BOY-FRIEND.
WHY DON'T I WATCH THEM WITH YOU?
HUH?
IT'S REFERENCE FOR OUR NEXT DATE, RIGHT?
THEN IT HAS TO DO WITH ME TOO.
YOH...
HAH!
THIS ISN'T THE TIME TO GET ALL CAUGHT UP!!
WANNA WATCH IT IN THE LIVING ROOM?
SURE!
I MUST MAKE YOH FEEL HAPPY ON OUR NEXT DATE!!
YOU ONLY RENTED OLD CLASSICS.
THE BASICS! WHEN IN DOUBT, GO BACK TO BASICS!
THERE'S YOUR SPORTY MENTALITY AGAIN...

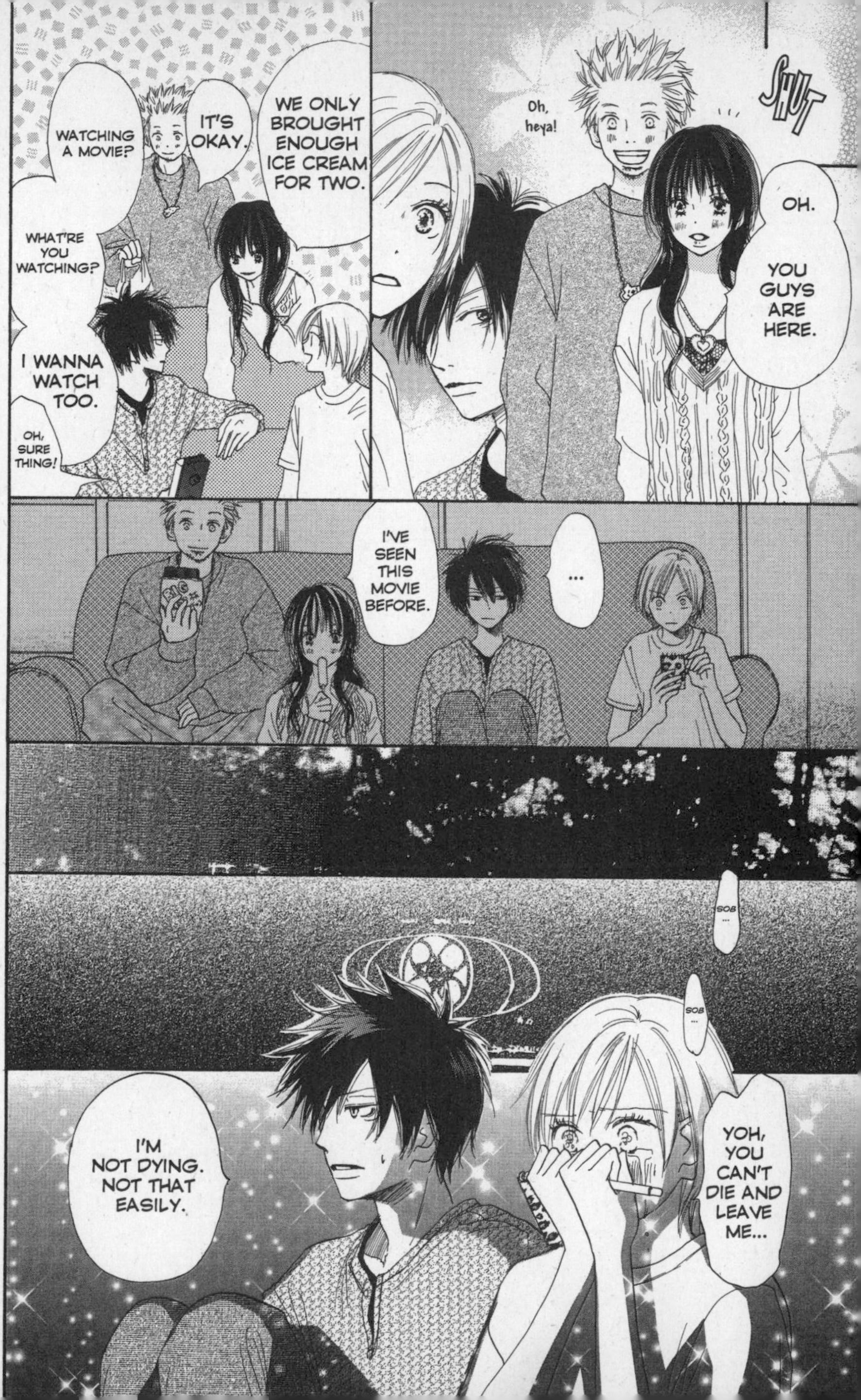
SHUT
Oh, heya!
OH.
YOU GUYS ARE HERE.
WE ONLY BROUGHT ENOUGH ICE CREAM FOR TWO.
IT'S OKAY.
WATCHING A MOVIE?
WHAT'RE YOU WATCHING?
I WANNA WATCH TOO.
OH, SURE THING!
...
I'VE SEEN THIS MOVIE BEFORE.
SOB...
SOB...
YOH, YOU CAN'T DIE AND LEAVE ME...
I'M NOT DYING. NOT THAT EASILY.

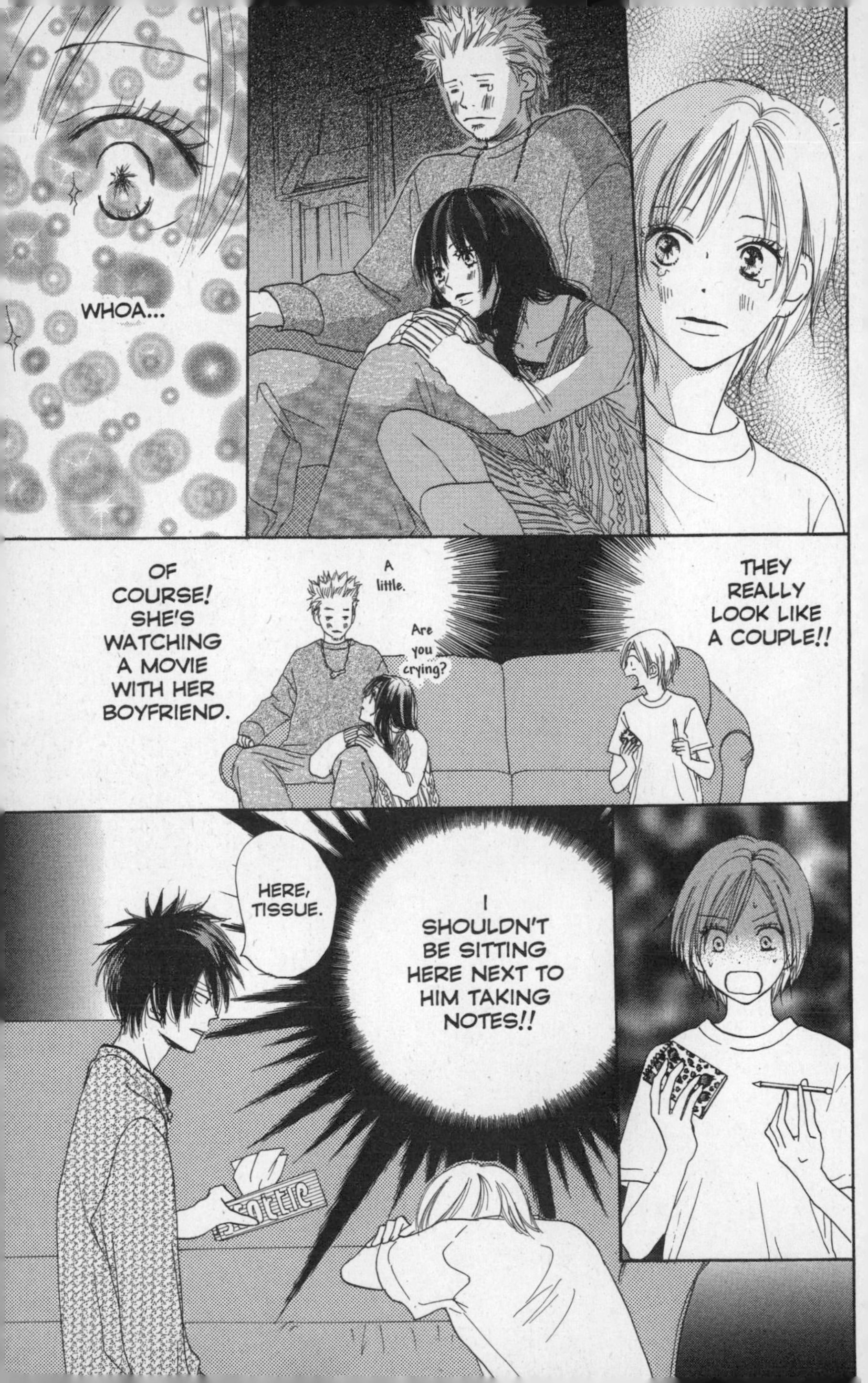
WHOA...
THEY REALLY LOOK LIKE A COUPLE!!
Are you crying?
A little.
OF COURSE! SHE'S WATCHING A MOVIE WITH HER BOYFRIEND.
I SHOULDN'T BE SITTING HERE NEXT TO HIM TAKING NOTES!!
HERE, TISSUE.

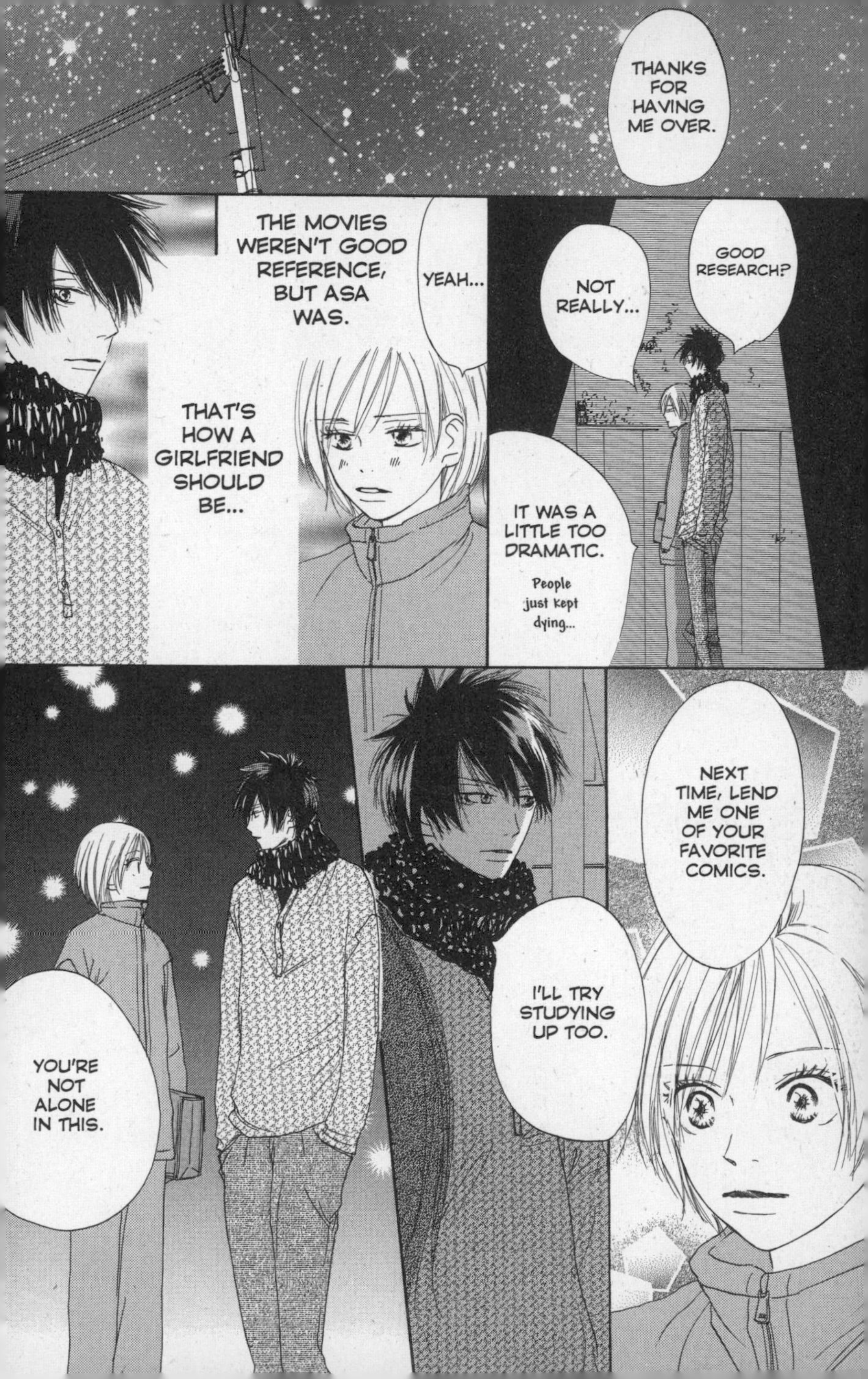
THANKS FOR HAVING ME OVER.
GOOD RESEARCH?
NOT REALLY...
IT WAS A LITTLE TOO DRAMATIC.
People just kept dying...
YEAH...
THE MOVIES WEREN'T GOOD REFERENCE, BUT ASA WAS.
THAT'S HOW A GIRLFRIEND SHOULD BE...
NEXT TIME, LEND ME ONE OF YOUR FAVORITE COMICS.
I'LL TRY STUDYING UP TOO.
YOU'RE NOT ALONE IN THIS.

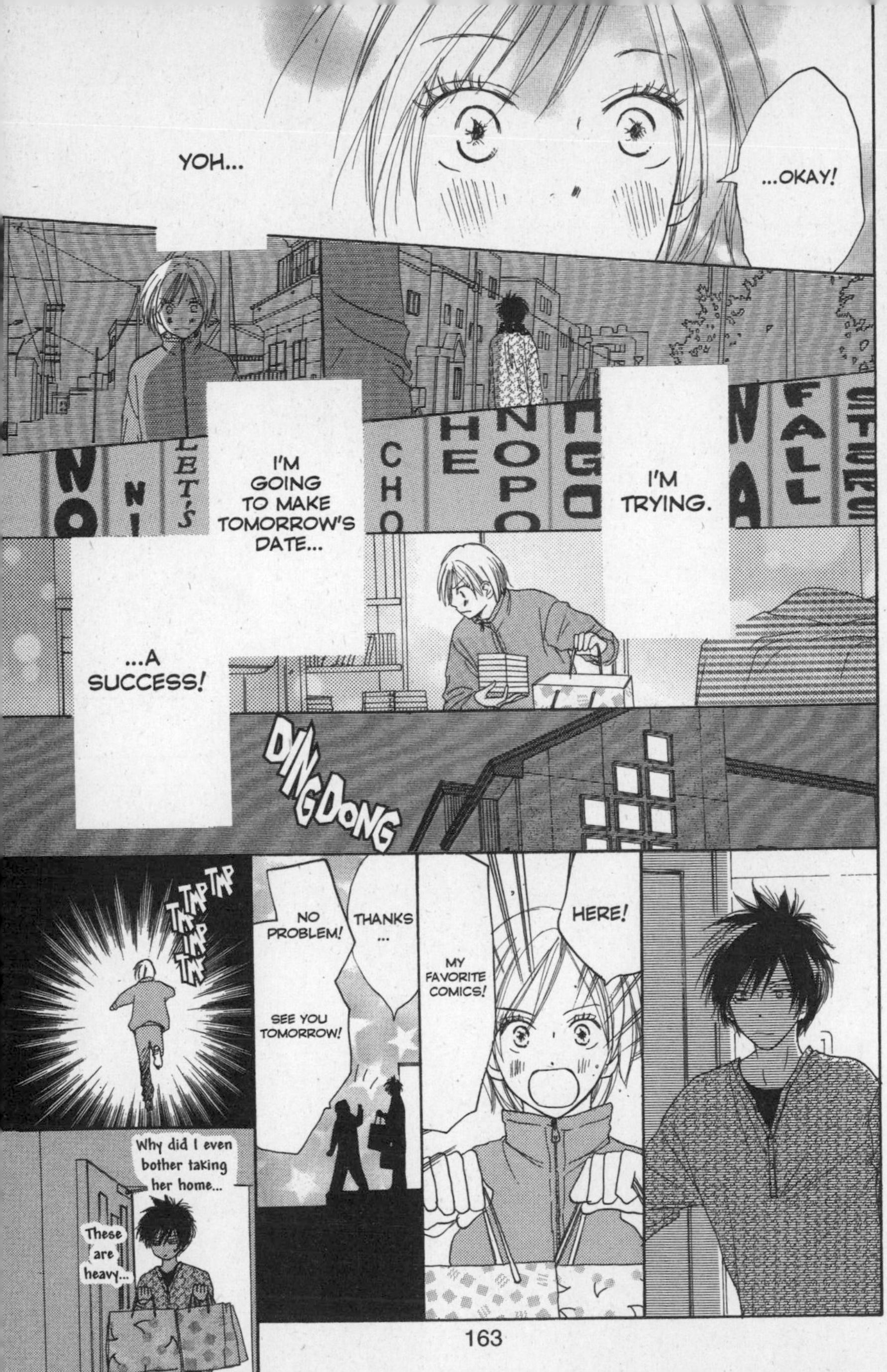
...OKAY!
YOH...
I'M TRYING.
I'M GOING TO MAKE TOMORROW'S DATE...
...A SUCCESS!
DING DONG
HERE!
MY FAVORITE COMICS!
THANKS...
NO PROBLEM!
SEE YOU TOMORROW!
TMP TMP TMP TMP TMP
Why did I even bother taking her home...
These are heavy...

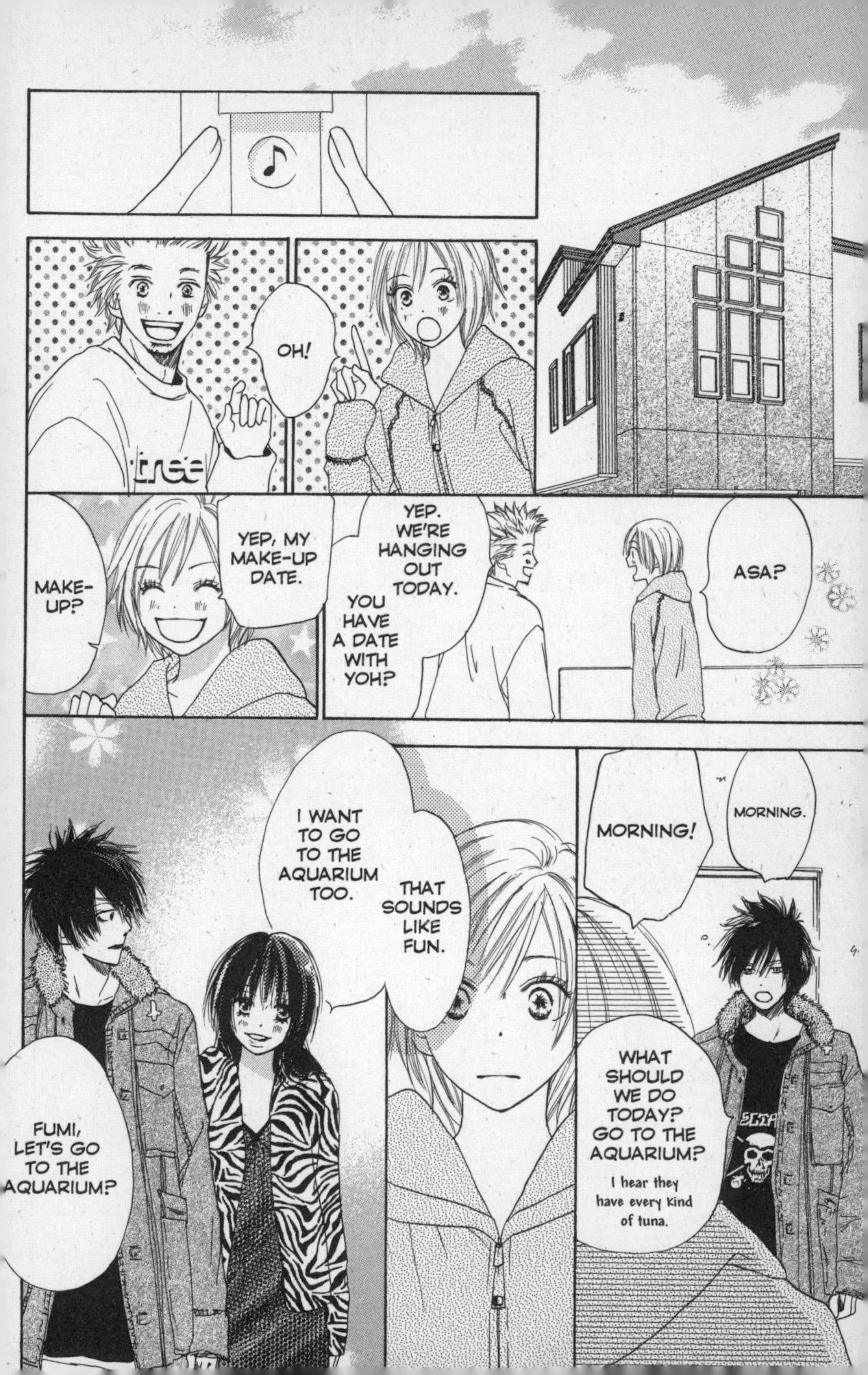
OH!
ASA?
YEP. WE'RE HANGING OUT TODAY.
YOU HAVE A DATE WITH YOH?
YEP, MY MAKE-UP DATE.
MAKE-UP?
MORNING.
MORNING!
WHAT SHOULD WE DO TODAY? GO TO THE AQUARIUM?
I hear they have every kind of tuna.
I WANT TO GO TO THE AQUARIUM TOO.
THAT SOUNDS LIKE FUN.
FUMI, LET'S GO TO THE AQUARIUM?

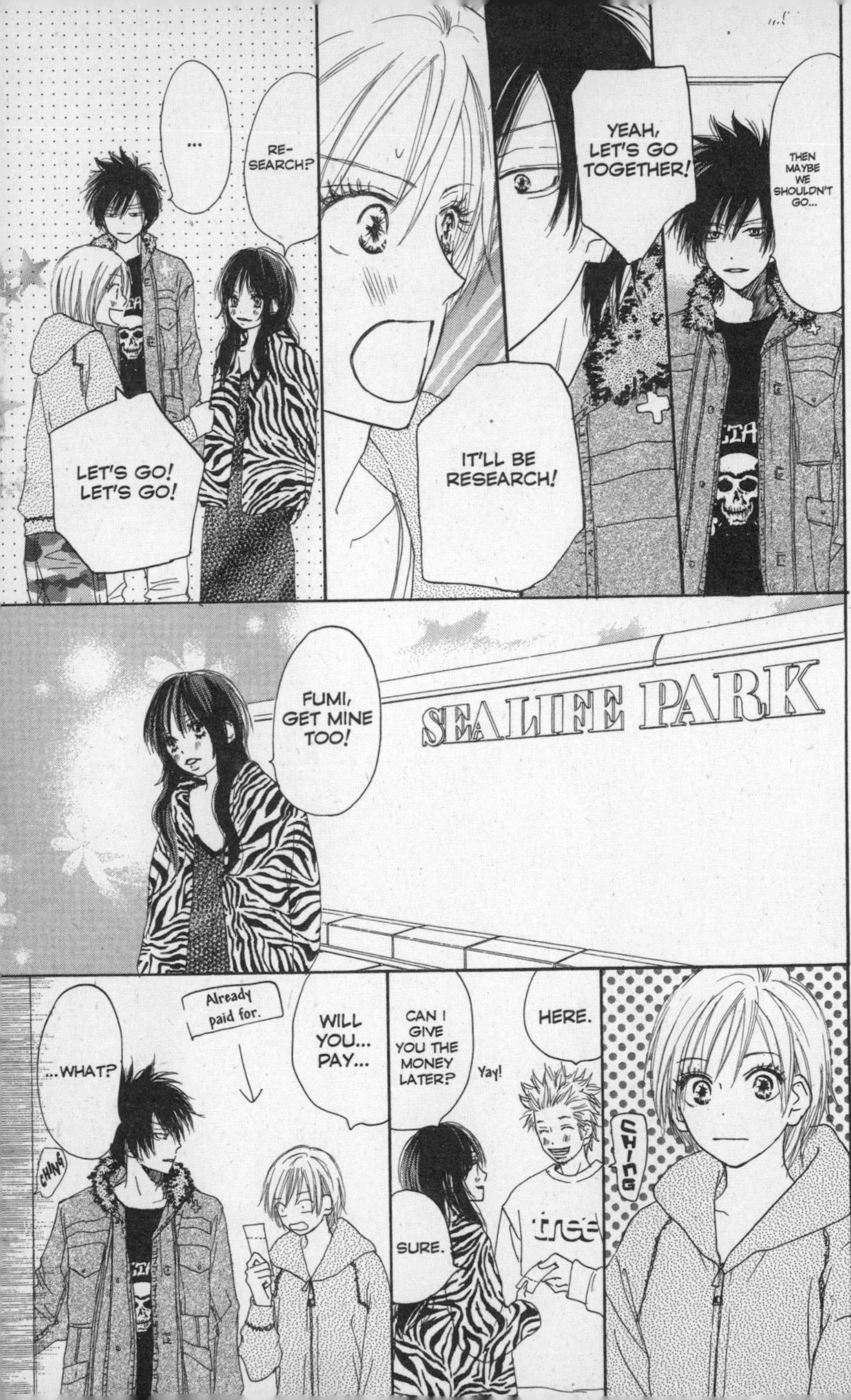
THEN MAYBE WE SHOULDN'T GO...
YEAH, LET'S GO TOGETHER!
IT'LL BE RESEARCH!
RE-SEARCH?
...
LET'S GO! LET'S GO!
SEALIFE PARK
FUMI, GET MINE TOO!
CHING
HERE.
Yay!
CAN I GIVE YOU THE MONEY LATER?
SURE.
WILL YOU... PAY...
Already paid for.
...WHAT?
CHING

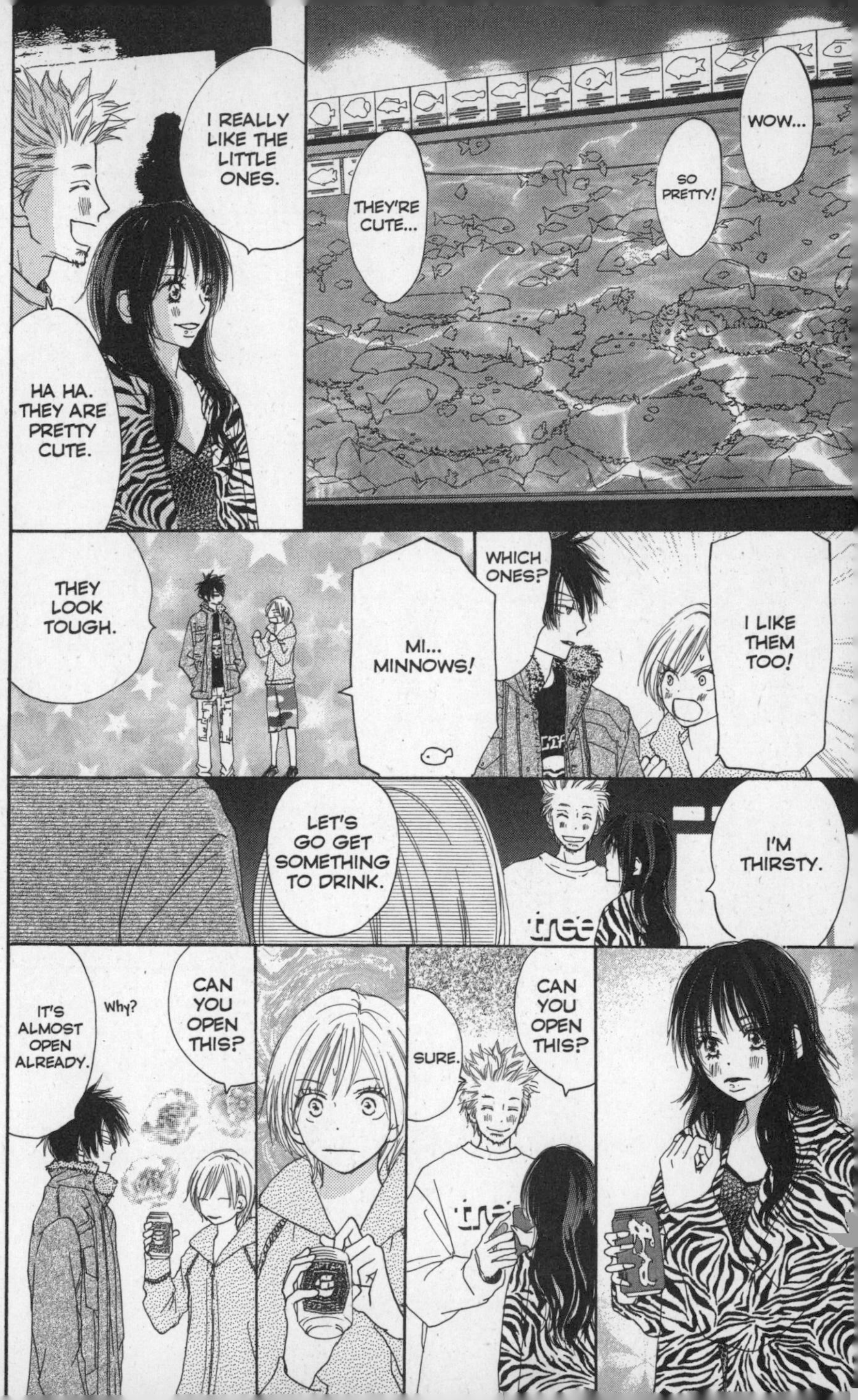
WOW...
SO PRETTY!
THEY'RE CUTE...
I REALLY LIKE THE LITTLE ONES.
HA HA. THEY ARE PRETTY CUTE.
I LIKE THEM TOO!
WHICH ONES?
MI... MINNOWS!
THEY LOOK TOUGH.
I'M THIRSTY.
LET'S GO GET SOMETHING TO DRINK.
CAN YOU OPEN THIS?
SURE.
CAN YOU OPEN THIS?
Why?
IT'S ALMOST OPEN ALREADY.

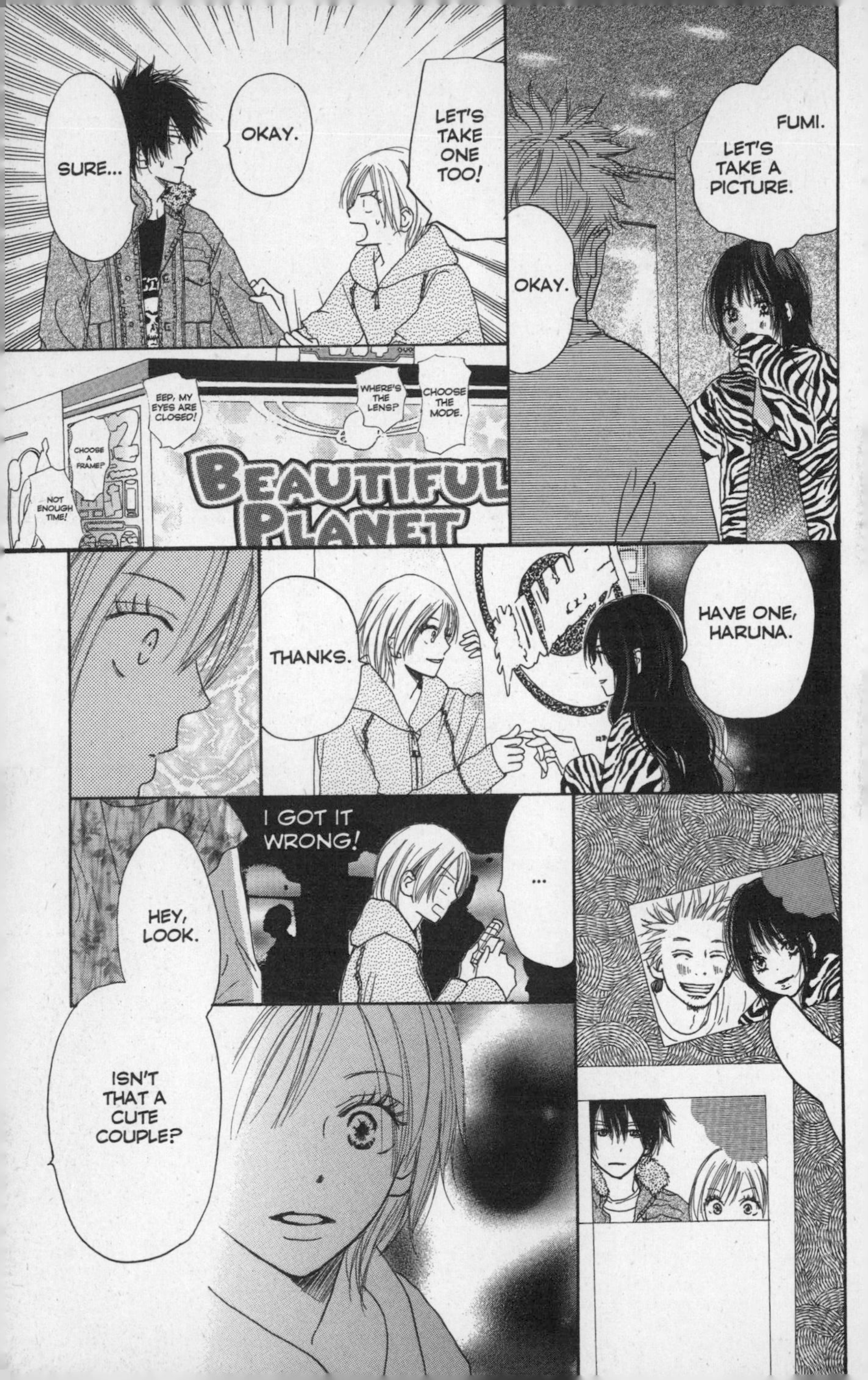
FUMI.
LET'S TAKE A PICTURE.
OKAY.
LET'S TAKE ONE TOO!
OKAY.
SURE...
CHOOSE THE MODE.
WHERE'S THE LENS?
EEP, MY EYES ARE CLOSED!
CHOOSE A FRAME?
NOT ENOUGH TIME!
BEAUTIFUL PLANET
HAVE ONE, HARUNA.
THANKS.
...
I GOT IT WRONG!
HEY, LOOK.
ISN'T THAT A CUTE COUPLE?

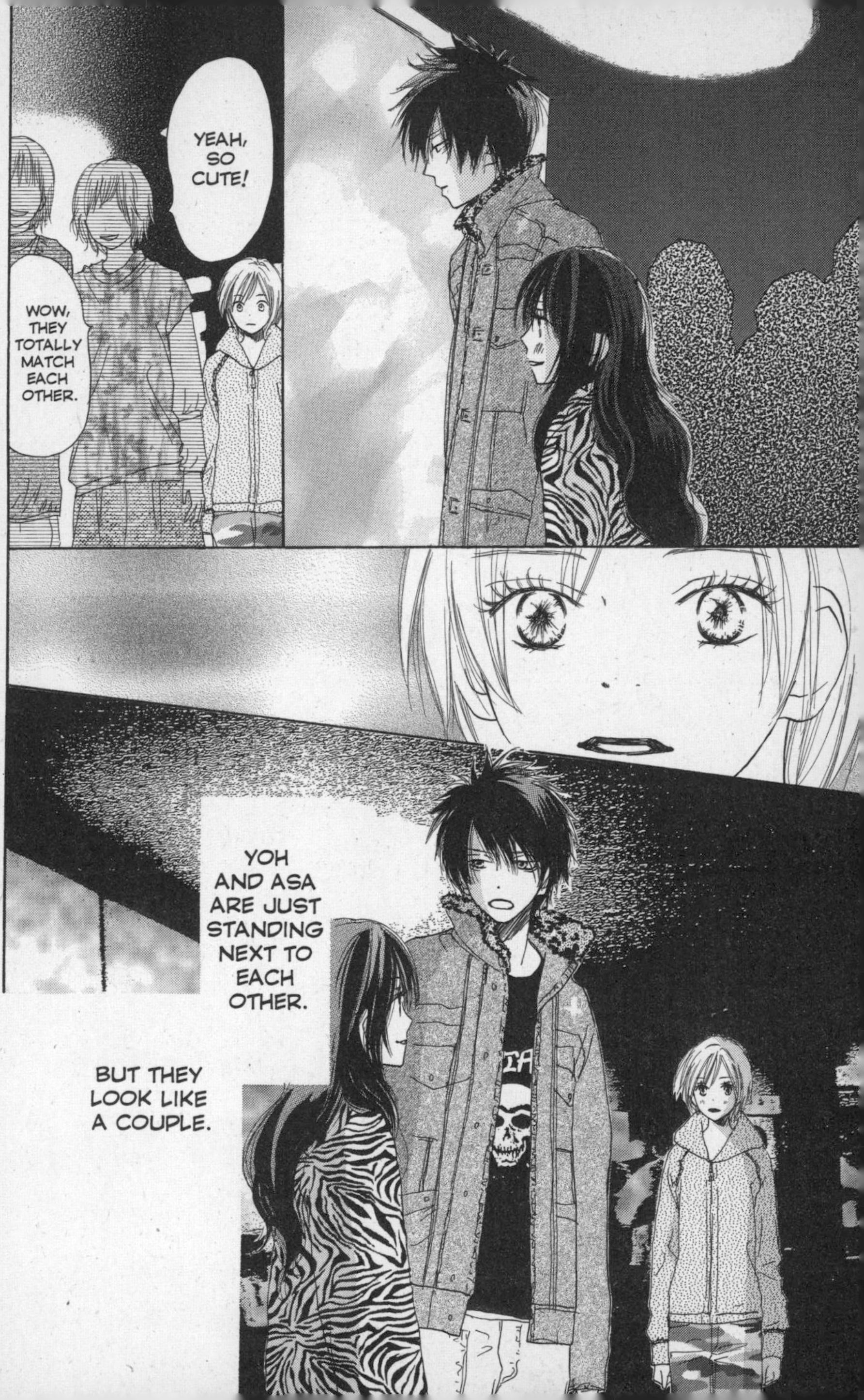
YEAH, SO CUTE!
WOW, THEY TOTALLY MATCH EACH OTHER.
YOH AND ASA ARE JUST STANDING NEXT TO EACH OTHER.
BUT THEY LOOK LIKE A COUPLE.

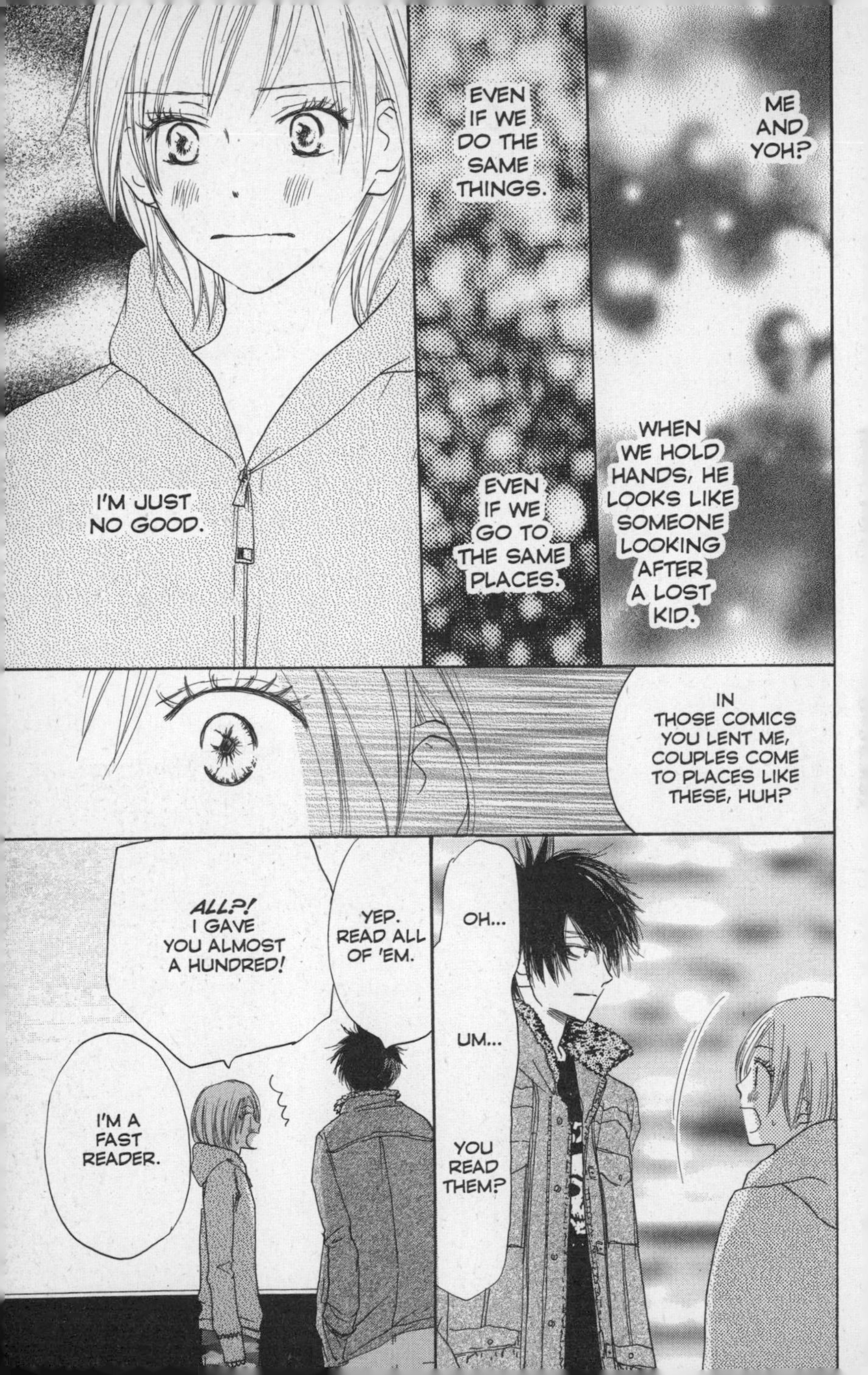
ME AND YOH?
WHEN WE HOLD HANDS, HE LOOKS LIKE SOMEONE LOOKING AFTER A LOST KID.
EVEN IF WE DO THE SAME THINGS.
EVEN IF WE GO TO THE SAME PLACES.
I'M JUST NO GOOD.
IN THOSE COMICS YOU LENT ME, COUPLES COME TO PLACES LIKE THESE, HUH?
OH...
UM...
YOU READ THEM?
YEP. READ ALL OF 'EM.
ALL?! I GAVE YOU ALMOST A HUNDRED!
I'M A FAST READER.

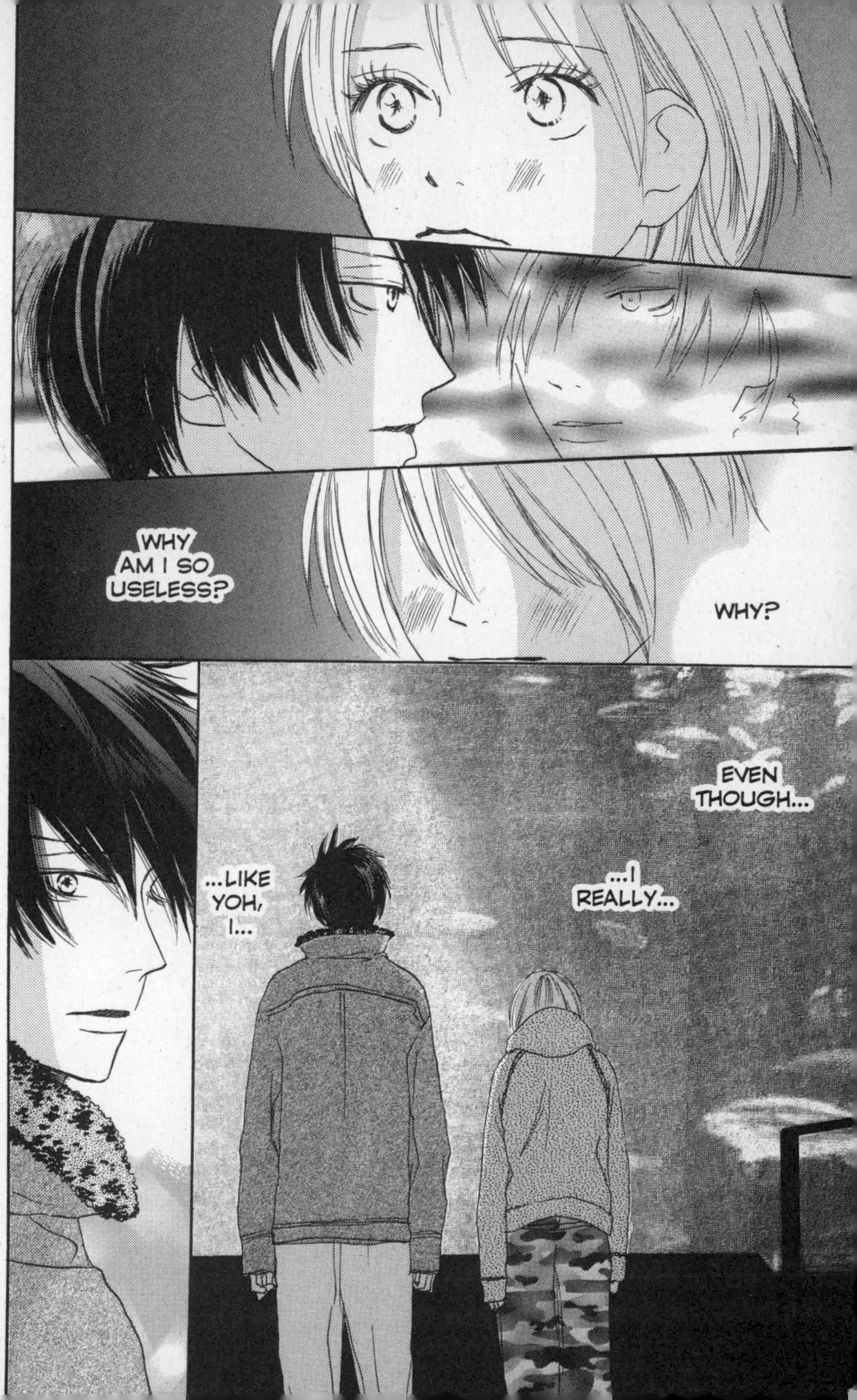
WHY?
WHY AM I SO USELESS?
EVEN THOUGH...
...I REALLY...
...LIKE YOH, I...

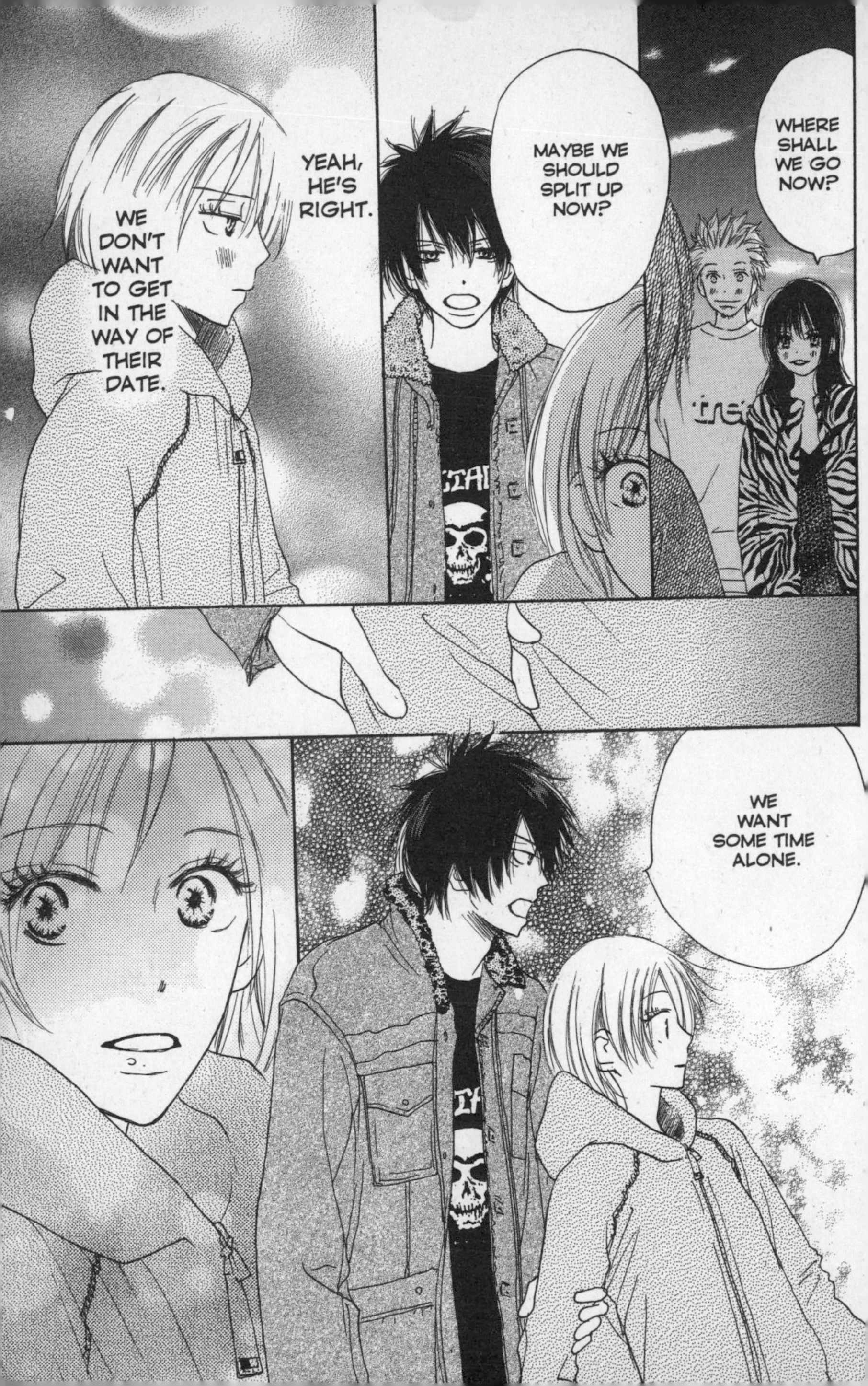
WHERE SHALL WE GO NOW?
MAYBE WE SHOULD SPLIT UP NOW?
YEAH, HE'S RIGHT.
WE DON'T WANT TO GET IN THE WAY OF THEIR DATE.
WE WANT SOME TIME ALONE.

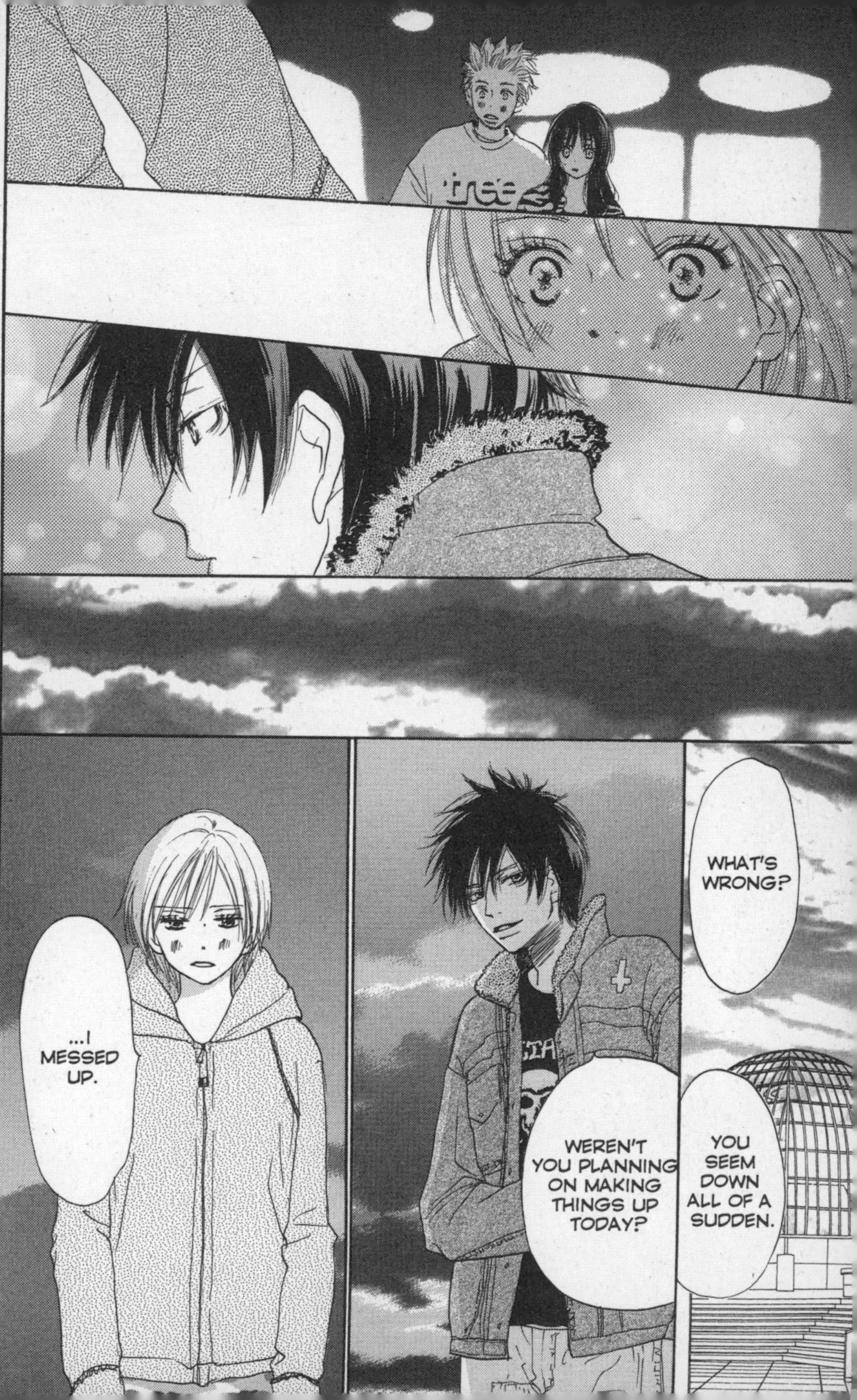
WHAT'S WRONG?
YOU SEEM DOWN ALL OF A SUDDEN.
WEREN'T YOU PLANNING ON MAKING THINGS UP TODAY?
...I MESSED UP.

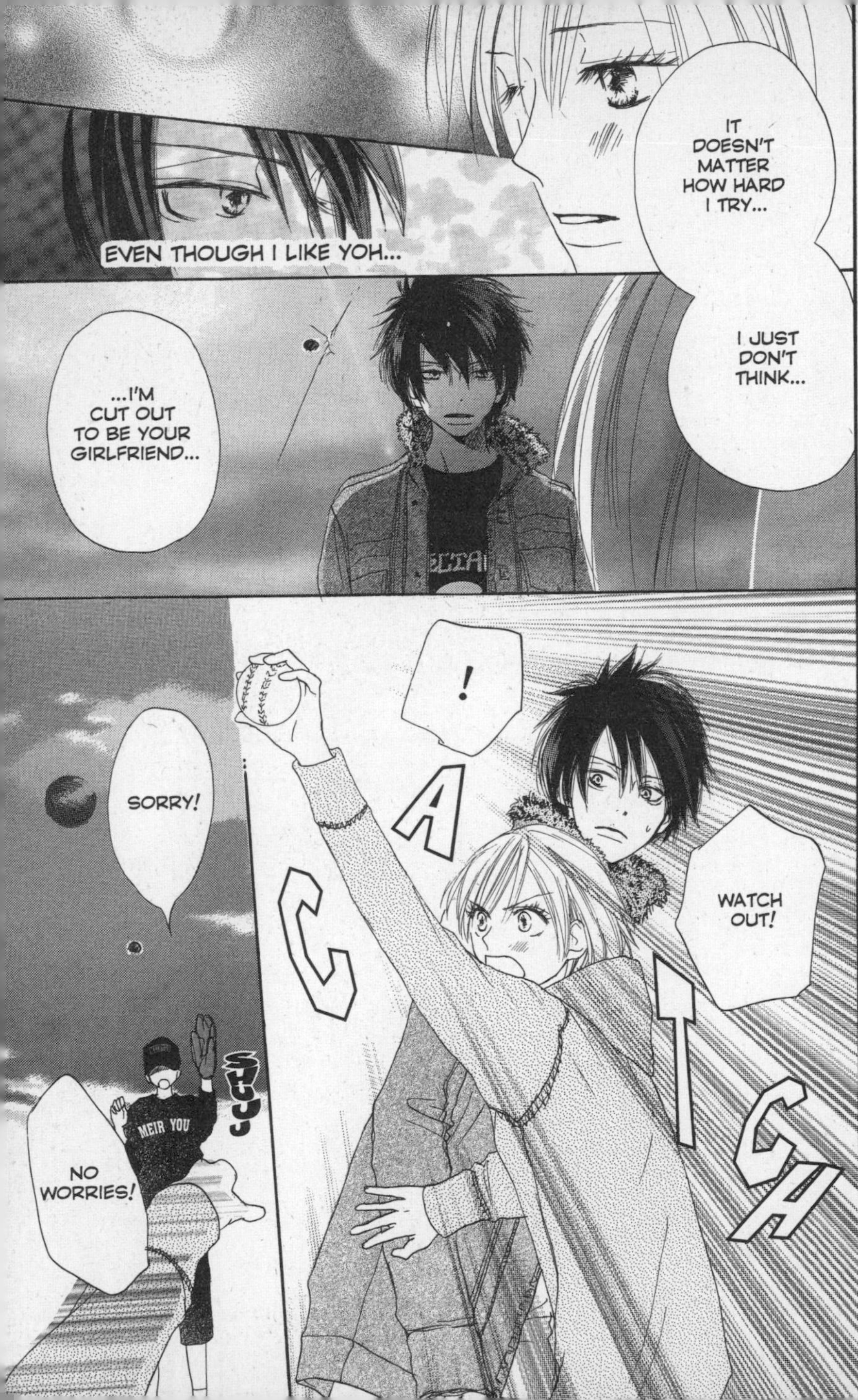
IT DOESN'T MATTER HOW HARD I TRY...
EVEN THOUGH I LIKE YOH...
I JUST DON'T THINK...
...I'M CUT OUT TO BE YOUR GIRLFRIEND...
!
WATCH OUT!
CATCH
SORRY!
SHUU
MEIR YOU
NO WORRIES!

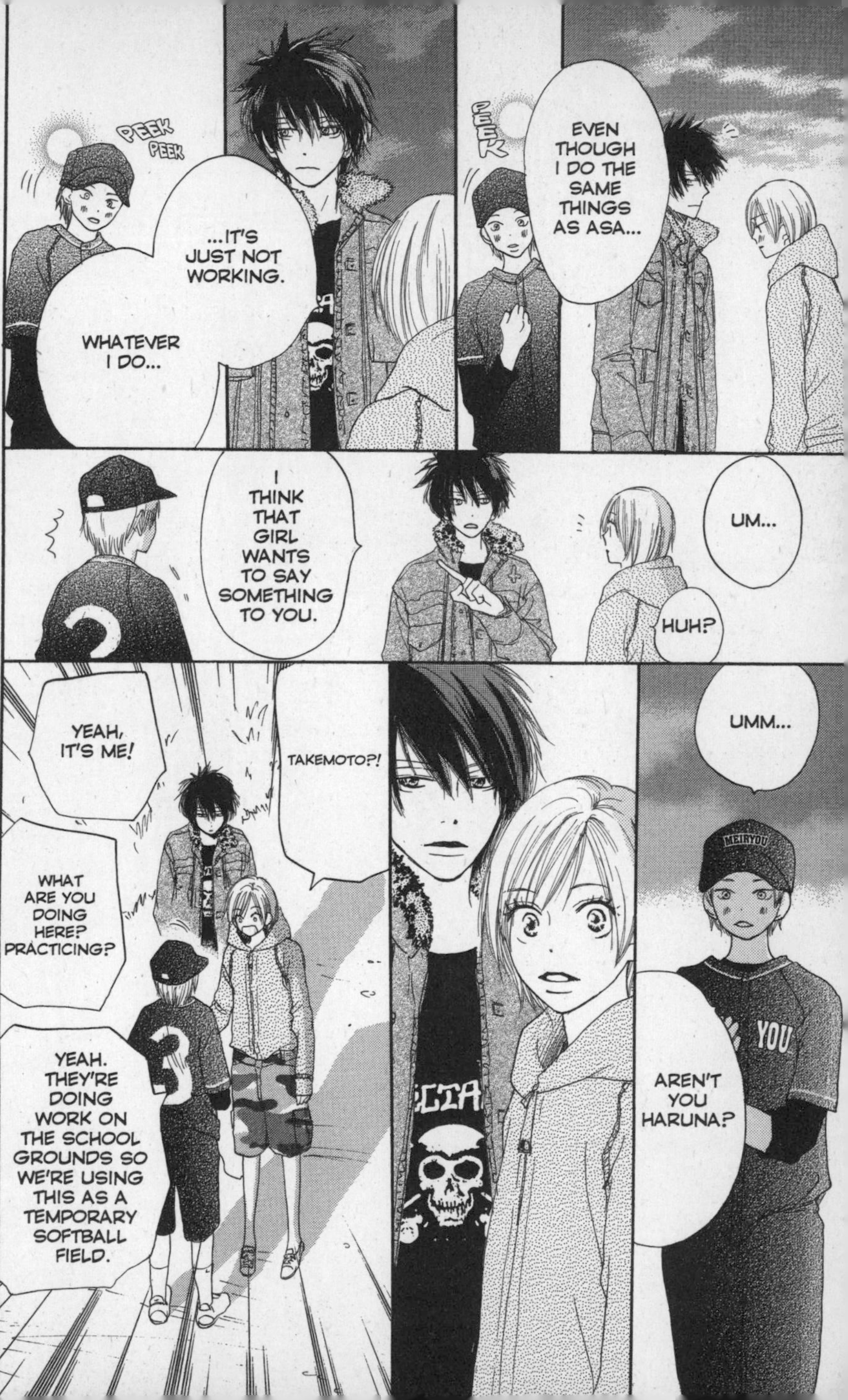
PEEK
EVEN THOUGH I DO THE SAME THINGS AS ASA...
PEEK PEEK
...IT'S JUST NOT WORKING.
WHATEVER I DO...
UM...
HUH?
I THINK THAT GIRL WANTS TO SAY SOMETHING TO YOU.
UMM...
MEIRYOU
YOU
AREN'T YOU HARUNA?
TAKEMOTO?!
YEAH, IT'S ME!
WHAT ARE YOU DOING HERE? PRACTICING?
YEAH. THEY'RE DOING WORK ON THE SCHOOL GROUNDS SO WE'RE USING THIS AS A TEMPORARY SOFTBALL FIELD.

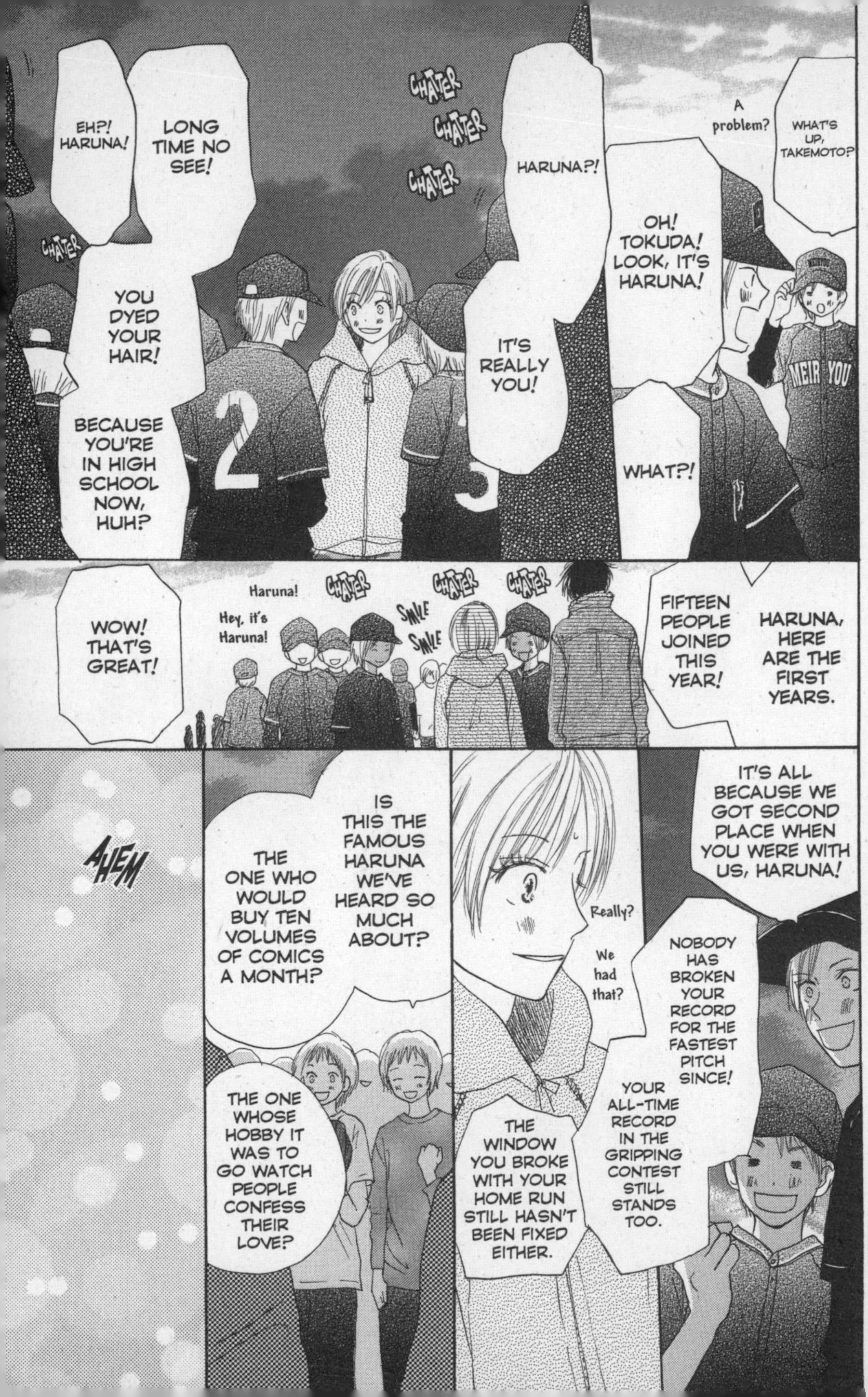
WHAT'S UP, TAKEMOTO?
A problem?
OH! TOKUDA! LOOK, IT'S HARUNA!
WHAT?!
HARUNA?!
IT'S REALLY YOU!
CHATER CHATER CHATER
LONG TIME NO SEE!
EH?! HARUNA!
CHATER
YOU DYED YOUR HAIR!
BECAUSE YOU'RE IN HIGH SCHOOL NOW, HUH?
HARUNA, HERE ARE THE FIRST YEARS.
FIFTEEN PEOPLE JOINED THIS YEAR!
CHATER CHATER CHATER
SMILE SMILE
Haruna!
Hey, it's Haruna!
WOW! THAT'S GREAT!
IT'S ALL BECAUSE WE GOT SECOND PLACE WHEN YOU WERE WITH US, HARUNA!
NOBODY HAS BROKEN YOUR RECORD FOR THE FASTEST PITCH SINCE!
Really?
We had that?
YOUR ALL-TIME RECORD IN THE GRIPPING CONTEST STILL STANDS TOO.
THE WINDOW YOU BROKE WITH YOUR HOME RUN STILL HASN'T BEEN FIXED EITHER.
IS THIS THE FAMOUS HARUNA WE'VE HEARD SO MUCH ABOUT?
THE ONE WHO WOULD BUY TEN VOLUMES OF COMICS A MONTH?
THE ONE WHOSE HOBBY IT WAS TO GO WATCH PEOPLE CONFESS THEIR LOVE?
AHEM

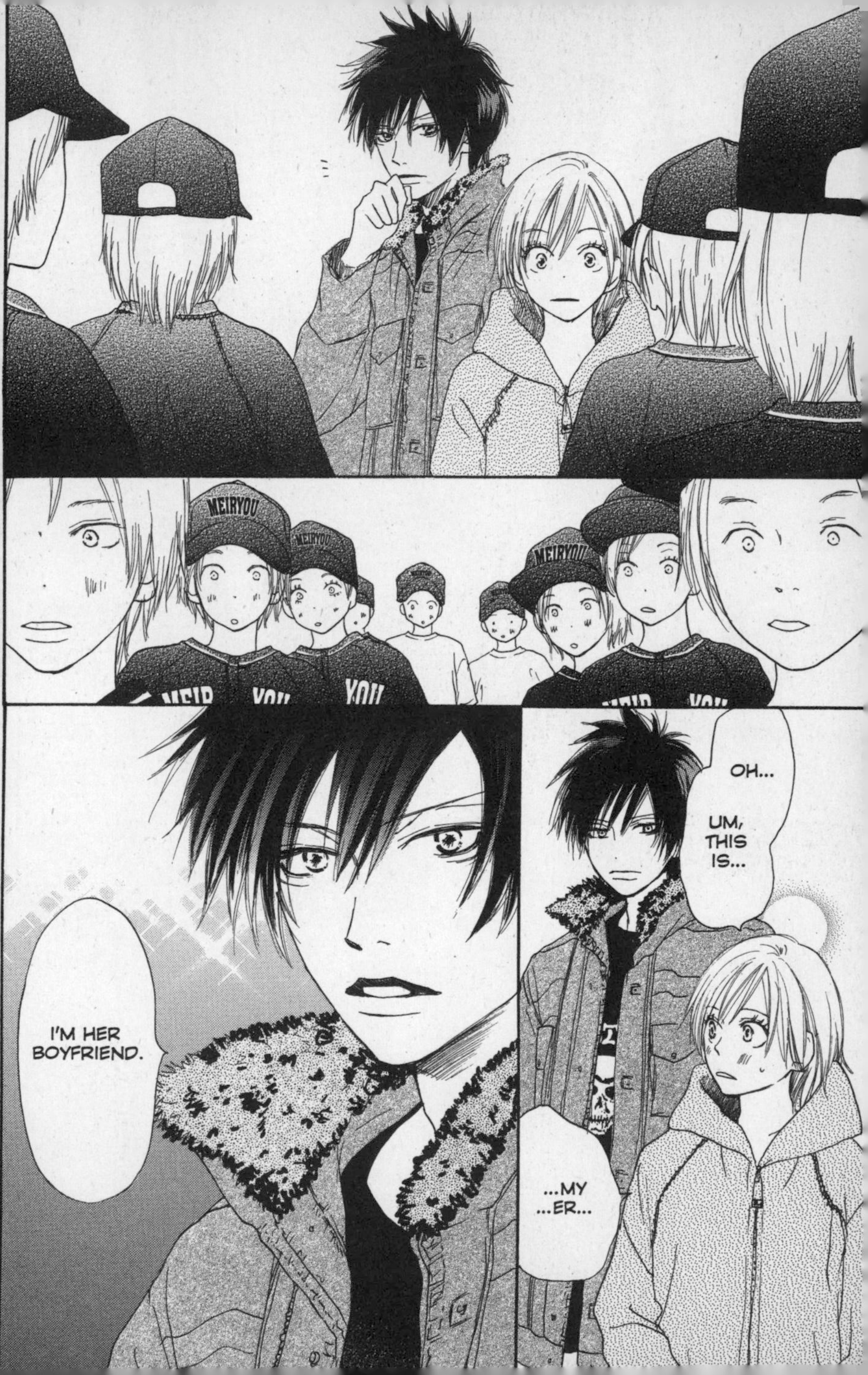
MEIRYOU
OH...
UM, THIS IS...
...MY ...ER...
I'M HER BOYFRIEND.

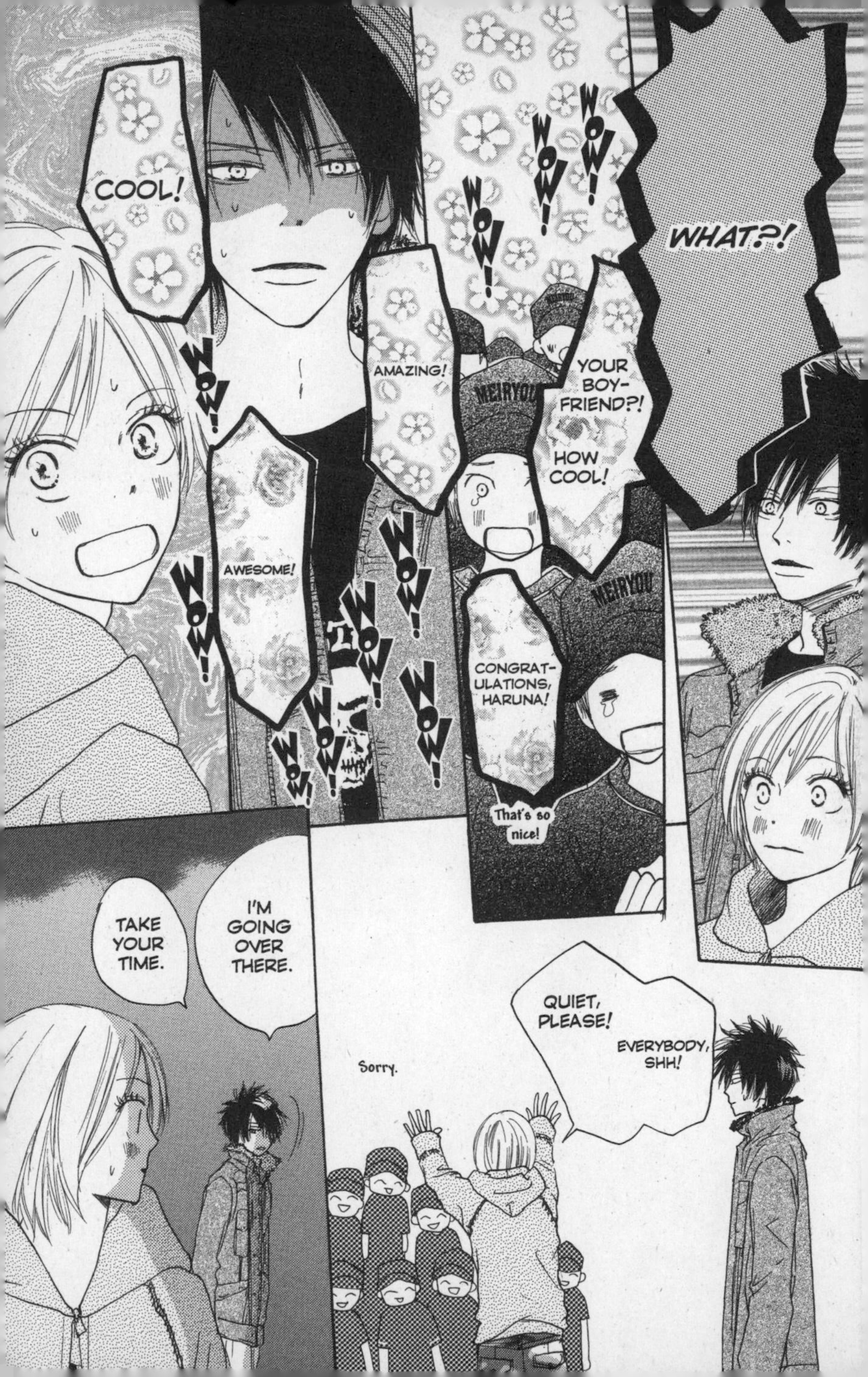
WHAT?!
WOW!
WOW!
WOW!
YOUR BOY-FRIEND?!
HOW COOL!
AMAZING!
CONGRAT-ULATIONS, HARUNA!
That's so nice!
COOL!
WOW!
AWESOME!
WOW!
WOW!
WOW!
WOW!
WOW!
WOW!
QUIET, PLEASE!
EVERYBODY, SHH!
Sorry.
I'M GOING OVER THERE.
TAKE YOUR TIME.

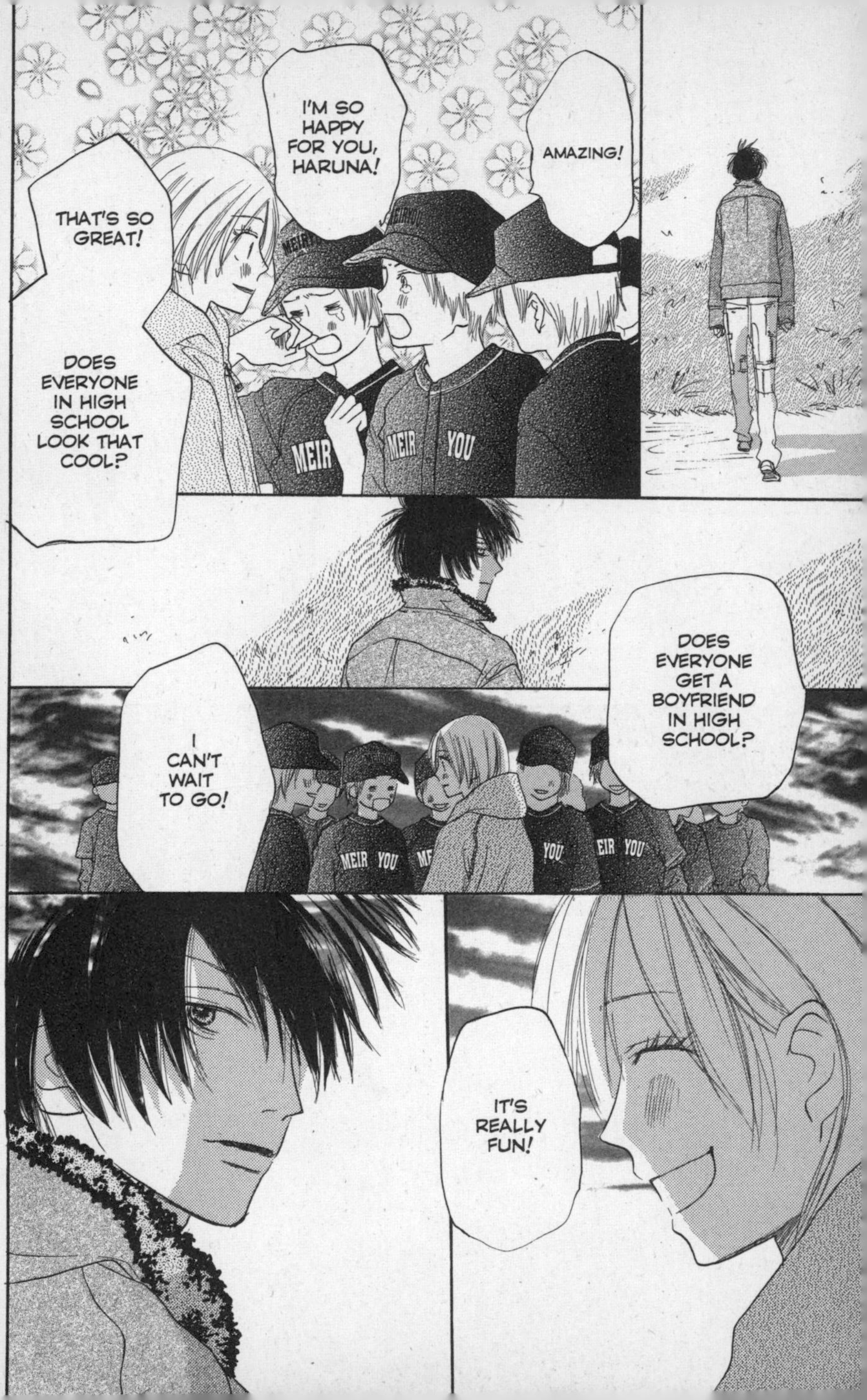
AMAZING!
I'M SO HAPPY FOR YOU, HARUNA!
THAT'S SO GREAT!
DOES EVERYONE IN HIGH SCHOOL LOOK THAT COOL?
DOES EVERYONE GET A BOYFRIEND IN HIGH SCHOOL?
I CAN'T WAIT TO GO!
IT'S REALLY FUN!

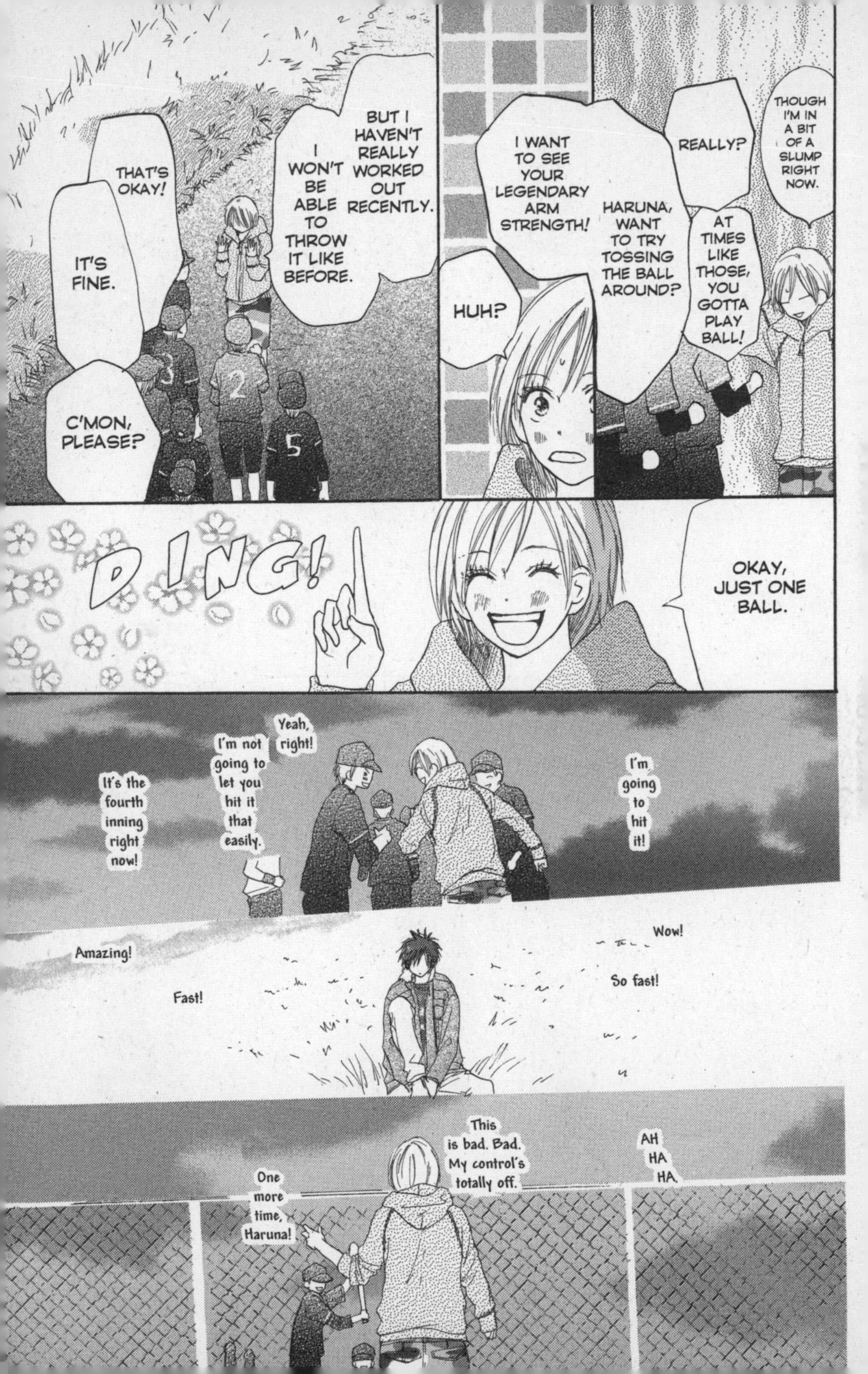

THOUGH I'M IN A BIT OF A SLUMP RIGHT NOW.
REALLY?
AT TIMES LIKE THOSE, YOU GOTTA PLAY BALL!
HARUNA, WANT TO TRY TOSSING THE BALL AROUND?
I WANT TO SEE YOUR LEGENDARY ARM STRENGTH!
HUH?
BUT I HAVEN'T REALLY WORKED OUT RECENTLY.
I WON'T BE ABLE TO THROW IT LIKE BEFORE.
THAT'S OKAY!
IT'S FINE.
C'MON, PLEASE?
OKAY, JUST ONE BALL.
DING!
I'm going to hit it!
Yeah, right!
I'm not going to let you hit it that easily.
It's the fourth inning right now!
Wow!
So fast!
Fast!
Amazing!
AH HA HA.
This is bad. Bad. My control's totally off.
One more time, Haruna!

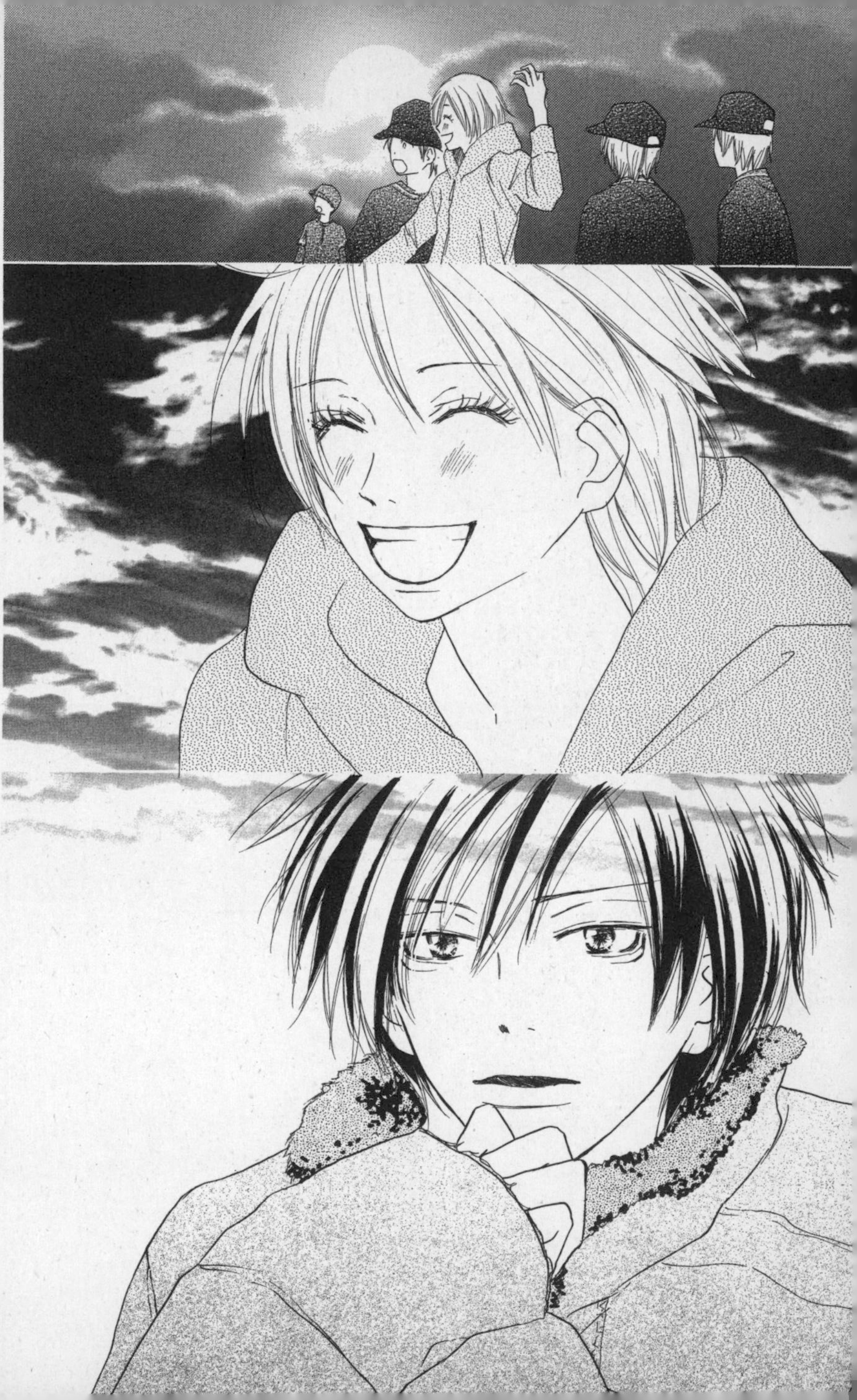

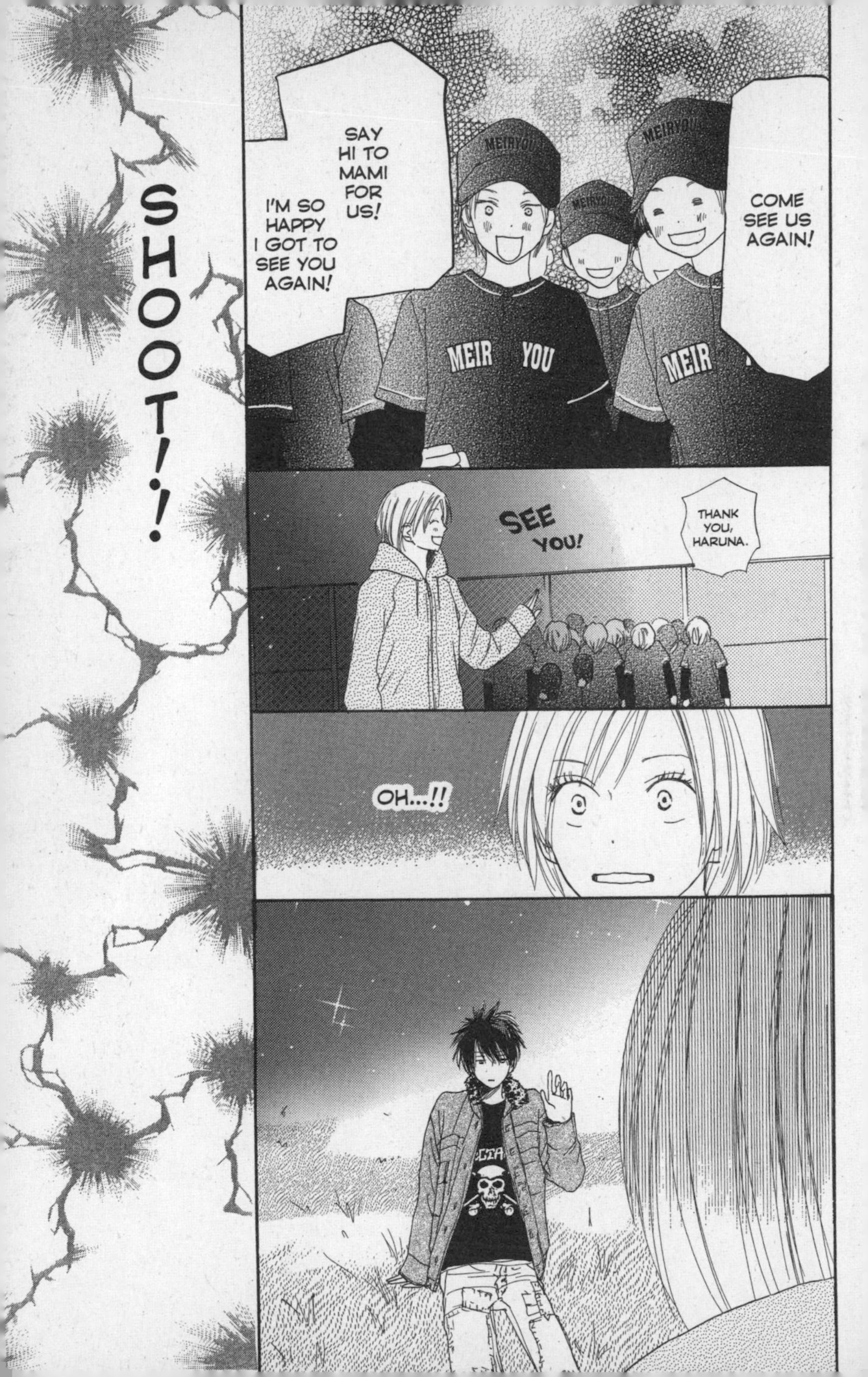
COME SEE US AGAIN!
SAY HI TO MAMI FOR US!
I'M SO HAPPY I GOT TO SEE YOU AGAIN!
MEIRYOU
MEIR YOU
THANK YOU, HARUNA.
SEE YOU!
OH...!!
SHOOT!!

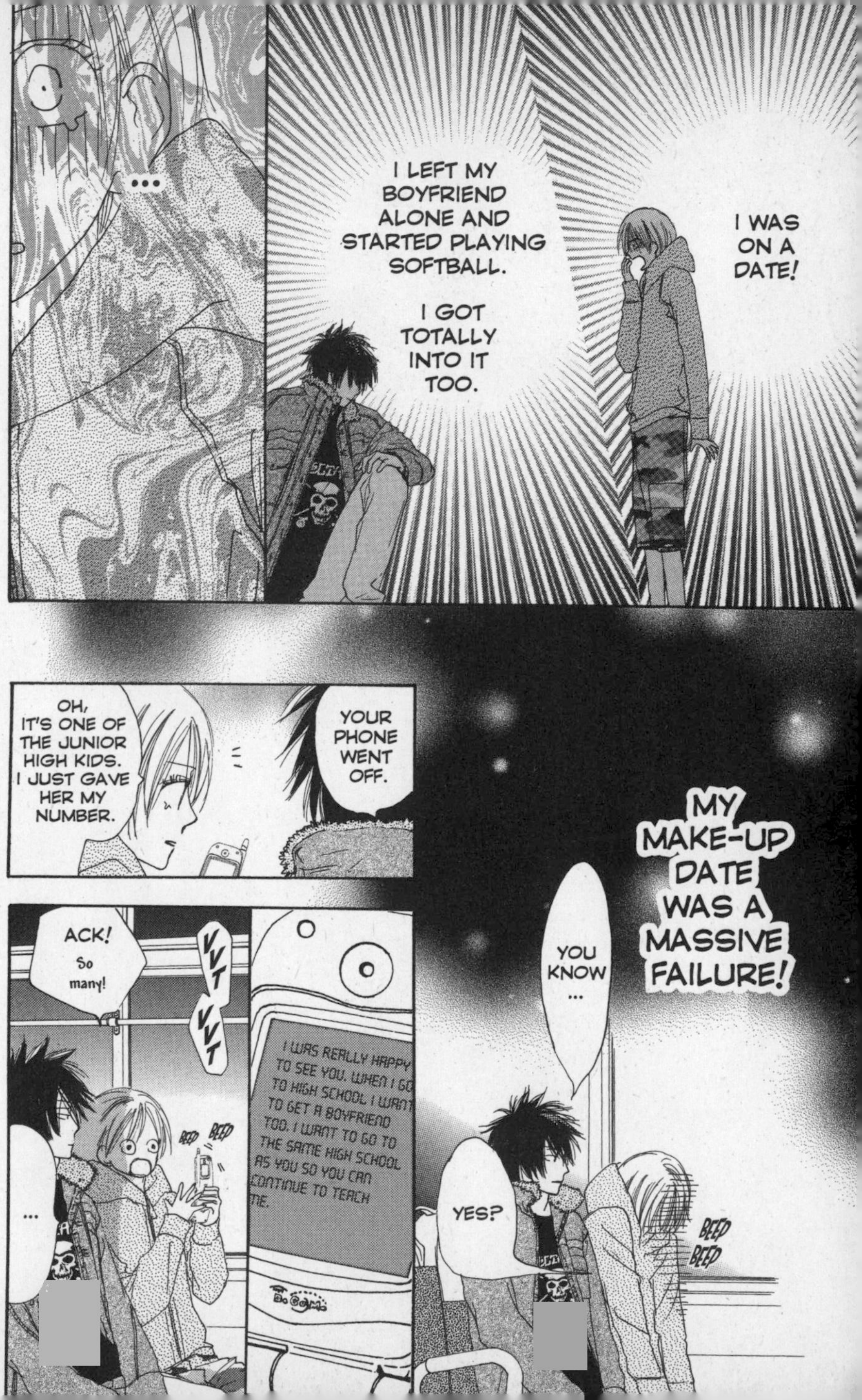
I WAS ON A DATE!
I LEFT MY BOYFRIEND ALONE AND STARTED PLAYING SOFTBALL.
I GOT TOTALLY INTO IT TOO.
...
MY MAKE-UP DATE WAS A MASSIVE FAILURE!
YOU KNOW...
YES?
BEEP BEEP
YOUR PHONE WENT OFF.
OH, IT'S ONE OF THE JUNIOR HIGH KIDS. I JUST GAVE HER MY NUMBER.
I WAS REALLY HAPPY TO SEE YOU. WHEN I GO TO HIGH SCHOOL I WANT TO GET A BOYFRIEND TOO. I WANT TO GO TO THE SAME HIGH SCHOOL AS YOU SO YOU CAN CONTINUE TO TEACH ME.
VVT VVT
ACK! So many!
BEEP BEEP
...

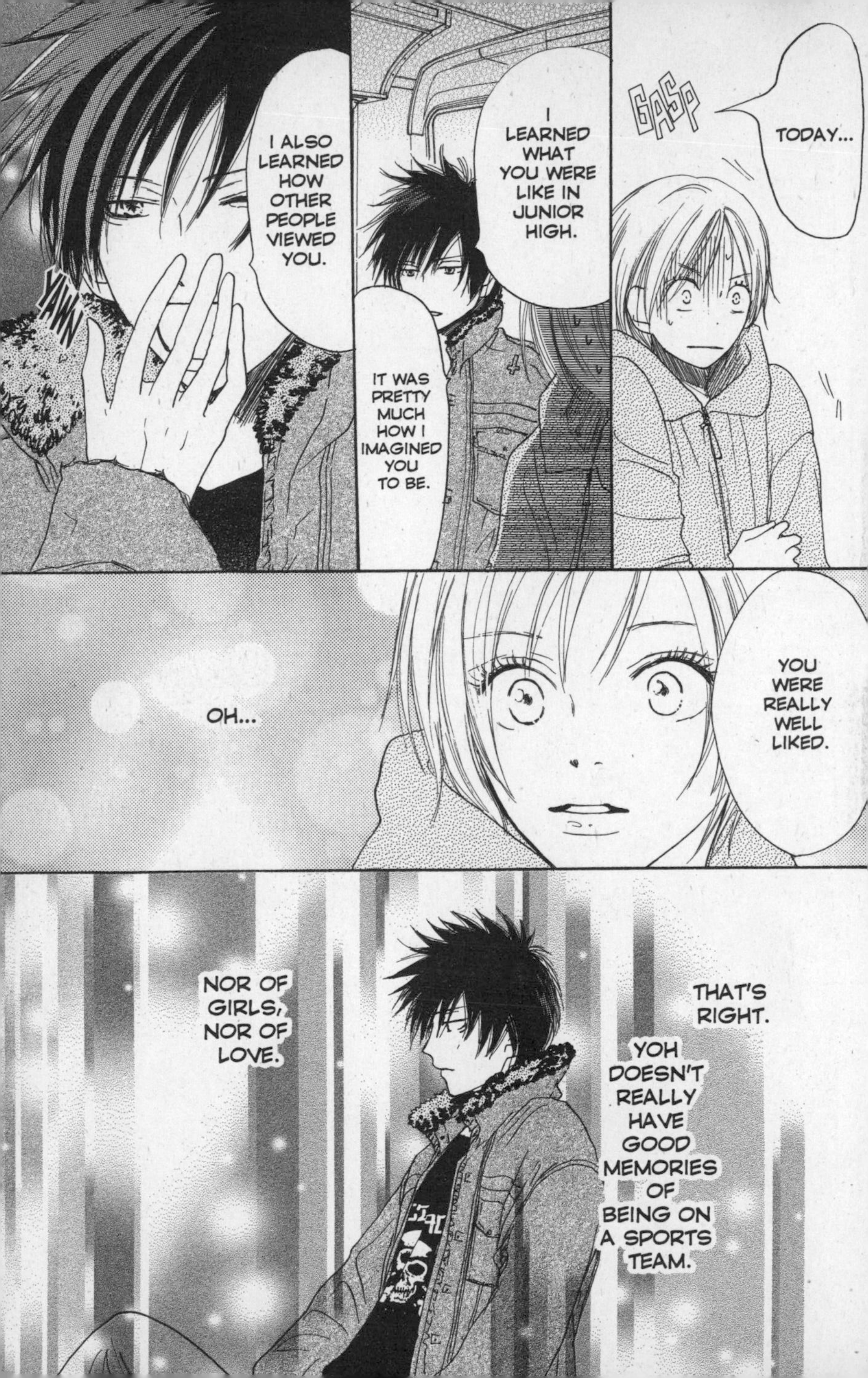
GASP
TODAY...
I LEARNED WHAT YOU WERE LIKE IN JUNIOR HIGH.
IT WAS PRETTY MUCH HOW I IMAGINED YOU TO BE.
I ALSO LEARNED HOW OTHER PEOPLE VIEWED YOU.
YAWN
YOU WERE REALLY WELL LIKED.
OH...
THAT'S RIGHT.
YOH DOESN'T REALLY HAVE GOOD MEMORIES OF BEING ON A SPORTS TEAM.
NOR OF GIRLS, NOR OF LOVE.

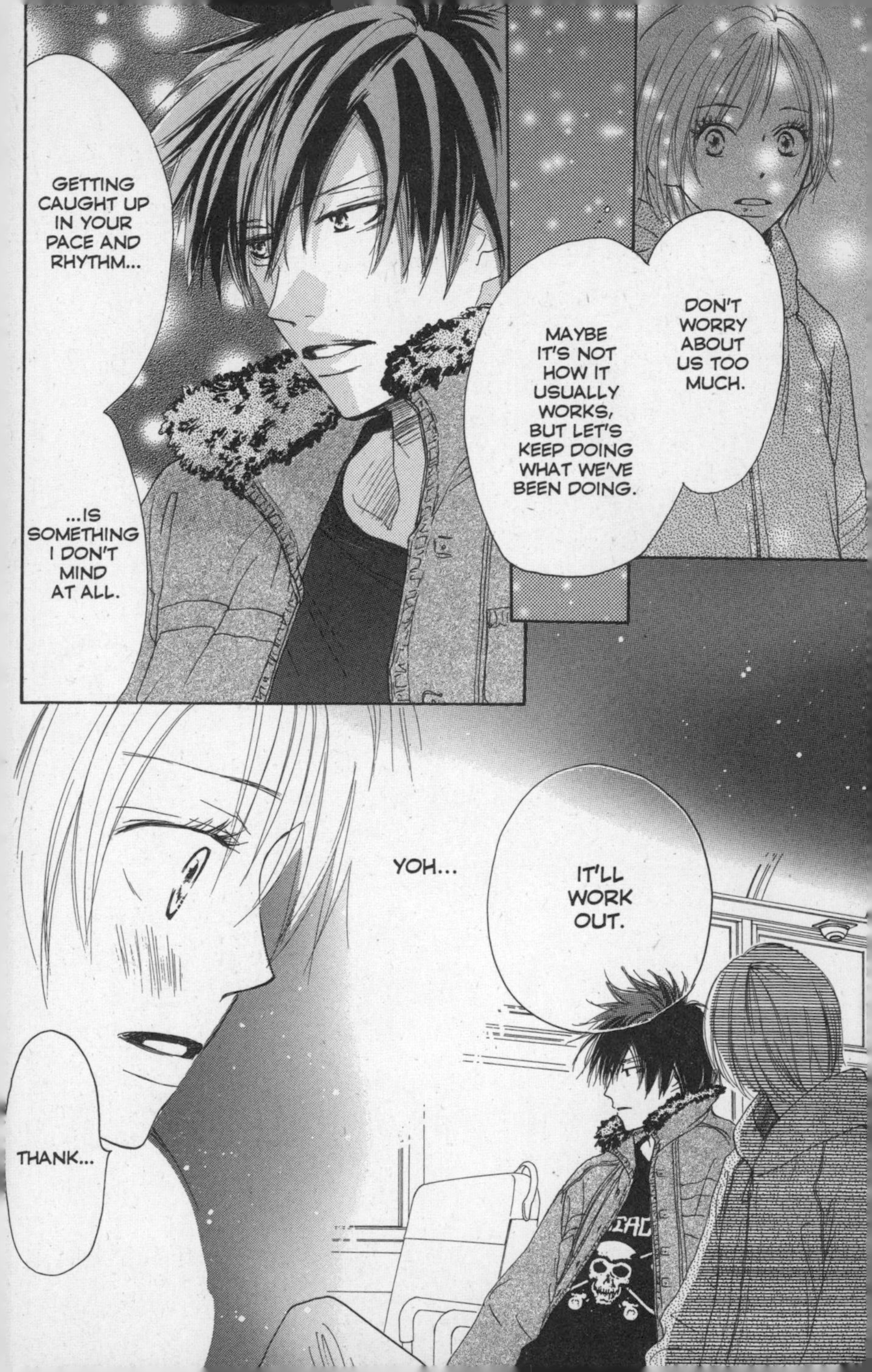
DON'T WORRY ABOUT US TOO MUCH.
MAYBE IT'S NOT HOW IT USUALLY WORKS, BUT LET'S KEEP DOING WHAT WE'VE BEEN DOING.
GETTING CAUGHT UP IN YOUR PACE AND RHYTHM...
...IS SOMETHING I DON'T MIND AT ALL.
IT'LL WORK OUT.
YOH...
THANK...

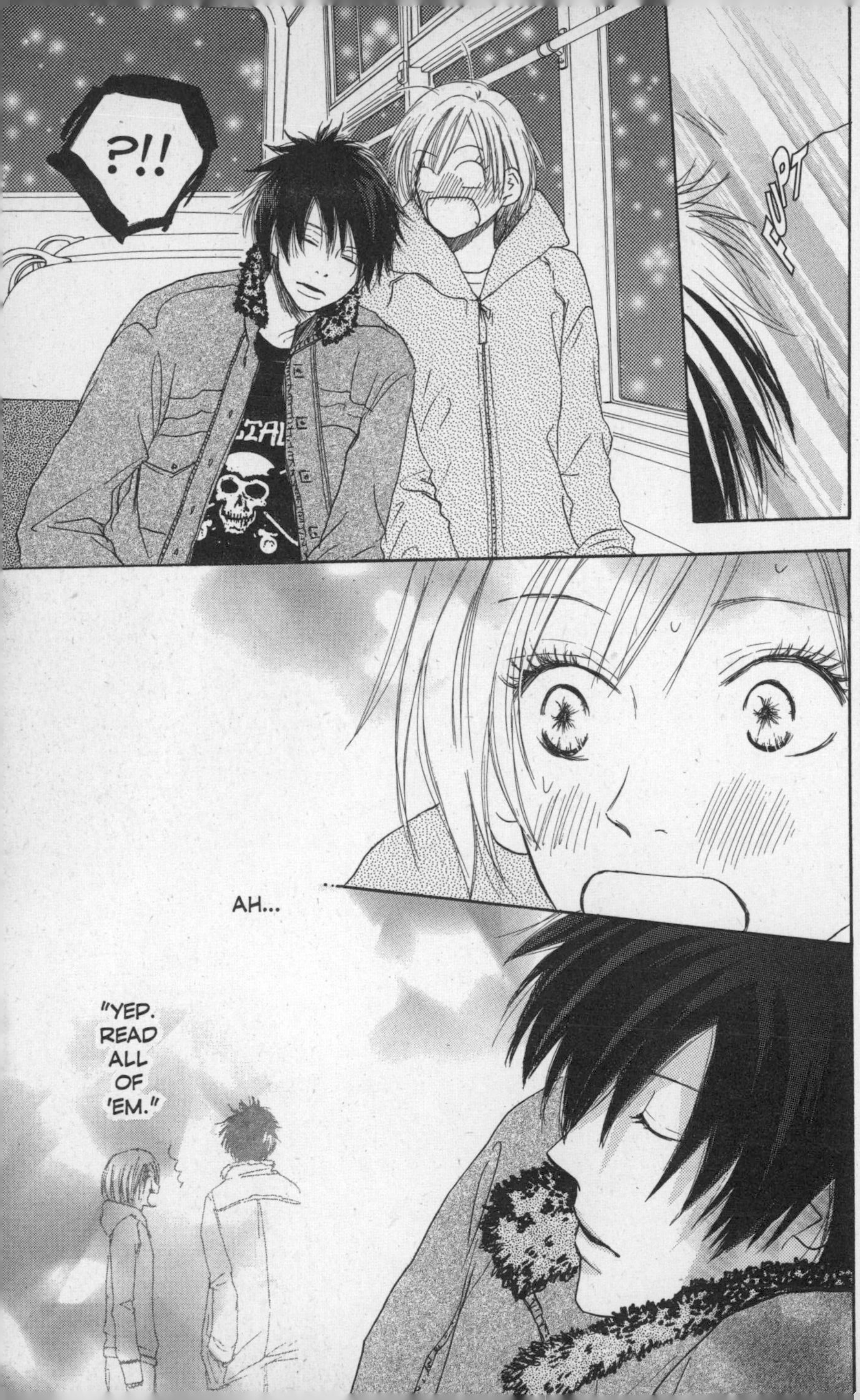
FUPT
?!!
AH...
"YEP. READ ALL OF 'EM."

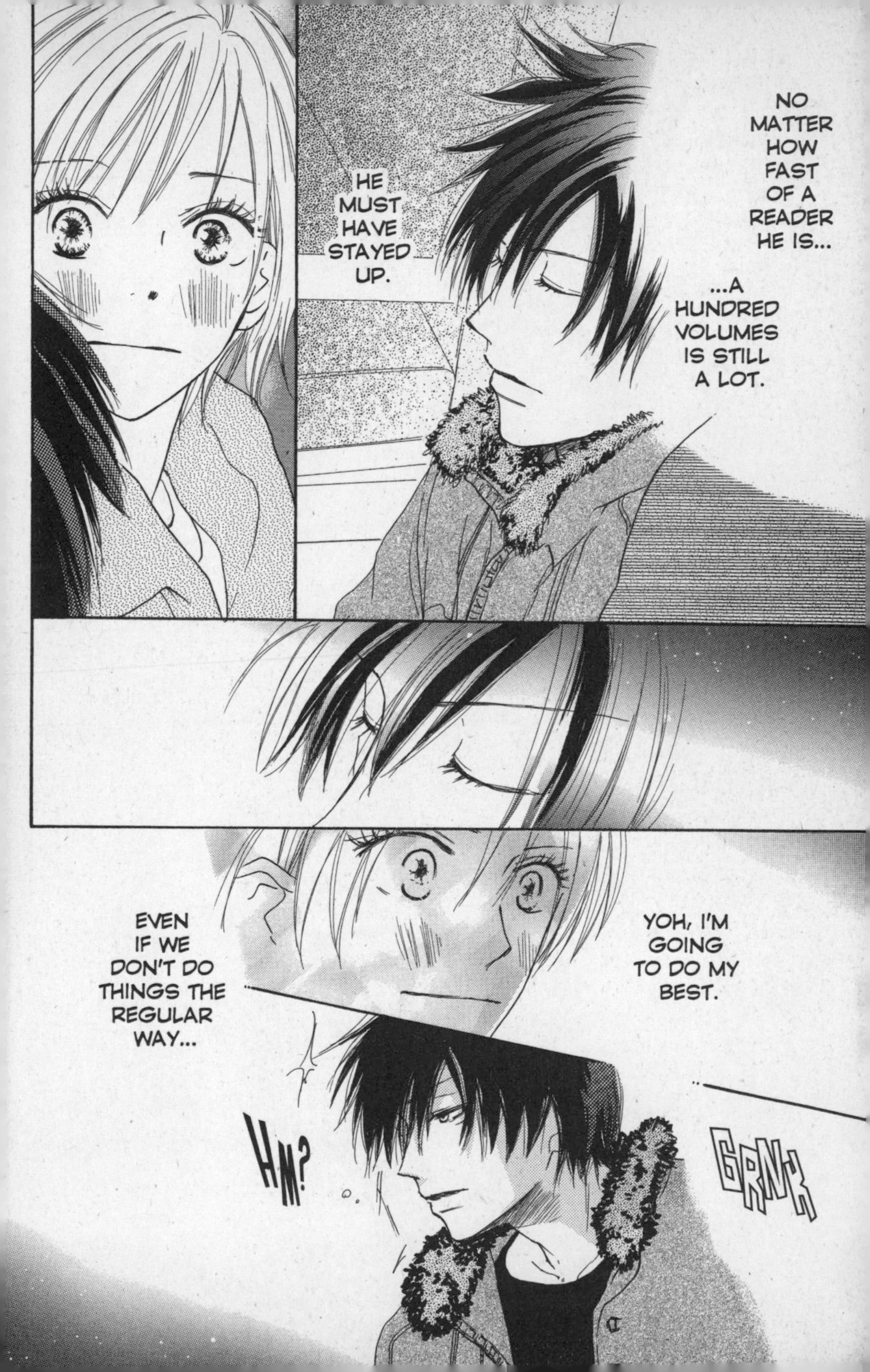
NO MATTER HOW FAST OF A READER HE IS...
...A HUNDRED VOLUMES IS STILL A LOT.
HE MUST HAVE STAYED UP.
YOH, I'M GOING TO DO MY BEST.
EVEN IF WE DON'T DO THINGS THE REGULAR WAY...
GRNK
HM?

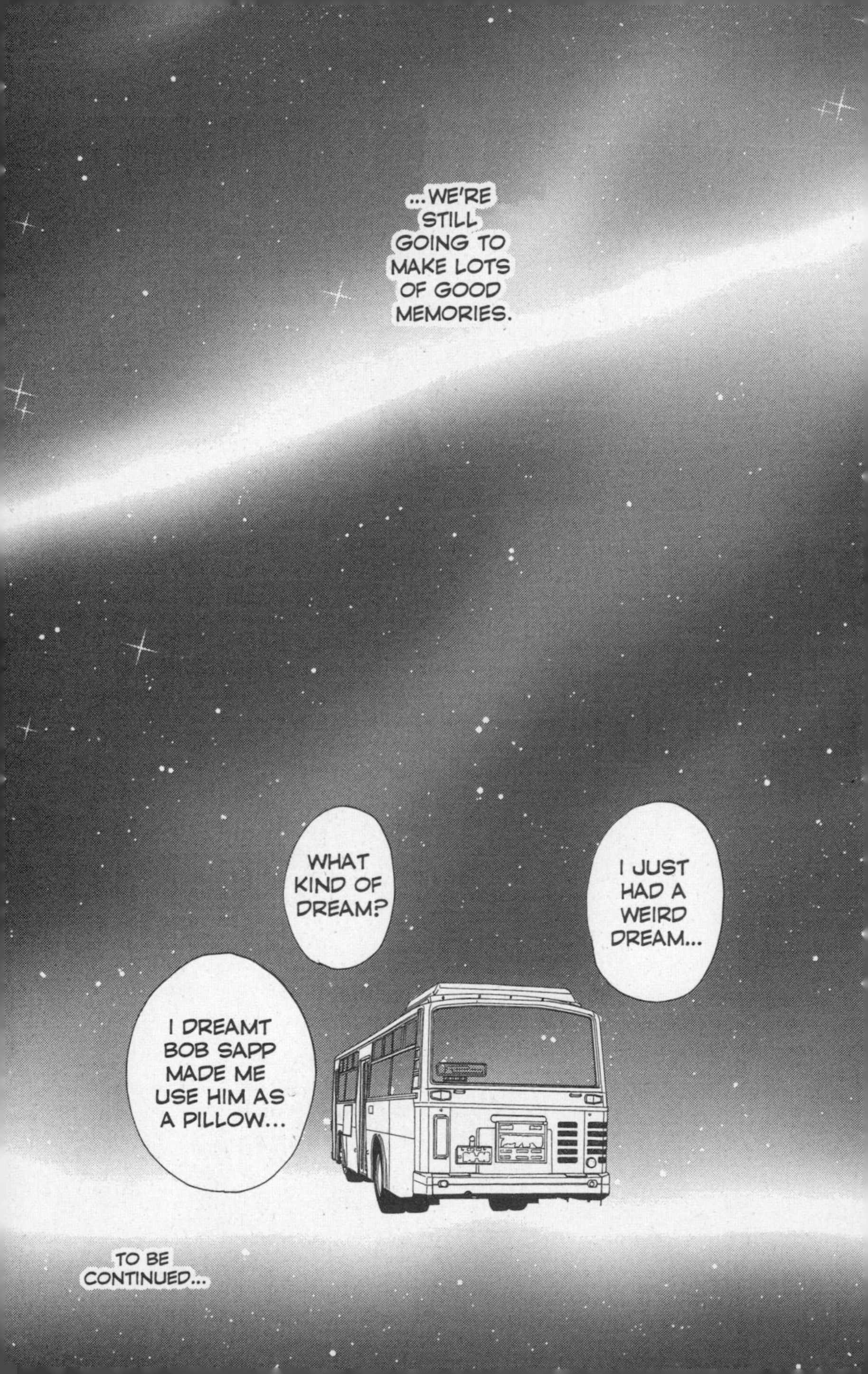
...WE'RE STILL GOING TO MAKE LOTS OF GOOD MEMORIES.
I JUST HAD A WEIRD DREAM...
WHAT KIND OF DREAM?
I DREAMT BOB SAPP MADE ME USE HIM AS A PILLOW...
TO BE CONTINUED...

My wisdom teeth are growing out, but I seem
to recall them being pulled out from those spots
before... I wonder if you can get wisdom teeth
twice? Last time when I had them pulled, it hurt
a lot. I wonder if it'll hurt this time? I can't just
leave them in there, can I? Ah, so scary...

– Kazune Kawahara

Kazune Kawahara is from Hokkaido prefecture
and was born on March 11th (a Pisces!). She
made her manga debut at age 18 with *Kare no
Ichiban Sukina Hito* (His Most Favorite Person).
Her other works include *Sensei!*, serialized in
Bessatsu Margaret magazine. Her hobby is
interior redecorating.

HIGH SCHOOL DEBUT
VOL. 3
Shojo Beat Edition

STORY & ART BY
KAZUNE KAWAHARA

Translation & Adaptation/Translation By Design - Gemma Collinge
Touch-up Art & Lettering/Mark Griffin
Design/Izumi Hirayama
Editor/Amy Yu

KOKO DEBUT © 2003 by Kazune Kawahara
All rights reserved.
First published in Japan in 2003 by SHUEISHA Inc., Tokyo.
English translation rights arranged by SHUEISHA Inc.

Printed in Canada

Published by VIZ Media, LLC
P.O. Box 77010
San Francisco, CA 94107

10 9 8 7 6 5
First printing, May 2008
Fifth printing, July 2011

www.viz.com   www.shojobeat.com

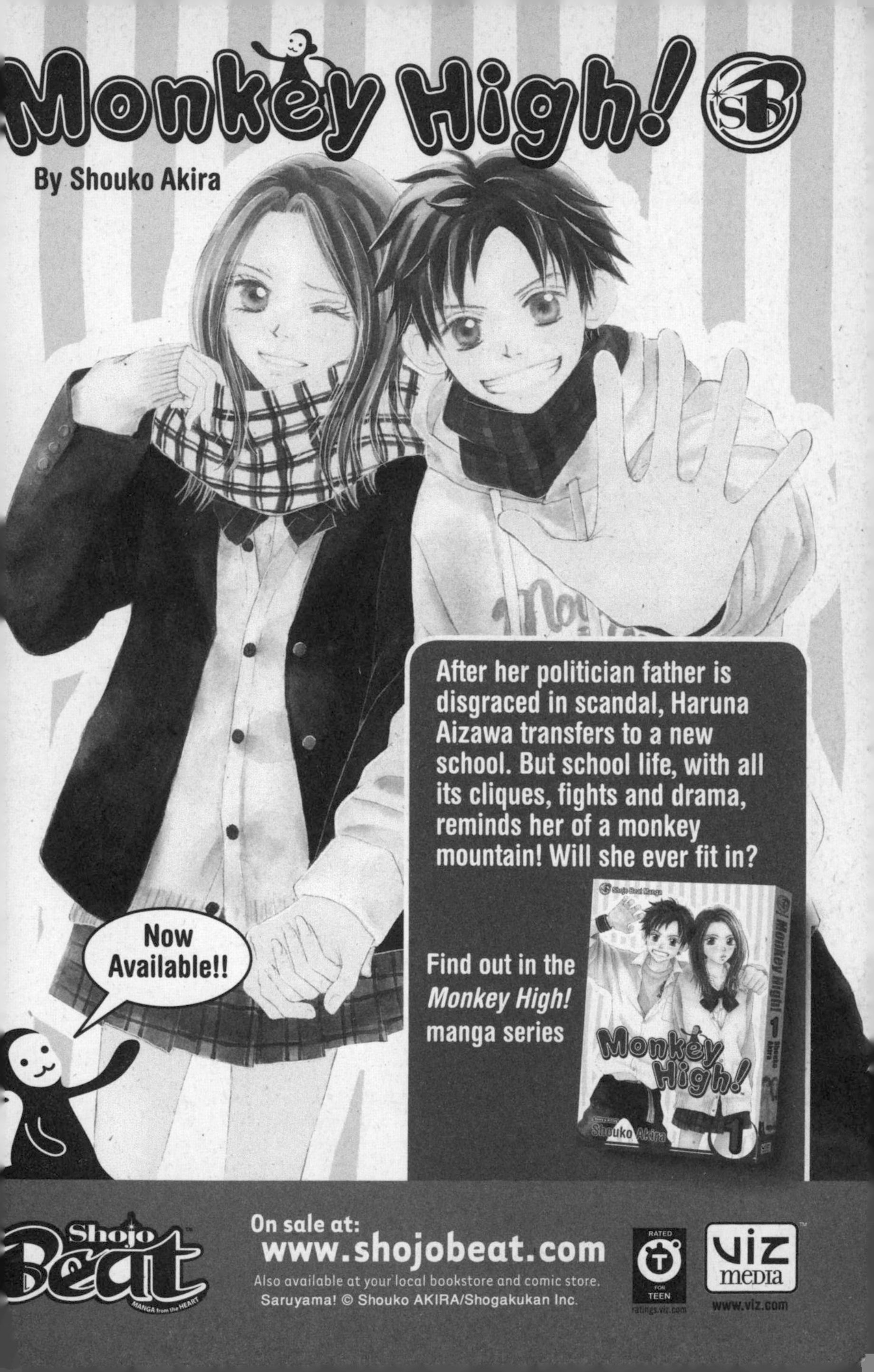
Monkey High!
By Shouko Akira
After her politician father is disgraced in scandal, Haruna Aizawa transfers to a new school. But school life, with all its cliques, fights and drama, reminds her of a monkey mountain! Will she ever fit in?
Now Available!!
Find out in the *Monkey High!* manga series
Monkey High!
Shouko Akira
1
Shojo Beat
MANGA from the HEART
On sale at:
www.shojobeat.com
Also available at your local bookstore and comic store.
Saruyama! © Shouko AKIRA/Shogakukan Inc.
RATED T FOR TEEN
ratings.viz.com
VIZ media
www.viz.com